# A Ministry of Enthusiasm

## Centenary Essays on the Workers' Educational Association

Edited by
Stephen K. Roberts

Pluto Press

LONDON • STERLING, VIRGINIA

First published 2003 by Pluto Press
345 Archway Road, London N6 5AA
and 22883 Quicksilver Drive, Sterling, VA 20166-2012, USA

www.plutobooks.com

British Library Cataloguing in Publication Data
A catalogue record for this book is available from
the British Library

ISBN 0 7453 1908 4 hardback
ISBN 0 7453 1907 6 paperback

Library of Congress Cataloging in Publication Data applied for

10   9   8   7   6   5   4   3   2   1

Designed and produced for Pluto Press by
Chase Publishing Services, Sidmouth, England
Typeset from disk by Stanford DTP Services, Towcester, England
Printed and bound in the European Union by
Antony Rowe, Chippenham and Eastbourne, England

SOUTH WALES MIN

# Contents

## 10 DOWNING STREET
### LONDON SW1A 2AA

I am delighted to write a foreword to *A Ministry of Enthusiasm*, a collection of scholarly essays marking the centenary of the Workers' Educational Association (WEA). This book celebrates the achievement of the WEA as a model for organising lifelong learning in the United Kingdom since 1903.

Learning throughout life has never been more important. We live in an increasingly competitive world where skills are the key to maintaining and improving our standard of living. But lifelong learning is much more. It contributes to our quality of life. It promotes active citizenship. It can help us end social exclusion by giving individuals and communities real hope of future prosperity and well-being. This is why we in the UK are working to create a learning culture, in which all participate, and from which all benefit.

The Government acknowledges the important contribution the WEA has made in the UK. We recognise the WEA's unique position as the largest voluntary provider of adult education in the United Kingdom. We help fund its activities through both central and local Government. My thanks go to everyone who helped put this book together. It offers an overview of the important themes in the WEA's history and relates the past to the present and future of the Association. More importantly it shows just how valuable a contribution the WEA has made to lifelong learning. I congratulate the WEA and its voluntary members on their achievements, and offer my best wishes for the future.

*Tony Blair*

December 2002

# Acknowledgements

I should like to thank my co-contributors for their willingness to produce their essays on time for this volume to appear in the WEA's centenary year; and those who volunteered memories and appreciations of the Association for the 'Voices' section. Lawrence Goldman deserves special thanks for arranging a seminar at St. Peter's College, Oxford, in 2001, which brought contributors together for enjoyable and useful discussions which fed into the making of this book.

I am grateful to the many branch secretaries and WEA activists who wrote to me with mini-histories and details of records relating to the WEA in their areas. In the event, very few of these could be used in a project so tightly defined as this collection of essays, but the exercise points the way forward for future historical projects to safeguard WEA history.

Above all, Mel Doyle, himself a historian of the WEA, has supported and nurtured this project from the outset, and I should like to place on record my grateful thanks to him for his encouragement and enthusiasm.

Finally, the WEA as a whole deserves thanks for sponsoring this collection. However, none of the views and opinions contained in this book embody official WEA policy. All contributors have been free to present their own interpretations of WEA history, and any errors and misjudgements that are contained in this volume are entirely the responsibility of individual authors and especially that of the editor.

Stephen K. Roberts

# Abbreviations

*Place of publication here and in all endnotes London unless otherwise stated.*

| | |
|---|---|
| *Adventure* | A. Mansbridge, *An Adventure in Working-class Education, being the Story of the Workers' Educational Association* (1920) |
| BL | British Library |
| *DNB* | *Dictionary of National Biography* |
| Fieldhouse and Associates, *History* | Roger Fieldhouse and Associates, *A History of Modern British Adult Education* (Leicester, 1996) |
| *Kingdom of the Mind* | A. Mansbridge, *The Kingdom of the Mind. Essays and Addresses 1903–37* (1944) |
| National Archive | University of North London Library, WEA National Archive |
| Price | T. W. Price, *The Story of the Workers' Educational Association from 1903 to 1924* (1924) |
| Stocks | Mary Stocks, *The Workers' Educational Association. The First Fifty Years* (1953) |
| *Trodden Road* | A. Mansbridge, *The Trodden Road. Experience, Inspiration and Belief* (1940) |
| WEA | Workers' Educational Association |

# Brief Chronology of the WEA: The First 100 years

**May 1898**: Speech by Albert Mansbridge at Co-operative Congress, Peterborough, calling on Co-operators to work with universities to establish educational programmes.

**Aug. 1899**: Paper by Mansbridge at conference of Co-operators, Oxford, during University Extension Summer meeting.

**Early 1903**: Articles by Mansbridge in *University Extension Journal*, on 'Co-operation, Trade Unionism and Extension'.

**16 May 1903**: Founding of Association to Promote the Higher Education of Working Men.

**22 Aug. 1903**: Conference of university bodies, trade unions and Co-operative societies, at Oxford, passes resolution that 'the necessary higher education of the working classes will be best furthered by an associated effort on the part of trade unions, Co-operative societies and educational authorities'.

**Dec. 1903**: 135 individual members, 11 affiliated Co-operative societies.

**6 Aug. 1904**: South-west District (not including Devon or Cornwall) committee formed, Exeter.

**Oct. 1904**: First branch formed, Reading, Berks.

**8 Oct. 1904**: North-western District committee first meets, Manchester.

**Mar. 1905**: Rochdale branch founded.

**Oct. 1905**: Name changed to Workers' Educational Association at 2nd national conference, Birmingham.

**1905–9**: First Scottish branch at Springburn.

**Spring 1906**: Mansbridge becomes first full-time secretary of WEA.

**1907**: Midland District formed.

**1907**: Provisional committee for South Wales and Monmouthshire District formed; first Welsh branch formed at Barry, Glam.

**10 Aug. 1907**: Joint committee of representatives of universities and WEA formed at Oxford conference after address by J. M. Mactavish.

**1907**: Constitution of central committee, Districts and branches adopted, providing much autonomy for Districts.

**1907**: WEA first in receipt of government (Board of Education) grant-in-aid.

**1907–9**: 1,000 people attend each of WEA London lectures on Westminster Abbey, the House of Commons and Parliament and People.

**24 Jan. 1908**: Tutorial classes start at Longton, Staffs.

**25 Jan. 1908**: Tutorial classes start at Rochdale, Lancs.

**Oct. 1908**: William Temple, bishop of Manchester, elected first president of WEA.

**Oct. 1908**: First number of *The Highway* published.

**1909**: WEA Women's Advisory Committee established.

**July–Aug. 1910**: First WEA summer school, Oxford.

**Oct. 1910**: North-eastern District established.

**1911**: Western District established.

**1912**: WEA central library founded, Toynbee Hall.

**1912**: Edinburgh branch founded.

**1912–13**: London District established.

**1913**: Eastern and South-eastern Districts founded.

**1914**: Yorkshire District established.

**1913–14**: WEA comprises 14 joint committees with universities, 145 classes, 3,343 students.

**Mar. 1914**: WEA founded in Australia.

**Jan. 1915**: First WEA study guides published.

**1915**: New constitution provides for autonomy of Districts.

**Winter 1915**: Mansbridge resigns as secretary, through ill-health.

**3 May 1917**: Conference at Central Hall, Westminster on WEA demands for post-war educational reform, lobbying for what became Education Act of 1918.

**1918**: Commonwealth WEA set up.

**1919**: Scottish District council established.

**1919**: Appointment of first woman tutor-organiser (Sophie Green), Kettering, Northants.

**1919**: South-western (Devon and Cornwall) District established.

**1919**: Midland District divides, into East and West Midlands Districts.

**1920**: WEA branch formed at Madras, India. By 1923 Associations had been formed in Australia, Canada, New Zealand, South Africa and Tasmania.

**1920**: Workers Educational Trade Union Committee (WETUC) formed.

**1921** North Staffs. District created from former West Midlands District.

**4 Mar. 1922**: WEA demonstration against 'Geddes cuts' in public services.

**1922**: Places reserved on WEA national executive committee for TUC, Co-operative Union and Club and Institute Union.

**1922**: First grants from Trades Union Congress (TUC) and National Union of Teachers (NUT) received.

**1923**: WEAs in existence in Australia, Tasmania, New Zealand, Canada, South Africa.

**1924**: WEA empowered to provide classes without collaboration with other bodies; acquisition of 'Responsible Body' status under funding regulations.

**1930**: New constitution placing supreme authority in national conference, which elects executive.

**1936**: Appointment of youth officers to work with 18–25s.

**Apr. 1939**: Circulation of *The Highway* at 20,000 under editor W. E. Williams.

**1942–5**: WEA in forefront of campaign for educational reform, leading to 1944 Education Act.

**1945–51**: 14 members of Labour government tutors, former tutors or members of executive; 56 WEA activists were MPs.

**1945**: New regulations relaxing conditions for government grant, relating grant instead to overall size of District programmes.

**Oct. 1945**: International Federation of Workers' Educational Associations (IFWEA) formed.

**1949**: WEA Special Conference on the theme of 'Education to Meet the Modern Needs of Trade Unions'.

**1949**: Trade union advisory committees in each District, trade union tutor-organisers appointed from central fund from per capita contributions from union members.

**1964**: WETUC wound up; WEA becomes provider of courses for TUC.

**1966**: Constitution changed to extend membership of the WEA to all WEA students, with shift of emphasis to a goal of addressing needs of 'adults', rather than 'workers' for education.

**1973**: Report of Sir Lionel Russell on adult education in UK recommends more tightly defined role for WEA in specific areas of provision.

**1975**: Report of Prof. K. J. W. Alexander on adult education in Scotland broadly echoes recommendations of Russell for WEA.

**1989**: Proposal of Conservative government that WEA funding should be brokered through LEAs.

**1989**: Start of NUPE Return to Learn, West Mercia District.

**1991**: Following a legal ruling that the WEA was a single employer, constitutional changes were adopted on which the WEA as a National Association was built. Districts in north and south Wales and in Northern Ireland feel unable to participate in the new structures and withdraw from the National Association. North Staffs. and Southern Districts amalgamated into others and lose specific identities. In

Scotland the three WEA Districts merged into a single Scottish Association, and the 'WEA England and Scotland' was born.

**1991:** The first of IFWEA's Regional bodies was established for Europe (EURO-WEA). The secretariat of EURO-WEA was later hosted by the WEA, soon followed by the establishment of a permanent WEA presence in Brussels.

**1992–3:** WEA now funded via Further Education Funding Council (FEFC), with emphasis on 'Schedule 2' provision.

**1995:** Start of WEA–UNISON Return to Learn scheme.

**1999:** Start of WEA's developmental programmes with employers in the public sector, the National Health Service Executive, and with the University for Industry (UfI Learn Direct).

**1999:** Research commissioned by the WEA suggested that there were some 1,600 formal educational partnerships across the Association.

**2001:** New membership scheme encourages participation in WEA by individuals.

**2001:** Demise of the FEFC, following the Learning and Skills Act, 2000, and the subsequent creation of the Learning and Skills Council (LSC).

1. Some delegates to the 1905 Birmingham conference. © WEA National Archive.

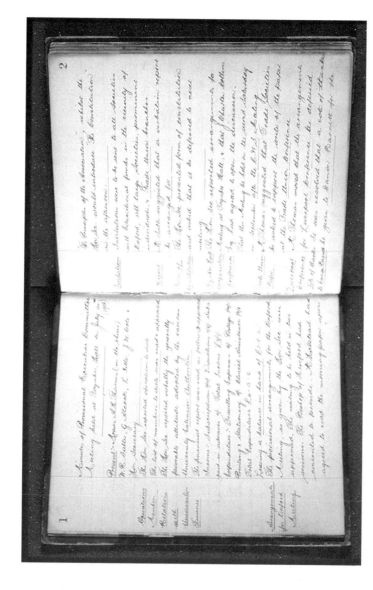

2. The first page of the first minute book, 1903. © WEA National Archive.

3. National officers at Toynbee Hall, 1909; clockwise from bottom left
Albert Mansbridge, L. V. Gill, T. E. Harvey, T. W. Price,
F. W. Cuthbertson, William Temple. © WEA National Archive.

4. Albert Mansbridge (right) in full spate, Sydney, 1913.
© WEA National Archive.

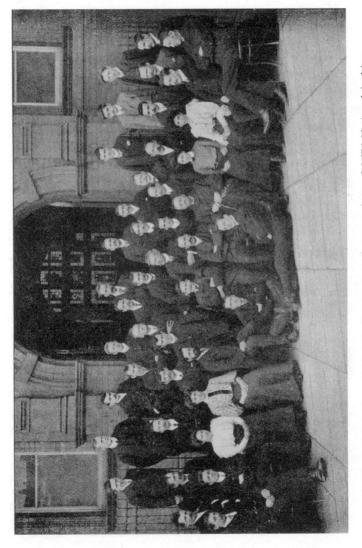

5. The Rochdale class, 1909: R. H. Tawney seated, centre, front. © WEA National Archive.

6. The ecumenical WEA: altar, St. Hilary Church, Cornwall, by Ernst Proctor
in memory of Gerard Collier, tutorial class tutor, quaker and pacifist.
© Philip Hills.

Pictures of Strikes and
Political Demonstrations
in Five Countries

BOMBAY

LONDON

7. *The Highway*, April 1936: photo-journalism on current affairs.
© WEA National Archive.

8. Elizabeth Monkhouse conducting a model WEA class, Olympia, 1959. © WEA National Archive.

9. Conference of field staff, 1969: Neil Kinnock (middle row, 7th from left) looks happy. © WEA National Archive.

10. Family learning group, WEA Clovelly Centre, Southampton 2002. © WEA, *Learning for Life*, Autumn 2002.

# Introduction

*Stephen K. Roberts*

The Workers' Educational Association was founded in the parlour of a Battersea clerical worker, Albert Mansbridge, in 1903. In 2003 it is the largest and most successful provider of educational courses for adults in the voluntary sector of the United Kingdom. This volume seeks to explain the continuing vitality of the WEA over a century of public service. From the outset, the Association was based on democratic principles. The relationship between teacher and students was conceived as one of a partnership, in which the syllabus was negotiated between them. In the early days of the WEA the classic example was the meeting of minds between university teacher and skilled working-class learner, from which both parties gained in intellectual development. A hundred years later, WEA tutors are drawn from a much wider social and educational pool of talent than was available in 1903; the aims and ambitions of students are as diverse as can be conceived. The principle of equality between the partners in a learning contract remains the same.

Democracy has from the outset also been a characteristic of WEA organisation. The classic expression of this through most of the Association's existence has been the local branch, in which a committee of volunteers took responsibility for room hire, course publicity and other local arrangements. The hiring of tutors was the task of either a regional WEA executive body, called the District, alone or in partnership with a university extra-mural department. By 2003 new forms of voluntary activity have emerged in some regions, such as Voluntary Educational Advisers (VEAs), who support students returning to learning. In other places the branch structure remains a vital component of WEA management. Each District has its own system of executive committees and councils, serviced by professional staff, and a central body, the National Association, co-ordinates professional and voluntary effort. In organisation as well as in the delivery of courses, therefore, the WEA retains a commitment to democratic principles.

The story of the WEA is not one of mere survival. It would be unrealistic to argue that it has been its commitment to democratic educational principles that has seen the Association through many vicissitudes over the century. An early injection of state funding for its core activities gave the WEA a standing denied its rivals within the meagrely-resourced structure of learning opportunities for adults. For most of its existence, the Association has been both a voluntary body and a component of the state education system. Before and just after the 1939–45 war, the WEA became an accepted element in the fabric of British educational and cultural life. Its tutorial classes in collaboration with universities were a mark of its seriousness to outsiders and a token of prestige to its members. Tutorial classes lasted years rather than months, and involved a commitment to the regular writing of essays: an extra-mural version of practice at England's oldest universities, particularly Oxford.

When William Temple wrote to Albert Mansbridge in September 1908, he assured the WEA founder that his was a 'ministry of enthusiasm'.[1] Temple had in mind the various ministries of the early church – healing, teaching and so on – knowing that the devout Mansbridge would understand the allusion. He meant his letter as personal encouragement for Mansbridge, who was in any case enthusiasm personified, but he also put his finger on what was to become a consistent quality of the WEA in its first hundred years, shining through successive evolutionary phases over the century. The Mansbridgean WEA, from 1903 to the founder's health collapse in 1915, was largely Liberal in political orientation, highly Christian in its leadership, and strikingly moralistic in tone. The second phase, often described as a recovery from the setbacks of the First World War, was a period of innovation in 'classroom' practice, organisation and extension of the WEA's territorial range. This was also the period of serious engagement with the educational needs of trade unionists. The 1930s and 1940s saw the WEA as a feature of mainstream national life in Britain, with its journal, *The Highway*, its prominent shop window. By most reckonings the 1950s and 1960s were disappointing times, as the WEA came to terms slowly with the Robbins expansion of higher education which pushed the Association to the sidelines. From the late 1970s the WEA returned to more precisely delineated goals, as it responded to more tightly defined government policies.

There can be few twentieth-century voluntary organisations as well studied by historians as the WEA, nor can there be many with more self-awareness of a historical kind. The WEA has from the outset produced histories of itself. The famous advice of E. H. Carr, 'study the historian before you begin to study the facts' was never more relevant.[2] An early – and many would agree with Lawrence Goldman, the best – historian of the movement was T. W. Price (1876–1945), a Rochdale warehouseman before he became secretary of the Midlands district of the WEA.[3] What makes his short history of the WEA's first 21 years so compelling is his pioneer's enthusiasm for the movement which had grown so rapidly: from origins in 1903 to a body in 1924 of over 23,000 students.[4]

What a contrast Price's slim volume makes with the 'chronicle of events' of Mary Stocks, produced in 1953 to mark the half-century. Price recorded a voluntary movement that had exploded into being, to surprise and delight its founders. Stocks wrote the history of a mainstream British social institution. The WEA had exercised a decisive influence on the Army Bureau of Current Affairs during the 1939–45 war, had been prominent in advocating the philosophy of integrated education that informed the 1944 Education Act, and could claim in *The Highway* an influential journal that had enjoyed a circulation figure of 20,000 in April 1939. The proudest boast of the WEA in 1945 could be that one of its vice-presidents, Arthur Creech Jones, was a government minister,

> fourteen members of the Government, including the Chancellor of the Exchequer [Hugh Dalton], were tutors, former tutors, or members of the WEA Executive. Fifty-six active WEA adherents, tutors or students ... were Members of Parliament.[5]

What a contrast between ex-warehouseman T. W. Price and Mary Stocks, principal of London University's Westfield College, member of many government committees and nationally-known panellist on BBC broadcasts such as 'Any Questions'. With a short memoir of the former captured in the *Dictionary of Labour Biography*, a notice of the life peeress and establishment figure Baroness Stocks in the *Dictionary of National Biography*, their own respective personal histories contribute a great deal to an understanding of how far, and in what direction the WEA had moved between 1903 and 1953.

It is noticeable that histories of the WEA since Stocks have been getting shorter and more focused. Overall treatments of the subject have either been deliberately brief, or have set the WEA in a wider context. Important texts here include Bernard Jennings's 1978 *Short History*, and Roger Fieldhouse's chapter in his 1996 *A History of Modern British Adult Education*.[6] Some have been histories of districts, such as those by Cecil Scrimgeour of the North Staffordshire district and E. C. Eagle of the East Midland District. Others have focused on smaller units, for example histories by W. J. Souch and Michael Turner of Reading and Bath branches respectively and Eve Rowley on the celebrated Longton branch.[7] Other approaches have included the biographical, such as Ted Mooney on J. M. Mactavish, and of course, Bernard Jennings on Albert Mansbridge. Jennings's study of the WEA in Australia suggests another line of enquiry, that of links between the parent WEA in the UK and offshoot Associations overseas.[8]

In the first tentative discussions of a centenary history, a volume of essays seemed to have more relevance than a full-length monograph. The format seemed to offer opportunities to explore aspects of the WEA's history in a framework that would allow more local studies, more concentration on particular problems and issues than could adequately be covered in a monograph study driven by issues of comprehensiveness and chronology. The editor is only too aware of the gaps. Most glaringly, the international, particularly European dimension, of the WEA's work still awaits its historian, and there is nothing on the history of the movement in Northern Ireland. There is perhaps less to apologise for in the emphasis in this collection on the early history of the movement. Simply as a human story, the early years are a compelling subject for general readers. The Edwardian beginnings of the WEA are worth dwelling on, if only to notice how qualitatively different British society was in 1903 viewed from the vantage point of 2003. Important elements of social change were visible between 1903 and 1924, when Price wrote his history. In 1903 the franchise had been extended to some but not all men and to no women. The Labour Party was only in existence as the Labour Representation Committee. In 1924 the vote had still not been extended to all women over 21, but for most of that year there was a first Labour government.

Nonetheless, the perspectives back to 1903 from 1924 and 1953 surely included important elements of social continuity. In 2003, by contrast, we no longer have a mass heavy-industrial working class, a clearly-defined social hierarchy, a trade union movement prominent in the counsels of power, or a Christian church able to command mass adherence. All these things of 1903 could still be discerned in the British social fabric in 1924 and 1953. Although there were objections, most obviously from women, to the first clumsy title of the Association, the existence of 'workers' or 'the working class' was not in doubt in 1903. As Chapter 5 shows, there could be frank strategic attempts to exclude middle-class people from WEA provision in the early years. More broadly, David Cannadine has convincingly argued that a view of British society shared across the social classes was that it consisted of three strata of upper, middle and working classes, if on occasion it could be collapsed into a simpler 'upper-class and lower-class' model. The language of class provided a powerful vocabulary for political discourse and social critiques in the Edwardian period, and was in no sense confined to Marxist or quasi-Marxist analyses.[9] This is not to say that all were happy with the title the WEA has kept over a hundred years. The change of name on 14 October 1905 seems to have been noted without comment by historians, but the recommendation from the national committee to the Birmingham conference (see plate 1) was that the name should be 'National Education Guild', a logical extension of the title borne by the Rochdale Education Guild when it was formed as a branch of the new Association.[10] Calls for a change of name, to something more bland or less class-conscious, have become a familiar litany at national conferences ever since, and are mixed up with periodic general social ill-ease with the language of class.

In tone, the cultural world of 1903 is every bit as distant from 2003 as the worlds of economics and politics. The dominant post-modernist register is that of irony, which pervades the mass media and makes moral pronouncements by politicians and most social commentators, unless from the far right, cautious and tentative. Mansbridge's pronouncements on the purposes of the WEA were consistently couched in moral and religious or semi-religious language. The volume of collected addresses of his *Kingdom of the Mind* (1944) illustrates convincingly how his world view changed little in essence over a period of 50 years. Temple and Tawney were equally steeped in a moralistic view of education and society, as Meredith Kwartin Rusoff shows in Chapter 4. The WEA in its first half-century was engaged in a moral critique of society. A motion of 1911 to national conference deplored the 'demoralising effects upon the minds of children resulting upon the exhibition of vulgar postcards' and urged WEA members to boycott offending shops. It is an example of what was to be an enduring interest by the WEA in wider educational issues, and of its willingness to contemplate social action in a moral cause. Yet what probably strikes the modern reader first is how trivial, even laughable, in the context of 2003, was the social ill that was targeted. As Derek Tatton argues in Chapter 13, there is plenty in modern mass culture for the WEA to develop a common critical perspective upon, but it has largely withdrawn from the field, presumably defeated by the scale of the enterprise.

The title of the WEA might suggest to the ill-informed that the WEA was in origins unambiguously left wing. It was certainly part of the labour movement, if by that is meant the movement to enhance the lives of working-class people. As Sean Creighton demonstrates in Chapter 2, the Association must also be seen as part of a rich culture of participative reform and self-help in local communities, nowhere more in evidence than in the south London of Mansbridge's youth and young adulthood. The most important strand of the range of labour organisations to influence the embryonic WEA was the Co-operative movement, but the WEA was not an unglamorous offshoot of Co-operation. Mansbridge's personal networks ensured that the fledgling Association was practically a youth movement at the outset, was heavily influenced by a particular strand within the English church and was not in a meaningful sense counter-cultural. While some early supporters were middle-aged in 1903, it is striking how young so many of the leading activists were. Mansbridge and Price were 27, Tawney was 23, Temple was 22, A. E. Zimmern (Oxford don and inspector at the Board of Education) was 24, Marion Phillips (early executive member and later Labour MP) was 22. A perception of the early movement was that it did good work with young men.[11] As is noted in Chapter 5, this is in striking contrast to WEA branches a hundred years later, which have (probably since the 1960s) been marked by an ageing membership, often unable to recruit younger newcomers. But it was not a youth movement *tout court*. Mansbridge had important establishment backers, who came to early WEA conferences, wrote letters to *The Times* and thus gave the WEA credibility well outside the labour movement where it might otherwise have been confined. Among these older men in their 50s and 60s who must have seemed like father figures to the young activists were Charles Gore, Anglo-Catholic bishop of Birmingham, Bishop William Percival (Tawney's former headmaster at Rugby), Oliver Lodge of Birmingham University and Samuel Barnett, first warden of Toynbee Hall.[12]

The church influence on the WEA in its infancy, and which numbered Mansbridge, Tawney, Gore, Percival and Temple among its adherents, was high Anglicanism, another surprising deviation from what might have been assumed. Nonconformity had its adherents in the WEA, of course, particularly in the regions. But Mansbridge had been drawn to cathedral services, first on holidays at Gloucester and later at Westminster Abbey, 'which became in very truth as a university to me'.[13] Bernard Jennings notes in Chapter 6 the influence of the Balliol philosopher T. H. Green on the thinking of the WEA leadership, and more immediate social networks were effective in spreading ways of applying intellectual resources to national questions of the day. One of these networks was the Synthetic Society, formed in London in 1896 by Charles Talbot, Bishop of Rochester, Charles Gore and others. 'The object was to get together representatives of as many sides of the intellectual world as could be managed, and to give them free utterance.'[14] Among the members who met to dine at the (Conservative) Junior Carlton Club were George Wyndham MP, R. B. Haldane, Oliver Lodge, T. B. Strong, William Temple and of course Talbot and Gore themselves: all of them subscribed to the aims and objectives of the WEA in the early years. The Association had from the outset friends in very high places.

The inclusion of Conservatives in the list of subscribing prominent individuals rounded up by Mansbridge and his colleagues is a further reminder of the limits of the labour influences on the WEA's founder. True, the WEA counted among its friends MPs who were trade union-sponsored supporters of the Labour Representation Committee: David Shackleton, Will Crooks and Richard Bell. But they were 'Lib–Labs' in political orientation: Shackleton became labour advisor to Winston Churchill in 1910, Bell denounced 'extremists' in his union for irresponsibility during the epochal Taff Vale dispute (to Mansbridge's approval).[15] Mansbridge's own politics remain opaque in accounts of him, but his views on Co-operation as a home for 'the better class of trade unionists', his belief that politics should be kept out of tutorial classes, his approval of men like Reuben George, a former soapbox orator ('down with all that is up!'), and Alfred Williams, a railway works blacksmith, both of whom had renounced political activity in favour of learning, suggests that he too was essentially a Lib–Lab in outlook, however discreet his pronouncements.

Under Mansbridge's guidance before 1914, the WEA could not be viewed as contributing to the socialist project, but from 1907 it was successful in attracting state money to provide workers' education. This was enough in itself to explain the personal crusade by Mary Bridges Adams against Mansbridge. As Bernard Jennings shows in Chapter 6, privately Mansbridge was nettled and angered by her persistence. There was more to her than Mary Stocks's belittling description, 'a certain Mrs Bridges Adams', would suggest. Her progressive Unitarian/feminist/socialist pedigree made her a formidable opponent. Mansbridge's chagrin must have been exacerbated by the knowledge that like him she had been a Co-operator, and counted Will Crooks as a supporter.[16]

Mary Bridges Adams was the WEA's earliest most persistent enemy, but nowhere was she able to deploy a case that the WEA did nothing for women. The Association has from the outset made an important contribution to women's education. Separate provision for women was organised from the earliest days of the movement, as Zoe Munby points out in Chapter 12, and is also clear from Chapter 5. The WEA was quick off the mark in appointing women tutors, some of whom had a clear and evident mission to extend educational opportunities for women at a time when they had not yet been given the vote. Professional women were active on the WEA's committee on the education of working women from 1907. Among them were Sophie Bryant of London University, E. P. Hughes of the Glamorgan Education Committee, J. P. Madam of the Co-op Union, Catherine Webb (noted by Sean Creighton in Chapter 2) and Ethel Snowden, wife of the Labour MP Philip Snowden.

The WEA under Mansbridge would have remained more conservative in outlook than in fact was to be the case under the national secretary J. M. Mactavish, whose own, basically Labour Party, outlook is described in Chapter 16. The 'Lib–Labism' of the period before the 1914–18 war gave way politically to a more clearly defined Labour identity in the politics of the country as a whole, and with the deaths or retirements from public office of so many of Mansbridge's earliest sponsors, as well as the founder's own collapse of health, the 'churchy' feel to the WEA gradually disappeared. What survived of quasi-religious imagery to provide the dominant motif of WEA self-fashioning between the wars and for years afterwards was the notion of 'the highway'. It was Mactavish who first called on Oxford to 'first make the highway, then use it', and the concept was a refreshing contrast to the notion of an educational ladder. The image of a broad highway along which people freely move towards educational goals is appealing and evocative not only of the Bible, but also of many mainstream writers in the literary canon. It so encapsulated the ethos of the WEA that it provided the perfect title for its journal, first published on 1 October 1908. Edited by various hands including Barbara Wootton, R. S. Lambert and D. A. Ross, it was transformed by William Emrys Williams (1896–1977) into a mass circulation 'poor man's *New Statesman*'.[17] In Chapter 7, John Atkins reveals how *The Highway* engaged often ambivalently with the issues of the day, and how it reflected the WEA's cautious approach to them.

The standard view of the WEA's experience during the years of the 1939–45 war is that the Association influenced forces education, and then the 1945 intake of the House of Commons. John Field's revisionist survey demonstrates that innovations and imaginative departures from the Board of Education regulations were too readily viewed by the Association's leadership as simply short-term expedients, a means of addressing the national crisis before normal service – the tutorial class system – could be resumed. Yet, as John Holford shows in Chapter 9, the 1953 report on trade union education reawakened the capability of the WEA to think the unthinkable which it thought it had left behind in 1945.

There seems little support from the contributors to this collection for the notion that the WEA was patronised by the state because of its potential for keeping workers quiet. As Bernard Jennings shows in Chapter 6, the WEA came to own the allegiance of many socialists; it was a successful movement because of its broad appeal. The view of Lord Eustace Percy, president of the Board of Education in 1925, 'that £100,000 spent annually on this kind of work [WEA and university extramural classes], properly controlled, would be about the best police expenditure we could indulge in' to stave off communism, was simply his view. As Jonathan Rose has recently argued, to have invested in the WEA as an agency of social control would have been a huge waste of money, since the motives and purposes of WEA students, the politics of its students, and the local allegiances it fostered, were beyond control.[18] The WEA has always been marked by a capacity to adjust to local and regional conditions. This has been a strength, as the Scottish and Welsh experiences, outlined by Rob Duncan and Richard Lewis in Chapters 10 and 11, show. Within Wales the character of the WEA in south Wales has been essentially different from that in the north. In Scotland the WEA's relationship with the state funding bodies has been notably different from that of England and Wales.

What WEA values can be sifted from its history to form an ingredient in the Association's future? An answer to this difficult question has been left to Julia Jones, in Chapter 15. Her conclusions are hers alone, just as personal as those of all the contributors to this book. Mary Stocks concluded her 1953 history with a reminder that the essence of WEA experience was the journey of a tutor 'at nightfall across an icebound shoulder of the Pennines, or through the murk of a November fog on country roads'.[19] All who have taught for the WEA will know what she means. Important though that commitment is, the WEA in 2003 would probably collectively prefer to reflect on the experiences of its students. In those experiences, and in the efforts of staff and voluntary members to sustain them, lie many histories and truths. Part of the purpose of this volume has been to subject some WEA traditions to close scrutiny. In doing so, all contributors would hope to uncover the makings of a rich WEA past that can be used by the Association's membership in its second century.

NOTES

*Place of publication London unless otherwise stated.*

1. BL Add. 65215, Mansbridge papers, Temple to Mansbridge, 26 Sept. 1908.
2. E. H. Carr, *What is History?* (1961).
3. *Dictionary of Labour Biography* v. 192–5.
4. Price, 68; *Trodden Road*, 60.
5. Stocks, 117, 126–7, 130–1, 143.
6. B. Jennings, *Knowledge is Power: A Short History of the WEA, 1903–78* (Hull, 1979); R. Fieldhouse, 'The Workers' Educational Association', in Fieldhouse and Associates, *History.*
7. C. A. Scrimgeour, *Fifty Years A-growing: A History of North Staffordshire District, the Workers' Educational Association 1921–71* (Stoke-on-Trent, 1974); E. C. Eagle, *The East Midland District of the Workers' Educational Association* (Nottingham, 1954); W. J. Souch, *A History of the Reading Branch of the Workers' Educational Association* (Reading, 1954); M. Turner, *A History of the Workers' Educational Association, Bath Branch, 1912–1987* (Bradford-on-Avon, 1987); Eve Rowley, *A History of the WEA in Longton* (Stoke-on-Trent, 1988).
8. T. Mooney, *J. M. Mactavish: General Secretary of the WEA, 1916–27: the Man and his Ideas* (Liverpool, 1979); B. Jennings, *Albert Mansbridge* (Leeds, 1973); Jennings, *The WEA in Australia. The Pioneering Years* (Sydney, 1998).
9. D. Cannadine, *Class in Britain* (2000), 106–26.
10. National Archive, WEA CENTRAL/1/2/1/1; Price, 24.
11. Dates from biographies in *Dictionary of Labour Biography* or *DNB*; Public Record Office, ED 119/1.
12. E.g. *The Times*, 25 Aug. 1903, 27 Aug. 1903, 6 Aug. 1906, 22 Oct. 1906, 27 June 1907, 17 Oct. 1908.
13. *Trodden Road*, 24–5.
14. O. Lodge, *Past Years* (1931), 172–3.

15. *Kingdom of the Mind*, 4; *DNB* for Shackleton and Crooks.
16. Jane Martin, 'An "Awful Woman"? The Life and Work of Mrs Bridges Adams, 1855–1939', *Women's History Review* viii (1999), 139–61.
17. *DNB* for Sir William Emrys Williams.
18. J. Rose, *The Intellectual Life of the British Working Classes* (New Haven, 2001), 257.
19. Stocks, 157.

# 1 The WEA – The Foundation and the Founder

*Bernard Jennings*

'With the intrepidity of youth I jumped up and urged an alliance between the two great forces there represented.' The forces were the Co-operative movement and university extension lectures, pioneered by Cambridge in 1813; the occasion was a conference held during the 1898 Co-operative Congress in Peterborough; and the speaker was Albert Mansbridge. He was in fact several years late for urging an alliance, and the twelve previous speakers in the debate had identified the reasons for the limited working-class response to university extension. They were finance, as the lectures had to be locally self-supporting, and alienation, as workers interested in education for the advancement of their class had learned to distrust middle-class benevolence. However, the 'young and enthusiastic Co-operator' was invited to present a paper on 'Co-operation and the education of citizens' at a Co-operative conference held during the Oxford Extension Summer Meeting in August 1899. This was his big chance, but he spoiled it by adopting an aggressive style, and seeming to blame the leading advocates of the Co-operative–university partnership for the difficulties against which they had been struggling. In his own words he was 'soundly trounced' and retired temporarily into private life.[1]

In later life Mansbridge laughed at his own youthful clumsiness, but always believed that he had been a pioneer in 1898–9. If he had paid more attention to the Co-operative heartland in the Pennine textile towns – Rochdale, Oldham, Todmorden and Hebden Bridge – he might have identified a WEA in embryo. Co-operative-backed extension courses (mainly Oxford) in these towns attracted audiences of several hundreds, which included small groups of earnest working-class students who sought opportunities for more progressive study. Attempts were made to form local federations of church and chapel educational societies as a base for extension activity. The most detailed scheme was put forward by Robert Halstead. He wanted school boards, democratically elected and locally with a strong Co-operative element, to be empowered to support extension lectures;

Co-operative societies to provide special libraries for adult students; and 'Student Associations', with an evangelical role, to be formed out of local organisations interested in adult education. Halstead was a four-loom fustian weaver in a producer-Co-operative mill in Hebden Bridge. Recognising the vital importance of education for the 'productive' cause, the Fustian Society was probably unique in devoting all of its educational funds to university extension.[2]

Whether or not the WEA was conceived in the Pennines, to be successful nationally it had to be born in or near London. Albert Mansbridge was brought up in Battersea, the youngest of four sons of a carpenter who rose to be a clerk of works. Scholarships took him to Battersea Grammar School, but he was forced to leave at the age of 14, in 1890, to earn a few shillings a week as an office boy. He later became a boy clerk in the government Department of Education, with the prospect, if he passed the required examination, of a modest but secure career as a second-division clerk.[3] Mansbridge, later to become a brilliant organiser, could not as a youth organise himself. He prepared erratically for four different examinations; in summer he played cricket frequently; and having joined the Church of England at about the age of 14 he was active in Sunday schools and the Band of Hope. At work he founded and edited the *Union Observer*, the journal of the Junior Civil Service Prayer Union. By the age of 17 he had developed a vocation for the Anglican priesthood, and he dared to hope that he might secure a place at Oxford or Cambridge. In 1894 he tried for a Co-operative scholarship tenable at Oxford, but was beaten by a candidate already at a university college. He found some consolation shortly afterwards by passing the examination to become a licensed lay reader.[4]

Albert Mansbridge found a partial substitute for a university in Westminster Abbey, where 'he heard with passionate delight the great preachers of the nineties'. One of these was Charles Gore, appointed canon of Westminster in December 1894. In the following Lent he delivered in the Abbey a series of lectures on the Sermon on the Mount, which were later published and became famous. Mansbridge wrote to Gore asking him to contribute an article to the *Union Observer*. Gore refused, but invited Mansbridge to his house. Over supper the young man met leading churchmen and others who walked at ease in the corridors of power. Their conversation enthralled him, and gave him for the first time a glimpse of a promised land of wisdom and authority which lay at the end of the road of learning.[5]

As a frequent visitor to Gore's house, Mansbridge found himself in the company of disciples of the Oxford philosopher Thomas Hill Green (1836–82). He had tried to rescue Christianity from the crisis caused by progress in scientific knowledge and the development of biblical criticism, by converting it into an undogmatic theology with as much concern for improving the conditions of this world as for securing salvation in the next. One Greenite product was the Christian Social Union, founded in 1889 by Gore, Henry Scott Holland and others, as a combined 'think tank' and pressure group for social reform. Green also provided practical programmes for the left wing of the Liberal Party, advocating both voluntary and state action to redress economic and social inequality.[6]

Having failed to progress in the civil service, Mansbridge had to leave the Education Department by the age of 20. In 1896 he became a clerk in the tea department of the Co-operative Wholesale Society. It was a dull and dead-end job, but it gave him a base for active work in the Co-operative movement, where he hoped to find an outlet for his idealism. In 1900 he married a fellow Sunday-school teacher, Frances Pringle, a loving wife and prudent housekeeper, who shared his ambition 'to do good work ... We both felt that we had to try to do something in addition to earning our living.' In 1901 he at last found a better job, as cashier of the Co-operative (now Permanent) Building Society. In the same year the Mansbridges had a son, John.[7]

Mansbridge was still searching for a field of practical idealism which could replace his frustrated vocation for the priesthood. He and Frances gathered a few friends together to form a Christian Economics Society. He published a pamphlet on 'The Ethical Basis of Co-operation'. He spoke occasionally at Co-operative meetings. In April 1902 he was one of the speakers at a conference of Co-operative employees held in Worcester, where he stayed with his old friend Charles Gore, the newly appointed bishop of that see. He seemed destined for the twin roles of minor Co-operative functionary and minor Co-operative evangelist. At the end of 1902, however, he sent an article entitled 'Co-operation, Trade Unionism and University Extension' to the *University Extension Journal*. Now aged 27, a husband and father with a responsible job, he had learned to control his own rhetoric, and select the most persuasive arguments. He took as his theme the social dangers of ignorance in the increasingly active working-class movement, especially the 'lack of thinking power in the rank and file'. It was in any case, he argued, a mistake to think only of immediate issues. 'Higher knowledge' would not only bring intellectual pleasure, it would guarantee 'right and sound action' in public affairs. The 'wise and forceful educational corrective' which was needed could best be provided by university extension.

The article appeared in January 1903 and was well received by both Co-operators and extension leaders. Mansbridge was encouraged to develop his ideas in two further articles. Halstead contributed an article in support, advocating an approach to trades councils, as most unions were debarred by their own rules from spending money on education. The extension administrators arranged for the four articles to be reprinted as a propaganda pamphlet. Having been advised that £50,000 would be needed to launch an 'Association to Promote the Higher Education of Working Men', Mansbridge now showed the quality which turns ideas into movements. He and Frances formed the Association at a meeting attended only by themselves and a group of friends. It was turned into a 'provisional committee of Co-operators and trade unionists' to plan the inaugural conference held in Oxford on 22 August 1903 (see plate 2).[8]

Amongst the gathering of extensionists and Co-operators, with a few trade union representatives, were some of the people who had criticised Mansbridge in 1899. This time the scripts were very different. The university spokesmen regretted their failure to reach the workers. J. A. R. Marriott, secretary of the Oxford Delegacy, thought that they had begun at the wrong end; the initiative must come from the people themselves. The keynote paper was read by Robert Halstead, who argued that

> working-class organisations framed for other purposes are now so large, and their officials so pre-occupied, that ... the higher education of their members inevitably finds a secondary place in their attention ... if the higher education of working men is to make desired progress, it will have to consolidate itself into a special movement, adopt a special organisation, form special objects of propaganda and appoint a properly equipped staff to carry out its purpose.

A constitution was adopted defining the objects as the promotion of the higher education of working men principally through university extension, the encouragement of all working-class educational efforts, and the development of an efficient school continuation system. Halstead and Mansbridge suggested the appointment of a 'suitable university man' as secretary, but the delegates insisted that the post should remain in working-class hands, and Mansbridge was elected as honorary secretary. The search for a person of appropriate standing to act as national president was not successful until 1908, when William Temple was elected (see plate 3).[9]

The gospel of the association was spread by a series of carefully organised conferences in different parts of the country, at most of which a local committee was appointed to develop the work. Mansbridge brought together progressive ecclesiastics, senior academics, politicians of different persuasions, Co-operators and trade unionists to declare their support. He kept in the background, believing that workers and their academic allies would know what was needed locally. The meeting at Manchester in October 1904, which led to the formation of the North-west District, involved the vice-chancellors of Manchester and Liverpool universities, and the presidents of the Womens' Co-operative Guild and the Manchester Trades Council. Mansbridge read letters of apology from several notables, to whom he had written in the hope of securing quotable replies. They included the prime minister, A. J. Balfour, and Winston Churchill, who was 'in full ... agreement with the objects of the association. It ought to be perfectly possible in this country for a man of high, if not necessarily extraordinary, intellectual capacity to obtain with industry and perseverance the best education in the world, irrespective of his standing in life.'[10]

Meetings at Reading in October and November 1904 produced the first branch. By the end of 1905 seven more had been founded, including one which called itself the Rochdale Education Guild, because the original title of the association was thought to be clumsy and sexist. In October 1905 the national name was changed to Workers' Educational Association. From 1 April 1906, when Mansbridge became full-time general secretary, the expansion accelerated, from 13 branches in June 1906 to 47 a year later. The healthy autonomy of these branches was reflected in the wide variety of activities which they promoted: lectures and classes in the arts and social sciences, nature-study rambles, reading circles, and courses for affiliated organisations, especially church and chapel societies.[11]

One WEA objective, uniting working-class organisations for educational endeavours, was succeeding to a remarkable degree. The other, promoting working-class extension courses, posed more difficulties. A few university institutions – Sheffield, Birmingham and Reading – were happy to provide courses for the WEA without worrying too much about the finances. Several branches which promoted conventional extension courses achieved some educational success at the expense of financial loss through charging a low fee. Mansbridge recognised that the WEA would have failed 'unless intensive class teaching up to University standard is developed'. Rochdale now staged a drama which gave him the lever he needed.[12]

The Rochdale Education Guild took over the work of the existing evening extension lectures committee, and continued to provide six-meeting Oxford courses on literary and historical subjects, which attracted average attendances of 500–600. When a course on Political and Social Problems was arranged, numbers fell to about 220, which, with low fees being charged, caused a serious financial loss. Furthermore, nearly all of the audience stayed on for the discussion class, and many wished to speak – an 'impossible proposition' according to Guild officer, T. W. Price.[13] Mansbridge promised Rochdale that if 30 people would pledge themselves to follow a course of study over two years, he would try to meet their needs. Over 40 recruits came forward. Mansbridge led a Rochdale delegation to seek the support of the chairman of the Oxford Extension Delegacy, Dr T. B. Strong. New College Oxford, where Mansbridge had found an invaluable ally in Alfred Zimmern, provided £300 to allow experimental tutorial classes to start. In January 1908 R. H. Tawney began to teach the first two tutorial classes, on Friday evenings at Longton in North Staffordshire, where a voluntary body as yet unconnected with the WEA had been developing extension work with the support of a generous LEA, and on Saturday afternoons at Rochdale.[14]

It was no accident that Oxford was the partner in this new venture. Marriott had warmly supported the WEA. A campaign for the reform of Oxford, designed both to raise its academic standards and democratise its entry, had been launched in 1906–7 by a group of young tutors, including Tawney, Zimmern and Temple, backed by Canon Barnett, warden of Toynbee Hall, and Charles Gore, now Bishop of Birmingham. Articles in prominent journals prepared the way for a debate in the House of Lords in which Gore urged the appointment of a royal commission on Oxford and Cambridge. There were other forces at work. Fifty-three representatives of Labour had been elected to the House of Commons in 1906, which made the establishment receptive to the argument that working-class political activists needed a better education. Church leaders, frustrated at their failure to achieve social reform by preaching and writing pamphlets, found Mansbridge's call 'seek ye first the education of the people and all things will be added thereunto' convenient as well as convincing.[15]

A conference on the theme 'Oxford and Working People' was held in Oxford on 10 August 1907, during the Oxford Extension Summer Meeting. Gore took the chair; 430 delegates from 210 organisations, including many trades councils and trade unions, attended. Papers read by Walter Nield, a prominent Co-operator, and Sidney Ball, fellow of St John's College, advocated a dual strategy, the provision of long tutorial classes and the admission of selected students from the latter to full-time study at Oxford, mainly following diploma courses lasting for one or two years. Ball argued that working-class leaders needed 'a social and political education such as no other institution than a university is in a position to offer'.[16]

The speech which electrified the conference was made by J. M. Mactavish, a Portsmouth shipwright, who declared: 'I claim for my class all the best that Oxford has to give. I claim it as a right, wrongfully withheld.' Workpeople should go to Oxford to train as missionaries 'for the great task of lifting their class'. For this purpose they needed new interpretations of history and economics. 'You cannot expect the people to enthuse over a science which promises no more than a life of precarious toil.'[17]

The most important speech was much quieter in tone. Robert Morant, permanent secretary to the Board of Education, explained that the board was 'looking for guidance from such an Association as is represented here to show us the way in which adult education can best be furthered. In particular we believe that it is to small classes and solid, earnest work that we can give increasingly of the golden stream.' This offer did not come out of the blue. Morant had been in close touch with Mansbridge, who had won him over with his combination of evangelical zeal and reverence for Oxford and Cambridge. He had recently arranged for Mansbridge to join the consultative committee of the Board of Education. One result of the 'golden stream' offer was the extension of tutorial classes from two years to three (which would probably have happened anyway) to qualify for the best rates of grant then available.[18]

The conference resolution requested the formation of a joint committee of 14 members, half appointed by the vice-chancellor of Oxford and half by the WEA, to devise a strategy. The press reports of the conference, well covered in the serious journals, stimulated further debate. In one article Marriott rejected the description of university extension as 'mere popular lecturing', and argued that the existing system could provide long courses for small groups of earnest students: 'It is entirely a matter of finance.'[19]

The WEA members of the joint committee included Mansbridge, Mactavish and two Labour/trade union MPs, C. W. Bowerman and David Shackleton. The seven university representatives might also have been chosen by Mansbridge. They included Dr Strong as chairman, Marriott, Zimmern, Ball and A. L. Smith of Balliol College. Zimmern and Mansbridge, joint secretaries, worked very closely together as the objectives were hammered out – a network of tutorial classes from which the ablest students would progress to full-time study at Oxford, and the design of largely new diploma courses in economics and political science. The real issue was who would control the administration of tutorial classes and the admission of working-class students to Oxford. Here Mansbridge set out deliberately to reduce Marriott to impotence. He had been a keen supporter of the WEA since its foundation, and had shown many kindnesses to Mansbridge. He was, however, a prominent Tory, and he objected to the idea that WEA students should 'if not tune the pulpits, at least choose the preachers'. Mactavish was afraid that Marriott would use the new system to send middle-class extension students to Oxford. Mansbridge wrote reassuringly, 'We do not fear him at all. He will not be allowed to even put his little finger in the new arrangements.'[20]

The report of the committee, *Oxford and Working-class Education*, published on 28 November 1908, has become a classic of adult education. It repeated the now familiar argument that

> The Trade Union secretary and the 'Labour member' need an Oxford education as much, and will use it to as good ends, as the civil servant or the barrister. It seems to us that it would involve a grave loss both to Oxford and to English political life were the close association which has existed between the University and the world of affairs to be broken or impaired on the accession of new classes to power.[21]

The report gave the WEA all it asked for, including the right of the WEA branch or 'a representative body of workmen' to have 'a controlling voice in the selection of a teacher' for a tutorial class. It was envisaged that most of the working-class students coming up to Oxford would read for one of the new-style diplomas in politics or economics. A permanent joint committee, with equal university and

WEA representation, had already been established in October 1908. It was to all intents and purposes independent of the Extension Delegacy, with its own officers and funds. Each partner was to meet half of the costs of providing tutorial classes, but grants from the Board of Education, LEAs and bodies such as the Gilchrist Trust were credited to the WEA side of the account.[22]

Marriott had persuaded the 1907–8 committee to tone down some of its criticisms of Oxford's extension work, but he still resented the 'grudging and inadequate recognition' of its contribution to working-class education. He was aggrieved at his exclusion from the management of the new schemes, and after drafting several notes of dissent, contented himself with a footnote to the report saying that he expressed no opinion on the administrative proposals. It is worth noting that Mansbridge's letter to Mactavish promising to freeze out Marriott was written only a few days after the first meeting of the committee. The episode shows that Mansbridge was not the simple-minded evangelist depicted in his own writings, but a skilful manipulator.[23]

Not all of the historians of this period have grasped the revolutionary nature of the 'workers' control' features of the Oxford scheme, but the point was not lost on the extension administrators at Cambridge (Dr D. H. S. Cranage) and London (Dr R. D. Roberts). Cranage kept the WEA at arm's length, and was very reluctant to establish a joint tutorial classes committee. Roberts thought that the WEA should confine itself to missionary work as a junior partner of university extension.[24]

Both the WEA and the tutorial class movement grew rapidly. By 1913–14 there were 145 tutorial classes, with 3,234 students, and some demands could not be met because of a shortage of funds. By 1914 the WEA had 179 branches, over 2,500 affiliated societies and nearly 11,500 individual members. At this period the WEA was, in many areas, an 'association of associations', with much effort going into provision for affiliated organisations. The Bristol branch, for example, organised in 1912–13 study circles led by WEA volunteers for 90 societies, including 16 Co-operatives. The students of tutorial classes in the Potteries went out to evangelise the neighbouring mining villages. By 1913–14 classes were being held in 24 centres with over 500 students, 70 per cent of whom were miners.[25] The working-class base of the WEA turned out to be more complex than the Co-operative-trade union alliance originally envisaged by Mansbridge and Halstead. The trade union movement accounted for 953 out of 2,555 affiliations in 1913–14, but that was only a small proportion of the possible number. The 388 Co-operative affiliations represented a much larger number of people and more consistent support. There was a wide variety of political and educational groups, but the third main element in the base consisted of religious groups, particularly adult schools and societies attached to churches and chapels.[26]

National statistics can obscure differences in the character and style of local branches. Rochdale adopted an all-party rather than a non-party stance. Prominent Conservative, as well as Liberal and Labour politicians, became honorary officers. Despite the burden of so much social harmony, the key workers in the branch, and the students of the first two tutorial classes, included a substantial proportion of committed socialists, members of the Independent Labour Party or the Social Democratic Federation. They were usually keen Co-operators and either nonconformists or ex-nonconformists, the latter carrying over into their socialist faith many of the values, certainly the idiom, of the chapel. Reading branch, by contrast, although fully committed to the WEA concept of objectivity, had a class-conscious, militant style. The branch president from 1906 to 1909 was a factory worker prominent in the SDF. The weekly public lectures on controversial issues often led to stormy discussions. Middle-class sympathisers were welcomed, but as supporters not beneficiaries.[27]

The expansion of the WEA owed a great deal to local and regional initiatives, e.g. branches evangelising neighbouring towns and villages, but Mansbridge put in an enormous personal effort. He wrote to Zimmern, apparently in December 1909,

> Today I am on my way back from a periodical rush. I have visited Nelson, Colne, Burnley, Manchester, Liverpool, Bolton, Preston, Halifax, Sheffield, Accrington, given 4 lantern lectures, interviewed 2 universities, met 5 tutorial class teachers, seen one class, attended one social, one WEA council meeting, helped to start one branch ... I really am most atrociously tired.

When Mansbridge was not talking he was writing business letters, advice to branches, articles for newspapers and journals. He emphasised the non-party and unsectarian character of the WEA on every possible occasion, and this was the subject of resolutions carried at every national demonstration. WEA members must pursue party-political objectives through the organisations, e.g. trade unions, affiliated to the WEA and not through the Association itself.[28]

The one exception was educational policy. In speeches and articles Mansbridge called for 'one system of schools unified upon a great highway in which there were no class distinctions whatever'. He demanded secondary education for all, with maintenance allowances for needy families; a school-leaving age of sixteen; access to universities for all who could benefit; a national system of crèches; and even paid holidays for all workers, so that they would be refreshed to enjoy opportunities for learning. He told a Church of England conference in 1912 that

> many working men and women are bitter because the Church has acquiesced in the existing economic order, the materialisation of our mental condition which spoils their lives, damages their children, throws up slums, produces starvation at one end of the scale and gross luxury at the other, and hating, as they must hate, the existing state of affairs, they hate the Church and reject the gospel of our Lord.

The remedy was for the church to work for 'the fullest and freest opportunities of education for all'.[29]

Mansbridge argued that his demands were not partisan, as no civilised person, of whatever political persuasion, could actually oppose the universal spread of the benefits of education. This was not, and is not, true, but radical educational policies offered a safety valve for pressures in the WEA to breach the 'non-party' rule. To most of the people who met him, Mansbridge's educational radicalism and burning zeal gave the lie to the accusation that his purpose was to draw the teeth of the workers and preserve the existing structure of class privilege.

In 1909 Mansbridge persuaded the universities involved in tutorial class provision to form the Central Joint Advisory Committee for Tutorial Classes, an effortless achievement according to William Temple, but actually won by skilful diplomacy in the face of opposition from Cranage and Roberts. At about the same time the Board of Education asked J. W. Headlam HMI and Professor L. T. Hobhouse to undertake a major inspection of tutorial classes. Their thorough and cautious report, published towards the end of 1910, concluded that with a few exceptions the quality of teaching conformed to 'the best standards of University work'. Mansbridge, however, criticised a small minority of tutors who used too narrow a range of textbooks. 'No [economics] class, for example, can afford to disregard either Marshall or Marx.' To ease the problem of book supply, Mansbridge, with the help of Canon Barnett of Toynbee Hall, formed the Central Library for Tutorial Classes in 1912. This grew into the National Central Library, now the British Library Lending Division.[30]

To Mansbridge the main deficiency of the tutorial class system was the limited scope for individual tuition. The need was met in part by the provision of summer schools, beginning in 1910 at Oxford. A wider question was access to full-time study. To the authors of the Oxford Report, the tutorial classes were intended to feed substantial numbers of students into diploma or degree courses. Only a handful of scholarships could be provided, and it was convenient for the WEA leaders when tutorial classes began to argue in favour of summer school scholarships for the many instead of full-time places for a few. A special WEA conference in May 1914 resolved that the 'growth and efficiency' of the tutorial class movement must have priority over opportunities for full-time study.[31]

In 1913 Albert and Frances Mansbridge went to Australia, and in the course of a four months' tour established the WEA in several states (see plate 4). Soon after his return Mansbridge was stricken with meningitis, from which he made only a slow recovery. He resigned the office of general secretary in 1915, to be succeeded by Mactavish. For the next 30 years he lived a very active life, helping to found the World Association for Adult Education, the Seafarers' Education Service, the British Institute of Adult Education and other bodies; making seven lecture tours in North America; lecturing and preaching widely in Britain; and writing many articles, pamphlets and seven of his eight books.[32] He retained his persuasive powers, an ability, which was almost a 'gift of tongues', to inspire quite different audiences with what was essentially the same message. In the course of time the message lost much of its dynamism, as 'education for emancipation' became 'education is emancipation', and his simple faith in the glory of education subsided into a series of slogans and platitudes. To judge the man on the basis of the latter would be a serious error. In between the enthusiastic but undisciplined young man, writing and speaking purple passages which contained little of substance, and the ageing, complacent sage, eloquent and persuasive but saying little of substance, was a quite different Albert Mansbridge, enormously energetic, enthusiastic, radical, subtle and sometimes ruthless.[33]

NOTES

*Place of publication London unless otherwise stated.*

1. *Trodden Road*, 58; *Co-operative News* 19, 26 Aug. 1898; *Oxford Journal* 19 Aug. 1899; *Oxford Chronicle* 19 Aug. 1899; N. A. Jepson, *The Beginnings of English University Adult Education* (1973), 24, 66, 81, 83. For a fuller account of the developments discussed in this chapter, L. Goldman, *Dons and Workers: Oxford and Adult Education since 1850* (Oxford, 1995), and B. Jennings, *Albert Mansbridge: The Life and Work of the Founder of the WEA* (Leeds, 2002).
2. R. Halstead, 'Working Men and University Extension', *Oxford University Extension Gazette* May 1893 and other articles in that journal Nov. 1890 –Feb. 1891; B. Jennings, 'Robert Halstead', in J. M. Bellamy and J. Saville (eds), *Dictionary of Labour Biography*, ii (1974), 54–9; B. Jennings (ed.), *Pennine Valley: A History of Upper Calderdale* (Otley, 1992), 183–6.
3. A. Mansbridge, *The Making of an Educationist* (1929),10–17; *Trodden Road*, 9–36.
4. *Trodden Road*, 24–36.
5. *Trodden Road*, 24–9.
6. Jennings, *Mansbridge*, ch. 5.
7. *Trodden Road*, 384–5.
8. *Co-operative News*, 12 Apr. 1902; *Adventure*,11–12; *University Extension Journal* Jan.–May 1903.
9. WEA, *The Working Classes and Higher Education* (conference papers, 1903), and *The Higher Education of Working Men* (conference report, 1903); *Co-operative News*, 29 Aug., 12 Sept. 1903; *Adventure*, 17.
10. *Co-operative News*, 13 Aug., 15 Oct. 1904.
11. *Co-operative News*, 8 Oct., 19 Nov. 1904; W. J. Souch, *The History of the Reading Branch of the Workers' Educational Association 1904–54* (Reading, 1954); *Adventure*, ch. 4.
12. WEA, Annual Reports 1905–7.
13. Price, 30.
14. A. Mansbridge, *University Tutorial Classes* (1913), 17–20.
15. Jennings, *Mansbridge*, chs. 3 and 5.
16. WEA, Papers submitted to the National Conference, 10 Aug. 1907; *Oxford Chronicle* 16 Aug. 1907; Goldman, *Dons and Workers*, 117–22.
17. *University Tutorial Classes*, 26, 194–7; Price, 37.
18. Oxford University Archives, Rewley House MSS, correspondence relating to the establishment of tutorial classes 1907–8 (hereafter tutorial classes 1907–8), R. Morant to Mansbridge 4 Dec. 1911 (which shows that Morant did attend the 1907 conference); BL Add. MS 65215, Mansbridge MSS.
19. J. A. R. Marriott, 'Oxford and the Nation', *The Nineteenth Century* lxii, July–Dec. 1907, 674–88.
20. J. A. R. Marriott, *Memories of Four Score Years* (1946), 139; tutorial classes 1907–8.
21. Sylvia Harrop (ed.), *Oxford and Working-class Education* (new edn, Nottingham, 1987), 141–2.

22. Harrop (ed.), *Oxford and Working Class Education*, 150–4, 158–60; tutorial classes 1907–8; Goldman, *Dons and Workers*, chs. 4 and 5.
23. Rewley House MSS, J. A. R. Marriott to Dr T. B. Strong, 26 June 1908, and memoranda, 'Workers Joint Committee' file; *Oxford and Working-class Education*, 131–4.
24. *University Tutorial Classes*, 16; *The Nation*, 5 Aug. 1911; Bodleian Library, Zimmern MSS Mansbridge to A. E. Zimmern 2 Mar. 1909 and n.d. [May 1910]; B. B. Thomas, 'R. D. Roberts and Adult Education', in B. B. Thomas (ed.), *Harlech Studies* (Cardiff, 1938), 23–30.
25. WEA, Annual Reports 1912–14.
26. WEA, Annual Reports 1913–14.
27. Rochdale Reference Library, Rochdale Education Guild Minutes 1905–10; *Rochdale Observer* 12 Apr. 1905, 18 Apr. 1908; S. Yeo, *Religion and Voluntary Organisations in Crisis* (1976), 253; University of Reading Library, Reading WEA branch records, correspondence 1950 about the pre-1914 branch.
28. WEA, Annual Reports 1905–10; *The Highway*, Dec. 1908; Zimmern MSS, Mansbridge to Zimmern, n.d. [?Dec. 1909].
29. WEA, Annual Reports 1907–14; *The Highway*, Dec. 1909–Feb. 1912; *Cambridge Independent Press*, 14 Aug. 1908; Mansbridge, *The Education of the People*, reprinted from the official report of the 1912 Church Congress.
30. F. A. Iremonger, *William Temple, his Life and Letters* (Oxford, 1948), 76–7; Cambridge University Library, Stuart House MSS, Cambridge Syndicate Letter Book Feb. 1909–Oct. 1911; *University Tutorial Classes*, 142–63.
31. *University Tutorial Classes*, 118–20; Rewley House MSS, Central Joint Advisory Committee Minutes 1910–12.
32. *University Tutorial Classes*, 99–110, 188–93; WEA, Annual Report 1912–13; National Archive, WEA Central EC Minutes 22 Sept. 1913 and AGM Minutes 16 May 1914.
33. B. Jennings, *The WEA in Australia, the Pioneering Years* (Sydney, 1998); Jennings, *Mansbridge*, ch. 8.

# 2 Battersea and the Formation of the Workers' Educational Association

*Sean Creighton*

Working-men today are all afire to act politically. Their Mecca is Parliament, their local temple the Municipality. The plank of their platform is labour representation. A taste of affairs highly to be desired, if it be the result of normal evolution pre-conditioned by wise education, but at present it bears no such evidence. If it be admitted, reasonably enough, that working men, as they stand, should be represented on governing bodies, it must also be admitted that lack of thinking power in the rank and file tends to nullify the good effects of such representation, however capable the representatives themselves.[1]

This formulation used by Albert Mansbridge in his *University Extension Journal* articles in early 1903, advocating an alliance between the Co-operative, trade union and university extension movements, is rooted in his upbringing in the 'municipal Mecca' of Battersea in south-west London. Battersea had a vibrant Co-operative movement throughout the second half of the nineteenth century, providing a strong base which enabled activists to contribute to a range of national Co-operative initiatives, such as the Co-operative Permanent Building Society and the Women's Co-operative Guild. This was in the context of a strong, organised working class which, under his leadership, saw John Burns elected to the new London Council at the end of 1888 and to Parliament in 1892, and which took control of local affairs through the Vestry from 1894 and the newly formed Metropolitan Borough Council from 1900 to 1909. This control was exercised in a Progressive Alliance partnership with Liberals.[2]

Albert's upbringing, schooling, and Co-operative and Congregational and later social progressive Anglican activities not only developed a sense of the importance of education for himself, but also for the working class as a whole. It was out of this unique combination of influences, of family, education, religion, and Co-operation within the Battersea political context of the concept of partnership between different movements, that Mansbridge formulated the idea that working-class education could be furthered by his proposed triangular alliance.

Albert's father Thomas Mansbridge, a building worker, and his wife Frances, came to London with their four sons in 1880, lodging for a short while in the Brixton/Herne Hill area, before settling in Battersea at 187 Battersea Bridge Road.[3] Aged 5, Albert started going to the infant boys' department of the local board school at Bolingbroke Road, and then from the age of nine to the Surrey Lane board school.[4] The Battersea the Mansbridges settled in was entering the last stage of its transformation from a largely agricultural and market garden area and rural retreat for the wealthy at the beginning of the nineteenth century to a dense and industrial part of the metropolis at its end. It was dominated by a tangle of railway lines going through Clapham Junction into Waterloo and across the Thames to Victoria and north-west London, by railway engineering works,[5] and a wide range of industries including flour milling and sugar refining; chemical, vitriol, vinegar and oil works; boat repairs, starch, gelatin, candle and crucible manufacturing. Laundering and munitions would soon join the list. Large numbers of workers and their families, like the Mansbridges, poured into the area. The population had risen from 5,540 in 1831 to 107,262 in 1881 and continued to rise through Albert's childhood and young adulthood to 160,000 in 1901. This dramatic transformation brought social problems in its wake. When the Mansbridges moved in, Battersea was called the 'sink hole of Surrey'. Unemployment and poverty were a constant threat. The Bridge Lane area near where they lived was known as 'Little Hell'.[6] The Thames-side areas, especially Nine Elms, were subject to frequent flooding.[7] Nine Elms, described as 'an island of shabby streets', had developed into a slum, whose population was largely Irish.

Having settled in their new home, Thomas and Frances would have become aware that Battersea had dozens of working-class organisations, including the lodges and courts of the friendly society benefit orders of the Oddfellows and Foresters, branches of smaller orders and local friendly societies, Friends of Labour loan societies, and trade union branches. All were training grounds in organisational financial management, and in participative and representative democracy. Many individuals were members of more than one type of organisation.[8] As both were convinced Co-operators and Congregationalists, and as he and most of his friends 'were keen trade unionists',[9] Thomas and Frances would have looked to see which organisations to join: the Bridge Lane Congregational Church, the Battersea and Wandsworth Co-operative Society, and the Amalgamated Society of Carpenters and Joiners. Albert was 'brought into contact with the Movement as a child'.[10]

Among the activities at the Bridge Lane Congregational Church were a Sunday school and Band of Hope. The Sunday school went on excursions to the rural areas on the edge of London, and had magic lantern shows. Albert recited poetry to the band, the young people's temperance group.[11] The minister of the church, Rev. Jarratt, preached the sermon at a church parade of the Battersea temperance societies in support of the Temperance Orphans' Asylum in Sunbury.[12] Albert's immersion in religion was supported at his board schools, to which he acknowledged a strong debt.[13]

Family life was intellectually stimulating and introduced Albert to a wide range of experiences and people. Home life was 'a background of quietness and peace'. 'It was not in any sense luxurious, rather the reverse, but nothing essential was ever wanting. Moreover, not only my parents, but my brothers also, brought to it interesting and adventurous people. There was no boredom; life was too full.'[14] His already wide horizons were further enlarged when aged eleven he entered Sir Walter St. John's middle school as a scholarship boy, and then a year later Battersea grammar school.[15] It brought him into contact with boys whose fathers belonged to the professional class,[16] and he was particularly friendly with the son of Henry Bradley, one of the editors of the *Oxford English Dictionary* and the President of the Philological Society.[17]

These rich experiences were reinforced by his parents' membership of the Co-operative Society. Started in 1854 as the workmen's stores at Price's candles works between the Thames and York Road, it had opened up its membership from 1865 and changed its name in 1872. By 1881 it had developed a wide range of activities, including a provident fund to support aged members, mainly widows, in 'adverse conditions'. Its main store and office was at 2 Plough Road near the candle works, and a shop on Battersea Park Road served mainly railwaymen. This link with railwaymen was personified in John Pilcher, a founder member of the Amalgamated Society of Railway Servants (ASRS), who was to write about Co-operative affairs for its newspaper, *The Railway Gazette*, and was a prominent member of the Battersea Society.[18]

Battersea Co-operative Society had a committee of management elected every six months along with two non-committee members acting as auditors. Thomas Mansbridge was an auditor of the second half of 1895, although unable to attend the audit meeting.[19] In 1882 the society set up a committee of nine members to plan Co-operative education activities. This included selling the *Co-operative News* at half-price, distributing copies of the *Metropolitan Co-operator* free, holding weekly discussions and public meetings, inserting occasional articles on Co-operation in local papers, organising tea and social meetings, and forming a branch of the Women's Co-operative League, later Guild. These activities were to be funded by a grant of between 1.5 and 2.5 per cent of net profits. Thomas Mansbridge served on the education committee for at least one period in 1888, while Frances was a member of the Guild.[20]

Thomas Webb, a founder member of the society was full-time secretary until 1890, and president from 1890 to 1896. He was active in Co-operative ventures outside Battersea, especially the Co-operative Permanent Building Society of which he was president from 1884.[21] Albert held Webb in high respect. 'His ripe wisdom was expressed with a kindliness which he showered upon all. Children, of whom one was the present writer, knew him as a friend.' He was 'the most prominent Co-operator in the south of England. He was a veritable "Prince in Israel".'[22] Webb's son Arthur became assistant secretary of the Battersea and Wandsworth Society in 1884, and was collecting agent for the building society. Even after becoming the building society's national secretary in 1892, he continued to come to the Battersea office to collect subscriptions. On Arthur, Albert wrote: 'If ever a society was built with one man at its centre and focus, it is the Co-operative Permanent Building Society.'[23]

The secretary (later president) of the Battersea branch of the Women's Co-operative Guild, of which Frances Mansbridge was a pioneer member, was Thomas Webb's daughter, Catherine. Meetings were held at the society's bakery. Catherine went on to be a leading national Co-operator and worker for women's organisations.[24] As he did at the Band of Hope, Albert recited poetry at guild meetings. 'Imagine a small boy of five or six years old standing there ... pouring out the sentiments of mature poets.'[25] By the time he was 12, in 1888, the Battersea Co-operative Society had a central stores and office, three branch shops, a butchery, provided a banking service and ran clothing and coal clubs. The society had 1,256 members. The Mansbridge family probably took part in May 1889 in the procession around the neighbourhood to celebrate the opening of the new bakery, led by the Anchor Co-operative brass band.

It was on this firm basis of organised collective self-help and mutual activity that the politically aware members of Battersea's growing working class built up a range of political organisations, which at the end of 1888 saw a spectacular electoral breakthrough. The main bodies exercising local government and poor law functions were the vestry, the Wandsworth District Board of Works on which vestrymen sat, and the Wandsworth and Clapham Board of Guardians. The electoral basis of the vestry and the guardians was tiny.[26] The early 1880s saw the establishment of several radical Liberal associations and activities by the social reform, clerical Guild of St. Matthew's. Many others will have shared the view of local radical W. J. Norton: 'So long as the people remain drunken and ignorant, so long will the wealthy tread them down. Until the workers take their own affairs in their own hands, their cause will be practically negligent.'[27] Radicals began to be elected to the vestry, among them (from 1882 until 1891) Thomas Webb.

For general election purposes Battersea was part of the parliamentary seat of Mid-Surrey up to 1885. The growing radical mood became clear during the 1880 parliamentary election when the Shaftesbury Park estate residents showed their political preferences by using a Conservative election meeting to endorse overwhelmingly the Liberal candidates.[28] Thomas Mansbridge appears in the electoral register for the Battersea constituency of the new parliamentary borough of Battersea and Clapham created in 1885. This comprised two constituencies, the largely working-class Battersea in the north, and the better-off Clapham constituency south of Lavender Hill and the Clapham parish. Political issues taken up by the radical and Liberal organisations included the case for borough status, and against government policies in Ireland. Leading activists spoke at demonstrations in Hyde Park, and were on the councils of the Land Nationalisation Society and League. About 5,000 marched from Battersea to a Hyde Park reform demonstration in June 1884. The Battersea branch of the National Secular Society was very active. One of its members, John Burns, a member of the executive of the Social Democratic Federation (SDF), gave a talk at the Secular Society on the causes of poverty, which led to the establishment of Battersea SDF.[29] In a few short years, its work would transform Battersea's working-class politics.

The establishment of the Battersea parliamentary seat in 1885 presented both Liberals and Conservatives with a serious political and organisational challenge. They had quickly to re-organise their structures around the new constituency boundaries. The Battersea Liberal and Radical Association was formed in May 1885 with Thomas Webb elected as first treasurer.[30] Because Battersea had been going through such a fast rate of change, the local establishment had no deep-rooted methods of social control and was unable to keep pace with the changes. The Association chose Octavius Morgan, director of one of the major local employers, Morgan Crucible, as its candidate. He was elected that year as Battersea's first MP.[31]

Much has been written about the activities of Battersea SDF-ers John Burns and Tom Mann, including Mann's formation of the 8-hour campaign, and Burns's involvement in the November 1887 demonstrations in Trafalgar Square.[32] By 1888 Battersea SDF had developed sufficient support to have members elected as vestrymen.[33] It then put Burns forward for one of the two Battersea seats on the newly created London County Council (LCC). Burns was elected to one seat with 3,071 votes, and James Tims, secretary of the Metropolitan Radical Federation (set up in 1886) to the second with 2,307. Both men had built a strong foundation of political support and organisation, rooted in supporters and activists sharing a common political view of how social change could be achieved.

As Albert went through his early teens, Battersea was centre stage in the dramatic growth of 'new unionism' after 1888. Burns and his colleagues Tom Mann and John Ward played leading roles in the matchgirls' strike, gasworkers' strike, the strike for the 'dockers' tanner', the formation of new national unions like the Gas Workers and General Labourers, the General Railway Workers, the Navvies', Bricklayers', Labourers' and General Labourers' Union, and the National Federation of Labour Unions.[34] Among the many improvements won by local workers was a reduction in hours agreed by the Co-operative Society for its employees.[35]

Tom Mann transformed the London Trades Council into a veritable labour parliament for all London's workers. He was instrumental in its taking part in the first May Day demonstration in 1890, in which 200,000 people participated.[36] On the LCC Burns advocated the 8-hour day, direct employment in place of the use of contractors, and the adoption of a fair wages clause in all council contracts. He worked closely with the radical/Liberal Progressive councillors. The pace of events and the level of activity in Battersea was such that you can sense the collective adrenalin pumping round, with activists heady with success that events were going their way. It was in this atmosphere that Albert Mansbridge left school aged 14 to start work in March 1890 in the East End for a cod-liver oil and guano merchant.[37] By now Thomas was earning sufficient money as a builders' foreman to move into better housing at 21 Rosenau Road.[38]

Battersea once again became prominent nationally when John Burns was elected to Parliament as Battersea's MP in 1892. He had worked since August 1889 to gain Radical and Liberal support for his parliamentary candidature, through building up a set of alliances and new organisations, especially the Battersea Labour League. One of its aims was educational: 'the diffusion of economic, social and political knowledge'.[39] The last three years up to 1892 had convinced Burns that it was through alliance building that real practical improvements could be achieved. As he wrote in the March 1892 issue of the journal *The Nineteenth Century*: 'Much that was considered utopian and impractical three years ago is being secured, and much more is on the verge of realisation.'[40] He did not compromise by obtaining Liberal support. He made it clear that he was standing as an independent Labour candidate and as a Social Democrat and was elected with 5,616 votes to the Conservative's 4,057.

Once in Parliament Burns did not neglect the further development of the local movement. On his suggestion the Labour League initiated the Trades and Labour Council in 1894.[41] Members included the League, the SDF, radical/liberal organisations and both 'old' and 'new' trade union branches. The Trades Council established a local election committee with the Liberals, which fielded a united slate of candidates standing as 'Progressives', and won control of the vestry. Among those elected were men like Alfred Sellicks and Arthur Raynor who were active nationally in their trade unions, while Sellicks was an active supporter of Co-operation.[42]

From 1888 to 1894 Battersea activists were therefore in the forefront of setting a new agenda for the organised working class and new organisations. That agenda was not limited to the need for workers to organise to improve their conditions at work, but also for wider social change, labour representation and a new role for local and central government. The practical implementation of municipal socialism as more than just a combination of municipal liberalism and enterprise, was in part made possible by the new form of political organisation that emerged as a result of new unionism. Burns and the others helped create opportunities and openings for decisive political action, if others in the movement had the vision and energy to exploit them. New unionism was a seed bed for new political, economic and social developments. Battersea Labour League took the view that

> it is not too much to say that, had every district in the United Kingdom done as well as Battersea in the duties of Parliamentary, County Council, School Board and Municipal representation, and the general education of its citizens in respect of economic, social and kindred matters, the fundamental change in the bases of society for which we have worked, do work, and shall continue to work, would today be within measurable distance of realisation.[43]

The movement now faced a new set of challenges related to exercising and retaining local political control, running services, and setting the rates, as well as continuing the basic work of trade union organisation and defence and improvement of working conditions. There was also an awareness that while the aim of employing direct labour had great merits, there were also potential dangers if workers developed negligent attitudes. It had hard lessons to learn, just as the Co-operative Society had already found in its capacity as an employer when its workers campaigned for the 8-hour day. There were inevitable tensions, disputes, and fallings out within the Alliance and the Trades Council.[44]

The Trades Council remained active in its own right on trade union and general issues affecting the working class, as well as being the leading force within the Alliance both in the vestry and the board of guardians, which it considered the Progressive and labour members helped to humanise. It backed the anti-vaccination campaign from 1896. It supported local, regional and national trade union struggles in Britain, like those of the engineers and south Wales miners. It took an interest in international affairs, and affiliated to organisations like the Workmen's Housing Council and the National Federation of Workmen's Trains Committee.[45]

While this political breakthrough was under way in Battersea, Albert had changed jobs in 1891 becoming a boy copyist at the Inland Revenue and then with the education department in Whitehall.[46] Already knowledgeable about the Co-operative and trade union movement, it is in this period that the third component of his conception of an educational alliance began to be built, through conversion to Anglicanism and immersion in university extension education, in which social reform Anglicans were active.[47]

He attended university extension classes on chemistry at Munt's Hall in Clapham Junction in 1891, then economics classes at the new Battersea Polytechnic:[48] Burns and Octavius Morgan were among its governors.[49] He went on to study chemistry, political economy and elementary Greek at Birkbeck College,[50] civil service classes at King's College, and took the Greek test at Oriel College, Oxford, for the Co-operative movement's Neale Scholarship. By now he linked his Christianity with his Co-operative background. 'I believed in it as an expression of Christianity in trade', he asserted; he 'had constant sympathy with trade unionism'.[51] He changed direction again, further immersing himself in the Co-operative movement, becoming a clerk in the tea department of the Co-operative Wholesale Society in Whitechapel.[52] He 'began to experience even more deeply how ... unsatisfied were the educated needs of working men and women'.[53] His work brought him into contact with the 'old-time Co-operative leaders such as ... Thomas Webb of Battersea'.[54]

He wrote articles and attended classes in Co-operative and industrial history.[55] From 1897 he began to teach industrial history at the CWS to his fellow workers.[56] He represented the Battersea Society at the summer meeting of Co-operators in May 1897.[57] In 1898 he became an instructor for the higher evening commercial education opportunities provided by the London school board.[58] Meanwhile the Battersea Society began to go into a period of decline; a deep rift had been caused by the committee's refusal in 1898 to sack the general manager, which led many members to resign. Although the manager in fact left in January 1899, there was no upward turn.

During his years of self-education and teaching, Albert developed the idea that

the teaching of Economics, Industrial History and Citizenship could be carried on so much better in Co-operation with the University Extension Movement as to justify my claim that Co-operators should cease trying to do it in isolation, and should rather concentrate on the teaching of Co-operative Principles and Techniques, in itself an enormous task, necessitating a college for the purpose.[59]

As winner of a Co-operative Exhibition, he attended a special educational conference being held as part of the Peterborough Co-operative Congress during Whitsun 1898.[60] This led to the invitation to read a paper entitled 'Co-operation and Education in Citizenship' at the August 1899 Oxford University extension summer school.

Meanwhile, Battersea was once again going through a period of ferment and national attention, as a result of the opposition of Burns, the Trades and Labour Council and most of the organisations in the Progressive Alliance to the British involvement in the Boer War in South Africa (1899–1902).[61] Albert seems to have been immune to all this. In 1901 (until 1905) he became cashier for the Co-operative Permanent Building Society, 'a society based on true ideals of house production and owning'.[62] Albert spent many Saturday afternoons at Co-operative meetings and was a delegate at annual conferences, often speaking on education. In the years 1901 to 1903 the Battersea Society made no profits. Albert was aware of the spiral downwards. In 1901 he made an impassioned appeal to the members:

> Co-operators of Battersea! let us – ere our Society feels its strength passing; whilst it still can realise power – develop enthusiasm for real Co-operation; look, in a business-like way, to our shops; education wherever possible; above all, take upon ourselves the legitimate burden which municipal Battersea forces upon us.[63]

But the decline continued. In 1902 the provident fund cash payments were replaced by paying beneficiaries in goods from the shop for a year. By early 1903 the Society's membership was down to 954.[64] In 1904 the Society made a loss, sales dropping to under half of the 1896 peak.

During the last year of decline, 1903, Albert and his wife Frances were so busy in establishing the WEA that they had no time to devote to helping the society, other than through Albert's representing it in relation to the WEA. Now firmly 'convinced that the future of England would depend largely upon the development of education in the widest possible sense among working men and women, who constitute by far the largest proportion of the population',[65] he developed his ideas in the *University Extension Journal* early in 1903.

His continuing personal educational search had led him to classes at Toynbee Hall settlement in Whitechapel, of which Charles Gore was a supporter.[66] Under its founder and warden, Samuel Barnett, the settlement had helped support the dockers in their strike of 1889, and assisted unorganised workers' groups. It 'called attention to the evils of casual labour, the horrors of overcrowding, the injustice of low wages, and the cruelty of the workhouse instead of old age pensions to the veterans of industry'.[67] At home in 52 Winsham Grove, Albert and Frances set up their 'Association to Promote the Higher Education of Working Men'.[68] On 14 July 1903 they and their Co-operative and trade union friends set up a provisional committee. Its members were A. H. Thomas, a brushmaker, George Alcock, a trustee of the ASRS who became its first historian,[69] their friend and neighbour William Salter, W. H. Berry, Frederick Rockell, J. W. Cole and Leonard Idle, the latter two both Co-operative employees. This provisional committee's first meetings were held at Toynbee Hall.[70] With the help of university extension leaders, the committee organised an inaugural conference in Oxford on 22 August.[71] Among those the conference elected to the committee to take over from the provisional committee were Albert (as founder and as representative of the Battersea and Wandsworth Co-operative Society), Alcock, and George Dew, the London County Council alderman and member of the Amalgamated Society of Carpenters and Joiners. Like Thomas Mansbridge, Dew had come to London from Gloucester, and he was also a leading official in the mutual Hearts of Oak Building Society.[72]

While the WEA's fortunes grew, so those of the Battersea Society continued to fade, but it was able to celebrate its Jubilee in 1904. By the end of the year, with the society making a loss of nearly £690, and with membership now at 691, Albert and Frances moved to Ilford. It is ironic that the society out of which the WEA developed was unable to revive, and foundered in 1908. The local Women's Co-operative Guild did not go down with it. The mushrooming of working-class organisations from the mid-1880s, particularly of trade unionism in the 1890s, and the heavy involvement of working-class activists in the council and the board of guardians and in national trade union and Co-operative organisations, played its part in depriving the society of organisational talent. The society's fate should also be seen in the context of an increasingly complex politics around alliances and labour representation. The Progressive Alliance itself was also going through a crisis, finally suffering a rout at the polls in 1906, from which it took three years to recover. One of the defeated candidates, Frederick George Barns, had been a Co-operative Society committee member in the 1880s and 1890s.

The Battersea Society's collapse was obviously a setback but not the end of Co-operation and educational activity in Battersea.

University extension classes continued to be held at the Polytechnic and the town hall.[73] Stalwart Battersea Co-operators Leonard Idle, John Pilcher, and William Salter and his wife became members of the WEA, as did Arthur and Catherine Webb, although they no longer lived in Battersea.[74] Catherine went on to chair the advisory committee on the education of working women, set up at the 1905 annual conference (see plate 1).[75] Salter became secretary of the WEA's South London branch.[76]

In May 1907 Battersea Trades and Labour Council affiliated to the South London WEA branch.

> From the reports we have received it is evident that good work has been, and is being done, lectures have been given upon economic and historical subjects, the same being well-attended, and highly appreciated by those interested in those subjects, visits to places of interest in the Metropolis have been arranged, and their historical associations thoroughly described and explained by competent lecturers. A Social Survey Committee, to study the social life of the Borough has been formed, and as they intend to be very thorough in their investigations, no doubt a good result will be obtained.[77]

By 1910 the Battersea branch consisted of 89 individual members and three affiliated societies including the Labour League, the Liberal and Radical Association, the Trades and Labour Council, and seven trade union branches.[78] One of the activities in 1910 was a visit by a number of members to the Hampstead Garden Suburb home of Mrs Barnett, the widow of the canon, where they chatted with Albert Mansbridge until late in the evening.[79] Having emerged from Battersea, the WEA found it received its support in return.

NOTES

*Place of publication London unless otherwise stated.*

1. A. Mansbridge, 'Co-operation, Trade Unionism and University Education', *University Extension Journal* 1903, quoted in *Kingdom of the Mind*, 1–2. The author would like to thank Stan Newens and Michael Ward for help with source material. His own privately published work cited here is available from 18 Ridge Rd, Mitcham, CR4 2ET.
2. S. Creighton, 'From Political Exclusion to Control. Radical and Working-class Organisation in Battersea 1830s–1918' (privately published, 1999).
3. Leonard Clark, intro. to *Kingdom of the Mind*, x.

4. *Kingdom of the Mind*, xi.
5. For details see E. Course, *London Railways* (1962); J. B. Atkinson, *The West London Railways* (1984); T. Sherwood, *Change at Clapham Junction. The Railways of Wandsworth and South West London* (1994); B. K. Cooper and R. Antil, *LSWR. A Tribute to the London and South Western Railway* (1988); J. N. Faulkner, *Clapham Junction* (1991).
6. Quoted in C. Wrigley, 'Liberals and the Desire for Working-class Representation in Battersea 1886–1922', in K. D. Brown (ed.), *Essays in Anti-Labour History* (Basingstoke, 1974).
7. J. Thomson and A. Smith, *Street Life in London* (1973),12–13.
8. S. Creighton, 'Working-class Loan and Benefit Society and Political Organisations in Battersea c. 1850–1894', unpublished paper at the Ninth British–Dutch Colloquium in Labour History, Bergen, 2–4 Sept. 1994; Creighton, *Ancient Order for Foresters in Battersea and Neighbouring Districts* (privately published, Agenda Services, 1999); *Friends of Labour Loan Societies. An Introductory Essay* (privately published, Agenda Services, 1999).
9. *Trodden Road*, 47.
10. *Trodden Road*, 40–1.
11. *Trodden Road*, 13–14.
12. *South London Press*, 27 June 1885, 7.
13. BL Add. 65338, A. Mansbridge, '"Let There Be Light": A Laymen's View of the Church Militant' (?unpublished paper), 5, 42.
14. *Trodden Road*, 43.
15. Admission No. 810. London Metropolitan Archives, LMA ACC 23/199, Sir Walter St. John middle school admission book.
16. *Trodden Road*, 19.
17. Mansbridge, '"Let There Be Light"', 43.
18. *Kingdom of the Mind*,169–172; S. Creighton, 'Battersea: The Municipal Mecca', in B. Lancaster, P. Maguire (eds), *Towards the Co-operative Commonwealth. Essays in the History of Co-operation* (1996); J. Pilcher, *History of Battersea and Wandsworth Co-operative Society* (1904).
19. Battersea and Wandsworth Co-operative Society, *Eighty-second Half-yearly Report to end of Dec.1895*.
20. Battersea and Wandsworth Co-operative Society, *Sixty-seventh Half-yearly Report to End of June 1888*.
21. H. F. Bing, 'Webb, Thomas Edward' in J. Saville and Joyce Bellamy (eds), *Dictionary of Labour Biography*, i, 343–4.
22. A. Mansbridge, *Brick upon Brick. Co-operative Permanent Building Society, 1884–1934* (1934), 45–6; photo, 47.
23. Mansbridge, *Brick upon Brick*, 55–6; photo, 73.
24. Joyce Bellamy and H. F. Bing, 'Webb, Catherine' in John Saville and Joyce Bellamy (eds), *Dictionary of Labour Biography* ii, 396–8. Profile in *Lloyds Weekly*, 29 May 1904.
25. *Trodden Road*, 13–14.
26. Janet Roebuck, *Urban Development in 19th-century London. Lambeth, Battersea and Wandsworth, 1838–1888* (1979).
27. *The Radical*, 4 Feb. 1882, 3.

28. Janet McCalman, 'Respectability and Working-class Politics in Late-Victorian London', Australian National University thesis, 1975.
29. The branch is described in detail in W. S. Sanders, *Early Socialist Days* (1927).
30. *South London Press*, 16 May 1885.
31. Morgan Crucible Company Ltd., *Battersea Works 1856–1956* (1956).
32. For Burns see: K. D. Brown, *John Burns* (1977); J. Burgess, *John Burns: The Rise and Fall of a Right Honourable* (Glasgow, 1911); A. Page Grubb, *From Candle Factory to British Cabinet. The Life Story of the Right Hon. John Burns* (1908); W. Kent, *John Burns. Labour's Lost Leader* (1950). For Tom Mann see: Dona Torr, *Tom Mann and His Times. Vol. One: 1856–1890* (1956); J. White, *Tom Mann* (Manchester, 1991).
33. E.g. C. Marson, *Putney and Wandsworth Borough News*, 19 May 1888.
34. S. Creighton, 'Battersea and New Unionism', *South London Record*, iv (1989).
35. *Dictionary of Labour Biography*, ii, 396–8.
36. Sean Creighton, 'The First May Day', *History and Social Action*, privately published, May 2001.
37. *Trodden Road*, 12; *Kingdom of the Mind*, 146.
38. Electoral registers at Wandsworth Local History Collection; Public Record Office, 1891 Census.
39. Battersea Labour League, *Report and Statement of Accounts for the Year Ending Dec. 1894*, in Wandsworth Local History Collection.
40. J. Burns, 'The London County Council', *The Nineteenth Century*, Mar.1892, 496–514.
41. B. Rudder, *Builders of the Borough. A Century of Achievement by Battersea and Wandsworth Trades Union Council from 1894 to 1994* (Battersea and Wandsworth Trades Union Council, 1992).
42. *The Labour Annual 1898*, 205.
43. Battersea Labour League, *Report and Statement of Accounts ... 1894*.
44. SDF member F. D. Summers wrote a pamphlet 'The Socialists Work on the Battersea Vestry, Scathing Exposure of the Battersea Labour League, Showing How they Hamstrung the Progressive Horse and Backed the Car of Progress into the Ditch of Reaction' (1896). Sean Creighton, 'Labour. The Problem of Alliances. The Experience of Battersea 1900–1929', *History and Social Action*, iii, June 2002, privately published.
45. Battersea Trades and Labour Council, *Annual Report 1896-7-8*. In Wandsworth Local History Collection.
46. *Kingdom of the Mind*, 147.
47. BL Add. 65320, Mansbridge Papers, cuttings from *Union Observer*, 12, 14, 16.
48. BL Add. 65346, Mansbridge Papers, notes, chronology of education and experience.
49. Battersea Polytechnic Opening Ceremony Brochure, Feb. 1894, Wandsworth Local History Collection.
50. *Kingdom of the Mind*, 128.
51. *Trodden Road*, 40–41, 47.
52. *Kingdom of the Mind*, xii.

53. BL Add. 65346, biographical notes about Albert Mansbridge drafted by Leonard Clark, Sept.1939 (File C), 5.
54. '"Let There Be Light"', 49.
55. *Trodden Road*, 41.
56. *Adventure*, 10.
57. *Co-operative News*, 15 May 1897.
58. *Trodden Road*, 52.
59. *Adventure*,10.
60. *Kingdom of the Mind*, xiii.
61. R. Price, *An Imperial War and the British Working Class* (1972); C. Wrigley, 'Battersea Republicanism and the 1902 Coronation', in *Republicanism and War in Battersea*, Wandsworth History Workshop, 1993.
62. *Trodden Road*, 45.
63. Add. 65320, 34, news clipping.
64. *Co-operative News*, 28 Feb.1903, 232.
65. *Trodden Road*, 48.
66. London Metropolitan Archives LMA/A/TOY/21: J. J. Mallon, 'The Story of Toynbee Hall', reprinted from *Social Services Review* Jan. 1939, 3.
67. 'Story of Toynbee Hall', 5–6.
68. *Adventure*, 11–12; BL Add. 65346, File C3, undated note of period from 1889, 3.
69. G. W. Alcock, *Fifty Years of Railway Trade Unionism* (1922).
70. *Adventure*,12; National Archive, WEA CENTRAL /1/2/1/1.
71. *Co-operative News*, 29 Aug. 1903, 1053–4; *Adventure*, 14, 31.
72. London Metropolitan Archives, LMA P18.4, 'Members of the London County Council 1889–1925', LCC June 1925, 97; '"Let There Be Light"', 38.
73. *Co-operative News* 16 July 1904; Battersea Polytechnic Prospectus of Day and Evening Classes 1908–9, Wandsworth Local History Collection; J. L. Taylor, 'The Battersea Tutorial Class on Sociology', *The Highway*, iv, no. 28, Jan. 1911, 57–8.
74. National Archive, WEA CENTRAL/4/2/2/4, Association for the Promotion of Higher Education for Working Men, *Second Annual Report, List of Members and Statement of Accounts, 1 Jan. 1905*, 38–42; WEA, *Third Annual Report and Statement of Accounts, July 1906*, 25.
75. Price, 27.
76. *WEA, Annual Report* 1907.
77. Battersea and Wandsworth Trades and Labour Council, *Report for 1907*, 13.
78. *WEA, Annual Report* 1910.
79. *The Highway*, ii, no. 24, Aug. 1910, 175.

# 3   The First Students in the Workers' Educational Association: Individual Enlightenment and Collective Advance[1]

*Lawrence Goldman*

It is a truism of educational history that we always learn more about teachers and educational administrators than about students. Who the students were, where they went on to, what they thought of their education, and what they believed in more widely, are the questions we often want answered but frequently cannot even ask in the absence of relevant sources. The institutional and official evidence with which historians usually have to work can rarely bring alive the actual experience of being educated. Historians of the early years of the WEA, however, are fortunate that this was a movement that was conscious of its originality and of its place in history. Its leaders thought deeply about their aims and methods and investigated the early classes to see if they were achieving their ambition to open up higher learning to groups and individuals who had been deprived of contact with the national culture. They wanted to know the identity of those who attended and their feelings about the 'experiment in democratic education' – R. H. Tawney's phrase – in which they were all involved. For their part, the students kept their own records of their experiences, for this was such a break with all precedent in their lives, and spoke openly about their educational interests and ambitions. Thus, if we focus on the first tutorial classes in the half-dozen years before the First World War we find considerable material that describes and explains the experiences of the early students of the WEA. Most of the material in this chapter relates to classes that the WEA organised jointly with the University of Oxford, beginning in 1908. Oxford had provided support, patronage and funds for the WEA from the Association's foundation at a conference in the university on 22 August 1903.[2] When Mansbridge and his fellows began to devise a means of intensive learning for the most committed and active students, it was to the University of Oxford that the WEA turned.

The lecture courses that most WEA students attended in the Association's first years had intrinsic limitations. Audiences were often very large, running into hundreds, and discussion was therefore difficult; lecture courses on different subjects followed each other at random; written work was optional; the whole educational experience lacked intensity. The tutorial class, on the contrary, was limited to a maximum of 24 students, met weekly for three years to follow a planned syllabus, demanded regular essays from the students, and was, in many respects, self-governing. The students had a role in choosing the subjects studied and the tutor who taught them. Its essential features were described in the famous '1908 Report', *Oxford and Working-class Education*, which was drafted by a joint committee of seven representatives from the WEA and seven from Oxford following another conference in the city in August 1907 at which the university had pledged its support for the WEA's attempts to enrich and enlarge the educational experience of its students.[3]

In January 1908, while the joint committee was sitting, two experimental classes began at Rochdale in Lancashire and Longton in the Potteries of North Staffordshire in response to representations received from both towns to move beyond the constraints of university extension lectures. That autumn the new Oxford Tutorial Classes Committee, established by a statute passed by the university's Congregation on 27 October 1908, organised six further tutorial classes. As was always intended, the model pioneered in Oxford spread rapidly to other universities which were beginning to engage in extra-mural education and which established similar partnerships with the WEA. By 1909 Cambridge, Manchester, Liverpool, Leeds and Sheffield had all begun tutorial classes.[4] By the end of the 1913–14 session there were 14 joint committees, some 145 classes and 3,343 students in the new movement. Just over one-half of the classes, 74, were in the category of 'social history and economics'; 22 were studying modern history, 11 were in sociology, and 10 were in political science. There were also 17 literature classes.[5] It was estimated that 47.5 per cent of the students were from the manual working class.[6]

By 1909 Oxford had established eight tutorial classes in Chesterfield, Glossop, Littleborough, Longton, Oldham, Rochdale, Swindon and Wrexham. When Mansbridge and William Temple, the WEA's first president, investigated these classes in a report on their first year, they found that the 237 students enrolled in them 'were mainly manual workers, with an intermixture of school teachers and clerks, together with secretaries of working-class organisations'.[7] Of the students 59 per cent were drawn from three trades: engineering, textiles, and building. There were 32 clerks and 12 teachers in the classes, as well. All but 21 of the students were men, and just over 60 per cent of the whole group were under the age of 34. Indeed, over half the students were between 25 and 34 years of age, which confirms a later description of 'the ordinary tutorial class student' as 'one who has after the elementary school gone to manual work and who after some years of such work desires systematic and higher education'.[8] In contrast to the recent history of the WEA, only 14 students were aged over 45. As the Tutorial Classes Committee explained: 'the personnel of the existing eight Tutorial Classes may be said to be recruited almost entirely from the younger and more energetic members of the manual working-class, who are keenly alive to the civic questions and desire to improve their knowledge of them by impartial study.'[9]

As the first two Oxford tutorial classes formed the model for those to come, they merit detailed consideration. Both were in 'industrial history', specifically 'the social, industrial and economic history of England, with special attention to the seventeenth, eighteenth and nineteenth centuries'. Economics and economic history were central to the curriculum of the new movement because, above all, workers 'wanted to know something of the forces which had made them what they were'.[10] Tutorial classes were an exercise in understanding where working-class communities had come from, and thinking about where they might be going. A later report by the education inspectorate into Oxford's programme noted that working-class students 'have been willing to read "economic" history, or "social" history, or "industrial" history in the belief that such special studies would throw light on immediate problems of social life'.[11] As John Dover Wilson, the great Shakespearean scholar and founder of the *Journal of Adult Education* explained of the period before the First World War: 'For the majority of adult students in those days, economics was the natural, the inevitable, gateway to knowledge. For any working man of more than average intelligence, what is called "the social problem" had to be tackled first, before anything else, and economics seemed to offer the key to it.'[12]

Both classes were taught by R. H. Tawney. He was then living in Glasgow and would leave the city on a Friday morning for an evening class at Longton. He would stay the night and then go on for a Saturday afternoon class in Rochdale (see plate 5), returning home on Sunday.[13] Tawney later described a tutorial class as 'the nucleus of a University established in a place where no University exists'.

> Thanks to the fact that they are small, tutor and students can meet as friends, discover each other's idiosyncracies, and break down that unintentional system of mutual deception which seems inseparable from any education which relies principally on the formal lecture. It is often before the classes begin and after they end, in discussions round a student's fire, or in a walk to and from his home, that the root of the matter is reached both by student and tutor.[14]

At Rochdale, Tawney met a class 'almost, if not entirely, made up of "workmen" in the strictest sense of the term' in the words of the class secretary, L. V. Gill.[15] Another student, T. W. Price, then working at a local bleaching works, was more precise:

> There are in the class 12 iron workers, 8 skilled and 4 unskilled, and 3 joiners. All the chief branches of the cotton industry are represented, spinning, weaving, bleaching and finishing. There are also 2 carpet weavers, a wool-sorter, a spindlemaker, a shuttlemaker, a printer, a housepainter, a picture-framer, an accountant's clerk, a cashier, a teacher, 2 journalists, and an insurance agent. Of the lady students one is a clerk, one a dress-maker, one a schoolmistress, and the fourth is a working-man's wife.[16]

Gill wrote to Mansbridge after the first class that: 'Tawney captured them right away.' He wrote again, after the second class, to explain that 'it is a case of love at first sight on both sides. His lectures are brilliant, illuminating, simple, lucid, eloquent.'[17] Price apparently 'went home as if I were walking upon air and was so exuberant that my wife wanted to know what was the matter with me.' It wasn't just that Tawney was 'the right man for teacher ... we [also] have the right kind of men and women in the class ... men and women in earnest'. After only two weeks there was no going back: 'None of us, now that we have become acquainted with Mr. Tawney & his methods, will be contented any longer with the ordinary University Extension lecture; we want lectures that will stimulate us to work, not lectures that are half popular entertainments.'[18] J. W. Henighan, a general labourer, was wonderfully expressive:

> At nearly half-past two Gill entered the room followed closely by a young man wearing the gown; he was the much debated tutor ... Briefly, Tawney stated his opinion of what the class should be, and without more ado delved deep into his work. My first impression was of surprise, first at his youth, and secondly at the sweet affable charm of his presence. There was none of the academic manner about him; none of that air which is so inclined to freeze; he was one of us. We had expected the frigid zone; we were landed at the equator. Tawney is not a teacher: he is a man with a soul.[19]

One of the students had already taken a degree and he ended a reflective letter to Mansbridge with the judgement that 'from the teaching point of view and seriousness of students, I think our class compares favourably with real University work.'[20] But difficulties were inevitable. Henighan advised preparatory instruction in composition before future classes: 'In the case of workmen, essay-writing is the greatest difficulty, so few being able to express their thoughts in writing.'[21]

After the last class of the session, Alfred Wilkinson, a Labour councillor from Rochdale and a member of the WEA/Oxford joint committee, wrote to Mansbridge to sum up: 'Tawney has captured not only the heads but the hearts of his scholars; if you can get [another] don like him, we can turn England upside down in a few years' time.'[22] Tawney, for his part, also wrote a report on the first session of the Rochdale class. He noted the great improvement made by the students over the term and the excellence of the 'first five or six' of them whose work 'was on a level with that in the honour schools of the only Universities with which he is acquainted'. He also took the opportunity to call for improved secondary education on general grounds and so that tutorial class students would have the necessary skills of composition, and for a reduction in overtime so that students would have leisure for study.[23] In his confidential report to the Delegates in Oxford, Tawney emphasised the quality of the best students whose 'power to grasp general ideas and to write forcibly and fluently was most striking'.[24] It is doubtful if he exaggerated their talent: Gill went on to become secretary of the

WEA's North West District and Price became secretary of the Midlands District and the Association's first (and best) historian.[25] One of the two journalists in the class was A. P. Wadsworth, who went on to edit the *Manchester Guardian* and write distinguished histories of the cotton industry.[26] When A. L. Smith, then a Modern History tutor at Balliol College and a key figure in adult education over the next generation, wrote to one potential donor to solicit funds, he praised the 'remarkable work' produced by the Rochdale students and offered to show copies of their essays as proof.[27] When Alfred Zimmern, another sympathetic Oxford don and later professor of International Relations in the university, paid a visit to Rochdale in April 1908 he received 'a royal welcome': 'Price gave me the finest tea I ever had in my life, and we spent a jolly evening at the Club. I was really impressed with the class ... and Tawney's treatment of the subject is masterly.'[28]

The Longton Class was rather different in social composition from that at Rochdale 'being representative of all sections of ... the middle and working classes' and as such was undoubtedly more like the majority of tutorial classes to follow.[29] It comprised 'a gardener, a plumber, a potters' thrower, a potters' decorator, a basket-maker, a miner, a mechanic, a baker, several clerks, a librarian, a grocer, a miller's agent, a railway agent, a clothier, insurance collectors and elementary school teachers'.[30] In fact, there were 17 of the last category among a total of 38 in the class. Certainly the Longton class was unrepresentative of the local employment and social structures, but, as Tawney explained, the social divisions within the class were more apparent than real: 'Teachers, elementary and secondary, are often the children of work-people and marry them; while their salaries are so low as to place them, at any rate at first, in an economic position inferior to that of many artisans.'[31] A similar point was made in the first report of the Tutorial Classes Committee by Mansbridge and Temple: the clerks and shop assistants enrolled in the classes were 'not usually classified as "workpeople"', but the majority of them still 'belonged to working class families'.[32] It is also worth noting the presence in the class at Longton of a knot of seasoned campaigners from the local branch of the Social Democratic Federation, the avowedly Marxist organisation: this may explain why Tawney was warned against 'setting up a den of iniquity' when he met one local public official to discuss a venue for the class![33]

At Longton, as in Rochdale, Tawney won universal acclaim: 'The lecturer was the right man in the right place and is evidently experienced in dealing with audiences of workpeople. He was lucid and eminently pure-minded in his treatment of the subject, and possessed the faculty of being able to capture and hold the interest of the class.'[34] However, the surviving sources on the Longton class are rather more honest and detailed on the problems encountered. The class secretary, Edward Stuart Cartwright, wrote to Mansbridge in November 1909 to explain:

> We are trying hard here to keep the class up to a high level. There are several of the newer members who find the subject very stiff owing chiefly to their defective preliminary education ... One thing this has brought home to me, personally – how very difficult and distasteful the mere physical act of writing is to a miner or a potter. I can see this is a very big initial obstacle to surmount. I felt weary in spirit last night when it was brought home to me what spade work had to be done before the Tutorial Classes movement can begin its work proper.[35]

Because most of the students 'had little practice in composition', Tawney himself did not 'think it wise to press them too hard to write papers'.[36] A few months later Cartwright identified the greatest difficulty as 'the unstable conditions of life of the ordinary industrial student, with sometimes long and sometimes irregular hours of work, and the uncertainty of employment'.[37] Zimmern, writing about workers' education in North Staffordshire in 1914, itemised 'the ravages of overtime, the anxieties of unemployment, the suspicions of foremen and managers, the difficulties of obtaining quiet for reading and writing' as enemies of the working-class student.[38]

One of the students in Tawney's class in Wrexham expressed the frustrations of worker students in a letter written to Mansbridge to ask leave to withdraw from the group:

> Having had practically no education I am handicapped at every point, the rules of grammar, composition, punctuation, and the sequence of historical persons and events are so absent from my knowledge as though they did not exist; for instance, I could not at the present moment say who was Queen Victoria's father, nor who preceded her in the monarchy and when I hear such names as William of Orange, Pitt and Sir Walter Raleigh, I don't know until I search for their history whether they were Primates, Pirates, Peers or Premiers. Of course, until I joined the Economics class I

had never found it necessary to know anything about them
because my life had been spent in a sphere in which the only
important thing seemed to be the devising of some scheme
whereby one could escape from what seemed to be the inevitable
end of one's fellow workers, viz., poverty and that old British
institution, the workhouse.[39]

Another poignant letter of resignation from a student in a later
Oxford tutorial class at Littleborough set down the health problems
of a husband and wife who 'both go to the Mill', thus presenting
another set of difficulties that militated against workers' education
– chronic medical conditions that afflicted many of the manual
working class.[40]

Reports on the first Oxford tutorial classes give graphic insight
into the disabling effects of fatigue, unemployment, poor housing,
illness and poverty that disfigured working-class life in the first years
of the century. The first annual report on Oxford's tutorial classes
gave an example of a student in Tawney's Longton class who worked
for 626 hours in nine weeks in early 1909, and concluded that 'the
long hours of labour' were the 'greatest single obstacle to the
extension of adult education'.[41] Tawney's own reports on his classes
in 1909–10 inveighed against the 'systematic misuse' of overtime by
some employers: 'A very promising student in one of my classes has
worked from 6 a.m. to 9 p.m. every day from October to March, with
the result that even when he can attend the class he is too worn out
to read or do the requisite number of essays.'[42] The class secretary at
Littleborough in the same year noted the 'most discouraging effect'
of unemployment on the students: 'their minds have never been free
from worry and depressing thoughts of the morrow.'[43] At Longton
in 1908, eight students ceased to attend the class between October
and Christmas, and 'the chief reason was unemployment.'[44] One
tutor apparently 'watched individual students, who began work with
enthusiasm and capacity, gradually sink through unemployment
into a state of mental despondency and distress in which every
thought of education gradually disappeared before the question,
"How shall I earn a living tomorrow?"'[45] In such circumstances tutors
also functioned as social workers. F. W. Kolthammer of Brasenose
College was teaching Oxford classes in Chesterfield, Glossop, Hanley,
Huddersfield and Oldham in 1910. He recorded that

For one man, keen and hard working, I found permanent employment on a Labour Exchange; for another (a political victim, turned out of home as well as from work) I have found jobbing work and may soon find permanent employment; another I sent to Fircroft [College] for educational improvement till chances improved. In some cases I have not been able to help; emigration was the refuge.[46]

The problems were offset by the mutual support, cameraderie and sheer enthusiasm which developed. At Rochdale, after the Saturday afternoon class, Tawney used to have tea and spend the evening at the home of one of the students, 'and on these occasions other members of the class would crowd into the house to the limits of accommodation – and even beyond – and the discussion would often go on until the early hours of the morning'.[47] It was the same at Longton. Cartwright recalled a particular scene:

The class meeting is over, and we sit at ease, taking tea and biscuits ... Talk ranges free and wide – problems of philosophy, evolution, politics, literature. Then R. H. T. reads to us Walt Whitman's 'When Lilacs Last in the Dooryard Bloom'd'; this moves a student to give us his favourite passage from the same source: 'Pioneers! O, Pioneers!' Another follows, quoting from a poem from Matthew Arnold that evidently has bitten him ... And for some of us as we sit listening, a new door opens.[48]

That was written in 1929 and echoes what Cartwright wrote after three years of work in Longton in 1911: 'The tutorial class has made for something more than mental training, it has made for the development of the human spirit; and for many of us opened the door to a wider and deeper life.'[49]

It is only the language of personal transcendence and idealism that can capture the experience of learning for these adult scholars. A love of learning for its own sake, a sense of spiritual enrichment through self-development and increasing knowledge, and a distaste for a materialistic approach to education, are remarkable aspects of the testimony provided by both tutors and students in these early classes. Mansbridge later described 'the old, original faith' of the Association in this way: 'that man is destined, if he would live aright, to develop his mind and body in the power of the spirit, not because it will serve some specific purpose, but because it is the law of his being.'[50]

Education was 'spiritual food'.[51] As he wrote in one of the articles in which he first projected the WEA in early 1903, it would lead its votaries 'to the beautiful and the true, where alone citizenship can be realised'.[52] One student from Tawney's first tutorial class in Longton, North Staffordshire, wrote of 'a higher ideal, a higher mode of life, a nobler purpose' in 1909.[53] Two years later another student in the class wrote of it opening 'the door to a wider and deeper life'.[54] For both men the experience of studying economic history with Tawney was pivotal: they left local employment and took up careers in adult education, one as a teacher and the other as an administrator.[55]

According to Mansbridge: 'There are miners and factory hands in the North who don't care twopence about increasing their wages or living in bigger houses or wearing finer clothes, but who can discuss Greek History with men like Alfred Zimmern, Greek poetry with men like Gilbert Murray and Greek philosophy with men like W. H. Hadow.'[56] One such was 'a Manchester Socialist', interviewed in 1918. He was:

Dead against materialism ... I want to live in my spirit. I want to feel more, and to see more deeply into the truth of things. I want to enjoy my spiritual life. Take away the life of the soul – take away the books, the music, and the plays, and I don't want to live ... The Socialism of the future is not the economic revolution; its not the Marxian idea; it's the movement of man's soul towards a more enjoyable existence through and for his reason.[57]

Idealism did not necessarily compromise political radicalism; rather, it confirmed among worker scholars that political mechanisms and economic instrumentalities would not be enough for social emancipation. As a miner from Castleford explained: 'I became an enthusiastic member of the [Workers' Educational] Association, losing none of my socialism, but seeing for the first time in my life that the basis of human existence is spiritual.'[58] An elite of working people, starved of contact with the national culture, often uncomfortable in the unenlightened milieu from which they came, were yearning for contact with a world of ideas beyond the immediate confines of working-class life – ideas that might free them in a personal sense by opening up the 'higher life' to which so many referred, and which might serve as the basis for the wider liberation of the class as a whole.[59]

Yet the desire for self-cultivation on the part of many autodidacts in the early WEA was balanced by an equal commitment to the communal advance of working people: the consciousness of collective endeavour was equally profound. At the 1907 conference in Oxford, Philip Snowden, later a Labour chancellor of the exchequer, had placed emphasis on class rather than individual advancement – 'I would rather have better education given to the masses of the working classes than the best for a few. O God, make no more saints; elevate the race'[60] – and the 1908 Report was insistent that this was its aim. In obtaining a university education, it was argued: 'it must not be necessary for workpeople to leave the class in which they were born ... What they desire is not that men should escape from their class, but that they should remain in it and raise its whole level.'[61] This seems to have been an especially important issue for the representatives of the working class on the 1907–8 Joint Committee. At one of its preliminary meetings the Labour MP, David Shackleton, made it clear that, though he 'had no desire to bind a student down to his original machine', nevertheless 'the important point was that he should return to his class' and take a position of responsibility within it.[62] At a meeting in Balliol in January 1908 at which members of the Committee came before members of the college to explain their project, J. M. Mactavish, who followed Mansbridge as general secretary of the WEA, made the same point: 'What the working classes need, is that raising not of individuals, but of the average level; and they look to Oxford, first, to make the highway and get it used; then to train the sons of the people, aye, and their daughters too.'[63]

The WEA named its magazine *The Highway* to emphasise its mission to construct a broad path 'along which the average man and woman can travel towards a larger life' rather than an 'educational ladder' by which the lucky or talented few could escape their origins.[64] The early students rejected the idea that three years of study in a tutorial class should end in individual qualifications and 'testamurs' for the successful.[65] The students in the original tutorial classes were also resistant to the idea that some of their number might qualify for scholarships to study at Oxford, even though this was an explicit aim in *Oxford and Working-class Education*. The Rochdale class rejected the idea of three of its members going to the university in 1910. In the following year H. H. Turner, the professor of astronomy in Oxford and another friend to the movement, visited both Rochdale and Longton to reassess the mood and found that the majority of students, especially at Rochdale, were still against the idea of prize scholarships for the best. Turner quoted one Rochdale student to give a flavour of their opinions:

> Workers have as much right in Oxford as anyone, but not in ones and twos ... Present proposition bad. We who have never had a fortnight's holiday in our lives have suddenly dangled before us the chance of a year or two at Oxford, which one is to get & another not. Tell the Committee straight we absolutely refuse this offer, thanking them for nothing.[66]

Opinion at Longton had been more divided, however, and in 1913 the class wrote to the Tutorial Classes Committee in Oxford to endorse the idea of scholarships, though only under specific conditions. Longton students remained against the idea of prizes for the few in principle, but they 'would not have the same objection to a student proceeding to the university with the definite object of becoming a Tutorial Class teacher'.[67] Funds were found to bring Albert Emery, a potter, and Maud Griffiths, an elementary school-teacher, to Balliol and St. Hilda's Hall respectively in October 1913.[68] Emery lacked classical languages and did not read for a degree but spent three years studying Modern History under A. L. Smith before he took up tutorial class teaching in Sheffield. Later he became a tutor for the Oxford Committee and went back to the Potteries, where he taught until the 1950s. As a colleague wrote in 1949: 'Old Emery was a constant reminder of the ability of one of their own to make his university training available to industrial workers.'[69] Griffiths, meanwhile, passed the University Diploma in Economics and Political Science with a distinction, and then took up employment as a social worker at Bournville, the Cadbury company town, in the absence of any immediate opening in adult education.[70] That these two adult scholars did go to Oxford is less significant than the rejection of individual advancement as a goal of the movement by the students themselves. Collective good took precedence over individual advantage; the ethos was co-operative rather than competitive. As such, the early workers' education movement was overtly opposed to the fundamental philosophy of the national educational system.

Perhaps the finest example of the camaraderie and the collective endeavour of the early tutorial class students was the North Staffordshire Miners' Higher Education Movement, started in 1911 by the students of the first Longton class. It was an evangelizing movement, intended to bring adult education to the isolated mining communities to the north and west of the Potteries.[71] As Zimmern explained in 1914:

> These villages are for the most part difficult to reach and are thus removed from all contact with the ordinary opportunities of civilisation. The university tutorial class students three years ago discerned in these semi-industrial villages a great field for missionary work, and as this coincided in point of time with a demand for higher education which came from the miners themselves, the two parties were quickly brought together and a new educational movement set on foot.[72]

It started with a meeting at the Stoke School of Mining in May 1911 where members of the Longton tutorial class met representatives from some 20 neighbouring mining villages. Tawney gave an address on 'Higher Education Considered Apart from Industrial Training'.[73] Cartwright, joint secretary of the scheme for its duration, wrote to Oxford to appeal for assistance and described the project as 'the education of a whole coalfield'.[74] The Longton tutorial class students organised it and were themselves the tutors, passing on the knowledge and insight they were gaining from Tawney to other workers.[75] Eight of the ten 'class leaders' in the first year were students from the Longton class – a miner, a colliery weighman, a potter's engineman, a potter's decorator, a railway telegraphist, an elementary schoolteacher, a secretary and a clerk. They included Cartwright, Albert Emery and Maud Griffiths, and they all remained members of Tawney's tutorial class while going out and teaching themselves.[76] After the first year, students from other tutorial classes that were beginning or in process in the Potteries assisted and shared the work. It was not successful in all locations, but the first classes reached approximately two hundred students and by 1916–17 the Movement was serving 650 students in 27 centres.[77] In 1921 the Movement voluntarily merged into the newly established North Staffordshire District of the WEA.

Could the WEA be at one and the same time an agent of spiritual uplift and of political and social liberation? As Bernard Jennings has suggested, Mansbridge promoted both simultaneously; in his view, education was necessary for social emancipation but it was also an individual emancipation in itself.[78] The subsequent institutional and

ideological division in workers' education after 1909, which led to the
foundation of the Marxist Plebs League and the Labour Colleges in
competition with the WEA, has sometimes encouraged a false
antithesis between the WEA's tradition of liberal adult education and
a class-conscious alternative designed to encourage fundamental
political change. In this version, the WEA is sometimes caricatured
as essentially focused on individual educational ends alone; beyond
introducing its students to the life of the mind it supposedly did not
go, apparently compromised by its association with the universities
and reliance on state funding which weakened its claim to represent
the communal aspirations of the working class.[79] Yet, if we listen to
the first students themselves, they evidently believed that the WEA
had to provide personal development and collective advance simultaneously, and they recognised no contradiction between meeting
the personal needs of individuals and the social needs of working
people more generally. To be sure, this was at the time, as it remains
today, a difficult balancing act. Yet, their experiences and eloquent
testimony make the dual tasks of the WEA, then and now,
abundantly clear. For the first students in the WEA the 'higher life'
denoted enlightenment and collective advance together and as one.

## NOTES

*Place of publication London unless otherwise stated.*

1. This chapter includes material first published in Lawrence Goldman,
   *Dons and Workers. Oxford and Adult Education Since 1850* (Oxford, 1995).
   It is reproduced by permission of Oxford University Press.
2. *The Higher Education of Working Men, Being the Official Report of the Joint
   Conference Between Co-operators, Trade Unionists, and University Extension
   Authorities, Held at Oxford, on Saturday August 22nd 1903* (1903).
3. *Oxford and Working-class Education: Being the Report of a Joint Committee
   of University and Working-class Representatives on the Relation of the
   University to the Higher Education of Workpeople* (Oxford, 1908).
4. Price, 38.
5. Ministry of Reconstruction, Adult Education Committee. Final Report,
   *Parliamentary Papers*, 1919, vol. xxviii, 54. The remaining classes were in
   'Philosophy or Psychology' (8); Biology (2) and Economic Geography (1).
6. Central Joint Committee on Tutorial Classes, Annual Report for 1913,
   cited in J. A. Blyth, *English University Adult Education 1908–1958. The
   Unique Tradition* (Manchester, 1983), 14.
7. BL Add. 65215, Mansbridge papers, vol. xxi, Albert Mansbridge and
   William Temple, 'Oxford University Tutorial Classes Committee. Report
   of First Year's Working', fos. 1–3.

8.  'Report of Committee on Applications by Extension Delegacy', Memorandum A, 1911, *Hebdomadal Council Papers, No. 92, April 23–June 27 1912* (Oxford, 1912), 141.

9.  Mansbridge and Temple, 'Report of the First Year's Working', fo. 4.

10. Stocks, 46.

11. *Board of Education. Report by H.M. Inspectors upon University Tutorial Classes under the Supervision of the Committee of the University of Oxford, for the Period Ending 31st July, 1924* (n.d.), Oxford University Archives, DES/F/2/1/8, 'Copies of Special Reports, Memoranda etc.', folder 3, 5.

12. J. Dover Wilson, 'Adult Education in Yorkshire', *Journal of Adult Education*, iii, 1 (1928), 58.

13. Stocks, 40.

14. R. H. Tawney, 'An Experiment in Democratic Education', *The Political Quarterly*, May 1914, 74–5.

15. National Archive, 'R. H. Tawney: Correspondence re Early Tutorial Classes 1907–8', 'Early Tutorial Classes', L. V. Gill to R. H. Tawney, 10 Dec. 1907.

16. WEA National Archive, WEA CENTRAL3/6/4,'Early Tutorial Classes', Box II, exercise book entitled 'Rochdale Class': 'The Rochdale Tutorial Class', MS. article by T. W. Price dated '1908' with Mansbridge's comment 'by a student who works in the bleaching works'. (The book comprises letters sent to Mansbridge from the first Rochdale class which he transcribed in his own hand.)

17. 'Early Tutorial Classes II', 'Rochdale Class', L. V. Gill to Albert Mansbridge, 26 Jan. 1908, 2 Feb. 1908.

18. 'Early Tutorial Classes II', 'Rochdale Class': T. W. Price to Albert Mansbridge, 2 Feb. 1908.

19. 'Early Tutorial Classes II', 'Rochdale Class': J. W. Henighan to Albert Mansbridge, 2 Feb. 1908.

20. 'Early Tutorial Classes II', 'Rochdale Class': Fred Hall to Albert Mansbridge, 7 March 1908.

21. 'Early Tutorial Classes II', 'Rochdale Class': J. Henighan to Albert Mansbridge, 14 May 1908.

22. 'Early Tutorial Classes II', 'Rochdale Class': Alfred W. Wilkinson to Albert Mansbridge (n.d.).

23. 'Early Tutorial Classes II', 'Rochdale Class': 'Tutorial History Class. Mr. R. H. Tawney's Report on the First Session' (press cutting, Rochdale source unknown). See also Tawney's report to the Oxford Delegacy on the class, 'Oxford University Extension. Reports of Lecturers, Examiners and Local Committees 1907–1908', Oxford University Archives, DES/R/3/37 fo. 739.

24. DES/R/3/37 fo. 740.

25. Price, *passim*.

26. 'Tawney on Wadsworth', *The Highway*, xlviii, Jan. 1957, 82. See also R. H. Tawney, 'A Fifty Year's Memory', *Manchester Guardian*, 5 Nov. 1956, 4.

27. A. L. Smith to Lord Balfour of Burleigh, 30 June 1908, Balliol College, Oxford, A. L. Smith Papers, 'Extra-Mural Work 1907–09'.

28. Oxford University Archives, DES/F/14/1, '1907–8 Joint Committee on Tutorial Classes', A.E. Zimmern to Albert Mansbridge, 8 Apr. 1908. See also Oxford University Archives, Edward Stuart Cartwright

Papers,'Records of Work in North Staffordshire': 'Report by Mr. Zimmern on the Rochdale Class', 4 Apr. [1908].

29. On the socially-mixed nature of Cambridge tutorial classes and their recruitment from the ranks of clerks, teachers and the lower-middle class generally, see Edwin Welch, *The Peripatetic University. Cambridge Local Lectures 1873–1973* (Cambridge, 1973),112.

30. DES/R/3/37, fo. 735, Report of the Local Secretary, W. T. Cope, in 'Oxford University Extension. Reports of Lecturers ... 1907–8'. See also 'Reports on Tutorial Classes', *Oxford and Working-class Education*, 105.

31. DES/R/3/37, fo. 732, 'Oxford University Extension. Reports of Lecturers ... 1907–8'.

32. Mansbridge and Temple, 'Report of First Year's Working', fo. 4.

33. H. P. Smith, 'A Tutorial Class Makes History', *Adult Education*, xxxi, 4, (1959), 271–3.

34. DES/R/3/37 f. 735, Report of the Local Secretary, W. T. Cope, in 'Oxford University Extension. Report of Lecturers ... 1907–8'. See also 'Reports on Tutorial Classes', *Oxford and Working-class Education*, 105.

35. DES/F/2/1/4, Cartwright to Albert Mansbridge, 9 Nov. 1909.

36. DES/R/3/37, fo. 732, 'Oxford University Extension. Reports of Lecturers ... 1907–8'.

37. Edward Stuart Cartwright Papers, 'Records of Work in North Staffordshire' (Box),'Longton Tutorial Class. Report for Session 1909–10', 3. See also Cartwright's report as local secretary for 1908–9 in DES/R/3/38, fo. 564, 'Oxford University Extension. Reports of Lecturers ... 1908–9'.

38. Alfred Zimmern, 'Education and the Working Class', *The Round Table. A Quarterly Review of the Politics of the British Empire*, xiv (Mar. 1914), 264.

39. DES/F/2/1/10, C. B. Caldecott to Albert Mansbridge, 26 Dec.1909, Tutorial Classes Committee Correspondence. For Mansbridge's less than sympathetic response, see DES/F/2/1/10, Albert Mansbridge to C. B. Caldecott, 30 Dec. 1909.

40. DES/F/2/1/1, Tutorial Classes Committee Early Papers vol. 1, John M. Vaughan to J. A. S. Walkden (class secretary at Littleborough), 16 Sept. 1909.

41. BL Add. 65215, fo. 7, William Temple and Albert Mansbridge, 'Oxford University Tutorial Classes Committee. Report of First Year's Working'.

42. *Tutorial Classes Committee Annual Report 1909–10*, 8.

43. *Tutorial Classes Committee Annual Report 1909–10*, 13.

44. Add. 65215, fo. 5n, Temple and Mansbridge, 'Oxford University Tutorial Classes Committee. Report of First Year's Working'.

45. Add. 65215, fo. 9.

46. Add. 65215, fo. 15.

47. Price, 33–4.

48. [E. S.Cartwright], 'Looking Backwards: A Tutorial Class Anniversary. By an Old Student', *Rewley House Papers*, ii (Oxford, 1929), 72–3.

49. E. S. Cartwright Papers, 'Longton Tutorial Class. Report on the work of the Past Session and also since the Commencement', 10 Apr. 1911, 2.

50. Albert Mansbridge, 'The Beginning of the W.E.A.', *The Highway*, xvi, no. 3 (Summer 1924),135.

51.  Albert Mansbridge quoted in Harold Begbie, *Living Water. Being Chapters from the Romance of the Poor Student* (1918),187.

52.  Mansbridge, 'Co-operation, Trade Unionism, and University Extension', *University Extension Journal*, 8 Jan. 1903, 53.

53.  Bodleian Library, Oxford, Zimmern MSS, 12, fos. 63–5, Albert Emery to A. E. Zimmern, 23 Aug. 1909.

54.  E. S. Cartwright, 'Longton Tutorial Class: Report on the Work of the Past Session and also Since the Commencement', 10 Apr. 1911, 2.

55.  Albert Emery left Longton to study Modern History at Balliol College, Oxford. He then became a tutor in Oxford's programme of tutorial classes in North Staffordshire. Edward Stuart Cartwright, a clerk, came to Oxford in 1912 as the organising secretary of the new tutorial classes committee and finally retired from that position in 1945.

56.  Begbie, *Living Water*, 187.

57.  Begbie, *Living Water*, 111.

58.  Begbie, *Living Water*, 136.

59.  See Stephen Yeo, 'A New Life: The Religion of Socialism in Britain, 1883–1896', *History Workshop Journal*, iv (Autumn 1977), 5–56.

60.  National Archive, 'Oxford Joint Conference on Education of Workpeople, August 10th 1907', MS minute book, fo. 77.

61.  *Oxford and Working-class Education*, 49–50.

62.  A. L. Smith Letters, Box 14, 'WEA', Oxford Joint Committee. Minutes of the Meeting held on December 27th and 28th 1907, 4.

63.  A. L. Smith Letters, Box 14, 'WEA', 'Report of a Meeting in Balliol College Hall on Sunday Morning 26 Jan. 1908', 5–6.

64.  Price, 45.

65.  Winifred Beaton, 'The Tutorial Class Movement', *The WEA Education Year Book 1918* (1918), 256.

66.  DES/F/2/1/8, 'Professor Turner's Report on his Visit to Longton and Rochdale, Jan 1911', 6.

67.  DES/F/2/2/3, 'Report on University Scholarships Held by Tutorial Class Students', Nov. 1916, 1, H. Jenkins and W. Morries to the Oxford Tutorial Classes Committee, 21 Feb. 1913.

68.  See Add. Ms. 65257, fo. 34, A. E. Zimmern to Albert Mansbridge, 19 Aug. 1913.

69.  DES/F/10/3/1, J. W. Campbell, Staff Tutor's File, J. W. Campbell to H. P. Smith, 11 Oct. 1949.

70.  DES/F/2/2/3, 'Report on University Scholarships Held by Tutorial Class Students', Nov. 1916, 6–14.

71.  See R. A. Lowe, 'The North Staffordshire Miners' Higher Education Movement', *Educational Review*, xxii (1970), 263–77. See also Ministry of Reconstruction. Adult Education Committee. Final Report, *Parliamentary Papers*, 1918, 296–309.

72.  Zimmern, 'Education and the Working Class', 267.

73.  H. P. Smith, 'Edward Stuart Cartwright. A Note on his Work for Adult Education', *Rewley House Papers*, III, no. 1 (Oxford, 1949–50), 20.

74.  Quoted in H. P. Smith, *Labour and Learning* (Oxford, 1956), 30.

75.  Cartwright, 'Looking Backwards. A Tutorial Class Anniversary', 69–70.

76. Smith, 'Edward Stuart Cartwright', 19.
77. Lowe, 'The North Staffordshire Miners' Higher Education Movement', 267–8.
78. Bernard Jennings, *New Lamps for Old? University Adult Education in Retrospect and Prospect* (Hull, 1976), 10.
79. For the most recent presentation of this case see Roger Fieldhouse, 'The Workers' Educational Association' and 'University Adult Education' and John McIlroy, 'Independent Working Class Education and Trade Union Education and Training' in Fieldhouse and Associates, *History*, 166–238 and 264–89. For a different view see Goldman, *Dons and Workers*, 163–90.

# 4   R. H. Tawney and the WEA

*Meredith Kwartin Rusoff*

Late in his life, the eminent historian and social critic R. H. Tawney liked to say that when

> asked where I received the best part of my own education, I should reply, not at school or college, but in the days when as a young, inexperienced and conceited teacher of Tutorial classes, I underwent, week by week, a series of friendly, but effective, deflations at the hands of the students composing them.[1]

This admission, in all its deference towards his students, reveals an essential truth about Tawney: he gained as much from his experience as a WEA tutor as his students did. Six years of teaching economic and industrial history to potters and weavers gave Tawney the foundation for a lifetime of social, political, economic and educational activism. By the 1920s, Tawney had become one of the nation's most important intellectual figures; his legacy of public and private service is unmatched by almost any of his fellow social critics. His undergraduate years at Balliol College and his service in the 1914–18 war greatly shaped Tawney's intellectual growth, but it was his experience with the WEA, particularly from 1908 to 1914, that led him to focus on equality as a national priority and education as one of the chief means to bring about that goal.

From his Oxford days to the end of his life, Tawney was consumed by the desire to improve society. In 1903 Tawney went down from Balliol to live and work at Toynbee Hall, the famous settlement house run by Canon Samuel Barnett in London's East End. Here he hoped to explore the roots of what was referred to as 'the social question', and come up with methods for creating a more just national community.

Over the course of his three years there Tawney tried (unsuccessfully) to find common cause with the residents of the East End while reporting on social conditions and educational issues. During his time in London he also taught a few university extension lecture classes at Toynbee Hall, including 'Social Aspects of Industry' in the autumn term of 1905.[2] A key aspect of Tawney's philosophy emerged at this time in response to his Toynbee Hall experience: his belief that giving the working class a real education was far more beneficial than concerts or poetry readings.[3]

In his quest to understand the position of the poor, Tawney studied the efforts of groups such as the Charity Organisation Society to provide palliative relief to the 'deserving' poor, and scrutinised the reports of sociologists and economists. Neither of these approaches seemed to him to be ultimately helpful. He later analysed these methods in his diary, kept from 1912 to 1914, as he struggled to combine his maturing Christianity and socialism with practical means of reform. 'The most pressing problem of our day', he argued, 'is that of economic right, not of economic facts. But during the last half century nearly all English thinkers have devoted their whole attention to the collection of facts, not to the examination of the nature of economic right.'[4] He complained bitterly that 'most modern prophets, Utopists, sociologists ... never tell us *why* we regard the present social order with disapproval, or *how* we may produce a social order in which the human conscience may find satisfaction.' Helping the unfortunate was 'good and necessary. But it is not the social problem.'[5] Tawney continued to search for a better means both to understand and fix England's social and economic crises.

Toynbee Hall was Tawney's first attempt at subordinating himself to the service of society, but he was, in the end, ambivalent about the experience. Fortunately, he soon found a better outlet for his wish to serve the public good. He clearly enjoyed teaching his university extension lecture classes, for in 1905 he declared to his friend William Beveridge that 'teaching economics in an industrial town is just what I want ultimately to do.'[6] Later that year, when Canon Barnett suggested that Tawney join the fledgling Workers' Educational Association, he leapt at the opportunity.[7] This was an organisation, he felt, that could help produce the more equitable society he desired. Tawney and his good friend William Temple, later archbishop of Canterbury, soon became deeply involved in the movement, with Temple serving as the WEA's first president and Tawney elected to the executive committee in 1905.

The great innovation of the WEA, with which Tawney's name will forever be associated, was the creation of university extension tutorial classes. Previously, university extension classes took the form of lecture courses sponsored by various universities, such as the courses Tawney taught at Toynbee Hall. In 1907 the university extension branch at Rochdale, which had joined with the new local WEA branch, demanded a different type of course, more like the personal, discussion-based tutorial method in place at Oxford and Cambridge. Albert Mansbridge promised the Rochdale workers that if they could find 30 students who were willing to commit to a two-year course of study (including the writing of fortnightly essays), he would get 'the best tutor in England' for them.[8] The Rochdale branch found 30 willing students, and Mansbridge turned to Tawney to lead this pioneering class (see plate 5). The Longton branch of the WEA then demanded the same type of course, which Tawney also agreed to teach.

Despite a real desire to teach, Tawney was nervous about the tutorial classes; letters from Mansbridge were full of reassurances. He told Tawney that more important than any 'scientific presentation of the subject' was that Tawney should 'make common cause with [the] class'.[9] Neither Mansbridge nor Tawney needed to worry much about that last point; according to L. V. Gill, the secretary of the Rochdale branch and one of the students in the class, 'Tawney captured them right away. He is splendid.' Another member of the class noted that: 'There was none of the academic manner about him ... he was one of us.' Even an outside observer saw that 'he has won the hearts of his pupils.'[10] At last, Tawney was in his element, doing what he most wanted to do, and succeeding admirably.[11]

Teaching in the WEA gave Tawney the opportunity to get to know a very different, if unrepresentative, segment of the working class. Compared to the poorest of the poor in London, these worker-students did not seem to belong to the same 'working class'. Perhaps this experience spoiled him and let him believe, at least before the 1914–18 war, that the working class could easily be converted to his Christian socialism. These seekers of knowledge became idealised figures in Tawney's mind. Unquestionably, his eager students, many of them very bright and anxious to learn, gave him a radically new view of the working class and its potential.

Tawney felt very strongly about the necessity for 'personal intercourse' and 'personal tuition' outside the formal class setting, and he and his students spent time getting to know each other outside the classroom.[12] Indeed, from the start of his WEA teaching, he 'would frequently arrange to have tea and spend the evening at the home of one of the students, and on those occasions other members of the class would crowd into the house ... and the discussion would often go on until the early hours of the morning'.[13] Unlike the artificial juxtaposition of Toynbee Hall in the East End of London, in the towns of the industrial North of England, workers and tutor came together willingly and eagerly: 'Fortunate teacher, who is sought and not avoided!'[14] One of the members of the first Rochdale class captured the essence of Tawney's experience: 'He is perfectly happy – in every sense – here.'[15]

The intimate rapport Tawney developed with his classes benefited both students and teacher. In the preface to his 1912 monograph *The Agrarian Problem in the Sixteenth Century*, Tawney acknowledged a great debt to the members of his tutorial classes, 'with whom for the last four years it has been my privilege to be a fellow-worker. The friendly smitings of weavers, potters, miners, and engineers, have taught me much about problems of political and economic science which cannot easily be learned from books.'[16] His students, in fact, personalised abstract ideas about industrialism, and they demonstrated in their daily lives some of the real flaws in Britain's social and economic system.

Tawney's quest for the spiritual peace that comes with 'finding one's work and doing it'[17] seems to have ended happily in his WEA groups scattered across North Staffordshire and Lancashire. The men and women of his classes came together in education, as he saw it, not for 'material success but spiritual energy ... not in order that they may become something else, but because they are what they are'.[18] Tawney was angered by those who questioned giving a humane education to workers:

'What,' said an educated man to the writer, 'you teach history and economics to miners and engineers? Take care. You will make them discontented and disloyal to us.' That division of mankind into those who are ends and those who are means, whether made by slaveholders or by capitalists, is the ultimate and unforgivable wrong, with which there can be truce neither in education nor in any other department of social life.[19]

Tawney was quick to point out that 'we do not want education for the workers, in order to make them better machines. We want it in order that they become better human beings, free men and free women.'[20]

Tawney was also adamant that education would better not just the lives of the individual students, but the working class as a whole, who would benefit through subsequent public service by these students. He was well justified in this belief. At the educational level, the students in his classes took it upon themselves to present lectures and papers to other workers in their towns, and then to workers in neighbouring villages. The North Staffordshire WEA District was later instrumental in helping found the University of Keele.[21] At a broader level, a 1938 survey demonstrated that the 2,174 former WEA students responding were currently serving in 2,342 positions, including 15 MPs, 13 mayors, 250 magistrates, 165 school governors and managers, and 1,490 people serving as county, city, borough, urban or rural district, or parish, councillors.[22] By the late 1940s Tawney claimed that 'no less than one in three of the Labour members in the present House of Commons has taken part in [WEA] classes.'[23]

Tawney's service as a WEA tutor gave him the foundation and direction for the rest of his professional life's work. Indeed, at the end of his life 'he acknowledged that the miners and potters in his first tutorial class had made a great impression on his mind and had coloured his thoughts and actions in later life.'[24] Required by the necessities of his job to become a historian, he ended up finding that history was the perfect springboard for his social criticism. His political views were deeply influenced by his worker-students and he later became '*the* Democratic Socialist *par excellence*', tirelessly striving to give the working class the opportunity to create a better future for itself.[25] Not surprisingly, education was one of the main planks of his socialist agenda and Tawney devoted much of his prodigious energy to reforming the nation's educational system at every level.

Tawney's involvement with the tutorial classes could not help but affect him at a time when he was trying to devise his own solutions to various social problems. During the dozen years between when he left Oxford and when he enlisted in the army, Tawney expended a vast amount of mental energy on formulating his own beliefs and world view, glimpses of which can be found in the pages of his diary. Not only did Tawney struggle to get to the roots of social discord and economic inequality, but – crucially – his theological views were also evolving. By the outbreak of the 1914–18 war, Tawney's views were basically settled. After his service in the war, he launched himself into the national political scene as the economic historian-as-public-moralist.

The heart of the nation's problem, Tawney decided, was one of moral principles; that is, the foundation of the entire socio-economic system was morally flawed. The cause of labour unrest, much on Tawney's mind, was 'not simply economic, nor party-political, but moral'.[26] After much searching for a source of moral standards,

Tawney settled on the God of the High Church. In his own mind, Tawney needed the concreteness of the Christian God. Further, he argued that 'the knowledge that God exists is a source of immense strength to man. ... What we want to know is what kind of God he is, and what he is like in ordinary human intercourse. This is what Christianity tells us.'[27] His religious views were uncomplicated and were mainly derived from the ethical thought of T. H. Green and the incarnationist teachings of Charles Gore, founder of the Christian Social Union at Oxford and later bishop of Oxford, who was a personal friend of Tawney.

In a long internal debate about the proper approach to social reform, Tawney declared that there are 'certain sorts of behaviour which we know to be right, and certain others which we know to be wrong ... This knowledge is, I would urge, the common property of Christian nations.'[28] For Tawney, it came down to a concept of the sanctity of the human spirit stemming from his belief that all people were created in God's image and had a spark of the divine in them. This idea is not, of course, unique to Christianity, but Tawney saw the Incarnation as the fulfilment of this idea.[29]

Tawney was something of an anomaly in his religious beliefs, fully embracing Christianity at a time when religious observance was rapidly declining. He exercised considerable influence in High Church circles, but he was not interested in doctrinal debates. In fact, he rarely discussed his spiritual beliefs at all. 'I dislike theology', he commented to Beatrice Webb, who noted in her diary that: 'Altogether, in his religious opinions, he remains a mystery to his free-thinking friends.'[30]

To his religious friends such as William Temple, however, Tawney was a welcome and potent voice of morality in a public arena that was notably irreligious. Albert Mansbridge was also a devout Anglican, a shared sympathy that overcame any disagreements the men had over WEA policy; Tawney told Mansbridge that: 'I regard you as one of my spiritual parents, though probably you would repudiate paternity.'[31] Although Tawney's beliefs were very private, they informed all of his public writings and work. Ultimately, when joined with his historical research, Tawney's Christianity led him to embrace socialism, not merely as a political programme, but as an entire way of life.[32]

If it had not been for the WEA, Tawney might never have become a world-renowned economic historian. In 1907, when Mansbridge tapped him to lead the first tutorial classes, Tawney was unhappily teaching theoretical economics at Glasgow University. When the first WEA tutorial classes asked for a course in economic and industrial history, he quickly found that this new discipline opened up whole new avenues of thought for him, despite his having little prior knowledge of the subject. By 1912, after teaching economic history in the WEA full time for four years, he concluded that 'the supreme interest of economic history lies, it seems to me, in the clue which it offers to the development of those dimly conceived presuppositions as to social expediency which influence the actions not only of statesmen, but of humble individuals and classes.'[33] As he continued his research and developed his various courses on economic and industrial history, he realised that the field also gave him a framework for his contemporary social questions and tangible evidence with which to bolster his arguments.

The study of history thus became a tool for Tawney. Most of Tawney's works stress that history is about the choices that people made. History, he wrote, is the result of human action: 'constantly violent, or merely short-sighted, or deliberately selfish, ... a form of social organisation which appears to us now to be inevitable, once hung in the balance as one of several competing possibilities'.[34] He used this idea to argue that the modern state of affairs was not preordained, for it was people's *choices* in the past that got the nation to its current point. This view served as a reminder to those who 'unconsciously assum[e] that what, in fact, occurred, is what must have occurred, and thus lending to the past an appearance of inevitability'.[35] Tawney was clearly not a Marxist historian, nor was he a supporter of the dominant Whig history that stressed a chain of glorious constitutional and political advances leading to a perfectly satisfactory contemporary situation.

By refusing to subscribe either to a mechanistic or to an optimistic view of history, Tawney's studies are marked by both scepticism and pessimism. History, in his opinion, 'is concerned with the study, not of a series of past events, but of the life of society. ... part of the historian's business is to substitute more significant connections for those of chronology.'[36] For him, this often meant tracing the development of ideas and ideology, with social and religious factors weighing as heavily as (if not more than) economic data. To focus overmuch on politics and constitutional development was anathema: 'Political societies are secondary, societies based on kinship, on economic needs, on culture and religion, are primary. The fundamental aspect of history is the growth, not of States, but of communities transcending them.'[37]

The most important function of history for Tawney was that it could illuminate the present. All contemporary problems have their roots in the past, and only with a thorough examination of those roots could modern problems be addressed properly. This was useful not only for himself, but also for his worker-students. As he noted in his diary, by teaching his WEA students industrial and economic history, he could try to overcome the relative complacency of the working class, '%₀ of [whom] have not got to the point of realizing that our present (though not all) inequalities are the creation of man not of God'.[38] Tawney was quite open about his desire to use history this way. In lectures and published works he acknowledged the 'truth in the paradox that all history is the history of the present; and for this reason each generation must write its history for itself. That of its predecessors may be true, but its truth may not be relevant. Different answers are required because different questions are asked.'[39] Given the right information about their past, Tawney believed that Britons would make better choices for the future of their society.

Tawney's research for *The Agrarian Problem* and *Religion and the Rise of Capitalism* led him to conclude that the simultaneous rise of capitalism and decline in the role of the church in the sixteenth and seventeenth centuries had allowed a whole host of problems to develop. The divorce of the Christian moral code from the world of business came in for Tawney's special criticism, for it had allowed the worship of God to be replaced by the 'worship of riches'.[40] Tawney believed that capitalism had it all wrong: 'The social problem is a problem not of *quantities*, but of *proportions*, not of the *amount* of wealth, but of the *moral justice* of your social system.'[41] Tawney's concern was not with wealth as such, but with the use to which it was put. Of course, for him this was a question of whether society benefited; if the answer was negative, then some other form of wealth creation or distribution was required. The political system, shaped by Britain's class system, was also, he felt, corrupted by the ideology of inequality.

Using both the study of history and incisive analysis of present conditions, Tawney laid out his morally-based critique of modern Britain. Equality and fellowship, such as existed in his tutorial classes, became the social expressions of his political and religious beliefs.[42] He argued that 'since even quite common men have souls, no increase in material wealth will compensate them for arrangements which insult their self-respect and impair their freedom.'[43] Equality of opportunity was an important element in his thought, and indeed in his life – his WEA work was one attempt to put that ideal into practice. He knew that inequality would never be completely eliminated, but he felt that equality 'should be sincerely sought. What matters to the health of society is the objective towards which its face is set', even if that objective is elusive.[44] When he complained about the gross inequalities prevalent in his society, he did not do so out of a blind obedience to the socialist ideals he embraced. Rather, he did so out of a keen sense of moral outrage stemming from the intersection of his religious beliefs with his experiences with the working class.

One needs only a glance at Tawney's commonplace book to see how his students and their working lives shaped his thoughts about contemporary social and economic matters. Tawney's sympathies clearly lay with workers who were at the mercy of profit-driven owners and managers. His WEA students personified the masses robbed of their dignity and stripped of their rights and liberties in the name of economic expediency. Early in his diary he noted that 'the indictment brought by workers against modern industry is in essence that brought in all times against slavery: viz. that under present arrangements men are used not as ends but as means.'[45] This theme reappears in all of his major works and essays.

Tawney considered his campaign to rescue workers from the tyranny of industrial wage-employment to be akin to the efforts of the nineteenth-century abolitionists.[46] Just as the early abolitionists were religiously motivated, so too was Tawney. He claimed that the 'gross inequalities' of modern society were 'an odious outrage on the image of God', which no Christian could possibly tolerate in good conscience.[47] As a Christian socialist, Tawney had to integrate his theology with his economic philosophy to create a programme of reforms that could both replace industrial capitalism and establish an ethically-based society. His goal was to 'find some formula expressing the attitude of all good men to social questions, which should be so entrenched in public conviction as to be drawn into dispute by no party'.[48]

Tawney's turn to socialism was encouraged by his WEA students, and they were never far from his mind as he shaped Labour Party policy and pressed for reforms. Unlike so many other socialist intellectuals, Tawney had personal and long-standing experience with members of the working class, which added strength to his social criticism. He believed that socialism, particularly labour-based movements, offered the best hope of restoring lost liberties and dignity to the working class. As the workers suffered the worst abuses of the industrial system, it made sense that those workers should be at the forefront of a change of organisation. Tawney wrote in 1912 that the labour movement 'really stands more than any other movement, for freedom today. What it demands is that men should not live their lives at the will of a master.'[49]

While most of the working class were generally discontented with contemporary society, Tawney felt that only the more perceptive members of the working class saw that the root of the problem was 'a violent contradiction between the external political order, and men's subjective conception of right'. This was the 'spiritual factor in human development, which our own economic age tends to forget, and forgetfulness of which is ruin. It is ruin for this reason; that it leads men to suppose that changes *within* the existing order, which improve material conditions, are a substitute for the change *of* the order itself which is felt or thought to be immoral.'[50] Unfortunately, as he saw it, the 'religion of inequality' had become a fact of life for all Britons, a 'national characteristic' that all classes seemed to accept, even the working class and their labour movement, which was supposed to stand for 'the ideal of social justice and solidarity'.[51] The challenge was to figure out the best way to change people's way of thinking in order to create a better society; not surprisingly, Tawney's experience led him to education as a key to curing many of the nation's ills.

Tawney tackled some of the thorny issues of social and economic reform in *The Acquisitive Society* and *Equality*.[52] Both of these works were considered 'socialist bibles' when originally published, although Tawney rarely used the word 'socialism' in *The Acquisitive Society*, nor did he overly stress nationalisation. What he desired was not any particular form of economic organisation, but the removal of 'the dead hand of private ownership, where the private owner has ceased to perform any positive function'. In fact, he criticised as 'absurd' those socialists who felt that any private ownership was evil; what was important was 'what sort of property it is and for what purpose it is used'.[53] Nationalisation was his preferred choice for certain large industries, such as coal mining, but he did not rule out other forms of ownership or management.

Tawney developed his socialist ideals further in his 1929 Halley Stewart Lectures, published in 1931 as *Equality*. Although Tawney's belief in equality stemmed in part from his Christianity, equality was more than a religious issue for him; it was at the heart of all of his ideas about social reform. In *Equality* he traced the historical underpinnings of the British social system, with special attention given to the class system and the economic causes of inequality. He then discussed, in great detail, what he called 'the strategy of equality': redistribution of income, provision of social services, and educational reform.

In the end, Tawney did not assume that simple administrative or organisational changes would be sufficient. This was a fundamental disagreement between Tawney and his friends the Webbs: 'This is where I think the Fabians are inclined to go wrong. They seem to think that you can trick statesmen into a good course of action, without changing their principles.' He felt that no social or political structure would remain standing for long without the will of the people behind it (or without brute force, which was not an option for him), because he held that the entire direction of society could only be altered from within; that is, the will to change had to come from the hearts of the people. Thus, the change in attitude had to take place not only within the ruling class, but also among the entire population: 'the attitude of individuals to each other is wrong, because we in our present society are living on certain false and universal assumptions. ... What we have got to do *first* of all is to change those assumptions or principles.'[54]

To transform those principles, Tawney emphasised three areas for his fellow countrymen to focus on: distribution of wealth, social services, and education. Educational reform does not appear to be an intrinsic part of a socialist's agenda, but for Tawney inadequate education was the final obstacle to a more equal society. He laughingly recalled that

When I first took part in the Labour Movement, some 18 years ago, my cultured friends used to express their contempt for an agitation so inimical to the interests of learning and to the life of the spirit. I find that today they more often complain that these barbarians demand education on a scale and of a quality which is likely to impose excessive burdens upon the tax payer.[55]

Redistribution of wealth and economic power were certainly critical, but without a change in the methods of and opportunities for education, a true community – a common culture – would never arise. Tawney's passion for educational reform came directly from his experiences with the WEA. Many of his worker-students had left school by the age of 14 to begin employment. Tawney deplored the economic realities that forced working families to pull their children out of school in order to support themselves. He argued that this situation had allowed two parallel, but unequal, educational systems to develop. One, for the majority of children, consisted of 'elementary' education, 'the education of a special class which would obtain no other'.[56] The assumption that all that the children of workers needed were the most basic skills 'is in itself a piece of insolence'.[57] The other system, for the privileged minority, provided primary and secondary education as a grounding for university or for a profession.

The continued existence of these separate systems was 'educationally unsound and socially obnoxious'.[58] Other than capitalism itself, Tawney felt that the educational system did the most to 'perpetuate the division of the nation into classes of which one is almost unintelligible to the other'.[59] He advocated a radical restructuring of the existing system into a universal course of schooling for all children from nursery school to the age of 16 or (preferably) 18. The advantages of this scheme were numerous, not least of which was that the most talented children from all classes would get the best training possible, and many more working-class students would be in a position to get a university education. Further, the intermingling of the classes would foster greater understanding between classes due to a common educational background.[60] The new secondary schools, he hoped, would function 'as an organ of mutual understanding and spiritual unity' and serve as 'the vehicle of a common culture'.[61] Mutual understanding was a critical factor for any society, but it was especially needed if Tawney's socialism had any hope of being realised.

Knowing that it would take a tremendous effort and many years until significant reforms took place, Tawney attacked the problem of education from a number of angles. From his first years out of school, Tawney began a lifelong press campaign urging educational reform from the primary schools up through the ancient universities. He wrote some two hundred articles and leaders on education policy, mostly in the *Morning Post* and the *Manchester Guardian*. He was the anonymous 'Lambda' who in 1906 penned a long series of critical articles on the need for reform at Oxford, published in the *Westminster Gazette*. He was also a key voice in the important report 'Oxford and Working-Class Education' (1908), which established the tutorial classes committee that sponsored Tawney's WEA classes.

Tawney also put his growing influence to work in the broader political arena, constantly pressing for education reform any way he could. In a speech to a local WEA group, he stressed his desire

> to see the mass of the people in England ... going on strike to assert their right to keep their children at school until they are 18 or 19, and to have sufficient income to enable them to do so. Education ought to be part of the standard of life which the Labour Movement exists to protect and to raise.[62]

He served on the adult education committee of the Ministry of Reconstruction at the end of the 1914–18 war, and was a private advisor to H. A. L. Fisher, sponsor of the 1918 Education Act. Tawney wrote two Labour Party policy statements on education, both issued as pamphlets: *Secondary Education for All* (1922) and *Education: The Socialist Policy* (1924), and worked on the Labour Party's education committee. Tawney also served on Henry Hadow's consultative committee at the Board of Education. In late 1926 the consultative committee issued what is referred to as the 'Hadow Report', urging a variety of reforms strikingly similar to Tawney's own suggestions, especially about raising the school leaving age. His stamp on this pioneering effort at reform has long been acknowledged.

To help gain acceptance for the Report, Tawney continued with his leader-writing, issued a pamphlet on *The Possible Cost of Raising the School Leaving Age*, and organised a conference on 'The Education of the Adolescent'.[63] He gave speeches on the issue and continued to press the programme of reforms publicly and privately. Though a watered-down Education Bill was defeated in the Lords in 1931, the stage was well set for educational reform in the future. The 1944 Education Act, which established uniform secondary education for all students, was a direct descendant of the Hadow Report. In the realm of higher education, Tawney's service on the University Grants Commission in the 1940s gave him the satisfaction of personally opening up the universities to more working-class students.

On an individual level, as a WEA tutor and later president of the WEA from 1928 to 1945, Tawney worked tirelessly to bridge the gap between education for the wealthy and for the workers. Unfortunately, his standards were perhaps too high or too unrealistic for the WEA as it grew beyond its founders' wildest dreams. Throughout his presidency, Tawney was frustrated by the Association's inability to recruit enough new teachers and tutors to satisfy the swelling demand for adult education. He was also afraid that the growing number of less-academic classes would weaken the quality and reputation of the WEA and keep worker-students from reaching their full intellectual potential because they were not being challenged.[64]

It is not surprising, then, that as both the first teacher of tutorial classes and as the WEA's first resident tutor, Tawney maintained a fierce loyalty to the tutorial class programme. He regarded tutorial students as the 'backbone of the organisation', and he gave possibly too much weight to tutorial classes' place within the WEA.[65] Of course, his own experience coloured his thinking. He believed that tutorial classes brought out the highest levels of student achievement and fulfilment. In order to attain that level of success, however, only the finest tutors would do. He argued that for a tutor to be effective, he (always 'he' for Tawney) must give his class 'most of his energy and interest, and must serve an apprenticeship to the work'. Tawney further stressed that a tutor 'makes a great mistake if he thinks that to teach Tutorial classes all he has got to do is to present his university lectures in a popular form. ... His task is to revise his own conclusions in the light of [his students'] and to supplement his ignorance by their experience.'[66] Tawney was very particular about having the right sort of person lead a tutorial class, and he stated bluntly that if, 'when a group applies for a class, we have not the right man for tutor, I should decline to send the wrong one, even though the result is that no class is held.'[67]

Evidence from his own tutorial classes testifies to Tawney's personal effect on his WEA students. At the end of his first tutorial session, one student in the Rochdale class exclaimed that 'Tawney [h]as captured not only the heads but the hearts of his scholars; if you can get a don like him, we can turn England upside down in a few years time.'[68] Later, long after Tawney had moved to the London School of Economics, 'his unfortunate successors who took the Longton Class found that the class, like Mrs. Grummidge [sic] in *David Copperfield*, was "thinking of the old 'un" and judging the young one by that impossible standard.'[69] As to his love and respect for his students, one WEA official commented of Tawney that 'I believe he thinks heaven will be populated exclusively by manual workers.'[70]

As he looked back on his life, Tawney 'very modestly ... said he never realised that what he had tried to do had apparently had such a great effect on so many men and movements.'[71] Chief among those movements was Tawney's beloved WEA. At the end of his teaching career, he humbly stated that 'I can never be sufficiently grateful for the lessons learned from the adult students whom I was supposed to teach, but who, in fact, taught me.'[72] After a lifetime of service to the WEA, Tawney continued to give after his death by leaving his entire estate, less a few small bequests, to the Association.

NOTES

*Place of publication London unless otherwise stated.*

1. R. H. Tawney, 'The Workers' Educational Association and Adult Education', lecture delivered on 8 May 1953, reprinted in *The Radical Tradition*, ed. Rita Hinden (1964), 82. The author wishes to thank T. W. Heyck, Carol Loar, and Sharmishtha Roy Chowdhury for their helpful comments on earlier versions of this chapter.
2. *Toynbee Record*, Nov. 1905.
3. See S. Meacham, *Toynbee Hall and Social Reform, 1880–1914: The Search for Community* (New Haven, 1987).
4. *R. H. Tawney's Commonplace Book*, ed. and with an introduction by J. M. Winter and D. M. Joslin, *Economic History Review* Supplement no. 5 (Cambridge, 1972), 3 Dec. 1913.
5. Tawney, *Commonplace Book*, 10 June 1912.
6. London School of Economics, British Library of Political and Economic Science, Beveridge Papers II a 106, Tawney to William Beveridge, 20 Sept. 1905.
7. For the WEA's relationship with Oxford during this period, see L. Goldman, *Dons and Workers: Oxford and Adult Education since 1850* (Oxford, 1995), ch. 4, which also includes much valuable information on Tawney.
8. *Adventure*, 37.
9. National Archive, WEA CENTRAL/3/6/1, Tawney correspondence re early tutorial classes 1907–8, Albert Mansbridge to Tawney, 3 Dec. 1907.
10. WEA CENTRAL3/6/4, L. V. Gill to Albert Mansbridge, 26 Jan. 1908; James Henighan to Albert Mansbridge, Feb. 1908; Charles Knott to Albert Mansbridge, 25 Mar. 1908.
11. One measure of his success was the work-product of his students. The final essays for each class were reviewed by outside examiners at Oxford. Of the first Rochdale class, 25 per cent of the essays were deemed to be of 'First-Class Honours' level, and the 1909 Longton class had 7 out of 18 essays pass 'with distinction'. Mansbridge, *Adventure*, 40; Oxford University Archives, Department of External Studies DES/F/2/1/3. See

Goldman's perceptive comments on the biases of the examiners in *Dons and Workers*, 133–4.

12. Memo from Tawney, Oxford University Archives, Department of External Studies, DES/F/2/1/8.

13. WEA CENTRAL/4/1/2/1, 'Workers' Educational Association. An Outline of its Growth and a Statement of its Needs' (1929), 15.

14. R. H. Tawney, 'An Experiment in Democratic Education', *Political Quarterly* (July 1914), reprinted in *The Radical Tradition*, 77.

15. WEA CENTRAL3/6/4, L.V. Gill to Albert Mansbridge, 2 Feb. 1908.

16. R. H. Tawney, *The Agrarian Problem in the Sixteenth Century* (1912), ix. Tawney wrote this book at the behest of the Oxford Extension Delegacy, in lieu of teaching a fifth class.

17. Tawney, *Commonplace Book*, 21 Apr. 1913.

18. Tawney, 'An Experiment in Democratic Education', 74.

19. British Library of Political and Economic Science, Tawney Papers 18/4, R. H. Tawney, speech at Tottenham County School (n.d., ca. 1945–6), 4; Tawney, 'An Experiment in Democratic Education', 72.

20. R. H. Tawney, 'Education and Social Progress', address delivered at the educational meeting in connection with the Co-operative Congress, 28 May 1912 (Manchester,1912), 7.

21. See National Archive, WEA Library Collections, university extra-mural work box, 'Oxford University Extension Delegacy Tutorial Classes Committee Report on the Second Year's Working to September 30, 1910'; and H. P. Smith, 'R. H. Tawney', *Rewley House Papers* (Oxford, 1962), 39.

22. WEA CENTRAL/4/1/2/2, 'The Adult Student as Citizen: A Record of Service by WEA Students Past and Present', with a preface by R. H. Tawney (1938).

23. Tawney Papers 16/5, Tawney, Lectures in the US on the Labour Government (n.d., ca. 1948), 6. The veracity of this claim is unknown.

24. J. Thomas, 'Salute to Professor R. H. Tawney' (report of Tawney's eightieth birthday celebration at the House of Commons), *Rewley House Papers* (1961), 6.

25. Hugh Gaitskell, address at the memorial service for Tawney on 8 Feb. 1962 at St. Martin-in-the-Fields, London, reprinted in *The Radical Tradition*, 211.

26. Tawney, *Commonplace Book*, 6 May 1912. See also 10 June 1912.

27. Tawney, *Commonplace Book*, 12 July 1914.

28. Tawney, *Commonplace Book*, 18 Sept. 1912.

29. See Tawney, *Commonplace Book*, 12 July 1914; and R. H. Tawney, 'Christianity and the Social Order', in *The Attack and other Papers* (New York, 1953), 182.

30. British Library of Political and Economic Science, Diary of Beatrice Webb, vols. 52–4, 21 Jan. 1938.

31. BL, Mansbridge Papers, Tawney to Albert Mansbridge, 3 Feb. 1943.

32. For more on Tawney's religious beliefs and how they shaped the rest of his thought and activity, see Meredith K. Rusoff, 'They Hoped For Yesterday: British Social Criticism in the Early Twentieth Century' (Ph.D. diss., Northwestern University, 2000), ch. 4.

33. Tawney, *Agrarian Problem*, vii.

34. Tawney, *Agrarian Problem*, 178.

35. Tawney Papers 4/1, Fragments of Ford and Chicago lectures.

36. R. H. Tawney, 'The Study of Economic History', *Economica*, Feb. 1933, 9.

37. R. H. Tawney, 'Introductory Memoir' to G. Unwin, *Studies in Economic History* (1927), lxiii.

38. Tawney, *Commonplace Book*, 26 Feb. 1913.

39. Tawney, 'The Study of Economic History', 10. Also Tawney Papers 3/1 and 5/2, Ford and Chicago Lectures, Lecture 1.

40. Tawney Papers 19/6, R. H. Tawney, Speech to William Temple Society, 5 May 1949, 6a.

41. Tawney, *Commonplace Book*, 22 June 1912. Emphasis in original. See also Tawney Papers 10/10, Tawney, 'The New Leviathan', 9 (an important manuscript book outline, never published, ca. 1914–19).

42. For a similar argument see Goldman, *Dons and Workers*, 160.

43. R. H. Tawney, *Religion and the Rise of Capitalism* (1926), 284.

44. R. H. Tawney, *Equality*, 4th edn (1952; reprinted, with a new introduction by Richard M. Titmuss, 1964), 56 (citations are to the 1964 edn).

45. Tawney, *Commonplace Book*, 6 May 1912.

46. See, for example, Tawney, *Commonplace Book*, 18 Sept. 1912.

47. Tawney, 'Christianity and the Social Order', 184.

48. Tawney, *Commonplace Book*, 7 Jan. 1913.

49. Tawney, *Commonplace Book*, 2 Dec. 1912.

50. Tawney, *Commonplace Book*, 6 July 1913.

51. Tawney, *Equality*, 39–40.

52. Unfortunately, Tawney was no theorist; he never worked out the details of his ideal society or of some of his important concepts such as 'liberty' or 'freedom'.

53. Tawney, *Acquisitive Society*, 86, 104.

54. Tawney, *Commonplace Book*, 2 Dec. 1912.

55. Tawney Papers 18/1, speech to schoolteachers (n.d.).

56. R. H. Tawney (ed.), *Secondary Education For All: A Policy for Labour* (1922), 25.

57. Tawney (ed.), *Secondary Education For All*, 33.

58. Tawney (ed.), *Secondary Education For All*, 11.

59. Tawney, *Equality*, 145.

60. See Tawney, 'The Problem of the Public Schools', in *The Radical Tradition*, 61.

61. Tawney Papers 18/4, Tawney, speech at Tottenham County School, 4.

62. WEA CENTRAL/4/2/2/12, education pamphlets, R. H. Tawney, 'The Educational Needs of a Democracy', speech to Yorkshire District WEA (n.d., ca. 1918–19).

63. J. R. Brooks, 'R. H. Tawney and Educational Reform in the Immediate Post-Hadow years, 1927–31', *Journal of Educational Administration and History* xx, no. 2 (July 1988), 3.

64. See WEA CENTRAL /4/1/1/16, R. H. Tawney, 'The Realities of Democracy', presidential address to the WEA, 7 Nov. 1936, 12–14; and his presidential address to the WEA, 18 Nov. 1944.

65. WEA CENTRAL /4/1/1/16, Tawney, 'Concluding Observations', speech to the WEA Jubilee Conference, Harrogate, May 1953.

66. BL Mansbridge Papers, Tawney to Mansbridge, 12 June 1923.
67. Tawney, 'The Realities of Democracy', 14–15.
68. WEA CENTRAL3/6/4, Alfred W. Wilkinson to Mansbridge (n.d., ca. Apr. 1908), report on Rochdale tutorial class.
69. A. D. Lindsay, 'R. H. Tawney, An Appreciation', *The Highway*, xxxvi (Jan. 1945), 51.
70. Quoted in J. R. Williams, R. M. Titmuss, and F. J. Fisher, *R. H. Tawney: A Portrait by Several Hands* (privately published, 1960), 29–30.
71. Thomas, 'Salute to Professor R. H. Tawney', 5.
72. Tawney, 'The WEA and Adult Education', 91.

# 5 The Evolution of the WEA in the West Midlands, 1905–26

*Stephen K. Roberts*

## ORIGINS

In the ambitious vision of its founders, the WEA was conceived as never less than a national movement. Eight 'branches' or 'centres' – the words were used loosely in the earliest days – were in existence by May 1905.[1] Historians of the movement have focused on places given totemic significance in the story (London, Rochdale, Longton), but much can be learned about the temper of the WEA by further local studies. This chapter considers the development of the WEA in the west Midlands, defined here loosely and geographically, not institutionally. In other words, we are considering territory (east–west, east Warwickshire to the Welsh Marches, north–south, Derbyshire to Oxfordshire), rather than the boundaries of the Midland or later West Midlands and West Mercia Districts of the WEA. Locally, as in the national sphere, the movement succeeded most effectively as an alliance between eminent individuals and local activists, and the WEA absorbed much from the civic culture of towns and districts where activity was rooted. Thoughtfulness, enterprise, enthusiasm and commitment were much in evidence from the outset.

The west Midlands, and particularly Birmingham, can claim a degree of significance in the founding of the WEA. Only one of the 'branches' noted in 1905 was in the Midlands – at Derby – but a great stimulus to activity in the region came with the second Annual General Meeting of the Association, at Queen's College, Birmingham, on 14 October that year (see plate 1).[2] It was at this conference that the Association shed its original title, 'Association to promote the Higher Education of Working Men', in favour of 'Workers' Educational Association'.[3] Queen's College was a medical school, associated with the newly-founded (1900) University of Birmingham. For the afternoon of the day's events, the 600 delegates and 400 unmandated enthusiastic individuals crossed the road to the Midland Institute. Both venues suggest links between the embryonic WEA and important existing educational currents in the Midlands. Birmingham was Britain's 'first civic university', and its departments

were, even as the WEA proto-activists met in conference, beginning
to transfer from the cramped city centre quarters to the imposing
range of buildings being built at Edgbaston.[4] The Midland Institute
had since 1855 been a centre for activities that would today be
described as adult educational. Charles Dickens had given 'readings'
of his *A Christmas Carol* there, and the Institute was an important
focus of the university extension movement.

The October 1905 conference, like the other early WEA public
meetings, was well-managed. On the Monday after the Saturday
meeting, the *Birmingham Daily Post* published a resolution passed
there. It called for joint action between universities and working-
class organisations to meet the need for workers' education. It had
been moved by Richard Bell, MP for Derby, and the bishop of
Birmingham. The list of subscribing bodies was impressive in its range
and number. There were representatives of the universities of Oxford,
Cambridge and Birmingham and of University College, Nottingham.
Leicester Working Men's College and Ruskin College, Oxford were
represented, as were the National Home Reading Union, the National
Union of Teachers and the Women's Trade Union League. There was
a strong regional and local voluntary input from the Midland section
of the Co-operative Union, the Midland Co-operative Education
Committee Association, Birmingham Trades Council, the
Birmingham Sunday Lecture Society and the Birmingham and
Midland Association of Adult Schools. The importance of the
resolution as a benchmark for collaboration is illustrated in the
copying of the pronouncement into the minute book of Birmingham
University's council, in 1909.[5] More immediately, the conference
marked the formation of a Birmingham WEA committee, whose
pioneering activities were reported to the central committee in
London by December 1905.[6] The new university provided lecturers
and free accommodation for evening lectures.[7] By May 1906, there
was WEA activity of an unspecified kind, presumably evening classes
along university extension lines, in Oxford and Coventry, as well as
at Birmingham. In 1907 W. J. Sharkey, formerly a brushmaker,
became the first salaried Midland WEA secretary, and indeed the first
salaried district secretary anywhere, at £7 12s. a year. The following
year, the WEA returned to Birmingham under the constitution
providing for a central association, districts and branches to elect
William Temple as first president.[8]

Oliver Lodge, head-hunted in 1900 by Joseph Chamberlain as
principal of Birmingham University, was poised to play a crucial role

in shaping the emerging WEA in the west Midlands, once the Board of Education approved new regulations to fund joint working between the association and the universities.[9] Birmingham University had run extension lectures on its own account from 1902–3, at Wolverhampton; and by 1905–6 had moved on to operate in Cheltenham, Coventry, Leicester, Lightwood (Staffs.) and Tamworth. The random scattering of venues suggests that then, as always, adult education activity had to be opportunistic in its scheduling. The university's total extra-mural programme that year amounted to 40 lectures. In 1909, the joint committee of the university and the WEA was founded.[10]

The Birmingham branch, which was effectively the central hub of WEA work in the Midlands, claimed a membership of 830 by 1911. It was the Birmingham of Joseph Chamberlain's unchallenged Liberal-Unionist supremacy: a town with a brand-new university and a brand-new Anglican diocese. In the early WEA work in Birmingham formal provision and informal work of a broadly educational character were blurred. There was a women's section, proudly reported to be 'by far the strongest in the country', a playgoers' club and a music section. The object of the playgoers' club was to 'educate the working class patron of the theatre and music hall to appreciate and demand good drama'. At some point, probably before 1914, a party of 100 WEA students took seats at the Birmingham premiere of George Bernard Shaw's *Caesar and Cleopatra*. A WEA orchestra was being formed in 1910 (it maintains a precarious existence today), and a WEA group won first prize the following year in a city-wide 'working girls' choir competition'. The excursions organised that year included one to Cadbury's 'model factory' at Bournville – 200 went on the visit, and 70 had to be turned away – and 60–70 went on visits to London and Oxford. Less demanding but even more popular was the 1910 whist drive at Handsworth, attended by over 500 people. The formal provision in Birmingham in 1906 consisted of evening lectures, run at Edmund Street, where the university, Queen's College and the Birmingham and Midland Institute formed a kind of intellectual quarter in the city centre. The numbers attending the lectures were again impressive: 60 for industrial history, 78 for a course on Russia. Interest was presumably fuelled by the 1905 workers' risings there, and in Bernard Pares (then it seems a Cambridge University extension lecturer), they had a Russophile teacher who became a world authority on his subject.

Even greater numbers – 400-plus – attended 'social study' lectures at the university.[11]

## UNIVERSITY TIES

In all of this activity, the patronage of supporters at the university was sought and nurtured. The 'moving spirit' (as the Birmingham WEA itself put it) of the women's committee was Mary Muirhead, wife of the professor of philosophy at Birmingham, John Henry Muirhead, himself a WEA supporter. Professor Granville Bantock was president of the music section, and university lecturers offered talks to give structure to the activities of the playgoers' club.[12] The concept of presidency was evidently important to Mansbridge, and doubtless to others of his WEA colleagues. Lodge had been approached as early as November 1904, before a Midlands WEA presence had emerged, to be president of the Association, and had declined, on the grounds that he was too busy to be anything other than a figurehead, when what was needed was an activist.[13]

There were practical reasons why patrons and partners were important. The WEA mounted no free-standing provision of its own. In 1906, the university ran the social study lectures, the city's education committee sponsored the industrial history course, and Pares gave his lectures on Russia at the expense of the Midland Institute. The Midland committee of the WEA at the time reflects in its composition the broad and strategic nature of support. The University of Birmingham, Cambridge Extension Syndicate, Oxford Extension Delegacy, University College Nottingham, Ruskin College, Leicester Working Men's College and the Director of Higher Education for North Staffordshire accepted places, but the presence of organised labour seems weak, with two Co-operative Society members, two from the National Union of Teachers and one from Birmingham Trades Council. As this last had 25,000 members, however, it was a gateway of access to the trade union movement, at least in Birmingham, and Sharkey was ready to travel to gather support from further afield, as in the case of Staffordshire Trades Council, which expressed interest that year. Furthermore, many more societies were affiliated than were represented directly on the Midland Committee. In 1906 affiliations had been received from 28 trade unions, 14 adult schools and 3 Co-operative societies.[14]

Mansbridge took an active interest in developments at Birmingham, and Sharkey supplied him with details of committee meetings. They were not always well attended: at one in 1906, only Professor Masterman, Sharkey himself and another were present, but this bore no relation to the speed and profusion of activity. Sharkey reported excitedly to Mansbridge on a public meeting in October 1906, at Queen's College: 'I broke the medical theatre last Tuesday. They were sitting on the stairs and in the gangways.'[15] But university patronage and Mansbridge's careful cultivation of the good and the great could hardly account for the sheer scale of interest in the WEA project that had blown up, seemingly from nowhere. In 1906 there were local groups connected with the Birmingham hub at Handsworth (then still outside the city boundary), Derby, Coventry, and at three places in Northamptonshire: Northampton, Rothwell and Kettering.

BRANCHES AND TUTORIAL CLASSES

The Birmingham branch was rather special in the WEA's evolution, because it drew on the stored dynamic charge of the October 1905 conference. More typical of early branches was that of King's Norton, in the Birmingham suburbs, founded in 1909, and whose records survive from 1911. There were 25 members of the branch in 1910–11, 43 in 1911–12. Organisationally, it was strong enough to support a council and a separate executive committee, a common pattern. The secretary in 1910 was Walter Hardy (1883–1959), a native of the area, who left school at 13 to take jobs in gardening and in an umbrella factory before finding work at Cadbury's in Bournville. President George Shann (1876–1919) had worked in a spinning factory at the age of 10. From 1904 he had taught at Birmingham University in economics and industrial subjects. He was involved with the Cadburys' Woodbrooke settlement, and was a member of the Workers' Union, a general union for the less skilled, which made great strides in the new cycle and motor car factories of the Midlands. Shann was also a local councillor, active in labour churches, the adult school movement, the ILP, the Fabian movement and above all the 'anti-sweating' movement: he was the first secretary of the Anti-sweating League. If this were not enough voluntary activity, after the council elections in 1911 he was also chair of the minority Labour group on Birmingham City Council. The King's Norton branch had powerful Cadbury links. It met at the recently-opened Ruskin Hall, in Bournville village, planned courses for the Bournville workers, and considered inviting George Cadbury Jr. to chair one of its meetings. Walter Hardy went on to a Cadbury-provided scholarship at the Cadbury-sponsored Fircroft College, and became agent for the first municipal Labour Party candidate in Selly Oak.[16]

The activities of the branch have a timeless quality about them, and suggest a pattern of voluntary working familiar to WEA branches everywhere. In 1910–11 a course on 'the health of the state' had been run successfully; for 1911–12 women members of the branch were to form a sub-committee to meet with the Social Service League to organise a course for which a work on hygiene was to form the key text. There was a women's committee, which reported in August 1911 that subjects 'of special interest to women' would be botany and English literature. The botany class was thought suitable for the spring, when rambles and open air study would be possible, and the following year it attracted 25 students. It was a 14-week course, each meeting of one-and-a-half hours' duration, and the tutor was paid 10s. 6d. per meeting. There had been a suggestion (from what quarter is unfortunately not recorded) that the botany class should be open to male students, and the branch agreed that the class be mixed. Nevertheless, the branch continued to sponsor courses aimed particularly at women, and the literature class duly started at the Bournville factory girls' pavilion: the name of the venue alone suggests that this was surely a women-only class. The tutor was a Miss B. Orange, from Birmingham University, and there were 53 on the register, 28 of whom were 'effective students' for grant purposes. It had been calculated by the branch that a class of 30 could produce £4 in grant, and it was therefore proposed from the outset as a grant-earning class. Publicity material was posted in the Bournville factory and in the 'syllabus' of Stirchley Labour Church.

By 1911, the tutorial class had become the 'gold standard' in the Midlands, as it was becoming so elsewhere. Students from the Selly Oak preparatory class and similar courses planned in 1912 in nearby Cotteridge and Selly Park would theoretically prepare for admission to the tutorial classes at Northfield and Stirchley. The joint committee of the WEA and Birmingham University ran its first tutorial classes in March 1910, two years behind Tawney's pioneering ones: there were initially three classes, all in Birmingham. They were added to a list of tutorial classes running in other Midlands locations in partnership with other universities: at Derby, Dudley, Hanley, Leicester, Sutton-in-Ashfield and (most famously) Longton.

The Northfield tutorial class had 20 students enrolled in October 1911, but the branch seemed uneasy with its university sponsor. It was reported at a meeting that month that at a conference of universities, 'opinion was expressed that tutorial classes should be primarily the concern of the universities'. King's Norton branch seems to have taken this as a serious threat to the continuation of the joint arrangements, and carried a resolution that Birmingham city education committee should recognise the tutorial classes, 'as far as educational policy is concerned in relation to the Northfield and Stirchley tutorial classes'. This vague resolution was in fact a prelude to a wholesale transfer; by January 1912, the tutorial classes, still with that name, were now running under the banner of the city council. The branch immediately regretted its haste:

> The classes tended to lose in status by the appointment of tutors ... by the education committee instead of the university ... These classes were looked upon as part of the system of evening classes and had not even the standing of Technical Schools.[17]

In order for tutorial classes to accomplish their mission, the appointment of tutors should lie with the WEA/University of Birmingham joint committee. By June, the branch was trying its best to retrieve the classes from the city education committee.

## LOCAL POLITICS

This WEA branch had a clear view of the superiority of itself and of tutorial courses, regarding both as the leaven in the lump of 'evening classes'. In tracing the rise of the WEA, the speed and scale of its spread is impressive, but in populous areas it never had the field to itself. In Birmingham in 1912 there were 21,344 students in day and evening classes, with 9,857 in evening provision. Much of it was vocational and technical, with groups of employers in the prime Birmingham trades – guns, jewellery and engineering – organising afternoon courses. The largest provider was the city education committee, but on the King's Norton branch's doorstep, Cadbury's at Bournville developed its own educational 'system' for the workforce, which WEA students could benefit from, and which the branch programme could only complement.

King's Norton delegates returned from the WEA conference in Manchester in 1911 to report two things of particular interest that had emerged there. One was that in the Bristol region, WEA reading circles had successfully been set up, and to the King's Norton branch this kind of provision suggested a way forward from the disappointments of formal classes failing to recruit. The second revelation was that it turned out that universities in Liverpool, Manchester and Leeds were providing more support to the WEA than Birmingham was.[18] This news came at an interesting juncture in the three-way relationship between the WEA, the city council and the university. The city council as a whole had never been as enthusiastic about the university's foundation as its first driving force, Joseph Chamberlain. Scepticism was prevalent among representatives of the labour movement, but when in 1911 Chamberlain called for an increase by the city council in its financial support for the new foundation, opposition from Labour quarters became vocal. According to a recent historian of the University of Birmingham, Labour councillors were by this time 'numerous', but they were still a minority: only six were successful in the 1911 municipal elections. Even so, there was popular disquiet in the city that working-class people received no benefit from the university, and some ratepayers queried the legality under the Technical Instruction Acts of 1889 and 1891 of rate support for the institution.[19] City rate support was only offered for one year in 1911, and the issue was a live one in the municipal elections in November.

There were other sensitivities which made the November 1911 city elections of interest to WEA activists. The university found itself caught up in controversy surrounding the extension of the city boundaries to include its new campus at Bournbrook, and this was to be a new council, increased in size. Labour was bound to organise a strong field in the contest: it was to be a 'miniature general election'.[20] The Birmingham WEA branch, with the support of its satellite groups at King's Norton and Handsworth, seized the moment to canvass support for its own interests. All candidates in the election were circulated with a typed sheet which described the work of the Association, and were asked whether if the city council decided to increase the level of support to the university, they would stipulate that more money for the WEA should be carved from the grant. Replies were received from 10 Labour candidates, 15 Liberals, 31 Conservatives and 11 Independents. All were positive expressions of support for the work of the WEA, except in the cases of 2 Conservatives and 1 Labour, who were opposed. The replies of a further 3 Conservatives and 1 Liberal were marked as 'doubtful'. Typical of the phrasing of the positive replies was: 'I consider the Association is doing excellent work and is worthy of much more financial support from the university than it has hitherto had.' The author was aspiring councillor Neville Chamberlain, later famous for appeasing mightier dragons than the Birmingham WEA branch.

The reasons for opposition are more interesting. Liberal candidate Harrison Barrow: 'Many of the [WEA] lectures which have been given have been attended almost solely by the middle and upper classes of society.' Conservative candidate T. R. Bayliss (irritably): 'I will not blindly tie myself to anything – must see its merits first.' A Progressive Liberal candidate (irrelevantly): was in favour of the higher education of children from poor families. Some opposition naturally picked up on the current controversies in the city's public life. Fred Hughes (Labour):

> I shall *not* vote in favour of any increased grant to the university from the city rates, at least till the university has shown that the money already granted is being used to bring its advantages within reach of the working class.

E. Marston Rudland (Conservative) thought the WEA deserved support, but could not support an increase in grant to the university without an inquiry into the university's finances. An Independent Labour Party candidate was sympathetic, but thought the university should be supporting the WEA better without any further help from the city, and offered the case of 'necessitous children' in Birmingham as a more urgent matter than adult education. Liberal J. L. Yates was opposed to city rate support for the university altogether.[21]

There was no division on strict party lines on this issue, in a city that was noted in any case for its generally consensual, Liberal–Unionist politics. The Birmingham WEA had linked itself irretrievably with the university on the question of funding, so that the sympathetic response of the ILP candidate who thought the WEA should be getting more money from the university without more city council help was marked as 'opposed'. In February 1912 *The Birmingham Daily Post* ran a leader calling for increased rate support from the city to the university if scholarships were established and if the university developed better links with the citizens, specifically through the WEA. By February 1913 the university had agreed to fund 15 scholarships in return for £15,000 a year indefinitely. In 1911–12 the university's grant to the WEA was £100; from 1912–13 it was £300. From 1911, the university allocated a large room to the WEA, used as a district office by day, and as teaching premises by night.[22]

## LABOUR MOVEMENT LINKS

The relationship between the University of Birmingham and the Birmingham WEA was close and had been kick-started in the earliest contacts between Mansbridge and Lodge. The Midland District of the WEA (1905–19) and then the West Midlands District (from 1919) were chaired by Birmingham University professors down to the 1950s. The role of organised labour is harder to trace, but an intending historian of the regional WEA may be misled into dismissing its significance because the sources are slighter and harder to come by. Nevertheless, in Birmingham the labour movement was a decisive force, particularly at branch level. W. J. Morgan of Birmingham Trades Council was probably the first trade unionist of standing in the region to become involved constructively: he worked with the influential Co-operator Robert Halstead (1858–1930) to establish the WEA District after 1905.[23] In 1910, there were seven societies affiliated to the District, the newest recruits being the Birmingham branch of the Amalgamated Society of Railway Servants, and the Railway Clerks' Association. The ASRS was the fourth largest union in the country, was in some regions becoming a focus for members with syndicalist views, and was in 1910 at the centre of a national rail strike. In fact, affiliations of societies to individual branches could outpace those of the District. The King's Norton branch appeared much healthier in this regard: the affiliating unions were Stirchley Amalgamated Society of Engineers, Stirchley Workers' Union, Northfield National Union of Teachers, and the National Federation of Women Workers. Beyond these lay an even richer vein of voluntary activity in the area: the Co-operative Education Committee, the Bournville Works Women's Social Service League and the Bournville Works education committee; several branches of the ILP, the East Worcestershire Labour Representation Committee branch, Bournville United Methodist Church and the local adult school.[24]

King's Norton was perhaps exceptional in its wealth of contacts, mediated as they were by Cadbury's benign influence and the impressive labour movement credentials of George Shann. Even so, affiliations rose generally in the District, so that by 1914 the societies represented on the Birmingham branch council included the

Tramway Vehicle Workers' Association, the Amalgamated Toolmakers, Birmingham Printers, as well as the adult schools, and the Women's Co-operative Guild. The following year, the Birmingham lodge of the Brotherhood of Arts and Crafts affiliated. The joint committee with the university included by 1916 delegates from the Chainmakers' Union, the Birmingham Industrial Co-operative Society education committee and the city council Labour group.[25] From among those coming from a trade unionist, non-academic background, who were prominent in the early decades of the WEA in this region must be singled out John W. Cuthbertson (1852–1931) of Handsworth, vice-chair of the District from 1912, treasurer during the 1914–18 war, and president of the Birmingham branch. He was by 1912 a JP and life governor of Birmingham University, and in 1910 took a WEA party to visit Belgium as tutor, having travelled extensively in Europe. He was one of the organisers of the 1911 questionnaire to city election candidates. A product of the adult school movement, he represented Birmingham at the founding of the Labour Representation Committee in 1900, presumably on behalf of the small metal-workers' union, the Metal Wire and Tube Society, of which he was salaried secretary.[26]

The suspicions of sections of the Birmingham labour movement towards the University of Birmingham in its early years have already been noted. Did this suspicion extend to the WEA itself, and did the university try to seduce the WEA from its social mission through the attractions of the playgoers' club and the music societies? In the earliest days of the District, the criticisms of the labour movement in fact fostered a sensitivity among the university leaders, especially in Oliver Lodge, on the question. In March 1911, the Midland Institute complained to the university about competition from WEA courses. An arrangement had prevailed whereby the Institute had run its courses there in the evening, and the WEA and the university had had the premises during the day. Their popular evening lectures and tutorial classes were now muscling in, and the lectures were cheap and well attended. Lodge's reply was written up in the university's council minutes. The joint committee would avoid subjects already covered by the Institute. WEA lectures were 'not to be advertised though ordinary channels, and middle class people are to be discouraged from attendance even if they hear about them'. The lectures were only to be advertised through working-class organisations, and 'the more expensive tickets previously issued to non working class members should no longer exist.'[27] The recognition of the existence of class divisions, let alone the explicit discussion of strategies around them, is surely one of the most striking differences between the world of 1911 and that of 2001, or even that of 1951.

## THE GREAT WAR AND ITS AFTERMATH

Until the 1914–18 war patterns of provision remained grounded in certain notions of what was appropriate fare for the WEA student. Courses in industrial history, economics and citizenship were the subject-matter 'gold standard', as the tutorial class became the talisman of delivery format. Literature was thought to be of special interest to women. Nevertheless, the Association continued to be on its guard to preserve its mission. At Nuneaton,

> A women's reading circle had been formed, but it was attended chiefly by elementary school teachers and could not therefore be regarded as satisfactory.[28]

During the war, there was a relaxation of subject-matter to appeal to new students. A series of ambulance classes was run at Small Heath (84 students) and at Five Ways. Folk-dancing was offered successfully at the women's settlement at Summer Lane in 1915, an area where a school in 1888 had pioneered the first cookery centre for girls.[29] Study circles were promoted during the war, and the subjects encouraged for their consideration were international relations, imperial problems, war finance, labour problems and the shape of education after the war.[30] A 'reading guide bureau' was mooted; a request with a stamped addressed envelope would elicit a reading list and advice on a reading strategy in certain subjects. The possibilities for junior WEA classes, aimed at 15–18-year-olds, 'in the usual WEA subjects' were discussed.

Inventive formats and widening ideas about subjects of study were a response to falling student enrolments during the 1914–18 war. In 1915–16, there were 34 classes attended by 448 men and 411 women. In 1919, there were 14 WEA branches running 18 classes and study circles with 239 men and 202 women enrolled. The gender balance remained roughly the same: between 45 and 47 per cent of the students were women. But the post-war recovery was strong and immediate: in 1919–20 student numbers were double what they had been the previous year. By 1925, there were 30 branches, 110 societies affiliated to the District, 1,600 individual branch members and 93 classes. In the WEA's provision of 'preparatory, one-year and termly classes', there remained a female student presence of 45 per cent of the total. The tutorial classes run with the university in 1925 appeared to appeal more to men: only 36 per cent of the students were women.[31] But this was no deep-seated failure of the programme to attract women students. The joint committee reporting seems to have been more alive to questions of gender balance than the WEA's own. Joint committee reports provide fitful statistical evidence, the WEA's alone, very little. In a political philosophy course of 1917–18, there were 10 men, 8 women; in a political science course of the same year, 10 men, 7 women; in economics, 16 men, 4 women; but in psychology, by contrast, 8 men and 12 women.[32] Building on the same observations made in King's Norton in 1911, the offering changed to accommodate subjects known to be attractive to a wide student group, which had to include half the potential 'market': women. In 1927–8, the largest categories of the District's provision were in literature (30 classes), economics (20) and psychology (12), with various kinds of history and social science trailing far behind. On the margins of the curriculum were Esperanto, folk-dancing, citizenship, German, hygiene and cookery (1 class each). This was the heyday of the District as 'by far the most powerful organisation for adult education in the Midlands of England'.[33] In 1936–7, when the West Midland District consisted of 44 branches offering 127 classes, there were more women than men in the tutorial and one-year courses: 650 women as against 490 men. Only in the short one-term courses was the pattern reversed: 248 men, 218 women. WETUC courses accounted for this.[34]

A conference on the higher education of women was held at Birmingham University in May 1922, attended by women's organ-isations, including WEA branches, but no more is heard of the women's committee after 1918.[35] The dominant culture of the WEA between the wars in this District was one in which serious study was promoted in tutorial classes, study of a preparatory nature offered in WEA classes, and the learning experience backed up by a range of social activities. These included the revived playgoers' club in Birmingham, and summer schools, rambles and outings. To judge from the 1926 souvenir publication, there was an earnest heartiness about these that probably characterised the movement as a whole: 'Living a fortnight, or even a week, in a big WEA family does imbue one with the community spirit.' The 'WEA family' was not as

dysfunctional as some might have supposed. It is striking how stable
was the pattern of key personnel. Herbert G. Wood, who left
Cambridge to build up the Woodbrooke settlement at Bournville,
and was the university's first professor of theology, was District chair
for 29 years. E. J. Studd, secretary of Todmorden WEA branch many
years before 1914, was district secretary from 1919 to well after 1945;
Gertrude Smallwood was assistant secretary of the District for nearly
40 years to 1952.[36]

In its struggle for the affections of Birmingham city council, the
university had reasons of its own for valuing the WEA as a token of
its honourable intentions towards workers. At first glance, its choice
of early full-time tutors for the joint programme might seem eccentric
as a strategy in this mission. The very first tutorial class tutor, from
1910–11, was an old Etonian, the Hon. Gerard Collier (1878–1923),
son of the 2nd Baron Monkswell (see plate 6). He had travelled the
world in 1903, and had been a professor briefly at the University of
Sydney. It may have been a coincidence that Collier was a
contemporary of Tawney's at Balliol. Whatever the influences on his
appointment, there was more to Collier than just his elevated
background. He was a friend of the explorer Gertrude Bell, and taught
economics and politics with an explorer's enthusiasm. He struck up
a rapport with Black Country groups, but retired to Cornwall in ill-
health in 1919. An altar to his memory in St. Hilary church there
records his efforts for peace during the 1914–18 war. Collier's widow
gave hundreds of his books to the Workers' Institute at Cradley Heath
– scene of the famous strike of women chain-makers in 1910 – after
his premature death.[37]

Surviving statistics have left a measure of how successful or
otherwise the joint committee tutors were in reaching workers. The
largest single groups among the 1917–18 tutorial class in political
philosophy were teachers (5) and clerks (6). Among the other
occupations (all one or two each) were those of cabinet-maker,
telegraph operator, engineer and works chemist. Collier's political
science class was dominated by 5 engineers (men) and 4 teachers
(women). In the Bournville psychology class there were (unsurprisingly) from the chocolate works, 4 women workers and 4 forewomen.
Among the men there were 4 engineers, a works chemist, 1 roadman
and 2 gardeners. Overall, engineers, clerks and teachers held sway.
Ten years on, forming the largest category of students were the
teachers (115 students), followed by 'housewives' (81), postal and
telegraph workers (73), clerks (70) and fitters and turners (39). Setting
aside the impenetrable social category of housewife, there is ample

evidence here that Tawney's working class was the aristocracy of labour.[38] There is no evidence that the District sought to develop its provision among the unskilled or dispossessed to counter or at least balance what was an inherent drift towards the lower-middle class.

Politically and economically, the West Midlands was not west Lanark or west Glamorgan, and the Birmingham WEA and the District machine which grew up around it absorbed much of the consensual traditions of a city which only first gave control of the city council to Labour in 1946. Away from the conurbation, WEA branches took on the character of their host communities. The Cheltenham branch, for example, was founded in 1925 after running a single class on economics in session 1924–5. Its chair in 1929 was Barbara Thomas, a minister of religion. The treasurer was an activist in the town's English Society, a vice-president was an assistant master at Cheltenham College, the public school, a handy source for tutors. One-year courses in geography, economic history and Esperanto were offered in 1925–6. Yet some of the culture of Birmingham had rubbed off. Folk-dancing was a course to be run collaboratively with the Women's Co-operative Guild, and the branch was hoping to entice either R. H. Tawney or Arthur Greenwood down to address a public meeting. In 1930 the branch brainstormed its list of possible future collaborators: Cheltenham Science Society, the Rotary Club, the Technical school, the YMCA, the Education Society, TocH, the Co-operative Society, the Historical Society, the trades council, brotherhoods and sisterhoods of churches and chapels, literary groups, discussion circles, adult schools, the Co-operative guilds, the public library and teachers' organisations. This was the whole gamut of voluntary activity in the town, and was more a publicity distribution list than an expression of social intent.[39]

GOLDEN STREAMS AND MUDDY WATERS

The issue of class and social mission could inform the Association's relationship with its Board of Education paymasters as well as with its avowed enemies on the Marxist left. Space does not permit a full consideration of the government–WEA District partnership, which is in any case handicapped by weeding at either the Board or the Public Record Office of the relevant files. But the case of Ascott-under-Wychwood in 1920–1 is illustrative. It was an area of rural north Oxfordshire where WEA classes had run since 1913. It was outside the Midland District, but was not far from Tysoe, within it, where a class had run from about the same time. In 1920–1 a series of ten lectures with the title, 'What the working people have done for themselves during the last century' was proposed. A tutor from Ruskin College, John Sharman, was identified. Board of Education grant aid was refused, as the course was not long enough. It bothered Board official W. F. Sheppard that the class seemed open only to WEA members: 'The [membership] restriction seems opposed to our general idea of the work the WEA is doing. I think that when we refuse recognition we ought to call attention to it.' Sharman wrote to protest: 'A struggling vicar is the only "non-worker" among them', and persuaded national secretary J. M. Mactavish to take up the case. Mactavish wrote to the Board to apologise for the disorganised state of the South-eastern District. The Board officials recognised that the village was 'a centre of light in a district that has been a dark spot in the sphere of adult education. Oxfordshire is notoriously backward in providing educational facilities for its own inhabitants.' Moreover, they sympathised with the argument that Sharman deserved support for having stepped into the breach to rescue a well-attended class short of a tutor. Then, unaccountably, Mactavish withdrew the appeal. The following year the class in any case received its grant (£5), but the fat PRO file shows how much official consideration could be devoted even to a single, non-tutorial 10-week class in 1921, and how issues of social purpose informed the debate.[40]

The earliest recorded attack on the WEA from Marxist quarters in the Midlands seems to have been when a proposed branch in Shrewsbury drew hostile comment from the Council of Labour Colleges in 1912.[41] In 1918, the case of Dr Segal showed the WEA at its most thin-skinned, but opportunistic. Under the auspices of the city Anglo-Russian society, Dr Segal was to give a course of three lectures at the university. The WEA was not involved, except that the lecturer worked frequently for the Association. After the first lecture in October 1917, the Bolshevik rising broke out, somewhat inconveniently. The course was suspended, 'until there was some clearer knowledge as to what was taking place in Russia'. *Plebs* magazine got hold of the story, and reported that Segal had been 'gagged' by the WEA and the university because he was pro-Bolshevik. District secretary T. W. Price reported the matter to the central WEA executive committee, which resolved on an article in *The Highway* and a reply to Fred Silvester, the Plebs League's Birmingham leading light, denying responsibility for cancelling the lectures. The WEA also declared itself keen to see the lectures resume, this time under its own auspices. Segal himself was more relaxed, and considered that no agitation was necessary on his behalf.[42] The partisans of independent working-class education in Birmingham were, even at their strongest, never more than a gadfly on the hide of the WEA. There were 12 NCLC classes in Birmingham in 1926, whereas across the District the WEA ran 93 classes on its own account, and another 79 classes under the joint committee. Fred Silvester in any case later turned up as a WEA course tutor.[43] At the height of this rivalry, the WEA preferred to fire salvoes from Big Joe, the university clock tower. The chair of the joint committee, Principal C. Grant Robertson, declared in 1926:

> To my mind, 'class economics' or 'class politics' are as absurd and dangerous as would be 'class Greek' or 'class chemistry' or 'class mathematics' – if such were possible.[44]

THE LEGACY

It is impossible to quantify the impact of the WEA regionally on the lives of citizens. What follows is virtually a postscript. From the 1930s to the 1950s the size of the West Midland District remained fairly constant. There were 44 branches in 1936–7, 40 in 1942–3, 46 in 1952–3. There were 43 branches in 1962–3, but by then other dynamics were at work, slowly reshaping the WEA. The most important partner, the University of Birmingham, established a department of extra-mural studies in 1945, and its ambitious new director wrote irritably: 'I am occasionally described as the university secretary of the WEA.'[45] In the climate of post-war university expansion, Birmingham no longer wished to be tied to the now tarnished gold standard of the tutorial classes with the WEA, and sought to build on its own not inconsiderable interest in independent initiatives.[46] In 1950 E. J. Studd, still in post after 31 years, called for a 'renewal of efforts to secure a greater demand for tutorial classes of a high standard'; by 1959 it was reported in the local press that 'a mild cold war' existed between the university and the WEA, although all denied it. The joint committee soldiered on, but there were 23 tutorial classes in 1953, only 8 in 1963. In the 1950s and 1960s the university was undoubtedly quicker at seizing opportunities than the WEA, which was encumbered by what had become the baggage of its traditions. To describe the psychology of the latter-day relationship between these old partners would require a borrowing of one of R. H. Tawney's sonorous sentences on Dives and Pauper.

From the late 1970s the WEA in the West Midlands (West Mercia District from 1991) began to re-invent itself. There was no conscious drawing upon the inheritance of the early decades: rather there was a relearning through experience of certain simple truths about the Association's social purpose. One of these is that the WEA works best when it has a clear vision of the target groups it seeks to work with. Another is that 'networking', to use a word which did not exist in 1905, is crucial to the well-being of a relatively small provider of adult education, and the evangelising of the early decades into other voluntary bodies is worth pondering. It is curious how the WEA seems to have to rediscover another simple truth evident from its history: that modes of delivery have to be matched to the needs of students. The 'new' twilight sessions, study groups and women-only provision of the 1980s onwards, to name but three types of course, are all found in the earliest years of the WEA's existence. There is much that is positive about the WEA West Midlands experience that can be drawn upon and used. The Birmingham WEA council elections campaign of 1911, the disregard for formalism in the WEA musical tradition in the city before and after 1914, and the rich voluntarist context of the King's Norton branch are just some case studies that provide valuable food for thought for the WEA activist of 2002.

## NOTES

*Place of publication London unless otherwise stated.*

1. National Archive, WEA CENTRAL 1/2/1/1, unpaginated, 19 May 1905.
2. WEA CENTRAL 1/2/1/1, unpaginated, 1905.
3. Price, 41.
4. E. Ives, D. Drummond and E. Schwarz, *The First Civic University: Birmingham 1880–1980* (Birmingham, 2000), 8, 42, 113.
5. University of Birmingham, university collection, council minutes 3 Nov. 1909.
6. WEA CENTRAL 1/2/1/1, 2 Dec. 1905.
7. University of Birmingham, university collection, 7/iv//6/11, *Report on ... the Joint Committee* (1928).
8. Price, 42.
9. *The Times*, 22 Oct. 1906; *DNB*; Ives *et al.*, *First Civic University*, 102–3.

10. Birmingham Central Library, Social Science Dept., Special Collections (hereafter BCL), BQ 374.9424 WEA/University of Birmingham joint committee annual reports, 1918–35, 4.

11. BCL, WEA Midland District annual report, 1910–11; minutes of Birmingham branch, 1911–12; *The Highway*, ii (Birmingham supplement, 1910); BL Add. 65215, W. J. Sharkey to Mansbridge, 26 Oct. 1906, attached minutes; university collection, 7/iv/7/5, *WEA Midland District Souvenir* (1926), 25; *DNB* for Pares.

12. BCL, WEA Midland District annual report, 1910–11; minutes of Birmingham branch, 1911–12; *The Highway*, ii (Birmingham supplement, 1910).

13. BL Add. 65215, Oliver Lodge to Albert Mansbridge, 11 Nov. 1904; *Trodden Road*, 66.

14. Add. 65215, W. J. Sharkey to Mansbridge, 26 Oct. 1906, attached minutes.

15. Add. 65215, W. J. Sharkey to Mansbridge, 26 Oct. 1906.

16. Birmingham City Archives, MS 1603/1, King's Norton branch minutes inc. note by M. B. Prettyman on Walter Hardy; *Dictionary of Labour Biography* ii. 339–40; *Victoria County History, Warwick* (hereafter *VCH Warws.*) vii. 50, 316.

17. MS 1603/1, 5 Jan. 1912.

18. MS 1603/1, Nov. 1911.

19. Diane Drummond, 'The New University', in Ives *et al.*, *First Civic University*, 136; *VCH Warws.* vii. 316.

20. *VCH Warws.* vii. 316; *First Civic University*, 136.

21. BCL AQ 374.94249: replies from municipal election candidates, 1911.

22. *First Civic University*, 137; university collection 7/iv/6/11, *Report on ... the Joint Committee* (1928), 8, 13; university council minutes vol. 8, 31 Jan. 1912.

23. *Midland District Souvenir*, 11; for Halstead, *Dictionary of Labour Biography* ii. 158.

24. MS 1603/2.

25. BCL, Birmingham branch minutes, 1914; Birmingham WEA council minutes, 1915–22, 2–4; Midland District minutes, 1912–20, 1 July 1916.

26. BCL Midland District minutes, 1912–20, 24 Apr. 1912, 11 Jan. 1913; *Midland District Souvenir*, 11; *The Highway*, ii (1910), Birmingham supplement; *Birmingham Despatch*, 13 June 1931; *Birmingham Gazette*, 18 June 1931; G. J. Barnsby, *Birmingham Working People* (Wolverhampton, 1989), 306, 486.

27. University council minutes, vol. 7, 29 Mar. 1911; vol. 8, 5 July 1911.

28. Midland District minutes, 1912–20, 31 Jan. 1914.

29. University council minutes, vol. 8, 31 Jan. 1912; Birmingham WEA council minutes, 1915–22, 2; *VCH Warws.* vii. 494.

30. Midland District minutes, 1912–20, 25 Mar. 1916.

31. West Midland District annual reports and financial statements, 1910–25; university council minutes, vol. 11, 1915–16; university collection, 7/iv/6/11, *Report on the Future Development of the Work of the Joint Committee* (1928), 15–16.

32. BCL, joint committee annual reports, 1918–35.

33. *Midland District Souvenir, 1905–26*, 6.
34. BCL, WEA annual reports, statements of accounts, 1936–60, for 1936–7.
35. G. J. Barnsby, *Socialism in Birmingham and the Black Country 1850–1939* (Wolverhampton, 1998), 348.
36. Midland District minutes, 1912–20, 21 June 1919; *Midland District Souvenir*, 22–3; BCL WEA annual reports and statements, 1948–9, 1960–70, for 1962–3, 1967–8; university collection, 14/ii/1, inaugural lecture by H. G. Wood.
37. *Balliol College Register 1833–1933* (Oxford, 1934), 237, 291; *DNB* for Monkswell; *Midland District Souvenir*, 16; pamphlet by Philip Hills on Gerard Collier in St. Hilary church, 1999.
38. Statistics in BCL, joint committee annual reports, 1918–35, for 1917–18, 1927–8.
39. Gloucestershire Record Office, D4227/1, WEA Cheltenham branch minute book, 1925–51.
40. Public Record Office, ED 41/373.
41. Midland District minutes, 27 Apr. 1912.
42. WEA CENTRAL/fi/1/3; Barnsby, *Socialism in Birmingham and the Black Country*, 346–7.
43. West Midland District annual reports; Barnsby, *Socialism in Birmingham and the Black Country*, 346.
44. *Midland District Souvenir*, 6.
45. J. Aitken, *Without Walls: Half a Century of Extramural Work* (Birmingham, 1995), 9.
46. See for example the university's ambitious plans for a day release programme for trade unionists in 1918–19: university collection, 7/iii, vice-principal's report to council, 1918–19, 12.

# 6 The Friends and Enemies of the WEA

*Bernard Jennings*

The success of the WEA and the tutorial class movement can be attributed in part to the breadth of the influential support which they received. Sir Robert Morant, permanent secretary to the Board of Education, and R. B. Haldane, who became lord chancellor, were not only powerful supporters but also personal friends of Mansbridge. Together with Rosebery, Alfred Milner and the Webbs they were prominently identified with the cult of national efficiency. At first sight there was little common ground, in relation to workers' education, between the 'ladders' of the efficiency group and the 'highway' advocated by the WEA. However, the group's advocacy of a 'national minimum' of nourishment, health and education, seen as essential for both national security and social harmony, fitted in well enough with the WEA objective of 'the elevation of the whole body of workers ... not raising people out of their class, but raising them and their class at the same time'.[1]

'Raise, not rise out of' was an expression of class solidarity, but it also provided reassurance to the privileged. Charles Masterman depicted the latter as afraid of being overwhelmed by the uneducated, so 'it lies awake at night listening fearfully to the tramp of the rising host.' A working class steadily improving both materially and morally was much less of a threat. 'Educate your people', declared Haldane, in a passage quoted approvingly by Mansbridge in one of the articles which launched the WEA, 'and you have reduced to comparative insignificance the problems of temperance, of housing and of raising the condition of your masses'. The reference to temperance is the key to understanding the passage. Haldane did not mean that the educated workers would take power and achieve a social revolution. He meant that educated people did not have social problems.[2]

The Christian Socialism of Charles Gore, Mansbridge's mentor, and William Temple, the first national president of the WEA, emphasised the incompatibility between contemporary capitalist values and Christianity. Temple argued, in a journal of the Christian Social Union in 1908, that the 'great sins' of the age were 'sins not

97

of the individual but of the citizen ... we must substitute a Co-operative basis for the existing competitive basis of society ... It is urged that Socialism is too ideal. – "If you want to get the best out of a man, you must appeal to his self-interest." Now if that is true, Christ was wrong.'[3]

It was only a short journey from Christian socialism to the ethical socialism propounded by Sidney Ball, the principal founder (1895) of the Oxford Fabian Society, who played a key role in the creation of the tutorial class movement. In an article on 'The Moral Aspects of Socialism', Ball argued that a spiritual change was needed if any reform of the industrial structure was to succeed. 'Just as democracy is the most difficult form of government, Socialism is the most difficult form of industry because [of] the amount of education – in ideas and character – that is required before any sensible advance can be made in the direction of Co-operative industry.' Tawney's views were close to those of both Temple and Ball:

> economic privileges must be abolished, not primarily because they hinder the production of wealth, but because they produce wickedness ... To preach in public that Christianity is absurd is legally blasphemy. To state that the social ethics of the New Testament are obligatory upon men in ... business affairs is to preach revolution.[4]

Another ally of the WEA was L. T. Hobhouse, whose joint report with J. W. Headlam HMI on the pioneer tutorial classes became a minor classic of liberal adult education. He was a close friend of Sidney Ball, who may have recruited him to the cause. In 1907 he became the first professor of sociology in the University of London. He and J. A. Hobson had become the leading intellectual spokesmen for 'New Liberalism', the 'new' recognising that the distribution of economic power had become so unequal as to erode the freedom of the individual. Like the Christian and ethical socialists, the New Liberals were strongly influenced by T. H. Green. The Greenites combined a faith in the ability of intelligent workpeople to build a better society from the bottom upwards, through Co-operation, friendly societies, trade unions and adult education, with a reluctance to create a dominant state apparatus. In Hobhouse's words 'democratic collectivism' was greatly to be preferred to 'benevolent officialism'. Modest state support for voluntary collective action through the WEA was therefore sound in principle as well as in practice.[5]

There was some opposition to the tutorial class movement from academic conservatives. The selection of both subjects of study and the teachers by working-class students would be 'destructive of progress in knowledge'. 'Some of the topics to be studied are distinctly dangerous. For instance, "the Carbonari" and "Bakounin and the Anarchist Parties" are scarcely edifying subjects to be taught to workmen.' Working-class students would feel out of place in Oxford, and their admission would destroy the character of the university. Mansbridge could afford to ignore such criticism, but he was more susceptible to sniping from the left. Mrs Bridges Adams, a political associate of Will Thorne, leader of the gasworkers' union, was a dissident voice at WEA open meetings. She claimed that Mansbridge was a paid agent of the 'establishment'. Publicly the WEA leaders laughed off this improbable delegate of the gasworkers' union, but in private Mansbridge was less restrained: 'The Bridges Adams opposition is more furious than ever – lies, misrepresentations, the devilments of the pit – are all brought to bear.'[6]

In the long term a more serious threat to the WEA project came from the provision of Marxist adult classes. From about 1900 the Social Democratic Federation had been running classes in economics in London, Glasgow and other towns. One of the London students, Tommy Jackson, went on to become a popular freelance lecturer. In his engaging autobiography he describes how a 'sermon' he gave in a Methodist chapel in Chopwell, County Durham, on the text 'Isaiah was a Bolshevik', led to an invitation from the local Labour College to give a series of lectures on the Principles of Socialism. The audience grew to fill every seat, gangway, staircase and window sill in the Co-operative Hall.[7] In 1903 nearly all of the SDF branches in Scotland seceded to form the Socialist Labour Party, taking most of the educational work with them. One of the students involved, Thomas Bell, graduated to become a class teacher. His method was to direct the study, paragraph by paragraph, of key Marxist texts, so that after six months each conscientious student became a potential tutor. Also in 1903 John Maclean joined a surviving Social Democratic Federation branch in Glasgow, and began taking classes in Marxist economics and industrial history. A schoolteacher who completed a part-time degree in 1904, Maclean was one of the outstanding figures in workers' education in the early twentieth century, with a devoted following. Several of his courses recruited over a hundred members, and as many as five hundred attended his main lecture course in economics and industrial history.[8]

Neither Maclean's nor Bell's methods would be strange to Scottish learners. Maclean was the evangelical preacher; there can hardly have been much interactive learning with groups so large. Bell was the catechist. Maclean gave the Sunday sermon, Bell took the weekly bible class. Whatever their achievements, there was a world of difference, in terms of the triangular relationship of tutor, students and source materials, between WEA tutorial class methods and those used by Maclean or Bell.

The Labour College mentioned by Tommy Jackson was not a building but an association, with its roots in a secession from Ruskin College in 1909. Ruskin Hall, Oxford (College from 1907) was founded in 1899 by the Americans Walter Vrooman, with the financial support of his wealthy wife, and Charles Beard. Vrooman became principal of the Oxford hall, which was intended to be the headquarters of a nationwide system of workers' education, involving branch halls, local lecture courses and learning by correspondence. The five or six branch halls were short-lived, but Beard, who established his base for a time in the north-west of England, had considerable success with the extra-mural programme. Short lecture courses were given; by 1902 about 4,000 students had registered with the correspondence department; and the students formed local study circles to discuss the material for their monthly essays. The circles and classes were grouped together in the Ruskin Hall Educational League. Of the 34 branches 18 were in Lancashire and Yorkshire, often meeting in Co-operative premises, and drawing in working-class extension students. Some of these won essay prizes, earning a short stay in Oxford. The sense of fellowship was strengthened by regional gatherings of the 'leaguers'.

All this had happened before Mansbridge wrote the articles which led to the founding of the WEA, but any possibility that the Ruskin network would play a major part in promoting a Co-operative-extension partnership was torpedoed by Vrooman. Charles Beard went on to become one of the leading American historians of his generation, but Vrooman scoffed at both academics and university extension in the pages of the Ruskin Hall journal, *Young Oxford*. 'Ruskin Hall Extension ... gives the great truths of science and history in simple speech and form.' The elimination of the 'speculative element' in learning would bring a university training within the reach of everyone, even 'the seemingly duller lads'.[9]

Fortunately Vrooman left the detailed management of the Oxford hall to the warden, Dennis Hird. He was a former Anglican clergyman who had found that the life of a country parson was not ideal for a free-thinking socialist. Vrooman and Beard returned to the USA in 1902; Hird became principal with H. B. Lees Smith as vice-principal; and *Young Oxford* expired. Relations with the University of Oxford improved. Most of the branches of the Ruskin Hall Educational League merged happily with the WEA, and within a few years several leading supporters of the WEA, including Sidney Ball and Labour MPs David Shackleton and C. W. Bowerman, had joined the council of Ruskin Hall.[10]

Under Hird's genial guidance, Ruskin prospered. By 1907 the college had about fifty students, all staying for at least one academic year. However, tensions began to build as increasing numbers of students became ardent socialists. They enjoyed Hird's lectures on sociology, a major element of which was the study of evolution, on which he had written a popular book. They disliked Lees Smith's lectures on economics, although acknowledging his ability as a teacher, because his adherence to current free-market theories was just as dogmatic as that of the left-wing students to Marxism. The latter formed their own study circles to work through Marxist texts. Lees Smith began a campaign to raise academic standards, through a narrower curriculum and regular written work. He was opposed by Hird, but gradually gained ground because Hird had other interests. He had a small farm at Bletchley in Buckinghamshire, which was presumably the source of the produce which he sold to his own college. He was a county magistrate in Buckinghamshire, and went away frequently to address socialist meetings.[11]

In 1907 Lees Smith was appointed professor of economics at University College, Bristol, but did not relax his grip on Ruskin. He became chairman of the executive committee and adviser on studies. To replace himself on the staff he arranged, apparently without involving Hird, for the appointment of Charles Buxton, aged 23, as vice-principal, and Henry Sanderson Furniss, aged 39 but with virtually no teaching experience as he was nearly blind, to lecture on economics.[12]

In September 1907 Lees Smith tried to marginalise Dennis Hird even further, by proposing that his teaching subjects should be changed from sociology and evolution to literature, rhetoric and temperance. (Hird had previously held an appointment in the Church of England's temperance movement.) The students protested, and the executive committee rejected the proposal. Approval was given, however, to requirements for regular essays and quarterly revision papers, and first-year students were forbidden to speak in public unless their academic work was satisfactory. Sanderson Furniss came to realise that he and Buxton were intended to carry on Lees Smith's campaign against Hird. They were, however, ill-equipped to do so, or to provide an antidote to the Marxist ideas which Furniss criticised without knowing much about them, They knew little about teaching, and less about working-class life.[13]

The Ruskin militants feared that, as a result of the deliberations of the joint committee which produced the report *Oxford and Working-class Education* in November 1908, the college, and workers' education in general, would be 'taken over' by the university. The proposals went no further than opening the new diplomas in economics and politics to Ruskin students, but any kind of curricular control would have been anathema to students who wanted only Marxist theories taught. The chancellor of the university, George, Lord Curzon, visited Ruskin, and made 'a most charming and tactful speech with which everyone was delighted', according to Furniss, but stalked out after being rebuked by Hird, according to the militants. In fact the recorded statements of Hird and Curzon were not very different, and could have been woven into the same speech by Mansbridge. 'To ask Ruskin College to come into closer contact with the University is to ask the great democracy whose foundation is the labour movement, a democracy that in the near future will come into its own and ... bring great changes in its wake' (Hird); 'The men I see before me represent the class to whom has been given the vote, and who because of their numbers, are the ruling power in the nation. It is supremely important that having the power they should also have the education' (Curzon).[14]

Tensions mounted in Ruskin during 1908. Only a minority of students took the first revision papers in April. Matters came to a head when, on 9 October 1908, the militants in alliance with Hird and another member of staff, Alfred Hacking, resolved at a meeting held in Oxford to form a league of past and present students and sympathisers (soon to be named the Plebs League), which would campaign for a closer identification of the college with the Labour movement. The college authorities appointed a sub-committee to took into its affairs, and asked its staff in the meantime not to become involved with the Plebs League.[15]

The sub-committee, reporting apparently in February 1909, rejected an accusation that Hird had deliberately identified the college with socialism; he had merely been guilty of 'some indiscretion'. He should, however, stop selling kitchen garden produce, provisions and books to the college. Sanderson Furniss was criticised for bias and ignorance, and the appointment of another lecturer in economics, more familiar with working-class views, was recommended. The relative mildness of the criticisms implies a belief that reconciliation was possible, but this was effectively sabotaged by what Sidney Ball described as the 'continued agitation' of the Plebs students. It was decided that either Dennis Hird, or his opponents on the staff, must go. Hird was dismissed for failing to maintain discipline. He was given six months' salary (£180) in lieu of notice, plus a pension of £150 a year for life. The decision of the executive committee was confirmed by the college council on 31 March, but in the meantime a majority of the students had voted for a boycott of lectures until Hird was reinstated and Buxton and Bertram Wilson, the college secretary, dismissed.[16]

The Ruskin authorities decided to close the college for a fortnight and then re-admit any students who would sign an undertaking to observe the rules. Of the 54 students 44 did so. They included several members of the Plebs League, which seems to have had 20 or more adherents before the closure. The atmosphere remained tense, the 'loyalist' students publishing a pamphlet attacking the 'rebels'. A rival Central Labour College (CLC) was established in Oxford in August 1909 (it moved to London in 1911). Hird became principal, without salary as he had his pension. The Plebs League and the CLC launched a campaign to attract the ideological and financial support of the trade unions.[17]

An early casualty was the truth, as the Plebs League and some sympathetic journals claimed that Hird had been dismissed for refusing to change his teaching subjects from sociology to literature and temperance, a proposal rejected by the executive committee in 1907. Albert Mansbridge and his associates publicly disclaimed responsibility for the internal affairs of Ruskin. Privately they blamed Hird's preaching of socialism, or as Mansbridge put it less charitably in a letter to a French friend, 'the low-down practice of Dennis Hird in playing upon the class consciousness of swollen-headed students embittered by the gorgeous panorama ever before them of an Oxford in which they have no part'. There is no evidence that Hird's teaching was more biased than that of Lees Smith or Sanderson Furniss.

Furthermore, the Plebs League was planned before Hird knew anything about it. He may have been the victim, as well as the hero, of the militants' campaign.'[18]

The ensuing battle for the support of the Amalgamated Society of Railway Servants and the South Wales Miners Federation, from whose ranks several of the Plebs leaders had come, was one of the few which Mansbridge lost. He loved talking to railwaymen, and many WEA branches had secured the affiliation of the local ASRS, but during tours of south Wales he failed to overcome the 'bitter and implacable opposition' of the Plebs faction. The ASRS (National Union of Railwaymen from 1913) and SWMF transferred their scholarships from Ruskin to the Central Labour College, and provided the only consistent support for the latter until its closure in 1929.[19]

Ruskin College was quick to learn the lessons of the dispute. A new constitution was adopted in 1909, vesting the government of the college in a council consisting of representatives of trade unions, Co-operative societies and other working-class organisations. The new principal was Dr Gilbert Slater, a distinguished social historian who had been Labour mayor of Woolwich.[20]

The Plebs League and CLC started extra-mural classes, including some in Rochdale. The two tutorial classes lost only one member, even though many of the students were members of socialist parties. However, the National Council of Labour Colleges, founded in 1921, became a serious rival to the WEA. Jim Millar, its energetic general secretary, kept up a flow of criticism over four decades with a remarkable economy of literary effort. The WEA argued that there was room for both an 'educational' and a 'propagandist' body in workers' education. The only choice was between capitalist education and socialist education, replied the NCLC.[21]

The developments of the period 1907–9 – particularly the 1908 report *Oxford and Working-class Education*, the tutorial classes and joint committee system, the Ruskin dispute and its aftermath – have been regarded as the defining episodes in the interpretation of the history of workers' education in the first half of the twentieth century. Some historians have been misled by partisan or defective sources, for example, overlooking Tommy Jackson's 'health warning' that his autobiography represented 'a *bona fide* recollection, either of actual experience or hearsay'. Jackson has Hird introducing Marxist economics to the Ruskin curriculum in response to student demand; refusing an instruction from the governors to exclude it; with the students boycotting Dr Slater's classes – all untrue.[22]

Brian Simon relies upon Jackson and Plebs sources. He quotes only one of the conflicting accounts of Curzon's visit to Ruskin. He mentions the student petition against the proposed change in Hird's teaching subjects, but does not make it clear that the proposal was rejected. The termination of Hird's appointment is described without any reference to the compensation and pension.[23]

Some of the brief references to these developments beg a few questions. For example, John Saville:

> What we have in these years is both the attempt to channel working-class education into the safe and liberal outlets of the Workers' Educational Association and Ruskin College, and the development of working-class initiatives from below; and it is the latter only which made its contribution to the socialist movement – and a considerable contribution it was.[24]

There is no doubt that the 'establishment' preferred the WEA and Ruskin to the Labour college movement, a fact exploited quite brazenly by the WEA in the 1920s. Temple, Tawney and A. D. Lindsay all warned the Board of Education and the LEAs that unless they supported the WEA and respected its academic freedom, workers' education would fall to the NCLC. However, most of the WEA branches in industrial towns were formed as a result of 'working-class initiatives from below', if we include, in addition to trades councils and union branches, the Co-operatives and chapel societies which were mainly, although not exclusively, working class in composition. The occupational analysis of the early tutorial classes reads like a guide to the distribution of industry – ten coal miners, six glass workers and five railway workers in Castleford, Yorkshire; 30 cotton workers out of a class of 36 in Nelson, Lancashire. Some of these 30, mainly young men, went on to become the Labour establishment of a town dubbed 'Little Moscow'. They would have been surprised to learn that the WEA made no contribution to socialism.[25]

Carolyn Steedman, writing about Margaret McMillan, comments: 'In 1909 McMillan provided Mansbridge with public support over the Ruskin College crisis, when claims for a worker-directed education came into sharp conflict with the WEA brand of education.' This is to ignore both the high degree of 'workers' control' provided by the joint committee system, and the autonomy of WEA branches. Her source is Jonathan Rée's *Proletarian*

*Philosophers*, according to which the 1908 Oxford Report was produced jointly by the WEA, the university and Ruskin College; and after the strike 'nearly all of the Ruskin students ... seceded from the college.' The correct figure is 10 out of 54, although several more left or were expelled at a later date.

On the broader issue Rée explains: 'The aim of the WEA was to direct the aspirations of proletarian autodidacts towards a Green-tinged corporate state', the Green being, of course, T. H. Green. Were Tawney's students autodidacts when they were writing essays at home? Mansbridge was 'himself a lower-middle-class autodidact, always tormented by the consciousness that he never had the opportunity of a university education'. Tormented? Always? Even the middle-aged sage, lionised on his North American lecture tours, who had served on the Royal Commission on Oxford and Cambridge, the statutory commission on Oxford and many similar bodies, was a member of Oxbridge senior common rooms and received five honorary degrees?[26]

Anne Phillips and Tim Putnam correctly attribute the authorship of the Oxford Report to the university and the WEA, but give the date of publication as 1907. They refer to 'state initiatives in working-class political education, such as represented by the WEA'. Argue if you will that the state welcomed, or even suborned, the WEA; to describe it as a state initiative is nonsense. They state that in 1907 the Ruskin authorities were worried about the threat to their endowment fund of £265,000, built up by selling the idea of a 'safe' education. No source is given for this figure, which is described by Harold Pollins in his history of the college as 'ridiculous'. He explains that by 1914 the endowments amounted to £1,221.[27]

Some prominent members of the labour college camp found no difficulty in being fair to the WEA. John Maclean wrote, 'the WEA ... simply has for its object the creation of intelligent workers. Personally I wish to see all opportunities for self-development opened to the working class. But I am specially interested in such education as will make revolutionists.' In their book *Working-class Education* (1924) Frank and Winifred Horrabin give an objective and accurate account of the clash of ideologies. They recognise the sincerity of left-wing activists in the WEA, while hoping to persuade them in due course to join 'Labour's own educational movement'.[28]

Bias and a lack of charity have not been found only on the Plebs side, as the quotation above from Mansbridge testifies. Mary Stocks wrote in her 1953 history of the WEA:

There is no doubt that Marx's *Das Kapital* was, and still is, an exceedingly impressive book especially to those who are not able fully to understand it, or having understood it, are not able to relate it to its historical background. At any rate this was the kind of teaching demanded by an ardent group of Ruskin College students.[29]

The errors and distortions of some pro-Plebs writers have tended to associate the WEA and the Oxford reformers with the disorganised pre-strike regime at Ruskin College. The Marx-hungry militants were not challenging tutors of the calibre of Tawney, Henry Clay and W. T. Layton, but the ill-equipped pair of Buxton and Sanderson Furniss, with the easy-going Dennis Hird, having been marginalised by the machinations of Lees Smith, unable or unwilling to control the situation. The argument 'who is not with us is against us' too readily becomes 'those who are against us are much of a muchness'. Committed socialists in the WEA argued that without access to the universities, the workers would receive an inferior education, and that the joint committee system gave them control over their own learning. In later years, when the NCLC had become less doctrinaire, some tutors worked happily in both rival movements, and a few people suggested that, because of its success in reaching the workers, the NCLC might function as the 'primary school' of workers' education, passing on the keener students to WEA/university classes. It was not to be.

Frank Pickstock, who was for many years the officer in charge of joint committee work at Oxford and was active in Labour politics in the city, commented,

The enormity of the innovation which the Tutorial Classes Committee represented is often too little understood – democratic power to working class students in sharing in (with an effective power of veto) planning the syllabus, selecting the tutor, managing the classes and equal sharing in the governing committee. This was democracy with a vengeance, and when you realise how doubtful and equivocal the Oxford reformers were about democracy, the more you realise what a momentous step 1908 was. Once the classes were in being, the students, the working men, took over. They were without any doubt Labour (in the general sense as it was then known) many of them socialist, and this was reflected in all sorts of ways ... above all their influence on tutors ... I have little doubt that it was contact with students of tutorial classes that resulted in tutors making the transition from liberalism to labour.[30]

The transition is, of course, less significant if the Labour party is seen as a device to contain, and not promote, the development of socialism. This is the thesis advanced by Ralph Miliband and applied to the present matter by Roger Fieldhouse in his paper 'The 1908 Report: Antidote to Class Struggle':

> The WEA/tutorial class movement was welcomed by the establishment as a bulwark against revolutionism, a moderating influence and a form of social control. It helped to channel and reduce pressures and conflict, neutralise class antagonism and integrate the working class into British society – just like its 'partner' the Labour Party.[31]

A clear distinction should be drawn between writers, of whatever ideological stance, who are scrupulous in their scholarship, and those critics of the WEA and Ruskin who have an unconscious affinity with the authors of medieval monastic chronicles whose motto seemed to be 'never let the facts spoil a good moral tale'. In fact monastic history offers a closer parallel, in what might be called the Gasquet Syndrome. The books of Abbot Francis Gasquet were criticised for bias in the selection of evidence and technical errors in the transcription of documents. But those who walk in the correct ideological path need fear no criticism, and to prove the point Gasquet was made a cardinal.

As a postscript to the great ideological battles of the Edwardian era, Jim Millar rejoiced in 1945 when large numbers of NCLC tutors and students were elected as Labour MPs – 9 became ministers, alongside 14 WEA tutors and students. To quote Chushichi Tsuzuki, 'The NCLC Marxists ... searched for a British way to socialism and found it in the Labour Party and trade unions.'[32] The antidote to class struggle had been swallowed once more. In his retirement, Jim Millar used to complain that the only people who remembered his birthday and sent him Christmas cards were in the WEA. Difficult as it is to obey the Christian injunction to 'love your enemies', to be loved by one's lifelong 'enemies' must be an even harder cross to bear.

NOTES

*Place of publication London unless otherwise stated.*

1.  G. R. Searle, *The Quest for National Efficiency: A Study in British Politics and Political Thought 1899–1914* (Oxford, 1971), 1–13, 62–5, 75–8; A. Mansbridge, 'The Functions of a Modern University', *University Review* vi. no. 33, 165.

2.  C. F. G. Masterman, *The Condition of England* (1st edn 1909, Methuen edn 1960), 53; R. B. Haldane, *Education and Empire* (1902), 32–6.

3.  W. Temple, 'The Church and the Labour Party', *Economic Review* Apr. 1908, 196–200.

4.  S. Ball, 'The Moral Aspects of Socialism', *International Journal of Ethics* vi. (Apr. 1896), 290–332; J. M. Winter and D. M. Joslin (eds), *R. H. Tawney's Commonplace Book* (Cambridge, 1972), 30–1, 53, 61; R. H. Tawney, *The Acquisitive Society* (1921), 227–8.

5.  L. T. Hobhouse, *Democracy and Reaction* (1904), 227–9, *Liberalism* (n.d. [1911]), 149–50, 159, 'The Historical Evolution of Property, in Fact and Idea', in C. Gore (ed.), *Property, Its Rights and Duties* (1913), 21–2, and leader in the *Manchester Guardian* 7 July 1899, quoted in P. F. Clarke, 'The Progressive Movement in England', *Trans. Royal Hist. Soc.*, 5th series, xxiv (1974), 167.

6.  See articles in *The Times* 25 Jan. 1909, *Morning Leader* 2 Dec. 1908, *Fortnightly Review* xciii (1913), 766–78, and *The Nineteenth Century* lxv (Mar.1909), 521–34; *Trodden Road*, 68; Bodleian Library, Zimmern MSS: A. Mansbridge to A. E. Zimmern, (n.d. [May 1910]).

7.  T. A. Jackson, *Solo Trumpet* (1953), 60–4, 90, 97,143–4, 153, 156–62.

8.  T. Bell, *Pioneering Days* (1941), 56–7; J. Broom, *John Maclean* (Loanhead, 1973), 58–65; Nan Milton, *John Maclean* (Bristol, 1973), 40–1, 149.

9.  *Young Oxford* i–iv; H. Pollins, *The History of Ruskin College* (Oxford, 1984), chap. 1; B. Jennings, 'Revolting Students – The Ruskin College Dispute 1908–09', *Studies in Adult Education* ix, no. 1, Apr. 1977, 1–16.

10. E. B. Forrest, 'A Labour College', *Independent Review* ix. no. 31, Apr. 1906, 80–90; H. Sanderson Furniss, *Memories of Sixty Years* (1931), 89–90; National Archive, WEA Central EC Minutes 14 Oct., 2 Dec. 1905.

11. Furniss, *Memories*, 86–7, 90, 97; H. B. Lees Smith, 'Economic Theory and Proposals for a Legal Minimum Wage', *Economic Journal* xvii (1907), 508–9; W. W. Craik, *Central Labour College* (1964), 38–9, 52–4; J. Lawson, *A Man's Life* (1944), 102; Ruskin College MSS, Ruskin College Strike Records vol. 1.

12. Ruskin College Strike Records vol. 1; Craik, *Central Labour College*, 28, 51–2; Furniss, *Memories*, 83, 92; W. H. Seed (ed.), *The Burning Question of Education* (Oxford, 1909); Committee of Ruskin Students, *Ruskin College and Working-class Education* (Oxford, n.d.); R. Lewis, 'The South Wales Miners and the Ruskin College Strike of 1909', *Llafur*, ii. no. 1, Spring 1976, 57–72.

13. Furniss, *Memories*, 83–5, 92–4, 100–1; Seed, *Burning Question*, 7,12.

14. Seed, *Burning Question*, 8–11; Furniss, *Memories*, 92.

15. Strike Records vol. 1; Furniss, *Burning Question*, 95; Craik, *Central Labour College*, 61–2; *Clarion*, 4 Dec. 1908.
16. Strike Records vol. 1; Furniss, *Burning Question*, 94–100; Craik, *Central Labour College*, 64 and ch. 5; Ruskin College, Annual Report 1909; *Oxford Chronicle* 11 Dec. 1908.
17. *The Story of Ruskin College* (3rd edn Oxford, 1968), 17; Craik, Central Labour College, 77–84; Furniss, *Burning Question*, 103–10; *Ruskin College and Working-class Education*; *Railway Review* 6 Aug., 3 Sept. 1909.
18. Craik, *Central Labour College*, 72–5; *Clarion*, 2 Apr., 8 May 1909; National Archive, WEA Council Minutes 10 Sept.1909; Oxford University Archives, Rewley House MSS, Tutorial Classes Committee Papers 1909–11: Mansbridge to G. Riboud, Apr. 1909; P. S. Bagwell, *The Railwaymen* (1963), 676.
19. Bagwell, *The Railwaymen*, 678–9; *Railway Review* Apr.–Oct. 1909; Rewley House MSS, Tutorial Classes Committee Early Papers i, Correspondence relating to the establishment of tutorial classes 1907–8: J. C. Finch, Barry ASRS, to Mansbridge 16 Dec. 1907, and J. Murgatroyd to Mansbridge 4 Dec. 1908.
20. Ruskin College, Annual Report 1909–10; Strike Records, vol. 2.
21. National Archive, WEA Central EC Minutes 11 Jan. 1909; Tutorial Classes Committee Early Papers 11, Rewley House MSS; B. Jennings, *Knowledge is Power: A Short History of the WEA 1903–78* (Hull, 1979), 31–3, 37; J. P. M. Millar, *The Labour College Movement* (1979), chs. 3 and 4.
22. Jackson, *Solo Trumpet* vi, 150–1.
23. B. Simon, *Education and the Labour Movement 1870–1920* (1974), 318–25.
24. J. Saville, *The Labour Movement in Britain* (1988), 32.
25. Jennings, *Knowledge is Power*, 16, 37–9.
26. Carolyn Steedman, *Childhood, Culture and Class in Britain: Margaret McMillan 1860–1931* (1990), 180; J. Rée, *Proletarian Philosophers: Problems in Socialist Culture in Britain 1900–40* (Oxford, 1984), 19–21.
27. Anne Phillips and Tim Putnam, 'Education for Emancipation: The Movement for Independent Working-class Education 1908–28', *Capital and Class* x (1980), 22–4; Pollins, *History of Ruskin College*, 36.
28. Nan Milton (ed.), *John Maclean, In the Rapids of Revolution: Essays, Articles and Letters 1902–23* (1978), 123; J. F. and Winifred Horrabin, *Working-class Education* (1924), 56–68.
29. Stocks, 50.
30. Letter, Frank Pickstock to B. Jennings, n.d. received 18 Dec. 1979, copy in WEA National Achive.
31. R. Miliband, *Capitalism and Democracy in Britain* (Oxford, 1982) and *Parliamentary Socialism* (2nd edn, 1972); R. T. Fieldhouse, 'The 1908 Report: Antidote to Class Struggle?', in Sylvia Harrop (ed.), *Oxford and Working-class Education* (new edn, Nottingham, 1987), 45.
32. Millar, *Labour College Movement*, 131–2; Chushichi Tsuzuki, 'Anglo-marxism and Working-class Education', in Jay Winter (ed.), *The Working Class in Modern British History* (Cambridge, 1983), 198–9.

# 7 'A Hard Rain's A-gonna Fall': The National Association and Internationalism 1918–39

*John Atkins*

Oh, where have you been, my blue-eyed son?
Oh, where have you been, my darling young one?
I've stumbled on the side of twelve misty mountains,
I've walked and I've crawled on six crooked highways[1]

On 6 June 1913, ten years after founding the WEA, Albert and Frances Mansbridge travelled to Australia (see plate 4) to encourage the growth of WEAs on an international basis.[2] The previous year, WEA President William Temple had visited Adelaide, speaking about the tutorial class system. This push from the cradle helped to stimulate development in already fertile soil, so that by 1919 membership-based WEAs were up and running in Australia, Canada, New Zealand, and South Africa.[3]

International co-operation – the desire to collaborate with and nurture workers' education organisations in other countries – has been a recurrent strand in WEA activities throughout the 90 years since Mansbridge's first voyage. The second and more obvious manifestation of the WEA's internationalism has been the plethora of courses, schools, and publications devoted to international affairs.

Events between the two world wars, and the intellectual soul-searching which followed the 1918 armistice, should have provided a rich stimulus to the international activities of the National Association.[4] Far from being a 'highway of diamonds' though, the period up to the outbreak of the Second World War proved to be pitted with obstacles, and in a general sense was quite barren in so far as internationalism was concerned.

THE SPIRIT OF ADVENTURE IN EDUCATION

The particular intellectual legacy of Albert Mansbridge strongly permeated the WEA post-1918 despite his having left office. As Bernard Jennings has noted, from this point on Mansbridge and the

WEA drifted apart – but there was no intellectual rupture.[5] Whilst his legacy continued to have an impact throughout the Association it does not wholly account for either the problems or failures encountered in the WEA's international activities. As a resonance though, it is the starting point for appreciating the source of ideological constraints upon the WEA's internationalism.

A belief in truth as a realisable, fixed, and elevated entity was a fundamental building block used by Mansbridge in his essential contribution to the WEA. For him truth would be revealed through the educational adventure 'into an unexplored region, or beyond the bounds of ascertained or recorded truth'. Truth is thus the product of an adventure 'to rediscover and reveal vital knowledge and principles which have been obscured either during the preoccupation of other days, or because a forgetful people has turned in other directions'. Whatever the path of the adventure, 'once truth is uncovered it is magnetic and does its own work.'[6]

Education in Mansbridge's terms was the process of applying knowledge to lead to achievable truth – 'reaching out to higher things'. Thus,

> The field of education is a common upon which all men can meet and exercise rights, no matter what their differences may be in ordinary activities of life. They may differ in politics, even in religion, but, if they be one in their determination to reach out to things which are eternal [i.e. truth], then they may unite to promote the great democratic adventure which needs the best thought and action of every individual.[7]

The evangelical side of Mansbridge is clear in such moments: 'The educated man can do no harm to the community. The band of the educated work their way to "Zion with their face thitherwards".'

The centrality of Mansbridge's contribution helped create the historically unfortunate conjuncture associating his belief in truth as a high ideal with the WEA's non-sectarianism and non-party political constitutional stance. At times, including the period under review, this has had an inhibiting impact upon the WEA's external relations and activities, by creating the conditions for passivity or inability to act decisively. It has fostered in parts of the Association a view that the WEA can only be political (in a non-party sense) if it reflects and gives space to any ideology or political tendency wishing to be heard. Because, following Mansbridge's logic, truth can only be arrived at when *all* voices have been heard.

At the same time Mansbridge and to a greater extent the emergent WEA were rightly seen as serving the cause of reform and democracy. Without this the WEA would not have attracted the active support and participation of many social forces, most notably from within the labour movement.

Whilst Mansbridge alone cannot account for the ideological heritage of the WEA, it is this mixture of apolitical idealism and anticipated commitment to social purposes that created the basis for an inner tension at its heart. The ferment of the founding years contained enough intellectual elasticity to allow quite different concepts of education and politics to be contained within the one organisation. The non-party, non-sectarian stance provided a unifying platform that at the same time allowed social objectives to be at the heart of the evolving WEA mission. It also was to be the major factor allowing the WEA to receive public funding for its work. The problem was that, while Mansbridge sought to give the WEA a spiritual mission others had no difficulty adhering to the WEA constitution whilst ascribing to it a much more practical purpose, firmly rooted in directly addressing the social and economic problems of early twentieth-century Britain.

For its first 15 years the WEA, particularly at national level, was intellectually constrained by the influence of, and deferment granted to, Mansbridge. Only with his departure could the WEA begin to work though a more fully developed intellectual position – one which would allow the 'social imperative' to temper the application of the 'all voices' approach to politics as the mechanistic interpretation and didactic reflection of the WEA's non-party, non-sectarian stance.

If the WEA was to have an international dimension to its activities, that dimension needed to be based upon some very clear principles. If the WEA's first international forays were judged very successful it was because the aim was absolutely simple – to spread the gospel. However, there needed to be something more to give the WEA as an organisation an active international policy, something which connected with the whole organisation and not just a spiritual belief. There especially needed to be something more because other forms of workers' education were developing globally outside the WEA model. While the WEA remained constrained by a proselytising approach to internationalism it was not going to find it an easy matter to launch itself fully in international relations and activities.

A MEANS TO CO-OPERATION

Responding to a communication from the WEA in Australia, the executive committee of the National Association considered how to link WEAs globally early in 1919.[8] The executive committee meeting of 24 January agreed to propose a resolution for discussion by the WEA central council meeting the following day. As a consequence the central council instructed the executive 'to consider a scheme for linking up ourselves with similar organisations throughout the world, and in connection with this, to consider the World Association for Adult Education'.[9] Following this decision the executive committee considered matters further at its meeting of 28 March 1919 and agreed four resolutions which were later published in full in *The Highway*.[10] These were:

1. Steps should be taken to supply information of the aims and work of the WEA to other countries, and information should be secured as to what is being done in other countries on similar lines.
2. The Workers' Educational Association in other parts of the Empire should be approached with a view to their co-operation in a scheme of federation.
3. A conference with the World Association for Adult Education should be arranged with a view to common action and sympathetic policy.
4. Working class and educational bodies in other countries should be approached with a view to an inauguration in those countries of national organisations of a similar type to the WEA.[11]

Clearly a head of steam was building up. So much so that it produced the only extant international policy document of any length produced by the National Association during the inter-war period. Entitled 'Memorandum on the WEA and its "Foreign Policy"' it was produced by Arthur Greenwood, then chairman of the WEA's Yorkshire District and member of the executive committee, who was shortly to become the secretary of the Labour Party's research department.[12]

Greenwood's memorandum examined the case for the WEA's nationally engaging in international work along the lines of the four resolutions, but was prescient in elaborating the wider constraints and considerations requiring prior consideration. Essentially his argument was that the WEA's energies and resources were still very much required to meet the needs of the immediate work to establish the WEA, and secure its objectives, in the United Kingdom. In seeking to present a positive case, but with explicit reservations concerning capacity and appropriateness of the WEA taking on certain roles, Greenwood though was at pains to underline the WEA's commitment to workers' education:

> It is to be remembered that the W.E.A. is a *worker's* association and therefore it is specially interested in the education of workers. It has no special and direct interest in education amongst other classes, whether in this country or abroad. It is not that adult education amongst all classes is not desirable; but the association has adopted a title which emphasises its predominant interest in working-class education, and its activities have been largely directed towards winning labour support.[13]

It would be wrong to view Greenwood's reservations as placing national success and achievement above international activity. Rather, he was expressing concern about being distracted and diverted down non-working-class paths, especially in relation to the World Association for Adult Education. He was also strongly cautioning against the WEA's biting off more than it could chew at a time when its horizons and potential were expanding. Greenwood himself was just about to become centrally involved in the establishment of the Workers' Educational Trade Union Committee (WETUC) – probably the single most important development in the inter-war period that brought the WEA into organic relationships with the British Labour movement.[14]

In fact Greenwood offered perhaps the then most cogent public statement on the benefits to the WEA of having an international dimension:

> I do not think that the WEA can or should maintain an attitude of 'splendid isolation', for to do so would deprive us of the experience of others, and the sustaining influence of enthusiasm on the part of co-workers in the cause of adult education abroad. Moreover it is probable that direct association with educational labour movements in other countries would increase our prestige and strengthen our position with the labour movement in this country.[15]

Greenwood's memorandum was accepted 'in principle' by the WEA executive committee meeting on 23 May 1919. Additionally a sub-committee was set up to put into effect the four resolutions adopted two months earlier.[16]

The question of organising an international conference was discussed at a special meeting of the central council on 17 and 18 October 1919 and the Executive Committee was given the authority to convene 'a Conference of WEA representatives from all parts of the British Commonwealth, to which representatives from workers' educational movements in other countries may be invited'.[17] Not until the Annual Report for the year ending 31 May 1920, however, was it made clear that the executive committee had not found it practicable to arrange the proposed conference.[18]

Whilst conference delegates from abroad would have been required to find their own transportation costs, the WEA as conference convenor would have been responsible for a large part if not all of the organisation and administration costs both before and after the event. Without any specific reason being given, lack of capacity seems the most likely reason for the National Association staff not being able to carry out the mandate of the executive committee. In fact the National Association had considerable experience of facing financial shortfalls. Staff reductions had occurred at the WEA central office as recently as 1918, and in the same year the possibility of abandoning publication of *The Highway* was considered.[19]

Nevertheless the desire to foster international links was not entirely ruled out. For example the WEA played host to an organiser from the Swedish WEA (ABF), visiting WEA summer schools in England for three months in 1921.[20] Also in mid-1919 it had been reported that contact had been established with the United Labour Education Committee in New York.[21]

If the WEA itself had difficulty underwriting the birth of a new international association, help appeared to be at hand from other quarters. An invitation was received to attend an international conference on labour education to be held in Brussels on 16 and 17 August 1922.[22] Convened by the Belgian Committee on Labour Education (*Centrale d'Education Ouvrière*) the conference was seen as an opportunity to exchange experience.[23] The serving WEA general secretary, J. M. Mactavish and H. H. Elvin, WETUC treasurer and secretary of the Clerks Union, were delegated to represent the WEA/WETUC. It is worth noting that Mactavish and Elvin were also asked by the Trade Union Congress to present a report on its efforts to develop workers' education activities. Thirty-four representatives attended the conference. From the United Kingdom in addition to the WEA, the Co-operative Union, Ruskin College, the Central Labour College, the Scottish Labour College, and the National Council of Labour Colleges all sent delegates.[24]

The conference discussed and adopted three resolutions. The first concerned the exchange of students between Labour Colleges, and the possibility of establishing an international (trade union) fund for this purpose. The second resolution called for renewed effort on the part of all organisations represented at the conference, and as such gave an opening to the British Labour College movement representatives to take to the continent their ideological struggle with the WEA.[25]

Speakers representing the Labour College movement tried to include as a part of the second resolution the phrase 'independent working class education' in place of 'working class education', and instead of urging those present to continue their efforts for 'the furthering of the economic and political emancipation of the working class', it was proposed that efforts should be dedicated to 'the efficient conduct of the struggle against National and International capital'.[26] Following discussion it was clear that the delegates from outside of the United Kingdom were nonplussed by the pedantic-seeming nature of the argument designed solely to embarrass the WEA, and the proposed amendments were not put to a vote.[27]

In retrospect – and it should have been obvious at the time – the third and final resolution adopted unanimously by the conference was much more important:

> This Conference requests the *Centrale d'Education Ouvrière* of Belgium to take steps to ensure the maintenance of relations between the organisations here represented until the holding of the next Conference which it is decided shall be held two years hence, and to consult with the Amsterdam Trade Union International on the possibility of creating a permanent clearing house for the International Education Movement.[28]

As a national organisation in search an international structure this final conference resolution could have been a vehicle for pursuing the existing national WEA policy mandate. Attendance at the 1922 conference had been global, and those organisations represented were clearly able to bear the cost of sending delegates. Travel costs aside, there was nothing which would have prevented the newly established WEAs from the dominions participating in future conferences. It was also clearly the case that the Belgian Committee on Labour Education did not see itself as a permanent secretariat for any future conference or supporting structure.

Nor was the Amsterdam Trade Union International (better known as the International Federation of Trade Unions) a more enthusiastic standard-bearer. As its conference observer was at pains to make clear in her first conference intervention, the IFTU 'was not directly concerned with Workers' Education'.[29]

The field was thus open. However, even had some been tempted to fill the breach, the WEA's leading figures were going to be politically constrained by the Association's inner tension between commitment to social purpose and apolitical constitutionalism. It was one thing to be given a mandate to speak on behalf of the TUC, quite another to think of offering to head up an international network comprised primarily of trade unions in which at least one political party would also have had a stake. In other contexts this tension rebounded most publicly upon Mactavish as general secretary who more than once was 'slapped on the wrists' for what was viewed by some within the WEA as his too pro-Labour commitment.[30]

Despite their own reticence, and possibly because there was no alternative, the IFTU set up a provisional committee to take forward the decisions of the Brussels conference. Almost two years to the day (15–17 August 1924) a follow-up conference was held in Oxford, at Ruskin College. Although the conference was convened in the name of the IFTU, it has been claimed that the WEA/WETUC was largely responsible for the venue and thus in effect acted as the host.[31] If so, it is further evidence of the WEA's desire to promote international co-operation from behind the scenes, avoiding the risk of inner tensions coming to the surface. As the TUC-nominated British delegate on the IFTU provisional committee, J.W. Bowen (general secretary of the Union of Post Office Workers), was at that time a leading figure in WETUC, the claim for the WEA's role is clearly not without foundation.

The 1924 World Conference was a much larger and noisier event with 59 delegates from 20 countries attending. Providing further evidence of the WEA's active role, Mactavish was, at the start of the conference, proposed as a member of its 'commission of reference', a type of standing orders committee. Jim Millar, general secretary of the National Council of Labour Colleges, immediately opposed this and the scene was thus set for a repeat of the type of wrangling seen in Brussels two years earlier. To try and draw the fire from the objectors Mactavish withdrew his name but, in any event, the next days saw the WEA under further sustained attack.[32] While it was a much more representative gathering than the 1922 conference, the decisions taken at Ruskin really did not move things much further forward. The most significant decision was to establish an International Federation of Labour Organisations concerned with workers' education.[33] In large part this was picking up from where the 1922 conference had left off, but now with a much clearer line of development.

It was agreed that an international education committee should be appointed to carry out the decisions of the 1924 conference, and that the committee should draw up a constitution for an International Workers' Education Federation. Specifically the committee was instructed to consult with international organisations representing the Labour and socialist, Co-operative, socialist education, and youth movements when drawing up the constitution. The resulting constitution would be submitted to a future inaugural conference. Until such time as the proposed Federation could be convened, the IFTU was asked to carry on its co-ordinating role. Writing in *The Highway* almost 18 months after the conference closed, however, the Secretary of the IFTU, J.W. Brown, announced: 'Plans were laid for a separate Workers' Educational International, but difficulties have arisen, and for the moment the scheme is in the melting-pot.'[34] However, the holding of the 1922 and 1924 conferences had clearly given impetus to the IFTU's own activities, because he also reported that the IFTU had started convening international summer schools, and had set up early in 1923 an education department responsible for producing a monthly education bulletin.[35]

In 1924, the WEA wrote to the IFTU suggesting either Germany or Austria as venues for a third World Conference.[36] It sent representatives to the first World Conference on Adult Education, organised by the World Association for Adult Education (WAAE) in Cambridge in 1929. Given, however, that Mansbridge was a leading intellectual force and president of the WAAE it is not surprising that the WEA played little part in the actual proceedings. One line from Mansbridge's presidential address perhaps sums up how far he had drifted away from the WEA – 'Adult Education is a supreme effort to replace the forces of spoliation by the forces of redemption.' One can only surmise that this rhetoric would have left the WEA delegates feeling uncomfortable to the point of embarrassment. Indeed the following year Tawney was urging fellow WEA executive committee members to attend the national conference of the British Institute of Adult Education, which Mansbridge would be chairing, 'in order to put forward the point of view of the Association'.[37] As far as the WEA was concerned the question of an international organisation, or convening international conferences, was now a closed item until 1943. At its annual conference that year, the WEA passed a resolution concerning the reconstruction of workers' education organisations in countries where they had been destroyed. Almost identical in tone to the earlier 1919 policy commitments this resolution led to an international conference in 1945, which saw the creation of the International Federation of Workers' Education Associations (IFWEA).

## SITTING IN THE TUMBRIL

Any organisation with radical intentions, especially one concerned with providing an educational dimension to the 'questions of the day', should reflect and refract the light of events around it. So far as the WEA as a whole is concerned this process will be evidenced primarily in its courses. To analyse mass-education provision and make something of the evidence, a detailed picture would be required of what went on in the classrooms, the materials used, the role and impact of the tutors, and the nature of student participation and its contribution. To cover the whole of a decentralised organisation, appreciating local circumstances as well as gaining valid overall national insights, is a major task – well outside of the scope of this chapter.

What we do have however is the evidence of nationally printed materials, especially the WEA journal, *The Highway*, which was open to contributions from WEA members, tutors, and students. As such it is therefore as good an indicator as anything else of the 'international spirit' of the WEA.

Throughout the inter-war period *The Highway* had regular items (articles, book reviews, and letters) on international events. Essentially they fall into two main categories – factual reports concerning the development of workers' education in other countries, and contributions directly commenting upon global social and political developments. The former show that the WEA continued to maintain and slowly enlarge its appreciation of other workers' education organisations. The latter indicate some of the problems besetting an organisation founded upon social concern, bound by a non-partisan ethos, yet faced with momentous events ultimately leading to world-wide conflagration.

The 1917 Revolution in Russia for example was commented upon in *The Highway*. In terms of immediacy and keeping up with events, however, it manages to give the clear impression of being out of touch or not wanting to address controversial issues. The first significant article on Russia post-1917 appeared in the November 1922 edition, well after the political changes and consequent foreign policy shifts of the new Soviet government – most notably in relation to the closing period and aftermath of the First World War. The November 1922 article took as its theme the rather drier subject of trade and the Soviet government's attempts to secure foreign loans.[38]

What contributions there were on international events in the 1920s were few in number and similar in approach to that of November 1922 – lacking hard, significant, social and political content. *The Highway*'s main journalistic rival, *Plebs Magazine* – the monthly journal of the Labour College movement – carried the first of a series of articles on the growth of fascism in Europe in June 1924. It took *The Highway* until November 1930 to make a similar intervention.[39] *The Highway*'s emphasis upon international developments in the 1920s was primarily upon adult and workers' education in other countries, including America, Australia, Russia and Sweden. Mary Stocks in her 1953 history of the WEA effectively condemns the 1920s by referring to the 1930s as the 'golden age' of *The Highway*.[40] Significantly it was a period of editorial stability with W.E. Williams taking on the editor's role for the whole of the decade. Circulation rose from 8,000 a month when he became editor to 20,000 in April 1939 (see plate 7).[41]

In the 1930s, with a new editor, *The Highway* was guided by Williams and allowed by the national leadership to become more opinionated if not polemical.[42] Two editions of *The Highway* in particular illustrate this trend. They also demonstrate the consequences that can arise when the search for truth through education using a rigid *laissez-faire* approach effectively sacrifices any social basis to political analysis on the altar of impartiality. The first was the January 1935 special issue devoted wholly to events in Germany, the second the edition of December 1937, which contained an article on democracy that used events in Spain as a point of reference.

Reaction to the Germany special issue was unlike anything previously experienced. Adverse comments were made about the pro-Nazi content of some articles. Some members of the WEA executive committee viewed the special issue as nothing less than a vehicle for Nazi propaganda, and a betrayal of the democratic faith of the WEA.[43] However, it is absolutely clear that Williams knew what he was about and where things might lead. As was usual the January 1935 issue was prefaced by the Notes and Comments section – customarily written by the editor. In it, although Williams took the unusual step of justifying, in advance, the content, readers were to discover in the following articles:

Many of the experts who contribute to this number are favourably impressed with the German experiment. That does not mean we are to accept their evaluations. ... Since Hitler came to power we have had few opportunities to find out what he is after ... We have been fed on atrocity stories as we were when the Bolsheviks were making their revolution, and as we were recently during the Spanish revolt. All of them may be true. Whether they are or not does not make one any less certain that they are only a part of the truth. What Hitler did to the Jews or Communists is no more the whole truth than what Lenin did to the Russian bourgeoisie. We may execrate both persecutions; but we may not say that these barbarities are all that there is in Bolshevism or National Socialism.[44]

His further observation in the subsequent issue of *The Highway*, that the special German number had 'made a stir', was verging on the disingenuous. Such was the feeling that some of the content had been strongly sympathetic if not pro-Nazi that probably for the first time ever the WEA's central executive committee felt it necessary to discuss and agree a resolution concerning the content of its journal:

That our adherence to the principle of Democracy be reflected in the next issue of *The Highway* by a statement to that effect.[45]

Williams was not present at the committee meeting which itself is perhaps an indication of the gap that was beginning to open up between himself as editor and the executive authority of the WEA.[46]

Eventually things were to get to such a state that by late 1937 the Association's national officers had to request the opportunity to meet with their journal editor once or twice a year.

This growing detachment though does not explain or justify events. Williams saw himself and indeed defended his actions as being wholly within the WEA tradition. His defence of the German special issue was given the following month in terms of its being within the democratic faith and practices of the WEA, expressing again his conviction that this literally requires all sides to a discussion, no matter how offensive, be given a hearing.

He seems to have been particularly stung by criticisms made by members of the WEA executive committee as he chose to mount his defence against their views:

> An educational organisation is concerned primarily with thought, not because it is indifferent to action, but because action is most likely to be effective if the thought which precedes it is fully informed. Its method is to provide opportunities for the expression of opinions of different minds, including opinions with which its members and supporters may strongly disagree.[47]

When these opinions touch upon the treatment and well-being of groups and individuals one would expect there to be an educational if not moral responsibility to ensure that at least all views are grounded upon verifiable fact and experiences. Good editorial practice should also demand no less. Otherwise the WEA might just as well open itself to all-comers to express their 'opinions', however bigoted or criminal.

While erecting his own moral vantage point, Williams could not resist snapping at the hands of those holding his editorial reins:

> Are we an educational society, or must we refuse to find room for the expression of opinions which we dislike for fear of arousing criticism – criticism often, it may be remarked, from the very people who had nothing but praise for *The Highway* when it published a Russian number which, as it turned out, was mostly pro-Bolshevik.[48]

Some of the executive at least must have sensed they could be in for more trouble.

So it proved to be with an innocuous-sounding article in the December 1937 issue of *The Highway* entitled 'The Foundations of Democracy', written by Arthur Bryant.[49] If the German special issue had caused 'a stir' then a veritable storm followed this time. The reaction arose from claims made by Bryant concerning events in Spain as justification and evidence for his arguments concerning democracy and dictatorship. In a highly charged description of life in Spain following the 1936 general election he specifically accused the Communist Party of ordering the burning of 36 of the 38 churches in the town of Malaga.[50]

Protests about the veracity of Bryant's claims, and their place in an educational journal, came in to Ernest Green, the WEA general secretary, as well as to Williams at his editorial office. These were reported to the finance and general purposes committee by Green on 7 January 1938. Having assured the presence of their editor this time, the committee took the unprecedented decision to include in future issues of *The Highway* a statement that articles expressed the views of the individual authors and not those of the editor or the WEA. In addition it was agreed that 'it would be useful for the Finance and General Purposes Committee to discuss matters of *Highway* policy with the Editor at the June meeting each year.'[51]

Public comment on Bryant's article first appeared in the February 1938 edition of *The Highway* along with the disclaimer insisted upon by the finance and general purposes committee. Undoubtedly under pressure from the adverse reaction, Williams used nearly two-and-a-half pages to justify his publishing of the Bryant article citing freedom of speech, the need to be fully informed by all opinions, and the WEA 'tradition' of accepting controversy within its educational practice, as his defence. Under pressure he certainly was, but he was certainly not bowed:

> To me personally these partisan protests, including those from tutors, W.E.A. officials and others who hold some authority, do not much matter. I have learned by now to look pleasant as I sit in the tumbril.[52]

In addition to Williams' lengthy statement of defence the February 1938 issue also contained two articles specifically refuting the arguments and claims previously made by Bryant.[53]

Later on, Williams went on to claim that of the 600 letters received concerning the publication of Bryant's article only three were critical.[54] This was a strange claim given that he himself quoted more than three critical responses as part of his self-justification in February 1938. While there is not the evidence to substantiate or properly refute Williams's claim about the level of support he received, it is clear that his actions put the WEA in a light from which its national leadership wanted to remove themselves. However, such was the success of *The Highway* in the 1930s, the same WEA leaders were loath to let the guillotine fall on their editor.

WHAT'LL YOU DO NOW, MY BLUE-EYED SON?

With hindsight one may jump to many a conclusion lacking an appreciation of the moral and intellectual turmoil of the 1930s. Even Williams as a staunch advocate of the WEA being non-political and open to all persuasions could see the vortex growing:

> Where it is vital and realistic, education is political. In the W.E.A. it has in that sense always been political – it has bent its members' minds to the prospect of realising in terms of party policy the social truths they have discovered. But the frontier between this position and that of party politics, save for sporadic 'incidents', has been kept intact. It comes to this: that in minor issues it is easy to remain non-partisan, in major issues it becomes increasingly impossible. This winter the W.E.A., with many another non-party non-sectarian society, may find itself in the political line-up.[55]

Without wearing anything looking vaguely like a badge on its sleeve *The Highway* during the inter-war period did cover a range of international topics from a social perspective, most often somewhere in the left-conservative to social-democratic range of opinions. There were, for example, articles on problems of the British Empire, imperialism, Europe, India, Germany, Russia, Africa and Spain.

Nevertheless, when one also considers the documentation concerning WEA educational and organisational policy there is a glaring absence of internationalism and international perspectives. It is hard to find a presidential address to a national WEA conference – most of which were given by R. H. Tawney – that contains any reference to an international issue. In the period 1931 to 1938 (there was then a gap until 1942) only three resolutions concerned international questions:

- Empire day celebrations (1933)
- Promoting 'fraternal feelings' between the nations of the world (1934)
- Democracy and intellectual freedom (1936).

Apart from the Greenwood memorandum and the unfulfilled executive resolutions of 1919 there was nothing, save *ad hoc* reaction, to give direction to the WEA as an internationalist organisation. The easiest and the most understandable rationalisation of this is that there was just too much else to do. The tougher view is that part of the explanation lies in the fact that difficult choices were never developed and followed through.

Commitment and action in an international context will inevitably take the WEA beyond its national domestic experience. The attempt to help establish and support British-style WEAs outside the United Kingdom was a highway that ultimately wandered into the sand. Even the cursory cataloguing of workers' education organisations around the world, which the WEA was able to make, showed very clearly that many models existed by the early 1920s.[56] Given that, the Association needed to ask of itself, and answer the question, 'what type of other national workers' educational organisations should it ally itself to?' Only by taking this step could the Association move from relations to substantial dialogue, from exchange of information to joint educational action. This is not to make grandiose claims for the WEA as a proto-supranational agency. Greenwood's stricture that 'the WEA, as such, cannot run the world' is as obvious today as it needed to be spelt out in 1919.[57] Yet, in deciding who to work with, the WEA would have had to confront its historic inner tension directly: the tension between the tradition that took non-partisanship as the justification for being an open house across the political spectrum *sine qua non*, and the tradition that believed social reform within a collectivist context gave to the WEA its core mission as a social force. The first tradition had no active analysis and response to unfolding world events in the 1930s, especially within Europe. Indeed, its danger was that it acted as a brake upon the development of WEA policy and, in a hegemonic position, could effectively immobilise the WEA as an organisation with social concerns and objectives. The second tradition never manifested itself in terms of expressed WEA activity and policy – at least at national level. Had the national policy commitment of 1919 been followed through, or the potential scope for development shown by the 1922 and 1924 conferences been taken up, then a basis upon which the second tradition could develop and apply itself would have been created. They were not, and it did not.

As a consequence defining moments of the inter-war period could be treated as 'free-for-all' educational exercises by the official organ of the Association, because as an *organisation* it had no practical international experience or commitment to give it grounding upon which to stand. This is not to say that finding an international expression to social commitment within an educational context is a simple and straightforward matter. It is not. But it was a task the WEA as a national organisation failed to address in the 1920s and 1930s. It took the outbreak and experience of the Second World War to bring back on to the table questions first posed over 20 years earlier.

NOTES

*Place of publication London unless otherwise stated.*

1. Bob Dylan, Copyright © 1963; renewed 1991 Special Rider Music.
2. *Trodden Road*, 72–4.
3. *The Highway* xi, no. 8.
4. The focus of this chapter is wholly upon national activities due to limitations of time available for research.
5. B. Jennings, *Albert Mansbridge and English Adult Education* (Hull, 1976), 18.
6. *Adventure* xiv.
7. *Adventure* xv–xvi.
8. The newly formed Federal Council of the WEA in Australia had in August 1918 agreed a resolution concerning co-operation with the WEA.
9. National Archive, WEA CENTRAL 1/2/1/3.
10. *The Highway* xi, no. 10, 103.
11. WEA CENTRAL 1/2/1/3: executive committee meeting 28 March 1919.
12. For Greenwood, *DNB*. He had been joint secretary of the government reconstruction committee on adult education set up in 1917 and was eventually to become a Labour MP in 1922 and Minister of Health in the 1929 Labour government.
13. *The Highway* xi, no. 10, 104–5.
14. WETUC was established as a joint national committee of the WEA and the Iron and Steel Trades Confederation in 1919 to develop joint educational activities. WETUC was soon to include other national trade union affiliates.
15. *The Highway* xi, no. 10, 104.
16. No separate minutes or documentation relating to this sub-committee have survived in the national archive. It clearly existed for some months though, as references to it as the International Committee can be found in other committee minutes for 1919.

17. Minutes of Central Council meeting, 17–18 Oct. 1919 (WEA CENTRAL 1/2/1/3).
18. *The Highway* xii, no. 11, 193.
19. Executive Committee meeting 12 July 1918 (WEA CENTRAL 1/2/1/3).
20. The visitor was Gunnar Hirdman who was later to become ABF General Secretary: *The Highway* xiii, no. 11, 175.
21. *The Highway* xi, no. 9. The United Labour Education Committee was an organisation established by trade unions.
22. The invitation was received by WETUC.
23. In opening the conference Hendrik de Man, general secretary of the Belgian Committee on Labour Education, reminded his audience that a Workers' Education Congress had been held in 1913 attended by delegates from half a dozen countries. *International Workers' Education (Embodying the Report of the International Conference Held at Brussels on August 16 and 17, 1922)*, published by the International Federation of Trade Unions (IFTU), n.d. 11. University of North London. TUC Archive, LC 5010.
24. Other representatives were from labour organisations in Australia, Belgium, Czechoslovakia, Denmark, France, Germany (including the German Social Democratic Party), Holland, Luxemburg, Switzerland and the United States. The IFTU attended the conference as an observer.
25. All existing general histories of the WEA make reference to the hostility and suspicion that marked and marred the public relationship between the WEA and the Labour College movement (i.e. the Central Labour College, the Plebs League, and the National Council of Labour Colleges). In essence the Labour College view was summed up in the second issue of its journal: 'The WEA cannot rise above the height of its source. It is hopelessly entangled in the class interests of those whose body and blood it is. It is founded on the fallacy that you can reconcile the interests of all classes in the State. Its boast is that it stands for a non-class view.' *The Plebs*, no. 2, Mar. 1909, 23.
26. *The Highway* xv, no. 1, Oct. 1922, 12.
27. 'Guns and sharp swords in the hands of young children.' The conference chairman (De Man) intervened in the debate with the remark that the question raised chiefly concerned the British delegates and as such he thought that the point of principle involved should be left to a future conference (*International Workers' Education*, 19). This is not to deny that the issues raised by the Labour College movement concerning the political independence and ideological perspectives of workers' education providers were irrelevant. Rather, that the so-called scientific examination of the characteristics of the WEA changed hardly a jot between 1909 and at least the 1950s. As such the case against the WEA became more and more superficial as time progressed – the swords became blunt and the aim of the barrels entirely predictable.
28. *International Workers' Education*, 20.
29. *International Workers' Education*, 15.
30. See the minutes of the Executive Committee for 28 April and 27 May 1922, WEA CENTRAL 1/2/1/5. The intermittent lack of confidence in Mactavish expressed by his peers has led to his being criticised for lacking

subtlety: B. Jennings, *Knowledge is Power* (Hull, 1979), 39, and being, in the words of Beatrice Webb, 'blunt, energetic, and somewhat commonplace' (quoted in Stocks, 70). Whatever view one takes, Mactavish stands absolutely on a par with other more celebrated WEA general secretaries whose health became part of the personal price they paid for service to the Association.

31. This is argued by A. J. Corfield in his history of WETUC, *Epoch in Workers' Education, A History of the Workers' Educational Trade Union Committee* (1969), 50–1.

32. Delegates from the Labour College movement never mustered more than 7 votes against 24 on any item put to a vote. The line of attack against the WEA was as usual in terms of its university connections and lack of policy commitment to class struggle as the basis for educational activity.

33. *World Workers' Education; Embodying the Report of the Second International Conference on Workers' Education Held at Oxford from August 15th to 17th 1924* (IFTU, Amsterdam, 1925), 51.

34. *The Highway* xviii (Jan. 1926) 56.

35. After a considerable time lapse the IFTU eventually convened a further meeting in Brussels on 16 June 1935 'to arrange for some kind of machinery which would give publicity and provide for the exchange of information between various countries in respect of Workers' Education'. A familiar pattern was followed in that the meeting asked the IFTU to convene a further conference on the issue in 1936: WEA CENTRAL 1/2/1/13, finance and general purposes committee, 21 June 1935.

36. WEA CENTRAL 1/2/1/7, finance and general purposes committee, 27 Nov. 1924.

37. *World Conference on Adult Education Cambridge 1929* ( WAAE, 1930) 29; WEA CENTRAL 1/2/1/9, central executive committee, 24 May 1930.

38. *The Highway* xvi, no. 2 (Nov. 1922), 24. See chapter 5 in this volume on how, over four and a half years earlier, the Russian Revolution had impacted upon the WEA more directly through events in Birmingham.

39. 'Danger Zone in Europe' written by the historian G. P. Gooch. *The Highway* xxiii (Nov. 1930), 11–13.

40. Stocks, 116.

41. Stocks, 116–17.

42. It was then current practice that the editor of *The Highway* be co-opted onto the WEA central executive committee. At the first meeting he was able to attend, Williams set out his policy as being 'namely, that *The Highway* should be rigorously non-party and unsectarian and should strike a proportion of all interests in the WEA': WEA CENTRAL 1/2/1/9, central executive committee, 18 Jan. 1930.

43. *The Highway* xxvii (Feb. 1935), 117–18.

44. *The Highway* xxvii (Jan. 1935) 85.

45. WEA CENTRAL 1/2/1/12, central executive committee, 12 Jan. 1935.

46. The fact that Williams had left full-time WEA employment by early 1934 to become secretary of the BIAE most certainly commenced or accelerated this process.

47. *The Highway* xxvii (Feb. 1935), 118.

48. *The Highway* xxvii (Feb. 1935), 118. Mary Stocks in siding with Williams after the event arrogantly dismissed his critics as 'a perceptible minority of fools'.

49. Sir Arthur Wynne Morgan Bryant (1899–1985), chief clerk to the Prince of Wales and later holder of various offices in the royal secretariat, lecturer in history, Oxford University Delegacy for Extra-Mural Studies, 1925–36; educational adviser (later governor), Bonar Law College, Ashridge, Herts., from 1929; writer of 'Our Note Book', *Illustrated London News*, 1936–85. *DNB*.

50. 'Almost everywhere off the beaten track the law ceased to give protection to those who dared to hold views that differed from those of the Communist and Anarchist bosses who controlled the local mob. In every small town and village the sign of the hammer and sickle was scrawled in letters of blood on the walls, and the mob stood in the street threatening with clenched fist those who passed by. Anyone, of whatever class, who was known to have Conservative sympathies or to be in the habit of attending Church or even of wearing a collar and tie, went in daily and nightly terror of attack. During those months murder, arson, theft and even rape went largely unpunished all over rural Spain. And in a great town like Malaga all but two of its thirty-eight churches were burned by the orders of the Communist party.' *The Highway* xxx (Dec. 1937), 40.

51. WEA CENTRAL 1/2/1/16, finance and general purposes committee, 7 Jan. 1938.

52. *The Highway* xxx (Feb. 1938), 99.

53. 'More Foundations of Democracy' by J. Hampden Jackson, and 'What Happened in Malaga?' by Sir Peter Chalmers-Mitchell, *The Highway* xxx (Feb. 1938). The latter article rebutted Bryant's claims one by one taking a rhetorical sideswipe in posing the question as to how a hammer and sickle may be 'scrawled in letters' – of blood or otherwise?

54. *The Highway* xxx (Mar. 1938), 129.

55. *The Highway* xxix (Nov. 1936), 2.

56. The following description of the work of the Swedish WEA (ABF) in the early 1920s illustrates the point well: 'The Swedish Association is a co-ordinating body, carrying on its work chiefly through affiliated bodies, the Communist Youth Association, the Communist Party, which have 16 and 23 per cent of their respective membership enrolled in study circles, the Confederation of Trade Unions (224 [study] circles), the Social Democratic Labour Party (190 circles), the Social Democratic Youth Association (21 per cent of membership in Study Circles), the Verandi Workers' Temperance Association, and others. The success of the work among young people is very remarkable.' *The Highway* xv, no. 5 (Feb. 1923), 66.

57. *The Highway* xi, no. 10, 105.

# 8 Survival, Growth and Retreat: The WEA in Wartime, 1939–45

*John Field*

Most historians of British adult education have concentrated on what they see as their subject's heroic moments. In mirror image, a minority of critical historians has dwelt on the darkest episodes of class betrayal. By either standard, the history of the WEA during the Second World War ought to be well-trodden ground. Starting as a conflict over European supremacy, the war rapidly evolved into a struggle for the values of democracy, freedom, fellowship and equality that the Association held dear. Even critical historians acknowledge that the Association expanded both its activities and its influence throughout the conflict. According to Roger Fieldhouse, the WEA's position caused such alarm that the authorities put it under pressure 'to conform' to an establishment view of the war.[1] As the war concluded, the WEA found itself in a remarkable position of strength, with a general election producing a parliament and government that were packed with WEA alumni, tutors and officers.[2]

In short, the WEA might be thought to have had either a very good or a very bad war, depending on your point of view. Yet remarkably little of this period has been examined in detail. Jennings's short history of the Association between 1903 and 1978 passes straight from the inter-war years to the Ashby report, devoting less than a page to the period between Munich and the Peace,[3] while Fieldhouse allocates one paragraph in his overview of the twentieth-century WEA.[4] This chapter redresses this imbalance, and examines the WEA's experiences during a war that witnessed enormous changes in the wider society to which the Association's educational efforts were directed. While previous conflicts had brought the threats of violent death and bereavement to many, their direct impact was usually limited to those who undertook active service, while the military objectives often appeared rather obscure or remote. The Second World War, by contrast, was a total war which was highly mechanised. It touched the lives of civilians of all classes as well as front-line fighting men, and because it required the full engagement of the civilian population it also became a struggle against domestic grievances and tribulations as well as the enemies overseas. As Angus Calder has famously said, this was a People's War.[5] Or so it came to be seen, with the WEA playing a key role in the process of constructing the war as a popular struggle for security and enlightenment.

This chapter explores this process in some detail. It is based partly on archival evidence in respect of the WEA and its trade union arm, WETUC, at national level. As well as the view from head office, I draw on archival evidence and a small amount of oral testimony from the Districts, and particularly from South Yorkshire. I ask whether the WEA was effectively brought under state control during a period of severe national emergency. I also examine evidence that, by accelerating the processes of democratisation and modernisation within British society, the war recast the immediate conditions which the WEA addressed. Finally, I consider the influence of the WEA on wider arguments for a stronger adult education system in post-war Britain.

## WEA ACTIVITY IN WARTIME

The WEA prepared carefully for the Second World War, but it did so on the assumption that its students would probably oppose the coming conflict. In a letter to branch secretaries, issued the day before Chamberlain returned from Munich to declare 'peace in our time', Ernest Green, WEA national secretary, reminded his audience that 'war is the child of greed, prejudice and intolerance. It is only by the spread of knowledge that the danger of war will recede.' Two days later, Green wrote again, urging branches to 'discuss ways and means of taking advantage of the tide of public opinion'.[6] A huge WEA rally in Sheffield in 1938 heard a speech by Konni Zilliacus, a Labour left-winger with a reputation for strong pro-Soviet sympathies, who drew on his experience as a member of the League of Nations secretariat, and spoke on 'The Working Class and the Efforts for Peace'.[7]

In short, the Association's pre-war thinking focused more on avoiding another brutal fight for imperialist domination than anticipating what might happen in the first war to be fought by assembly-line methods. But it did prepare. In March 1939, the Association's central executive committee (CEC) agreed to create an emergency committee, consisting of its national officials together with any members of the finance and general purposes committee (FGP) who were in London, to 'act on behalf of the Association in the event of War'. In reaching this momentous decision, the CEC had to consider whether it should first consult the Board of Education or the Districts; prudently, the members opted for the latter course.[8] In an upbeat article in *The Highway*, G. D. H. Cole argued for the fullest possible fulfilment of the WEA's programme, with classes being used 'as instruments for helping an important section of the public to think out its position in the light of current happenings'.[9]

In its earliest months, despite the planning, the war had a mildly negative impact on the Association's work. Even during the phoney war, which lasted until early 1940, shiftwork, overtime working, petrol rationing and the blackout all wrought havoc on the three-year tutorial class programme in the industrial cities. The CEC heard in November that Districts were organising two-thirds the number of classes they had run in the previous year, while WETUC reported that the Union of Postal Workers had found itself unable to continue with its educational activities.[10] On the whole, though, the WEA's officers had good grounds for feeling pleased with the Association's dedication and persistence, and publicly contrasted their work with that of the much reduced provision by local authorities.[11]

The onset of the *blitzkrieg* from May 1940 brought an end to all sense of normality. Whatever the prophetic skills of the WEA's leaders, though, little could have prepared the branch members in Deal, on the Kent coast, for what was to happen to their class meetings in the 1939–40 session. One class secretary reported reassuringly in May 1940 that 'The standard of work has been very good', if less than might have been the case but for the 'many distractions':

> During the actual class there have been explosions that have shaken the whole room and rattled the windows, but the class as a whole have been so keen and interested that work has proceeded normally, and the tutor not being so used to these things as the students has been wondering if they are guns, bombs or the local gasworks going up.[12]

Nor, as the blitz dragged on into the following year, were the earnest learners of Deal alone. Whatever else happened, the WEA could not hope to pursue business as usual. In autumn 1940 the CEC itself had to move its meetings from London to Nottingham; planned annual conferences were cancelled in 1939, 1940 (the latter following transport disruption) and 1941. The South Western District's offices and files were destroyed during the Plymouth blitz.[13] In Northern Ireland, the divisional committee of WETUC, bombed out of its Belfast offices by the Luftwaffe in spring 1941, did not meet again until June 1943.[14] The number of courses offered fell in 1940 from the reduced level of 1939 (though given the circumstances, the CEC felt that the programme was large enough for the Districts to be congratulated).[15]

With a German occupation apparently looming in weeks or days, the outlook for an organisation concerned with workers' education seemed, at best, bleak. In a confidential note drafted in June 1940, Green set out his view of 'The WEA and the Crisis' (a title he had used since the international tensions of the late 1930s as a heading for circulars to all branch secretaries). He anticipated that 'martial law and a curfew in most industrial and garrison centres' were likely to be followed shortly by invasion. In the event of aerial bombardment, the 'whole of the South eastern District, Kent and East Sussex, will be completely disorganised and unworkable'. In these dark circumstances, he believed that the central joint advisory committee should prepare to muster a 'mobile force of about 100 full-time tutors' to be deployed to areas where refugees or military personnel and industrial workers had swollen the population. *The Highway* should come under the immediate 'direct control' of the officers.[16] This was apocalyptic stuff, and Tawney made Green tone it down; the version which went to the CEC made no mention of control over *The Highway*, and contained new sections, including one on the WEA's attitude to the war. The leadership's view was now summarised in one line: 'The war must be won.'[17]

As the conflict entered a more settled period, the Association's work expanded and widened. It increasingly participated in a large-scale programme of adult education for servicemen and women stationed in Britain. Based on experimental work in Scotland and elsewhere, it developed innovative programmes for civil defence personnel, war workers living in hostels, and displaced persons. The WEA also explored new pedagogic approaches, as hard-pressed voluntary activists and tutors on the ground faced an influx of new students, most of whom had never encountered the WEA before, had no background in the trade unions or co-operative movement, and of whom many had not even been employed before.[18] Together, these changes represented a considerable challenge, and they pushed the WEA in new directions.

WEA interest in army education predated the hasty launch of the scheme in the Home Command by some months. Pressed by George Wigg (district secretary in North Staffordshire) and Arthur Creech Jones (vice-president), the officers lobbied in the last year of peace for an amendment to the military training bill allowing conscripts 'to retain freedom in their social and cultural contacts', and argued for the forces to permit educational activities funded by the Board of Education 'in co-operation with bodies such as the WEA'.[19] Following the outbreak of war, the Young Men's Christian Association (YMCA) convened a meeting in December 1939 leading to the creation of a new central advisory council (CAC) on adult education in H. M. forces. The WEA was represented on the CAC, along with other 'responsible bodies', arguing successfully for the regionalisation of its work with the same borders as the university extra-mural areas.[20] Green also persuaded the War Department to finance Ruskin College's correspondence courses for members of the armed services.[21] By all accounts, the armed forces scheme was an enormous success. By spring 1941, the War Office was funding 20 lectureships, as well as meeting the WEA's organising costs; some 4,200 lectures and 700 classes had been offered in January 1941 alone.[22]

The WEA was also quick to recognise the needs of people displaced by the war. In the autumn of 1939, it had developed localised provision for evacuees from the industrial areas, refugees from Czechoslovakia and civil defence workers.[23] During the blitz, classes were offered in London bomb shelters, and then elsewhere, including the Chislehurst caves in Kent.[24] In spring 1941, the Scottish District agreed to organise pioneer classes for industrial workers in hostels and camps.[25] In the autumn, national negotiations between the WEA, the Ministry of Supply and the Workers' Travel Association led to a scheme of adult education for migrant war workers living in government hostels.[26] Over the winter, the Districts considered proposals for a national scheme for the civil defence services.[27] By July 1942, ten Districts had offered around 100 courses for civil defence personnel and workers in war hostels; further growth was halted only by a shortage of tutors.[28] By January 1943, all Districts were involved in work with civil defence personnel, and some 346 classes had attracted over 7,500 participants. Over 100 courses had been arranged in war workers' hostels, plus 290 single lectures.[29] Yorkshire South District provided 25 lectures for firefighters in 1943–4 alone.[30] In Glasgow, the programme for civil defence workers included eight discussion groups along with continuing classes in drama, modern history and economics.[31] After the Allied invasion of France, the Eastern District proposed to work with German prisoners of war, to the reported consternation of the Foreign Office which claimed that WEA classes might infringe the prisoners' rights under the Geneva Convention.[32] In each case, the WEA asked for additional resources – often including the appointment of organisers – to undertake the work. As a result, the staff of the Association grew steadily between 1941 and 1945.

Finally, of course, branch work continued. Perhaps the best way of illustrating what happened is to look more closely at one locality. Yorkshire South District was relatively young, having been created when the old Yorkshire District was divided in 1929. By the time the war broke out, the District had 37 branches with 1,044 members and 22 affiliated societies; by 1944–5 there were 41 branches, 29 affiliations and 1,524 members. The overall growth rate was impressive, but it masked considerable churning; three branches, for instance, closed during the war (all in mining areas) and four more (also in pit communities) lost membership. With the sheer practical difficulties facing an ever more stretched body of tutors, voluntary activity was essential; where there was no branch life, the District was unable to mount a programme.[33]

Perhaps because of its location, the District maintained its activities largely undamaged by the outbreak of war. The last unemployed summer school was held at Hope, in 1939. In most other respects, the District simply altered emphasis, providing growing numbers of one-year and terminal courses, brains trusts, wireless groups, concerts and single lectures.[34] The District even sustained its summer schools, which were switched from Aberystwyth to Ashford, in the Peak District, where the staff and students slept in villagers' homes and ate in the village institute, and met in the chapel and school.[35] By 1945–6, though, the District had restored the balance, with a larger proportion of students in three-year tutorial classes than in 1939. In a particularly striking development, the District transformed itself into a campaigning body, throwing itself into rallies and lobbies on behalf of school reform and the Beveridge Report.

War also brought about changes in subject balance. While the mainstays in South Yorkshire continued to be industrial history, literature, economics and current affairs, from 1942 there was a leavening of courses around aspects of reconstruction. However, one experienced economics tutor recalls that even when established subjects formally remained as before, they 'lost shape' as tutors and students alike sought direct, contemporary relevance from their reflections.[36] The student body also changed somewhat, though the District remained overwhelmingly an organisation for working-class people: 44 per cent of all students were manual workers in 1944–5, a tiny decline from 46 per cent in 1938–9. Colliers accounted for 28 per cent of the student body when war broke out, and 24 per cent when it ended and, although there was some growth in the number of white-collar members (particularly clerical workers and school teachers), the most significant change was the influx of women. By 1945, for example, the category unhelpfully described as 'home duties and nursing' had almost overtaken coal miners as the largest single occupational group. Before the war, women had been a majority of students in only one District, North Lancashire and Cheshire. By 1945, the proportion of classes with a majority of women was sufficiently routine to attract comment from the Association of Tutors in Adult Education.[37]

The war also witnessed a partial feminisation of the WEA staff. In general, the WEA tried to protect its largely male organising staff from conscription, and to some extent it was successful. Still, wartime conditions opened opportunities for able women. The South-eastern District appointed Mrs Ivy Cooper-Marsh (a head teacher who had been made to resign on marriage) as acting district secretary in June 1941, replacing a male incumbent who had moved.[38] Mary Stocks became editor of *The Highway* in 1941, following the resignation of W. E. Williams (though two men were offered, and turned down, the post first).[39] A female organiser was appointed to lead pioneer work in Aberdeenshire in September 1941, and another proved outstanding at organising in hostels in Staffordshire.[40] Elizabeth Monkhouse (see plate 8), then of the Eastern District, led a famously successful programme of pioneer courses among construction workers living in hostels in Scotland.[41] The Scottish District subsequently appointed Monkhouse to a tutor-organiser post in North East Scotland (with a second woman taking a similar post in Glasgow).[42] When the Scottish District secretary became eligible for call-up, it was agreed that Monkhouse might stand in.[43]

In experimenting with new approaches to teaching and learning, the WEA was risking its history. In 1939, the CEC had agreed to a Board of Education suggestion that tutors should be discouraged from using broadcast talks as part of normal class activity.[44] In his earliest proposals for adult education in the armed forces, Green accepted that much would need to be 'of a pioneer character'.[45] Pioneer work, for the WEA, meant educational activities of a type not usually undertaken by the WEA (and, by implication, not covered by the Board of Education's regulations for funding purposes). Tutorial class teaching methods were never likely to work with these new groups. In a statement on the WEA's educational policy in wartime, the CEC accepted that it must be willing to learn from the experience of war, and modify its arrangements where relevant, in particular by offering short courses and single lectures.[46] In 1941 a Miss A. W. Smith reported from Scotland on the success of small-group work combined with the appointment of discussion leaders in a programme with women assigned to searchlight units.[47] In a pamphlet designed to present its work to people serving with the armed forces, the CAC spoke of 'growing interest in problems of reconstruction' combined with strong demand for 'short courses', with a preference for 'regular meetings of discussion groups' rather than lectures followed by question and answer sessions.[48] Yet, it was precisely the latter (along with regular written work) that the WEA had vigorously defended for much of its existence. The three-year tutorial class certainly did not disappear, but it was increasingly accompanied by new approaches.

As well as supporting the Ruskin correspondence scheme, the Association also developed its own resource-based learning. In 1940 the WEA launched a series of study outlines for groups such as trade union branches, and people serving as ARP wardens, for whom 'the organisation of formal classwork was not practicable'.[49] So popular were these that, despite paper shortages, several outlines had to be reprinted shortly after publication. Training for discussion group leaders was subsequently developed for use with ARP personnel and firefighters, leading to a decision to issue pamphlets on the conduct of discussion groups accompanied by a series of study outlines edited by Thomas Hodgkin.[50]

Of course, these changes had implications for funding. Public grant was only available for defined activities, strictly codified in regulations approved by the Board of Education. The central joint advisory committee reached agreement with the Board of Education on relaxation of the regulations in the autumn of 1940, so part of the grant could be reserved for 'informal activities'.[51] In 1942 the Association asked the Board to consider recognising classes that were undertaking surveys and other projects on reconstruction.[52] In many ways, the practice of adult education was taken forward substantially as a result of the new approaches, but by and large the Association thought of these changes as temporary adjustments. Once at peace, the predominant desire was to return as soon as possible to the old alliance with the universities, rooted in the tutorial class model.[53]

IDEOLOGY AND CONTROL

From the second year of the war, the WEA thrived. Its activities widened, its influence deepened and its reputation grew. The 1945 election, as already noted, marked a high point in the Association's achievements. Was this success earned at a terrible price? Had the WEA earned its wartime position at the cost of its independence?[54] Did it really kneel, as Fieldhouse alleges, before a largely conservative establishment?

Fieldhouse claims that the WEA's work with the armed forces was particularly vulnerable to powerful ideological pressures. He also suggests that the WEA was ultimately forced to bend to a climate in which independent, critical teaching was weeded out,[55] with the Home Command's role in the army scheme amounting to a 'political filter'. He provides a list of 'categories of tutors who were not acceptable to the Services', including all those expressing views that the military authorities 'considered subversive'.[56] This echoes the contemporary claims of J. P. M. Millar, secretary of the NCLC and perpetual enemy of the WEA, who saw the services education programme as confirming that the WEA was: 'For all practical purposes ... part of the state's educational machinery'.[57] For Millar, servicemen and women enrolled by the CAC were all 'conscripts', unmasking the WEA as a true ally of Colonel Blimp.[58] Fieldhouse's formulation presents a similarly crude and unsatisfactory view. Not only does it ignore evidence that interference from the armed services' chiefs was extremely limited and generally unsuccessful; it also runs together different periods in the war, and assumes that popular demands went entirely unheard for the full six years of armed conflict. Neither interpretation is consistent with the evidence.

There were certainly occasional attempts at controlling the armed forces programmes, but most came to nothing. At the outset, it was agreed that class attendance should be voluntary, and that the scheme should enjoy 'complete academic freedom'.[59] In the early years of the war, the WEA stood up to the Army Command on several occasions. It fought an attempt in Scotland to insist that the names of lecturers be submitted beforehand to the military authorities.[60] Early in 1941 there was a dispute between the WEA and the military authorities, who had withdrawn the permits of three lecturers on security grounds. Two permits were duly restored, but the Home Command in the Southern District refused to allow the third (J. R. Armstrong, a known pacifist and nudist) on to its premises. Although Armstrong was not a WEA employee, the Regional Council's work ground to a halt.[61] In a separate incident, the Association successfully backed a District facing down a chief air raid warden who was blocking classes in political studies.[62]

By the time the blitz was over, the Home Command had decisively accepted that its adult education classes would hear from all shades of political opinion. The London regional committee's panel of lecturers, for example, included entries for retired colonels, university lecturers, musicians, refugees and writers. Among these was the notoriously anti-communist and misogynistic novelist Arthur Koestler. Yet it also listed one J. T. Murphy (occupation given as 'inspector of factories'), whose background was solemnly given as 'leader of C.P. 1921–32; London correspondent of *Pravda* 1925–32'. Murphy was willing to speak on a long list of topics, including international reconstruction. Tom Wintringham, a communist and specialist on guerrilla fighting (listed as 'o.c. of O.T.C. International Brigade, Spain, 1937'), was also on the panel, offering lectures on 'methods of hunting tanks'.[63]

Nor were the armed services homogeneous. None of the services could have coped without promoting officers from backgrounds that might have seemed inappropriate in peacetime, including several WEA veterans. George Wigg, who had served as a regular soldier before becoming district secretary in North Staffordshire before the war, became a captain in the Army Education Corps. Addressing the CEC in spring 1941, Wigg complained that some Districts 'had not entered wholeheartedly into the work of Army Education', and urged them to develop courses 'informing the men on what the Nazi system stood for, and how it arose'.[64] Nor were all conscripts budding socialists; among other things, the WEA had to consider how it handled complaints of left-wing bias not only from Home Command but also from ordinary servicemen and women, along with others who choked with fury at any criticism of the Soviet Union.[65]

Fieldhouse suggests that, although direct intervention failed, all the pressures induced a general 'wariness and caution' which promoted conformity with establishment views.[66] There was indeed caution, at least in the early years of the war. For example, the Association circulated the CAC regional committees on what to do in cases of 'alleged indiscretion'.[67] Basic prudence, though, does not seem to have inhibited a wide range of views; for example, the CEC debated a new study outline on trade unionism in wartime, and after weighing up the arguments referred the decision back to the joint publications committee.[68] When *Trade Unionism and the New Social Order* eventually appeared in autumn 1942, it promptly sold out, and went into instant reprint.[69]

More generally, WEA–government relationships changed when the Conservative administration under Chamberlain gave way to the wartime coalition under Churchill. One episode cited by Fieldhouse involved a cautiously worded report by HMIs Dann and Jack on the teaching of 'controversial topics' in adult education, which then served as the basis for an internal minute in the Board of Education. This happened in early 1940.[70] At this stage, though, the WEA leadership was also cautious about the government. It refused an invitation from the Ministry of Information (MoI) to co-operate on a lecture service, explaining that 'the one thing it [the WEA] must do was retain its independence.'[71] Eventually, it agreed that, while the MoI might support public lectures, any funds would have to be passed through the Board of Education, and the WEA would maintain freedom to select lecturers, including individuals who had not been approved by the MoI.[72] Following the appointment of the coalition, the WEA's relationship with senior civil servants gradually changed. After a dispute between the WEA and a local chief warden, for example, the Ministry of Home Security wrote to all its civil defence staff recommending that they co-operate with the Association.[73] As with the Army Education Corps, several ministries appointed WEA staff whose skills might help mobilise the wider population behind the war (the MoI recruited the secretary of the South-eastern District into its Film Service in early 1941).[74]

Following receipt of the Dann and Jack report, the Board of Education enquired in summer 1940 about the WEA's treatment of 'subjects of strong political interest'. In response, the CEC reaffirmed the Association's views on academic freedom:

The principle which should guide Tutors is the same in war time as always. There is no obligation on a Tutor, any more than an individual student, to conceal from the class his personal opinion on burning questions which may come up for discussion. But it is his business to avoid propaganda, conscious or unconscious, and to be scrupulous not to use the class or allow the class to be used as a means of making converts to particular beliefs. ... That would at all times be an offence against the principles of the movement; and in the immediate future it is liable to imperil freedom of discussion throughout the whole field of adult education.[75]

The Association published study outlines by the likes of Walter Kendall, an iconoclastic and independently-minded Marxist; the communist Thomas Hodgkin edited bulletins for civil defence discussion leaders.[76]

There were tensions and conflicts aplenty. However, the evidence overwhelmingly depicts a WEA whose pragmatism was always tempered by the broadly left-leaning views of its leadership. For Fieldhouse, the Association's sin lay not in what it did not do: it failed to teach 'the revolutionary ideology of a fully fledged Marxist class analysis'.[77] It is true that there is a distinctly reformist whiff over programmes of lectures in Land Army hostels, projects on recon- struction in Yorkshire pit villages, and discussion circles on Beveridge's plans for a welfare state. Increasingly, the staple activities of the WEA provided a forum for serious-minded citizens to explore the ways in which they believed a peacetime Britain could and should seize the opportunities of reconstruction. Yet, the end result was rather to help stamp the great struggle into the wider consciousness as one not simply between two sets of powers, but as a people's war. Once the war was over, and reconstruction was under way, the people would require educated leaders who had thought carefully about such matters as housing, urban planning, and employment, who appreciated the need for free school meals and raising the school- leaving age, and who understood them in a broader social, economic and political context.

## WORKERS' EDUCATION vs. ADULT EDUCATION

In the late 1930s the WEA's leadership saw its alliance with the universities as the intellectual pinnacle of British adult education. Ernest Green had been general secretary for a decade when war broke out, and he was uncompromising in his defence of quality as against quantity. In his view, attempting to provide for the mass of working people – even the minority belonging to trade unions – would simply dilute standards. As Elsdon has noted, Green always wrote of Adult Education with upper case initials, thereby denoting the tutorial classes provided through the WEA and the universities.[78] War brought an immediate requirement for the WEA to adapt to new circumstances, and almost immediately the leadership was forced to decide whether it would gain more than it might lose by co-operating with other providers from whom it had previously stayed aloof. While it accepted that the argument for co-operation was tactically advantageous, the WEA's leadership was also keen not to lose sight of the Association's own best interests. This helped create the basis for barely-suppressed conflicts that were bound to emerge as soon as wartime conditions ended.

The WEA's pugnacity in defence of its turf against incursions from the left, and particularly from its rivals in the Plebs League and Labour Colleges, is well documented.[79] Its vigorous assertion of its claims over other adult education providers is less widely acknowledged. Yet, despite pressures for co-operation, relationships between the adult education organisations were tense from the outset. As early as October 1939, Green was worried that BIAE might offer to provide educational activities in the armed forces.[80] There was a more serious conflict with the YMCA, who initially developed the proposals leading to the army education scheme. While manoeuvring to maintain a leading role, WEA officers worried lest the YMCA's initial lead should in any way weaken their position. WEA national education officer Harold Shearman expressed public irritation in 1941 over the YMCA's claims, stressing that this was 'a co-operative scheme', and claiming that

The actual initiative from which the scheme developed, was taken by the WEA in the spring of 1939. ... though it is by no means always recognized in accounts which appear elsewhere of the original development of the scheme.[81]

Although exaggerated, Shearman's account contained a kernel of truth. Not only had the Association sought in spring 1939 for the Board of Education to fund educational work 'inside the Camps', but it had already suggested it 'would be able to co-operate with the YMCA, which had considerable experience in the last war'.[82] Subsequently, Green had drafted a detailed proposal for 'Education in Militia Camps and Camps for Conscientious Objectors'. However, the CEC Minutes record that: 'The matter was considered urgent as bodies not recognised by the Board of Education as "Approved" bodies were interesting themselves in the question.'[83] The WEA, and Green in particular, were already evidently anxious about the possibility of being outflanked by other bodies.

Although the WEA encouraged Districts to offer lectures to the services after the outbreak of war, it was essentially still acting alone, and its response to an offer of collaboration from the YMCA was distinctly bureaucratic, not to say frosty.[84] After reading an early proposal for libraries, discussion groups and other educational activities to be provided as 'mental comfort for the forces', Green wrote dismissively: 'I do not know who has framed the phrase "Mental Comforts for the Troops", but it seems to me a gross insult.' In fact, as Green surely knew, the proposal and phrase came from W. E. Williams, secretary to the British Institute of Adult Education (BIAE).[85] When the CAC was finally created, the YMCA's organiser, Basil Yeaxlee, became its part-time secretary, which can have done nothing to soothe ruffled feathers in the WEA. Green wrote privately in 1940 that there was

far too much YMCA atmosphere about the whole thing and a tendency for it to be turned into a popular lecture scheme with no recognition of educational standards whatever.[86]

In public, though, the Association's leaders had to swallow their pride.

Subsequently, the WEA found itself overtaken by events again during the creation of the Army Bureau of Current Affairs (ABCA). In setting up ABCA in 1941, the Army Education Corps recruited W. E. Williams (secretary of the British Institute of Adult Education) as secretary, and announced proposals for a general education in citizenship for troops. Green was furious at the War Office's failure to consult the WEA, and urged the CAC to refuse co-operation in its early stages.[87] This was all the more embarrassing to the WEA given that Williams was editor of *The Highway*; his offer to resign was rapidly accepted.[88] However, in a draft memorandum that Tawney had toned down, Green had already tried to oust Williams in June 1940, complaining that the journal was 'used to propagate personal theories of the Editor which are not shared by the Association as a whole, nor in line with its general policy'.[89] This episode simply increased the WEA's willingness to view other players on the field of adult education as potential threats, and in turn the WEA came to be regarded as a byword for complacent arrogance.

Mutual suspicion damaged irrevocably the prospects of collaboration over post-war policy for adult education. Brendan Evans has noted with surprise the absence of adult education as a campaigning issue in the later years of the war, at a time when the adult education organisations were actively crusading for reform of the British education system. Neither the 1943 White Paper nor the 1944 act used the term 'adult education', which was dealt with along with vocational training under the phrase 'further education'. The fact that the WEA went along with this, suggests Evans, 'bordered on complacency'.[90] Research into archival evidence suggests that the WEA had acted deliberately, in what must now be seen as a misguided attempt to outflank its rivals.

In 1943 the WEA officers sabotaged an attempt to draft proposals for a broadly based system of post-war adult education. In an account based both on the newly rediscovered archives of the Educational Settlements Association (ESA), and on Board of Education correspondence with the key actors, Konrad Elsdon has reconstructed this episode in considerable detail.[91] Elsdon suggests that serious debate over post-war adult education followed the somewhat cautious distribution (to a strictly limited audience) of the Board of Education's *Green Book* on educational reconstruction. Wider conditions were also propitious for post-war planning, in that the Luftwaffe's bombing campaign had passed its peak, and the entry of the Soviet Union and United States had removed the prospect of a German invasion, or even conquest, as had seemed entirely possible for most of the previous two years. The lively reception of the *Green Book* persuaded the government to issue a White Paper on educational reconstruction in the summer of 1943.[92] There was a broad consensus among the adult education community that the White Paper was inadequate in its treatment of their area. Among those who lobbied and spoke were Sir Richard Livingstone, a classicist and president of Corpus Christi College, who had become a passionate advocate of residential adult education, and William Temple, the archbishop of Canterbury, who convened a small group to meet in Oxford in January 1944 to draft plans for post-war adult education. Their aim was to secure a statutory basis for a national adult education system, involving the creation of local adult education centres run jointly by local education authorities, universities, and voluntary organisations including the WEA, co-ordinated by an independent national adult education council.

Tawney and Green in particular detested this scheme.[93] The WEA's main concerns had, though, been identified internally well before the broader national debate around the *Green Book*. As early as summer 1941 the CEC had created a small committee, chaired by A. D. Lindsay, master of Balliol College, to consider proposals for post-war adult education policy.[94] An initiative by BIAE to create a small committee on post-war adult education was given conditional support, on the understanding that it would report to the bodies that had sent delegates to the committee in the first place. In the WEA officers' view, 'it was inadvisable for such a committee to make a direct approach to the Board'.[95] In October 1941, Green drafted a confidential note on the 'dangers' of 'co-ordination' as proposed by the Board in the *Green Book* and elsewhere. For Green, the armed forces scheme showed:

> The danger to educational standards and social objective in trying to co-ordinate bodies which have such serious purpose with those whose entrance into the field of Adult Education could certainly be challenged if standards of work and social purpose were the criteria.[96]

The WEA's own committee met periodically over the following year, despite considerable disruption to transport. While it reached a consensus on the broad shape of a post-war system, it disagreed over the problem 'of co-ordination, and how this could be achieved while, at the same time, maintaining the independence and rights of the Association as a providing body'.[97] The sub-committee's report was subsequently amended by the CEC to remove references to the National Council of Social Service; and it attracted instant objections from the YMCA.[98] If there were not enough tensions already, Green then resigned from the BIAE's post-war planning committee, claiming that its recommendations were unacceptable.[99]

According to Green, Temple's plans for the Oxford meeting were circulated to the CEC at its meeting on 18 December 1943. If this was the case, it was not recorded at the time, and the first minuted discussion in the CEC was at the following meeting in February.[100] At this stage, Green was urging that no WEA delegate should be sent to the follow-up conference, which was subsequently cancelled.[101] The CEC then decided that Green himself should go to the next meeting, a much smaller affair than originally planned, and held in April 1944.[102] This meeting in turn appointed a small Standing Joint Conference on Adult Education, and the WEA (whose two delegates were Shearman and Green) duly took on the administrative task of arranging its next meeting, which took place in February 1945.[103] Green was still dissatisfied, however, reporting that the Board of Education had bypassed this process and 'consulted certain people about a National Institute of Adult Education'.[104]

It takes two to make a fight, and the WEA was not the only organisation pursuing its own interests. Among the WEA's friends, A. D. Lindsay proved unreliable. In 1941, Lindsay broke ranks with Green's hoped-for boycott of ABCA, sending Williams the names of possible tutors.[105] Two years later Lindsay joined Williams in drafting a British Association for the Advancement of Science report on post-war adult education in the universities. Defenders of the WEA position would have been alarmed by the report, which urged the universities to broaden their range of partnerships to include LEAs, and possibly replace the local joint committees with new adult education councils of some sort.[106] The University of Wales tried to withdraw from its existing arrangements with the WEA, an irritation which rumbled inconclusively on throughout the war.[107] Senior figures in the British Institute of Adult Education had expressed concern in autumn 1942 over the WEA's stance in respect of its own post-war planning group. According to one BIAE officer, 'too many educational bodies are preoccupied with ways and means of enlarging their own particular sphere of influence', with the risk that they would fail to learn 'from the several momentous experiments in popular education which this war has produced'.[108]

There were, then, good grounds for the WEA to feel threatened. Yet even to friends, the WEA's arguments sometimes sounded rather precious. A draft statement of the WEA's views on the war, approved by the CEC in June 1940, emphasised that the WEA's importance to the country was not to be measured solely by the number of its students but by their 'knowledge and power of self expression', which allowed them to 'enlighten and arouse a far wider circle'.[109] When the Association agreed to order 500 copies of Sir Richard Livingstone's *The Future in Education*, the general secretary proposed that the publisher should insert a statement to the effect that the WEA was 'not committed' to the views of the author; the FGP committee changed this to 'not necessarily committed'. Despite this qualified embrace, the membership bought the book in droves, and more copies had to be ordered.[110]

All of this feuding did the WEA considerable harm. In 1945, Sir Robert Wood, deputy secretary at the Board of Education, launched a remarkable attack on the WEA at the annual conference of the BIAE. His words were carefully coded, alluding to the 'intransigent tendencies of some of the voluntary bodies' who had successfully prevented attempts to secure co-ordinated provision of adult education after the war. Wood's comments were published by E. Salter-Davies, editor of the *Journal of Education*, who came from a local government background. Salter-Davies, contrasting the fate of the Temple proposals with the creation of the United Nations, claimed that the development of British adult education had been hindered by 'the apparent insistence of the WEA that it must always be accepted as the dominant power in any educational alliance', and insisted that 'a discussion group in a community centre is a no less vital kind of adult education than a university tutorial class'.[111] This theme was echoed by H. C. Dent, editor of the *Times Educational Supplement*. In a leading article, Dent stated that few would be found to 'challenge the justice of this indictment', and urged that the voluntary organisations should 'meet, with the same integrity of purpose as the work demands, the changing need provoked by new conceptions of the wider purposes of education'.[112]

At one level Green found it easy to repudiate the charges laid against the WEA, writing to the journals to claim that the Association was an enthusiastic partner in Temple's initiative.[113] Yet, as Dent pointed out, both the press coverage and Wood's original comments reflected a 'widespread conviction' in the field that the WEA was insisting on taking a leading role in adult education policy-making, then using that position to prevent public funding for other forms of adult education than the tutorial class.[114] If Dent was right, the WEA had managed to alienate a significant number of people who otherwise would have helped ensure that the WEA would assume a significant (if not necessarily the pre-eminent) place within a national adult education system. At the least, it demonstrated an organisational sectarianism and lack of vision that was extremely short-sighted, and ultimately did the WEA itself little good.

## CONCLUSIONS

At the outset of war, the WEA's activities were at risk, and its very survival was threatened. Over time, however, the Association managed to find a role for itself as a provider of education for service personnel, the civil defence services and civilian adults alike, while preserving what it could of its established partnership with the universities. It also carved out a place for itself as an advocate of post-war educational reconstruction. Whether serving as provider or advocate, the WEA thereby helped to promote and underpin the popular quality of the war, and shaped the way in which the war's objectives were redefined in terms of civic reconstruction rather than military strategy and geopolitical power.

It is important, however, not to present this in too positive a light. This chapter shows that in promoting what they saw as a most significant form of adult education, the WEA's leaders were fiercely protective of their guardianship of the intellectual high ground, and equally quick to pounce on any threat. In doing so, they profoundly alienated many other advocates of adult education, and arguably weakened the collective case for adult education as a key component of post-war reconstruction. Further, they firmly insisted that the best in adult education had a particular shape and size – namely the three-year tutorial class with a university teacher and compulsory written work. This was an admirably principled stand, but it meant that the WEA as an organisation was unable to learn collectively from the experience of innovation. The WEA's wartime activity with adults in industry, the armed forces and the civil defence services was written off as a short-term tactic, a concession to necessity, rather than as a rich and powerful laboratory in which new approaches might be tested. As a result, the Association not only earned itself a reputation for educational conservatism, but found itself increasingly outflanked in the later 1940s by other collective actors.

## NOTES

*Place of publication London unless otherwise stated.*

1. R. Fieldhouse, 'The Workers' Educational Association', in Fieldhouse and Associates, *History*, 178.
2. Mary Stocks calculated that in 1945 14 members of the government were tutors, former tutors or members of the WEA executive while 56 MPs were active in the WEA: Stocks, 143; see also B. Jennings, *Knowledge is Power: A Short History of the WEA 1903–78* (Hull, 1979).
3. Jennings, *Knowledge is Power*.
4. Fieldhouse, 'Workers' Educational Association', 177–8.
5. A. Calder, *The People's War: Britain 1939–1945* (1966).
6. National Archive, WEA CENTRAL/3/5/1, Green to Branch Secretaries, 29 Sept. 1938, 1 Oct. 1938.
7. WEA Yorkshire South, *Twenty-first Annual Report* (Sheffield, 1950).
8. WEA CENTRAL/1/2/1/19, WEA CEC minutes, 18 Mar. 1939.

9. G. D. H. Cole, 'The Watch on the Home Front', *The Highway* xxxii (1945), 9–10.
10. WEA CENTRAL/1/2/1/19, WEA CEC minutes, 18 Nov. 1939.
11. H. C. Shearman, 'The First Months: The WEA Carries On', *Adult Education* xii (1939), 77–84.
12. WEA CENTRAL/3/5/2, H. J. Orgar, class secretary's report, 30 May 1940.
13. WEA CENTRAL/1/2/1/20, WEA FGP minutes, 6 June 1941.
14. WEA Northern Ireland Offices, Fitzwilliam Street, Belfast, WETUC Northern Ireland divisional committee minutes, 23 June 1943.
15. WEA CENTRAL/1/2/1/19, WEA CEC minutes, 30 Nov. 1940.
16. WEA CENTRAL/3/5/2, E. H. Green, 'The WEA and the Crisis', 24 June 1940.
17. E. H. Green, 'The WEA and the Crisis', 24 June 1940; see also WEA CENTRAL/1/2/1/19, CEC minutes 29 June 1940.
18. A. J. Corfield, *Epoch in Workers' Education: A History of the Workers' Education Trade Union Committee* (1969), 72.
19. WEA CENTRAL/1/2/1/19, WEA CEC minutes, 20 May 1939.
20. WEA CENTRAL/1/2/1/19, WEA CEC minutes, 3 Feb. 1940.
21. WEA CENTRAL/1/2/1/21, WEA CEC minutes, 5 July 1941.
22. WEA CENTRAL/1/2/1/21, WEA CEC minutes, 1 Mar. 1941.
23. H. C. Sherman, 'The First Months: The WEA Carries On', *Adult Education* xii (1939), 82.
24. H. C. Shearman, 'The WEA in the Second Year', *Adult Education* xiii (1941), 190.
25. WEA CENTRAL/1/2/1/21, WEA CEC minutes, 1 Mar. 1941; WEA Scotland, *Twenty-third Annual Report, 1940–41*.
26. WEA CENTRAL/1/2/1/21, WEA CEC minutes, 5 July 1941, 8 Nov. 1941.
27. WEA CENTRAL/1/2/1/21, WEA CEC minutes, 8 Nov. 1941, 10 Jan. 1942.
28. WEA CENTRAL/1/2/1/21, WEA CEC minutes, 11 July 1942, 24 Oct. 1942.
29. WEA CENTRAL/1/2/1/21, WEA CEC minutes, 16 Jan.1943.
30. WEA Yorkshire South District, *Fifteenth Annual Report* (Sheffield, 1944).
31. WEA Scotland, *Twenty-sixth Annual Report, 1943–44*.
32. WEA CENTRAL/1/2/1/21, WEA CEC minutes, 14/15 July 1944, 17 Nov. 1944.
33. WEA Yorkshire South District, *Twelfth Annual Report* (Sheffield, 1941).
34. WEA Yorkshire South District, *Fifteenth Annual Report* (Sheffield, 1944).
35. Interview, Dick and Olive Whittington, Bessacar, 21 Dec. 1988.
36. Interview, Joseph Roper, Rotherham, 12 Oct. 1988.
37. 'Comment', *The Tutor's Bulletin of Adult Education* (July 1946), 4.
38. WEA CENTRAL/1/2/1/20, WEA FGP minutes, 6 June 1941.
39. WEA CENTRAL/1/2/1/20, WEA FGP minutes, 30 Sept. 1941.
40. WEA CENTRAL/1/2/1/20, WEA FGP minutes, 30 Sept. 1941, 19 Aug. 1942.
41. WEA CENTRAL/1/2/1/21, WEA CEC minutes, 24 Oct. 1942.
42. WEA CENTRAL/1/2/1/20, WEA FGP minutes, 9 Feb. 1943.
43. WEA CENTRAL/1/2/1/20, WEA FGP minutes, 18 Mar. 1943.
44. WEA CENTRAL/1/2/1/19, WEA CEC minutes, 18 Mar. 1939.

45. WEA CENTRAL/1/2/1/19, E. H. Green, 'Education in Militia Camps and Camps for Conscientious Objectors', 6 June 1939.
46. WEA CENTRAL/1/2/1/19, WEA CEC minutes, 29 June 1940.
47. WEA CENTRAL/1/2/1/21, WEA CEC minutes, 5 July 1941.
48. WEA CENTRAL/3/5/1, Central Advisory Council for Adult Education in HM Forces, no date (1941?).
49. WEA CENTRAL/1/2/1/19, WEA CEC minutes, 3 Feb. 1940.
50. WEA CENTRAL/1/2/1/21, WEA CEC minutes, 3 April 1943, 3 July 1943.
51. WEA CENTRAL/1/2/1/19, WEA CEC minutes, 14 Sept. 1940.
52. WEA CENTRAL/1/2/1/21, WEA CEC minutes, 11 July 1942.
53. Interview, Joseph Roper, Rotherham, 12 Oct. 1988.
54. Tom Steele describes 1945 as the point which 'finally induced the WEA to give up its class identity': 'From Class-consciousness to Cultural Studies: George Thompson and the WEA in Yorkshire', *Studies in the Education of Adults* xix (Leicester, 1987), 120.
55. Fieldhouse, 'The Workers' Educational Association' , 177–8.
56. Fieldhouse, 'Conformity and Contradiction in English Responsible Body Adult Education, 1925–1950', *Studies in the Education of Adults* xvii (1985), 126.
57. J. P. M. Millar, 'Do Your Own Thinking', *Plebs* xxxii (1940), 4; J. P. M. Millar, 'Propaganda and the Path to Power', *Plebs* xxxii (1940), 111.
58. J. P. M. Millar 'Statesmanship and Lying', *Plebs* xxxi, 169.
59. WEA CENTRAL/1/2/1/19, WEA CEC minutes, 3 Feb 1940.
60. WEA CENTRAL/1/2/1/19, WEA CEC minutes, 6 Apr. 1940.
61. WEA CENTRAL/1/2/1/21, WEA CEC minutes, 1 Mar. 1941.
62. WEA CENTRAL/1/2/1/21, WEA CEC minutes, 21 Mar. 1942.
63. London Regional Committee for Education among H.M. Forces, Panel of Lecturers (1944).
64. WEA CENTRAL/1/2/1/21, WEA CEC minutes, 21 Mar. 1942.
65. WEA CENTRAL/1/2/1/21, WEA CEC minutes, 5 July 1941.
66. Fieldhouse, 'Workers' Educational Association', 178; Fieldhouse, 'Conformity and Contradiction', 126–7.
67. WEA CENTRAL/1/2/1/21, WEA CEC minutes, 21 Mar. 1942.
68. WEA CENTRAL/1/2/1/19, WEA CEC minutes, 6 Apr. 1940.
69. WEA CENTRAL/1/2/1/21, WEA CEC minutes, 16 Jan. 1943.
70. Fieldhouse 'Conformity and Contradiction', 125–6.
71. WEA CENTRAL/1/2/1/19, WEA CEC minutes, 29 June 1940.
72. WEA CENTRAL/1/2/1/19, WEA CEC minutes, 14 Sept. 1940.
73. WEA CENTRAL/1/2/1/21, WEA CEC minutes, 29/30 May 1942.
74. WEA CENTRAL/1/2/1/20, WEA FGP minutes, 21 Mar. 1941.
75. WEA CENTRAL/1/2/1/19, WEA CEC minutes, 29 June 1940.
76. Kendall, who had been an extra-mural tutor for Sheffield until 1934, wrote Study Outline Number 5, *War and the Economic System* (1941).
77. R. Fieldhouse, 'The Ideology of English Adult Education Teaching 1925–50', *Studies in Adult Education* xv (1983), 28.
78. K. T. Elsdon, 'The Archbishop's Conference: Missed Opportunity or Vain Hope?', *Journal of Adult and Continuing Education* vii (2001), 14.
79. Fieldhouse, 'Workers' Educational Association', 166–84; L. Goldman, 'Intellectuals and the English working class 1870–1945: The Case of Adult Education', *History of Education* xxix (2000), 281–2.

80. WEA CENTRAL/3/5/2, E. Green to District Secretaries 3 Oct. 1939.
81. H. C. Shearman, 'The WEA in the Second Year', *Adult Education* xiii (1941), 191.
82. WEA CENTRAL/1/2/1/19, WEA CEC minutes, 20 May 1939.
83. WEA CENTRAL/1/2/1/19, WEA CEC minutes, 1 July 1939.
84. WEA CENTRAL/1/2/1/19, WEA CEC minutes, 18 Nov. 1939.
85. WEA CENTRAL/3/5/1, '"Mental Comforts" for the Forces: Memorandum by Mr W. E. Williams', n.d.; Green to Creech Jones, 19 Jan.1940.
86. WEA CENTRAL/3/5/1, E. Green to A. Creech Jones, 24 Sept. 1940.
87. WEA CENTRAL/1/2/1/21, WEA CEC minutes, 8 Nov. 1941.
88. WEA CENTRAL/1/2/1/20, WEA FGP minutes 8 Aug. 1941, 30 Sept. 1941.
89. WEA CENTRAL/3/5/2, E. H. Green 'The WEA and the Crisis', 24 June 1940; revised version 26 June 1940.
90. B. J. Evans, 'Further Education Pressure Groups: The Campaign for Adult Education in 1944', *Studies in Adult Education* xv, 92–102.
91. Elsdon, 'Archbishop's Conference', 13–29.
92. Board of Education, *White Paper on Educational Reconstruction* (1943).
93. Elsdon, 'Archbishop's Conference', 22–4.
94. WEA CENTRAL/1/2/1/21, WEA CEC minutes, 5 July 1941.
95. WEA CENTRAL/1/2/1/20, WEA FGP minutes, 30 Sept. 1941.
96. WEA CENTRAL/3/16, E. Green, 'Post War Adult Education: Problems for Consideration', 8 Oct. 1941.
97. WEA CENTRAL/1/2/1/21, WEA CEC minutes, 21 Mar. 1942.
98. WEA CENTRAL/1/2/1/21, WEA CEC minutes, 29/30 May 1942, 11 July 1942.
99. WEA CENTRAL/1/2/1/20, WEA FGP minutes, 9 Feb. 1943.
100. WEA CENTRAL/1/2/1/21, WEA CEC minutes, 18 Dec. 1943, 11 Feb. 1944; there was however a discussion at FGP: WEA CENTRAL/1/2/1/20, minutes, 17 Dec. 1943.
101. WEA CENTRAL/1/2/1/20, WEA FGP minutes, 2 March 1944.
102. WEA CENTRAL/1/2/1/21, WEA CEC minutes, 14/15 July 1944.
103. WEA CENTRAL/1/2/1/21, WEA CEC minutes, 17 Nov. 1944.
104. WEA CENTRAL/1/2/1/21, WEA CEC minutes, 21 April 1945.
105. WEA CENTRAL/1/2/1/21, WEA CEC minutes, 8 Nov. 1941.
106. WEA CENTRAL/3/17, British Association for the Advancement of Science, *Report on Universities and Adult Education*, 29 July 1943.
107. WEA CENTRAL/3/18, Green to WETUC members, 10 Oct. 1940; University Extension Board, University of Wales, Survey of Adult Education, 24 Sept. 1943.
108. 'Notes of the Quarter', *Adult Education* xv (1942), 3.
109. WEA CENTRAL/1/2/1/19, WEA CEC minutes, 29 June 1940.
110. WEA CENTRAL/1/2/1/20, WEA FGP minutes, 30 Sept. 1941, 6 Jan. 1942.
111. 'Notes and Comments', *Journal of Education* lxxvii (1945), 521–2.
112. 'Educating the Adult', *Times Educational Supplement*, 1 Dec. 1945.
113. *Times Educational Supplement* 8 Dec. 1945, *Journal of Education* lxxvii (1945), 588.
114. 'Comment in Brief', *Times Educational Supplement*, 8 Dec. 1945.

# 9 Unions, Adult Education and Post-war Citizenship: The WEA and the Construction of Trade Union Education

*John Holford*

'We are convinced that the WEA has learnt some all-important lessons in the way to educate for democracy'[1]

'How is this apathy to be overcome?'[2]

## INTRODUCTION

Something happened around the middle of the twentieth century which changed forever the WEA's relationship with the 'working class movement'. Through its first four decades or so, engagement with trade unions seemed second nature to WEA activists. When Mansbridge planned the 'Association to Promote the Higher Education of Working Men', his 'provisional committee' comprised 'Co-operators and trade unionists'.[3] At a meeting in Reading to establish what would become the first WEA branch, over 20 trade unions were represented.[4] In every town, trade unionists and active WEA members – many of them, at least – inhabited the same milieu of trade union, political and Co-operative meetings. It was clear to the Ministry of Reconstruction adult education committee that adult education developed 'most readily under conditions which facilitate the rapid development of other movements', and was 'weak where they are weak'.[5] For Mary Stocks, from a well-connected and well-to-do professional background, a welcome 'side-effect' of WEA teaching in the 1920s was a 'close association with the trade union movement, since most of the class members were keen trade unionists'.[6] The location of the WEA as part of the working-class or labour movement was, by common assumption, a fact of life.

By the 1950s a growing distance between WEA and trade unions was commonly noticed – if widely regretted. There were many indicators. In 1933 over 34 per cent of the students in WEA classes were manual workers; by 1951 it was under 19 per cent.[7] Between 1918 and 1943, the number of 'bodies' – chiefly trade unions – affiliated to the WEA declined by a quarter to just over 2,000. Since in the meantime the number of WEA branches had tripled, however, the average number of affiliations per WEA branch had fallen from over 13 to fewer than 3.[8] The trend was no secret. Eric Ashby described how

> here and there, in one place after another, a WEA Branch became moribund. It fell into the hands of a clique; it lost touch with the workers it was founded to serve and displaced them by the local bank manager, the schoolmaster, the curate, and the sort of cultivated ladies who flock to hear about bird watching and bring their knitting.[9]

In an influential contemporary book, Roy Lewis and Angus Maude saw the adult education movement growing from working-class roots, through university extension and polytechnics, 'until it culminated in that profoundly middle-class institution, the Workers' Educational Association'.[10] Were they teasing? Perhaps: but as Ashby's anecdote suggests, there was a kernel of truth.

What had happened? What should be done? WEA leaders faced these questions half a century ago; in this chapter we explore how they did so, and the answers they gave. We do so, however, from a particular angle. 'Where have all the workers gone?' was not an issue about trade unionists alone,[11] but the WEA's union links made them an unavoidable dimension. Educating trade unionists was not the WEA's private domain – others played a part – but the WEA's standing meant its thinking and decisions were significant. In its thinking, democratic aspirations mingled with practical needs. Although it was not clear at the time, the WEA was laying foundations for an approach – role education for union representatives – which dominated trade union education until at least the 1990s.

## WAR AND WORKERS' EDUCATION

In retrospect, the years before the Second World War seem the WEA's heroic age. When war broke out, an average of over 18 branches had been formed in each of the 35 years since the Association's formation: a total of 635. But war cast a different light. In a WEA leaflet of April 1940, R.H. Tawney saw democracy 'on the defensive'; its very survival at stake. '[We] must be determined', he argued, in what was almost a call to arms, 'that out of the welter of war and its sacrifices a real democracy and a new civilisation shall arise. ... It can only come if we multiply by tens of thousands the number of men and women capable of using the power which education alone can provide.'[12]

In this perspective, pre-war achievements seemed more modest, since

something like 18 million persons [are] insured under the National Health Insurance Acts and the total number of adults registered for all forms of further education in 1938 ... was just over half a million. Of those, less than one in every hundred were studying subjects which had a direct bearing on citizenship.[13]

Reflecting on the situation, wartime WEA leaders were struck by a contrast. Early WEA members had been the 'pick of the working class'. Their desire 'to learn about social, political and economic matters' stemmed from trade union and Co-operative activities. They were 'natural leaders', 'a small minority but ... of enormous importance'.[14] Three decades later, the quest for a new social order with education at its heart[15] called for a much larger cadre of active, engaged citizens. Unfortunately, workers' education now faced what its leaders saw as a general problem of working-class movements. Working-class élites – people like themselves – might lead, but ordinary working people seemed reluctant to follow. To the WEA, apathy about adult education seemed 'so widespread, the practical problem facing the movement is to stimulate demand'.[16]

In this light, trade unions presented just a particular case of a general problem. The 'cardinal weakness of most working class movements', according to a 1942 WEA pamphlet, was that 'the bulk of the members have no deep sense of loyalty to the organisation of which they are members', were 'often ignorant of its fundamental purpose' and 'took no active part in its administration'.[17] The trade union movement,

like all voluntary movements ... has its inactive members and its apathetic mass. Its problem, like that of all working class voluntary movements, is to inspire the mass of its membership with a sense of social responsibility.[18]

In the 'new social order' envisaged by Tawney and other wartime WEA leaders, working men and women would be central. There would be 'democracy in industry', as workers and trade unions took an active role in 'industrial control'.[19] The 'working class movement' should also be 'an educational force, potentially the most powerful instrument for ensuring the effective realisation of democratic responsibility'.[20] 'And ... the strongest single group ... if ... aroused and ... unanimously vocal in its demand for social justice', was 'the Trade Union Movement'.[21]

Would unions play this role? A 1942 WEA pamphlet on 'Trade Unionism and the New Social Order' suggested union membership 'may reach ten to twelve millions during the present war'. But wartime gains might be rapidly eroded as they had been after 1918. Was growth now to be

> a temporary acquisition of opportunists ... Or can it be ... used not merely to increase the size of the Trade Union Movement, but its power? The only way to ensure that the new membership becomes a source of strength is to educate it.[22]

If education was essential to union strength and to democracy, however, pre-war experience was not encouraging. By the late 1930s, the bulk of education for trades unionists was provided by three bodies: the WEA, its offspring and soulmate, the Workers' Educational Trade Union Committee (WETUC), and their sworn enemy, the National Council of Labour Colleges (NCLC).[23] Together, their provision was quite modest. In 1937–8, for example, 13,274 students attended NCLC classes,[24] and 4,459 the WETUC's.[25] For the WEA itself, we have no accurate figures on trade union students: 20,000 might be a reasonable estimate. This suggests that at most perhaps 40,000 trade unionists attended some kind of class offered by these bodies.[26] There were, however, over 6 million trade union members in 1938, over 4.6 million in TUC-affiliated unions,[27] and the classes were diverse in duration, teaching approach, quality and subject-matter.[28]

THE LESSONS OF WARTIME

In a 1942 Memorandum to the Board of Education, the WEA offered some sharp self-criticism. Its own experience 'proved that where the W.E.A. has experimented in "popularising" in its own special field of adult education, the effort has ended where it began and has led to no sustained educational activity'.[29] This was a circle to be squared. Fortunately, early in the war, new educational opportunities seemed to be emerging: changed social circumstances – military discipline, bombing, rationing and so forth; questioning of social institutions, as when 'evacuation shows up our failure to plan'.[30]

A deeply significant shift in thinking was taking place. In the pre-war WEA and WETUC, quality had come before quantity. Ernest Green, secretary of both through the 1930s and 1940s, had taken the view that 'long-term systematic work and high educational standards were the essence of workers' education'.[31] Efforts went into serious, academic class teaching, and into organising longer rather than shorter courses. During the 1930s the number of WETUC three-year 'tutorial' and one-year 'sessional' classes grew by between 50 and 100 per cent; the number of day and weekend schools remained more or less constant.[32] This approach was clearly not going to meet the WEA's new aims.

What new opportunities emerged? In 1941 T. L. Hodgkin described three new lines of development: educational work in the armed forces; lectures and classes among civil defence groups, and 'talks on Food and news-talks in factories'. He saw these as having three common characteristics:

- students had typically left school at 14, had no previous contact with adult education, and – without the 'conditions produced by the war'- would probably not have had any;
- classes were 'based on occupational groupings' and held in the workplace, so that 'a certain amount of group-consciousness already exists';
- there was a 'common focus of interest' and 'obvious starting point for discussion' in the war itself, and courses could 'turn upon problems directly relating to the war'.[33]

This seemed to answer the conundrum. If the Association were serious about 'creating an educated democracy', it was 'of vital importance to develop its educational work beyond the limits of the existing body of students'.[34]

Of course, 'standards' were not easily set aside. From the days of Mansbridge and the Oxford Conference, WEA commitment to the tutorial class had been instinctive.[35] Hodgkin distinguished between 'purposive' (i.e., not mere entertainment) and 'advanced' (rather than simple) education. News talks and short courses might be 'fairly simple' but they were not superficial.

> Problems such as that of the relation between Nazism and the German people, or the conditions of realizing a stable European order, or the economic issues involved in paying for the war, [were] ... purposive education since they involve an attempt to understand the nature of the social forces operating within the world in which we live. On the other hand, they ... can [and must] be treated in a simple and lucid way, ... in groups of this kind if students are to recognize them as having meaning and importance for themselves.[36]

The WEA developed a similar argument, in effect redefining 'standards'. The number of 'men and women capable of accepting moral responsibility and leadership in the democratic institutions of community life' must be 'considerably increased',[37] but 'popularising' the tutorial and sessional class would achieve this. Standards would be assured provided that 'the student contribute[d] to his own education by certain standards of intellectual discipline'.[38]

> The revolutionary events of the past few years have ... created a ferment in the minds of thousands of men and women who can never hope to aspire to leadership, but whose education is of vital importance if they are to know how to co-operate in strengthening the democratic way of life.[39]

Among this 'wider public' there was 'scope for activities of a more informal kind' which could be 'designed to stimulate mental effort' and therefore 'related to definite standards'. It was 'pioneer work': not 'an end in itself but a means to developing an interest in more advanced study'. It was also – a key feature from a WEA perspective – an avenue by which students should find 'scope for voluntary and social activity'.[40]

As the years passed, these dimensions were redefined, reinterpreted, often fudged, but this tension – standards and quality on the one hand, new opportunities and building a new social order on the other – was to prove lasting and intractable.

## TRAINING FOR DEMOCRATIC LEADERSHIP

New wartime experiences continued to fuel these perspectives. In part it was a triumph of the adult educational will, a victory of unbridled optimism over the modest realities of the pre-war record, but there was real achievement. The WETUC reflected in 1944 that the WEA's

> co-operation during the war in Army Education, and its experiments in Civil Defence work, work among Women's Land Army and Munitions Hostels on Government Building Sites, have catered for far more students that all the Trade Union Schemes no matter through what agency they have been provided. [T]he informal approach through Discussion Classes and short course classes, has brought into the Movement thousands of students who would not have been approached through the normal grant-earning classes.[41]

The new opportunities presented by the war, and required for the 'new social order', were not all of this kind. The WETUC also saw

> much greater scope for specialisation for selected individuals in the Trade Union Movement who are likely to occupy positions of responsibility and who can be provided with courses on Trade Union and Industrial Law, Trade Union Principles and Practice, History of special industries and research on case papers, charts and material for negotiation.[42]

Attitudes to this work were ambivalent. Sometimes, it was a 'technical approach to trade union problems', and 'quite properly the responsibility of the Trade Union Movement itself'.[43] The WEA should offer only the services of well-qualified tutors. Collaborative union–WEA summer schools and like events would also help 'to arouse the interest of the trade unionist in continuous educational efforts and to bring him in touch with the more intensive forms of class study'.[44] But it was only a taster compared to the real thing.

At the same time, there was an almost mystical identification of the 'self-governing democratic group'[45] with the notion that WEA education could become a mainspring for working-class and community leadership: 'a broadly based leadership and a wide participation in national and local affairs calls for a good supply of educated personnel.'[46] Unions were essential to national reconstruction and a new social order:

> In the post-war period, the voluntary good will which has made national unity possible for waging the war, may be considered less urgent and the Trade Union position in national life will be related not so much to its paper membership but to its active membership.[47]

The recipe for overcoming apathy was for 'every trade union branch in the country' to be 'deliberately engaged in some form of systematic education of its membership'.[48] Some argued for rethinking traditional WEA disdain for the technical and vocational. The proposed specialist courses implied 'a kind of vocational or technical emphasis but it is vocational only in relation to democratic action'.[49] This was the key. The assumption that two essentially separate spheres of education and training existed – the one broadly liberal and for its own sake, the other vocational and 'technical' – was not challenged, but the latter could now be justified for the wider good. The WEA now had 'a special task' in adult education:

> It is to train adults for democratic leadership. It is to equip the workers themselves to participate in social and political organisations, so that, in the words of our Statement of Policy, they 'may be able to relate their personal experience of industrial and local problems to a wider knowledge and understanding of public affairs'.[50]

## RETHINKING EDUCATION FOR CITIZENSHIP

What we see in the wartime WEA is a rethinking of how adult education and trade unions should relate. Unions were no longer simply partners; they had become a crucial challenge. The workers, their members, were too ill-educated, but unions were central to delivering a new post-war social order; yet at the same time wartime experience suggested social challenges, and the need to strengthen social institutions could be the vehicle for educational opportunity.

The WEA's rethinking evolved within a wider wartime reassessment of education, and in particular of adult education. Sir Richard Livingstone, for example, argued:

That almost any subject is studied with more interest and intelligence by those who know something of its subject-matter than by those who do not; and, conversely, that it is not profitable to study theory without some practical experience of the facts to which it relates.[51]

Experience of life, he believed, was 'necessary for the full and fruitful study of subjects like literature, history, politics and economics'. The 'cultural education' of young people was therefore 'very incomplete when they leave school'.[52] Livingstone advocated 'a compulsory part-time continuation system until the age of 18 for the great majority who left school at 14 or 15. This would prevent earlier education being 'largely wasted'and 'take them to the threshold of adult education, where the solution of our educational problem must be found'.[53]

This was manna to the WEA. Livingstone, to A.D. Lindsay, 'a very good man but a mild-mannered Tory',[54] was an influential establishment figure: president of Corpus Christi College, Oxford, vice-chancellor of the Queen's University, Belfast (1924–33), knighted in 1931, a frequently public speaker and broadcaster.[55] *The Future in Education*, published in Cambridge University Press's 'Current Problems' series in March 1941, was reprinted twice within six months. A 'W.E.A. Cheap Edition' was arranged: '1/6. 1/8 post free (three copies or over, 1/6 post free)'.[56]

Livingstone's argument was inextricably intertwined with an ethical view of education.[57] As the 'world adrift' had 'no standards, no principle to rule and discipline it',[58] the need was to strengthen training in 'character'. 'Our fundamental need and a chief task of education today is to form the right attitude to life and to give what our age lacks, clear values and definite standards.'[59] Of his views on how this could be achieved, only two need detain us here. First, a 'habitual vision of greatness'[60] was essential to all education:

The sight of goodness in life or in literature or history gives a standard and a challenge. If anyone has been able to compare the first-rate with the second-rate, his criticism will not be merely bitter and barren, but creative, born of a vision perceiving the good, dominated by it and desiring to bring it to birth.[61]

This was a highly élitist point of view,[62] of course, but not in a straightforward sense. 'Visions of greatness' were needed in all areas of society: everyone was 'capable of a virtue, and excellence, which consists of doing a particular job well, in being a good son or daughter, a good citizen, good in his occupation – whether it is that of Prime Minister or of shop assistant'.[63]

Second, citizens were 'made, not born'. From citizenship education – 'civics' – in schools, we should 'not expect much' because 'school is not the right time or place to give it'. '[A]ction and thought, living and learning naturally belong together ... [When] children are adults and have votes, let such instruction be available so that their votes can be used with intelligence.'[64]

The 'most important element in training for citizenship',[65] however, came informally, through practice and life rather than study: 'we become good citizens by doing what good citizens do.' In the family, 'we learn to live together as members of a tiny community.' But families exist everywhere: what had made the British 'not experts in the art [of citizenship] but perhaps more expert than most peoples'?[66] Religion, and institutional traditions such as parliamentary government provided a 'general social education'. But other institutions gave this 'a specific form'. The Scout and Guide movements, and the public school, were key examples, but:

> Another great school of citizenship in England is the Trade Union, where several millions of Englishmen learn to subordinate private wishes and opinions to a common policy, and a mass of individuals becomes a disciplined army. A strike may be inconvenient or even unjustifiable, but men who will throw up their work and livelihood for a common cause, possibly against their desire or even their judgement, have learnt one at least of the lessons of social education – how to act as a community.[67]

Livingstone's message, then, was clear. People learn best when they have experience; this was a general truth, but applied with more force to some kinds of learning than others. It applied especially strongly to learning 'citizenship'. In a 'world adrift', 'character' and 'standards' were needed. These were developed informally when people encountered 'habitual visions of greatness' and in social institutions – informal 'schools' of citizenship. In the latter, people learned because they practised citizenship as part of a community. Livingstone's views did not go unchallenged,[68] but this emphasis on the importance of practice in learning, and especially in the learning of democracy and citizenship, was to be found not only in the WEA,[69] but also in important areas of policy.[70]

## TRADE UNIONISM IN THE NEW SOCIAL ORDER

By 1945, the WEA had taken a critical look at its pre-war record in relation to trade unions, and judged it wanting. It had adopted – partly formally, partly unconsciously – a vision of a new post-war social order, in which trade unions would play a key part in a renewed and deeper democracy. To make this effective, more trade unionists must take up active roles, and would need better education. Wartime experience suggested this could be achieved by focusing on people's work, and by courses which engaged with their new democratic roles. All this was underpinned by some influential scholarship, and was in step with policy developments elsewhere. Of course, this summary draws common strands from a more diffuse reality; it plays down tensions and debates; it closes its ears to the caveats: but it reflects the WEA's optimism as peace came.

Did the 'new social order' arrive? Speaking to the WEA's 1947 Annual Conference, Tawney took a sanguine view. In contrast to pre-war 'stagnation':

> Democracy in the sense of management of affairs by common consent, by argument, discussion, and agreement has now extended its influence into spheres previously closed to it. Working-class bodies are confronted by problems which were visualised twenty years ago by theorists, but which now have become part of the everyday texture of ordinary life and activity.[71]

In this spirit, the WETUC had launched itself into 'weekly talks on related subjects, connected courses of short duration, study circles to discuss special topics, and similar informal methods for mixed groups of trade unionists, or for branches of particular unions'.[72] But these were quite modest in number – at least in relation to the 'swollen membership'.[73]

The promise remained unfulfilled, for two main reasons. First, only modest resources were available, and too often the results would 'disappoint and depress the many willing voluntary workers in our movement'.[74] Second, for many, the new work was not the real thing, 'not to be regarded as an end in itself but as a means to the end of encouraging trade unionists in larger numbers to undertake more sustained and advanced studies in WEA classes'.[75] Year after year, this theme recurred. Thus, for instance, the 1951 Annual Report:

> Stress upon long courses is essential. ... [I]t is the long course of study in a class that brings the best and most lasting, beneficial educational results. Class work is the vital requirement of the trade unionist. There is no short cut to real educational development in the individual, a determined solid effort must be made, the long pull must be faced. If this necessity of trying hard to build up one's educational resources is shirked then no effective progress is made.[76]

It was 'not easy to get trade unionists to give so much time to serious study', but it was 'our business never to give up trying', just as it was 'the business of short courses to encourage a proportion of students to proceed' to 'more serious work'.[77] These views were expressed in WETUC reports – that is, from the trade union arm of the movement: belief in the virtues of long, serious study ran deep.

In short, the WEA (and WETUC) had limited resources, and were divided about priorities. Also, as in all voluntary movements, the resources were largely unpaid men and women whose chief efforts followed their commitments. In fact, when the WEA reviewed its activities during the late 1940s, it concluded that the 1945 WETUC report had led 'educational work to be extended', but 'largely upon traditional lines'.[78]

Education for trade unionists had never been the sole preserve of the WEA and WETUC, but the war saw a significant development. Partly because the dispute between the WEA and the labour college movement was so bitter, the TUC had since the 1920s stood aside.[79] From 1944 this began to change, and in 1946 the TUC appointed a director of studies. Through the 1940s its programme remained small, but had significance beyond its size. The TUC had established an independent educational presence; with its own expertise, it began to develop its own views, policies and institutional interests.[80]

For the WEA the TUC was more than another competitor. Its authority was such that hostile competition – as with the NCLC – would be disastrous. The only feasible strategy was co-operation, and influence. In fact, the TUC had claimed to be 'fill[ing] a gap', not replicating WEA or NCLC provision, but offering 'practical' courses for 'officers and active members'.[81] Unfortunately, this 'gap' was exactly the area into which the WEA was also trying to move. Despite differences in emphasis and approach, the TUC had none of the baggage of Tawney – education for democracy and 'university standards' – but WEA and TUC were fishing in the same pond. WEA thinking in the post-war years reflected the need to engage with this territory, in harmony rather than competition, and the desire to influence others – including the TUC – in what it saw as a politically and educationally desirable direction.

## TOWARDS TRADE UNION EDUCATION

While for many in the WEA the new forms of education stood or fell by how far they won trade unionists to more 'serious' studies, for others their purpose was different. In this view, a new social order meant supporting the activity of trade unions themselves. Two principal trends emerged.

There was, first of all, a perspective from the Labour right – from the trade union establishment and its allies. The government knew best, and the role of union education was to ensure membership support for sound leadership policies. As time passed the need became pressing. By 1948, for example, when Herbert Morrison addressed the issue of 'Trade Unionism and the New Social Order' head-on in a speech to the London WETUC and WEA, he was speaking – albeit allusively – to trade union sceptics. Unions had found 'their place in the sun'; 'steady full employment' had been achieved; the 'large basic industries' were 'socialized'.[82] The union movement had 'functions which it never dreamed of before'. Unions had to 'become experts in productivity', and in 'pressing imperfect management whether in private or socialized industries'.[83] The trade unionist must now 'judge what is sensible and sound' and, with the help of 'advisers and experts ... give firm and public-spirited guidance to the rank and file', rather than 'exploit his immediate tactical advantage against the needs of the community and take a line as bad and selfish as the old employer did when he was on top'.[84]

By 1948 the Labour government was encouraging pay restraint – incomes policies would dominate relations between governments and unions for 30 years ahead. There was now 'no justification for any general increase in individual money incomes unless accompanied by a substantial increase in production'.[85] TUC leaders and government[86] believed consensus could be achieved along these lines. Education for trade unionists should therefore help build the new social order – on the basis that its key features had been established. Education should encourage and support trade unionists to play a constructive role.

Secondly, however, not all argument that education should focus on practical trade union problems came from the right. Bridget

Sutton, for example, saw the growth of trade union membership since 1939 as presenting 'an urgent need' for 'rank and file members' to obtain 'the necessary training and educational background to fill newly-created positions of responsibility and leadership'.[87] This meant thinking about 'the method of approach best fitted to present-day circumstances'.[88] Earlier WEA students had dealt with problems which needed long-term solutions, but in 1949 problems demanded 'an immediate answer and [could not] be the subject of long drawn-out discussion'. If the WEA did not change its approach, 'we shall find, as indeed we are finding already, that trade unions seriously concerned with education for their members' would be 'forced to make their own provision'.[89] Sutton was typical of a significant body of adult education opinion, especially among university tutors close to the Communist Party.

These two perspectives overlaid and intermingled with views about educating citizens in a revitalised democracy. If the euphoria of wartime had ebbed by the 1940s, for some the welfare state presented a potent, and present, new environment. Thus Harold Clay's presidential address to the WEA's 1947 Conference:

> In considering educational schemes for trade unionists, we have to envisage branches of study broader and deeper than anything contemplated a few years ago. Economic and industrial planning, and public control, have raised new issues, and these affect the worker both as a producer and as a citizen.

New conceptions were emerging about industrial relations. Joint production committees presupposed 'a new understanding by both sides of industry'. The 'relationship between technical, vocational and broad general education' needed re-examination.[90]

By and large, WEA leaders inclined to a positive view of post-war developments. Things might not be perfect, but they were a lot better; unions should act with restraint and responsibility, within the new structures. Thus, the idea that union officials and members should learn about new institutions, and how to make them work, was uncontroversial. Debate arose over how this should be done, who should do it, what role the WEA should have, and how it should relate to unions and the TUC; and, no less important, whether this was a sufficient education for a trade unionist.

## THE WORKING PARTY

By about 1948 or 1949, neither WEA nor WETUC was attracting the large hoped-for numbers: indeed the downward trend continued. This was no recipe for mass citizenship education. There was no new mass cadre of knowledgeable lay administrators for the welfare state. There was no mass education of responsible trade unionists – nor even of irresponsible ones. From a narrower WEA perspective, there were additional concerns. Trade unionism was not serving to strengthen the WEA's working-class membership, which continued to erode. As TUC and union provision developed, the risk was that even those trade unionists drawn into education would do so outside the WEA ambit, and thus become immersed in different, narrower, curricula and traditions.

There were three main responses to this threat. The first was simply – it was not simple, but efforts were made – to encourage better links between the WEA and trade unions. This took place at several levels: attempts to build closer official co-operation with the TUC, restructuring to draw the local work of WETUC closer to the WEA districts, resolutions and speeches at annual conferences. In May 1949, for instance, over a hundred delegates from 41 unions attended a special one-day conference on 'the educational needs of the trade union movement' and how the WEA could 'ensure that those needs are in future more effectively met'.[91]

The second response reflected WEA assumptions about the importance of 'standards'. This was the view that trade union courses were justified only by how far they were – or drew workers into – serious, long-term study. By the late 1940s, several prominent WEA leaders had 'retreated' to this traditional view, distancing themselves from an earlier openness to new approaches. Tawney, for example, opened the special 1949 conference by accepting that 'varying forms' of education may well be necessary for trade unionists, though 'each should, on its own special plane, be honest, thorough and sincere'. But he continued with a lament and a challenge:

> When I compare the adult students whom I knew thirty years ago with those of today, I am sometimes disposed to think that, though the former suffered from disabilities and disadvantages from which the latter are free, they were often inspired by a stronger sense of mission. They regarded education, not merely as a hobby or a pastime, but as a social dynamic, and were willing as

a consequence to make the sacrifices of time and energy to enable them to get to the bottom of the subject with which they grappled. ... The trade union movement has always played an active part in adult education. If it is to take a larger share in it in future, it is a modern version of that determined temper which it must seek to evoke. The business of all who are concerned with education is not to mislead our students by the mendacious pretence that it is a less exacting substitute for the cinema, dogs, darts or the intellectual austerities of the daily Press. It is to put them on their metal, to pitch our claims high, and to rely for a response not on the insignificance of the effort demanded, but on the magnitude of the reward which effort will bring, in the consciousness of new powers and an increased capacity for effective action.[92]

This was strong if conservative stuff, and left little room for doubt as to what real education comprised. The delegates present, at least according to *The Highway*, came to similar conclusions:

while the training of 'functionaries' was an important need in view of the wider responsibilities of the trade unions, this ... was a specialist job in which the unions themselves must play the major part. On the other hand ... special training ... could only be fully effective if the sociological background was ensured by a liberal education.[93]

The problem with this position was political. Union hands might be soiled with 'training', but the WEA's would remain clean; at the same time unions would be praised if they used 'liberal educational' approaches. WEA influence was limited – Tawneyesque rhetoric counted for little against the organisational imperatives of major unions.

The third response was, in the long run, to prove most influential. This attempted to chart, as it were, a 'third way' between a strongly academic approach – typified by the three-year 'tutorial class' – and practical training. It drew strongly on wartime hopes about citizenship. It drew on the view that union members should have a renewed role in a full-employment welfare state. It reflected experiments in teaching methods within both unions and universities,[94] enthusiasm for community development, and positive judgements of some of the post-war experimental work. It was also supported by many unions, as being closer to their institutional interests. Such influences led the 1951 WEA Annual Conference to establish a working party on trade union education.[95] Chaired by Arthur Creech Jones (a recent member of Attlee's cabinet), this high-powered group included five senior trade unionists (one a general seretary), two WEA district secretaries, the WEA's general and organising secretaries, and two 'academic advisers'.

The working party took on board much of the thinking which had developed over the previous decade. The tutorial class was of diminishing use to the trade union movement and its members 'We want an educational instrument and an educational technique for the non-academically minded, as effective and successful as the tutorial class was for the potentially grammar school minded.'[96] The solution they recommended would 'build on the immediate interests and experience of students', moving 'from the particular to the general by starting from common experience' and 'in mutual discussion gradually ... lay bare the conflicts of motive and principle and the obstinate material factors which are involved in a problem'.[97] There should be 'active participation'; a group had to 'find its own way, in good measure'. 'Frank expression of opinion and mutual and constructive discussion' were vital.[98] The report was rich with examples of good practice, many of them drawn from outside the WEA – from technical colleges, for example.[99]

THE END OF APATHY?

In the early 1950s, 'apathy' was again a hot topic. In a very influential 1952 book, Joseph Goldstein used the concept to analyse the problems of trade union democracy.[100] The following year Ernest Green's *Adult Education: Why this Apathy?* was published, based on research stimulated by his experiences as WEA general secretary.[101] The high hopes of wartime had not been achieved, and apathy remained a problem both for adult education and for the unions. The strategy now was to locate education in the experience of the trade unionist: it would relate to workplace and trade union problems, and build out from there.

As argued elsewhere,[102] the 1953 report underpinned a major strand of post-war trade union education. Approaches to 'role education' developed in several university extra-mural departments, particularly Oxford, in the 1950s and 1960s were close relations; the TUC's provision, as developed particularly from the late 1950s, shows direct descent. This is not the place to explore the impact and the implications of that parentage: there is a substantial literature arguing both pro and con.[103] The purpose of this chapter has been to uncover the thinking which led the WEA to abandon its flagship tutorial class as the principal vehicle for educating trade unionists.

Of course, for many in the WEA, as for Tawney, serious, in-depth study following the liberal curriculum of a tutorial class remained a 'gold standard'. But the 1953 report was the watershed. From that time on, the Association acknowledged – in policy, though by no means always in practice, and certainly not full-heartedly – that serving trade unions and the organised working class effectively called for a different approach. Sidney Raybould, a member of the working party but now best remembered as the ideologue of 'university standards', detected 'a sort of Gresham's Law' at work, making it 'very hard to secure an easy or lasting mixture, either in classes or [WEA] Branches, of workers with different types of educational background'.[104] Unless the WEA 'voluntarily limit[ed] its appeal', it would 'quite soon cease to be working-class', or 'to have any specific *raison d'être*'.[105] This was a drastic solution. The working party – and ultimately the WEA – preferred differentiated *raisons d'être*.

NOTES

*Place of publication London unless otherwise stated.*

1. WEA, 'Adult Education after the War' (unpublished confidential memorandum to the Board of Education, 1942), 36 (National Archive, WEA CENTRAL/4/1/2/3).
2. WETUC, *Workers' Education and the Trade Union Movement: A Post-war Policy* (1944), 4.
3. *Adventure*, 11.
4. B. Jennings, *Albert Mansbridge* (Leeds, 1973), 15.
5. *Ministry of Reconstruction. Adult Education Committee. Final Report* (Cmd. 321, 1919), 41. The Report does not refer only to the working-class movement, but this was its main emphasis.
6. M. Stocks, *My Commonplace Book* (1970), 158.
7. E. Green, *Adult Education: Why this Apathy?* (1953), 12.
8. District and national, as well as branch, affiliations are included; they cover all affiliations, but were preponderantly from 'working-class bodies'. For the detailed figures, which suggest that the trend was clear before the war, see *The WEA and the Working-class Movement. WEA Conference Report No. 2* (for WEA Annual Conference 1944), (National Archive, WEA CENTRAL/4/2/1/2). Evidence from the mid-1930s suggests 'much less contact than in the past' between trades councils

and the WEA: see A. Clinton, *The Trade Union Rank and File: Trades Councils in Britain 1900–1940* (Manchester, 1977), 181.

9. E. Ashby, *The Pathology of Adult Education* (William F. Harvey Memorial Lecture 1955) (Belfast, 1955), 10. Ashby entered a caveat: this 'generalised case history' was 'not typical; ... not even very common' – but he saw it as 'correct' for 'a few regions, and important and thickly populated regions at that' – implicitly, the exception represented the most significant 'truth' (*The Pathology of Adult Education*, 11).

10. R. Lewis and A. Maude, *The English Middle Classes* (1949), 57. Angus Maude later became a Conservative MP, and Paymaster-General under Margaret Thatcher. But not all on the political right shared this view: Colm Brogan, e.g., urged it to beware of 'the wide suspicion that its classes are treated as a training ground for the intellectual troops of the Socialist party' (*Daily Telegraph*, 3 July 1953).

11. See, e.g., the discussions in E. Green, *Adult Education: Why this Apathy?*; E. Ashby, *The Pathology of Adult Education* , and WEA Annual Conference reports of this period.

12. R. H. Tawney, *Can Democracy Survive?* (n.d. [April 1940]).

13. WEA, 'Adult Education after the War', 31. In 1938–9, the WEA enrolled 61,719 students in 3,511 classes, which implies that at most about one in ten WEA students were studying these (unspecified) subjects with a 'direct bearing on citizenship' in 1938–9.

14. WEA, 'Adult Education after the War', 30.

15. War saw major reassessments of social and economic policy in many countries: see, e.g. A. S. Milward, *War, Economy and Society 1939–1945* (1977); in Britain the Beveridge report (*Social Insurance and Allied Services*, Cmd. 6404, 1942) and the 1944 Education Act are more familiar than the WEA's.

16. WEA, 'Adult Education after the War', 31.

17. J. I. Roper, *Trade Unionism and the New Social Order* (1942), 28.

18. WETUC, *Workers' Education and the Trade Union Movement. A Post-war Policy. Report of a Special Sub-committee* (1944), 4.

19. Roper, *Trade Unionism and the New Social Order*, 28.

20. *The WEA and the Working-class Movement. WEA Conference Report No. 2* (for WEA Annual Conference 1944), 1 (WEA CENTRAL/4/2/1/2).

21. *Workers' Educational Trade Union Committee, Workers' Education and the Trade Union Movement. A Post-war Policy. Report of a Special Sub-committee*, 3.

22. Roper, *Trade Unionism and the New Social Order,* 28; emphasis in original.

23. Other organisations, such as Ruskin College, the Trades' Union Congress and various unions, played lesser roles. See J. Holford, *Union Education in Britain* (Nottingham, 1994), 15–56.

24. J. P. M. Millar, *The Labour College Movement* (n.d. [1979]), 252.

25. A. J. Corfield, *Epoch in Workers' Education: A History of the Workers' Educational Trade Union Committee* (1969), 248.

26. Figures for all three bodies must be treated with caution. They refer to student enrolments in classes, with all enrolments (from day schools to tutorial classes) counting equally. There was almost certainly a

substantial measure of double-counting. For the WEA, the estimate is very rough, based on the proportion of manual workers in the Association's overall student enrolment of just over 60,000.

27. R. Price and G. S. Bain, 'The Labour Force', in A. H. Halsey (ed.) *British Social Trends since 1900* (Basingstoke, 1988), 187, 191.
28. See Holford, *Union Education in Britain*, ch. 3.
29. WEA, 'Adult Education after the War', 32.
30. T. Hodgkin, 'Some War-time Developments in Adult Education', *Rewley House Papers* II(4) (Oxford, March 1941), 141.
31. Corfield, *Epoch in Workers' Education*, 65.
32. Corfield, *Epoch in Workers' Education*, 248.
33. Hodgkin, 'Some War-time Developments', 143.
34. Hodgkin, 'Some War-time Developments', 142.
35. See, e.g., S. Harrop (ed.) *Oxford and Working-class Education* (Nottingham, 1987; first published by Oxford University Press 1908); A. Mansbridge, *University Tutorial Classes: A Study in the Development of Higher Education among Working Men and Women* (1913).
36. Hodgkin, 'Some War-time Developments', 144.
37. WEA, 'Adult Education after the War', 32.
38. WEA, 'Adult Education after the War', 32.
39. WEA, 'Adult Education after the War', 32.
40. WEA, 'Adult Education after the War', 32.
41. WETUC, *Workers' Education and the Trade Union Movement: A Post-war Policy* (1944), 8 (WETUC/4/1/1/2).
42. WETUC, *Workers' Education and the Trade Union Movement: A Post-war Policy*, 8.
43. WETUC, *Workers' Education and the Trade Union Movement: A Post-war Policy*, 9.
44. WETUC, *Workers' Education and the Trade Union Movement: A Post-war Policy*, 10.
45. WEA, *The W.E.A. and the Working-class Movement*, 8.
46. WEA, *The W.E.A. and the Working-class Movement*, 10.
47. WETUC, *Workers' Education and the Trade Union Movement: A Post-war Policy*, 4.
48. WETUC, *Workers' Education and the Trade Union Movement: A Post-war Policy*, 4.
49. WEA, *The W.E.A. and the Working-class Movement*, 10.
50. WEA, 'Adult Education after the War', 36.
51. R. Livingstone, *The Future in Education* (Cambridge, 1941), 7.
52. R. Livingstone, *The Future in Education*, 33.
53. R. Livingstone, *The Future in Education*, 39–40.
54. Quoted in J. A. Blyth, *English University Adult Education 1908–1958: The Unique Tradition* (Manchester, 1983), 161. No source given. However, Livingstone himself wrote that though he was 'brought up in a conservative atmosphere and regarded Gladstone as an incarnation of evil', he was 'today ... a liberal'. See R. Livingstone, *Education for a World Adrift* (Padstow, 1988; first published Cambridge, 1943), 76.

55. H. M. Palmer, in *The Compact Edition of the Dictionary of National Biography* (Oxford, 1975), ii. 2755.
56. Cole, *Adult Education after the War*, 7 (advertisement).
57. R. Livingstone, *Education for a World Adrift*. This book flattered the WEA, asserting that 'the three most original British achievements in education are (in chronological order) the Residential [i.e., boarding or 'public'] School, the Workers' Educational Association and the Scout and Guide Movement' (26–7).
58. Livingstone, *Education for a World Adrift*, 9.
59. Livingstone, *Education for a World Adrift*, 60.
60. Livingstone, *Education for a World Adrift*, 33. Livingstone drew the expression from A. N. Whitehead, *The Aims of Education and Other Essays* (1932), 106: 'Moral education is impossible apart from the habitual vision of greatness.'
61. Livingstone, *Education for a World Adrift*, 36.
62. Without in any way detracting from this view, we may note in passing that Livingstone's view on the importance of 'habitual visions of greatness' chimes with much in WEA thinking, both pre-war and post-war: the liberal curriculum, the tutorial class, the charismatic tutor, and so forth.
63. Livingstone, *Education for a World Adrift*, 67.
64. Livingstone, *Education for a World Adrift*, 94.
65. Livingstone, *Education for a World Adrift*, 99.
66. Livingstone, *Education for a World Adrift*, 99.
67. Livingstone, *Education for a World Adrift*, 100.
68. See, e.g., Cole, *Adult Education after the War* (n.d.), which criticised Livingstone (with some, though not total, justice) for 'looking ... exclusively from the standpoint of the individual, regarded as an entirely isolated "personality" needing development', rather than in a 'group' or 'social' perspective (6). See also Blyth, *English University Adult Education 1908–1958*, 161–3.
69. E.g. H. C. Shearman, *Adult Education for Democracy* (1944) was strongly influenced by Livingstone.
70. We see it, for example, in three highly influential reports: Colonial Office, *Advisory Committee on Education in the Colonies, Mass Education in African Society* (HMSO Colonial No. 186; 1943); Colonial Office, *Advisory Committee on Education in the Colonies, Education for Citizenship in Africa* (HMSO Colonial No. 216, 1948); and UNESCO, *Fundamental Education: Common Ground for All Peoples, Report of a Special Committee to the the Preparatory Commission* (Paris, 1947).
71. R. H. Tawney, 'Programme for Action' (Speech to the WEA Annual Conference 1947), *The Highway* xxxix, Nov. 1947, 3.
72. WETUC, *Workers' Education and the Trade Union Movement: A Post-war Policy*; the 1947 *WETUC Annual Report*, 2–4 gives a list (albeit 'incomplete') of only 67 such 'short informal courses'.
73. Union 'density' (members as a proportion of the labour force) stood at 45.2 per cent in 1948, compared with 30.5 per cent ten years earlier; over the same period union membership rose from 5.1 millions to 7.7

millions – an increase of 50 per cent. See R. Price and G. S. Bain, 'The Labour Force', in A. H. Halsey (ed.) *British Social Trends since 1900*, 187.
74. *WETUC Annual Report 1950*, 9.
75. *WETUC Annual Report 1947*, 5.
76. *WETUC Annual Report 1951*, 14.
77. *WETUC Annual Report 1951*, 14.
78. WEA, *The Workers' Educational Association: A Review 1946–1952* (n.d.), 20.
79. This period is discussed in Holford, *Union Education in Britain*, 28–33.
80. Holford, *Union Education in Britain*, 58–60.
81. Quoted in Holford, *Union Education in Britain*, 59.
82. Herbert Morrison, 'Trade Unionism and the New Social Order', *The Highway* xl, Nov. 1948, 5–7.
83. Morrison, 'Trade Unionism and the New Social Order' 7.
84. Morrison, 'Trade Unionism and the New Social Order' 5–7.
85. House of Commons debates 4 Feb. 1948, cols. 1829–31, quoted in L. Panitch, *Social Democracy and Industrial Militancy: The Labour Party, the Trade Unions and Incomes Policy 1945–1974* (Cambridge, 1976), 22. See also *Statement on Personal Incomes, Costs and Prices* (Cmd. 7321).
86. Panitch, *Social Democracy and Industrial Militancy*, 21.
87. B. Sutton, 'The WEA and Trade Union Education', *The Highway* xl, May 1949, 172. Sutton, later the historian Bridget Hill, was then an Oxford staff tutor and member of the Communist Party. See also R. T. Fieldhouse, *Adult Education and the Cold War* (Leeds, 1985), 34.
88. Sutton, 'The WEA and Trade Union Education', 172.
89. Sutton, 'The WEA and Trade Union Education', 173.
90. H. E. Clay, 'Presidential Address Delivered to the WEA Annual Conference', 1947, in *The Highway* xxxix, Nov. 1947, 8.
91. R. H. Tawney, 'Education to Meet the Modern Needs of Trade Unions', *The Highway* xl, June 1949, 183. Speakers included Alan Winterbottom, the TUC's director of studies, and Ernest Green, WEA general secretary.
92. Tawney, 'Education to Meet the Modern Needs of Trade Unions', 184.
93. 'News of the Movement, by the General Secretary', *The Highway* xl, June 1949, 193.
94. These are discussed in Corfield, *Epoch in Workers' Education*, ch. 8.; Holford, *Union Education in Britain*, 145–50, J. McIlroy, 'The Triumph of Technical Training?' in B. Simon (ed.) *The Search for Enlightenment: The Working Class and Adult Education in the Twentieth Century* (1990), 208–18.
95. Corfield, *Epoch in Workers' Education* , 107–8. The resolution was moved by Ellen McCullough, Education Officer of the TGWU.
96. WEA, *Trade Union Education: A Report from a Working Party*, (1953), 42.
97. WEA, *Trade Union Education: A Report from a Working Party*, 58.
98. WEA, *Trade Union Education: A Report from a Working Party*, 63.
99. The report is discussed in more detail in Holford, *Union Education in Britain*, 144–50.

100. J. Goldstein, *The Government of British Trade Unions: A Study of Apathy and the Democratic Process in the Transport and General Workers' Union* (1952).
101. E. Green, *Adult Education: Why this Apathy?* (1953).
102. Holford, *Union Education in Britain*.
103. J. McIlroy is sharply critical in articles too numerous to list here, but see my *Union Education in Britain, 293–4*, which is broadly sympathetic.
104. S. G. Raybould, *The WEA. The Next Phase* (1949), 39.
105. Raybould, *The WEA. The Next Phase*, 50.

# 10 Ideology and Provision: The WEA and the Politics of Workers' Education in Early Twentieth-century Scotland

*Rob Duncan*

## INTRODUCTION

The very nature, provision, ownership and control of adult and workers' education were all highly controversial and contested areas in early twentieth-century Scotland. Conflict over workers' education in particular was a constant ideological battleground, not least within the organised labour movement. Accordingly, an interpretation of the bitter rivalry between the open, liberal pluralist WEA and the explicitly fundamentalist and socialist Labour College movement for 'independent working class education', which had a strong base in Scotland, will intersect the main narrative on the WEA and form an important dimension of the investigation in this chapter.[1]

The vision of the relatively small band of WEA pioneer activists and supporters in Scotland was consistent with that of the founding body in England. They sought to form a partnership between aspiring labour and the university sector, and to enlist recognition and financial backing from the central and local state, in order to gain working-class access to the broad stream of continuing education and higher learning, both for personal enrichment and collective social purpose. Over the years the declared objectives of the WEA and the struggle to implement them would be subject to close, often challenging scrutiny and interpretation from inside and beyond WEA circles.[2]

## THE SCOTTISH SCENE: EDUCATION AND INEQUALITY

From 1907, the WEA in England and Wales won official recognition and direct grant aid from the Board of Education, and additional financial support from local authorities and universities. However, in

Scotland a very different pattern prevailed. The Scottish Education Department (SED), all but a few of 1,000 school boards operating at parish level before 1918, and the four universities, were not prepared to fund the non-vocational, liberal adult education advocated by the WEA. Statutory and providing powers for adult education remained with the SED and also, after 1918, with the re-organised, few, enlarged local educational authorities. Until 1934 the statutory remit of the SED and of LEAs was confined to compulsory schooling and vocationally oriented evening classes for young workers under the Continuation Classes Code. Moreover, the anomalous position of the WEA in Scotland was shared by its potential partners, the Scottish universities who, unlike their English counterparts in the 1920s, were denied Responsible Body status for adult education provision.

However, the restrictive regulations of the state education regime in Scotland were underpinned by negative policies and downright hostility towards liberal adult and workers' education. Although progressives, Labour and socialist elected members did make some inroads into school board and local authority committees in urban Scotland, many of these bodies into the inter-war years still tended to be dominated by clergy, employers and small business types who held functional, utilitarian and often reactionary views about education. Their characteristic frame of mind was hostile towards social science subjects with potential for inculcating subversive views, particularly left-wing extremism.[3]

Leading Scottish Office officials displayed a patrician disregard for educational provision for adult workers. According to them, popular demand among workers for liberal education at or below university level was unproven, and therefore could not justify separate funding consideration. They held that, because of an open and democratic tradition of Scottish education, and the general availability of lower fees, scholarships and bursaries, the ladder of opportunity into university education was readily accessible to deserving young men and women from all social backgrounds, and could be seen in the number of university places taken by working-class students.[4]

Class and educational inequalities exposed this as colossal official complacency. In 1900 the mass of workers in Scotland had received only a few years of elementary schooling before entering waged work at 11 or 12 years of age. The school-leaving age in the 1900s was still 14, and for reasons of family economic necessity, low expectations and under-achievement, only a tiny proportion of working-class children were destined to progress to higher entry qualifications via secondary schools which, in any case, were few and far between in most areas of Scotland.[5] Given such exclusionary circumstances, serious-minded workers who sought learning opportunities for 'self-improvement' or for social and political purposes had to pursue their goals by their own means and, where possible, through their voluntary organisations, typically trade unions and Co-operative societies. As will be seen later, many also sought enlightenment and emancipation through the proliferation of political groups on the Labour and socialist left which, especially in Glasgow and the industrial heartlands of west and central Scotland, were increasingly organising programmes of events, lectures and classes on social and political issues.

ORIGINS AND RIVALRIES: 1905–18

In this milieu of potential demand for workers' education, the fledgling WEA had obvious opportunities, even if few resources, to mount a challenge for popular support. Yet, between 1905 and 1918, its limited record of growth in Scotland contrasts sharply with the significant profile of the movement in England. In this protracted formative period, five permanent branches were established, three in the university cities of Edinburgh (1912), Aberdeen (1913), Glasgow (1916); and the others in Dundee (1917) and Kilmarnock, Ayrshire (1917). In all five centres this was entirely the result of voluntary and material support from the labour movement, namely trades councils, individual trade unions and Co-operative organisations; from sympathetic university staff and schoolteachers; and through encouragement from school boards, particularly in Glasgow. Principal early champions of the WEA from the academic community were the progressive modernists Dr William Boyd, head of Education at Glasgow University from 1907; at Edinburgh University, Alexander Darroch, professor of Education, and J. F. Rees, then lecturer in economic history. All promoted liberal adult education for social purpose and citizenship.[6]

The WEA began in Scotland in 1905 when, following a visit by Albert Mansbridge, an interested group of teachers formed a branch at Springburn. This first Glasgow branch, which recorded 269 subscribing members, and generated several liberal studies classes under the School Board, lasted until 1909.[7] In October 1909 a large conference was held in Glasgow to debate and promote adult and workers' education. With Glasgow University principal, Sir Donald

Macalister, as chairperson, over 350 delegates from 182 organisations, including 59 trade unions, 44 friendly societies, and several Co-op branches formed a noisy, argumentative gathering which broke up without agreement.[8]

Nevertheless, the overall context of this meeting is important. Following the state funding breakthrough in 1907 and the 1908 report, *Oxford and Working Class Education* (both of which did much to launch the WEA in England), and the creation of the rival, Marxist-oriented, Plebs League, the conference had indicated latent demand for workers' education in the Glasgow area. However, the contentious deliberations had also signalled the growing rift between the liberal education concept as advocated by the WEA and university sector, and the proponents of independent working-class education.

In Glasgow this rivalry erupted from 1916 amid a mounting tempo of industrial militancy and anti-war unrest, as John Maclean and revolutionary elements in the British Socialist Party launched a campaign to mobilise labour movement support for a Scottish Labour College and a rolling programme of classes in Marxist education. At the inaugural rally of the Scottish Labour College campaign in February 1916, 496 delegates from labour and socialist organisations, trade unions and Co-operative societies committed themselves to developing an alternative socialist culture.[9] Maclean kept asserting that the state was fostering the WEA as a counter to the growing influence of socialist and Marxist ideas, citing the effect of Marxist education in the south Wales coalfield and in the industrial west of Scotland. His judgement here was endorsed by the alarmist conclusions of the 1917 Commission of Enquiry into Industrial Unrest.[10] Identifying the WEA as a reactionary influence, Maclean commented thus in late 1917:

> Now the WEA is being galvanised into activity in Scotland. Lord Haldane helped at the opening of the branches in Edinburgh and Dundee. More significant still, Dr Boyd of Glasgow University made a savage attack on Marxian education in Kilmarnock a fortnight ago when opening the Ayrshire branch of the WEA ... His speech, and he is president of the Educational Institute of Scotland, reveals quite clearly the exact motive underlying this new burst of WEAism.[11]

Of particular interest here is the thesis developed by Roger Fieldhouse that the state in early twentieth-century Britain officially and financially backed the WEA as a politically moderating influence on the emerging labour movement, as a sound investment against revolutionary Marxism.[12] If this thesis has any currency for Scotland, it would surely apply to the period 1916–26, characterised by a peak in industrial and political militancy and the demonstrable attraction of Marxist-oriented workers' education, especially in and around Glasgow. In the case of the struggling WEA in Scotland, however, there is no obvious evidence of any such direct source of political backing and bankrolling. Nevertheless, although some of its tutors, members and students were otherwise inclined, the prevailing ethos of the WEA was undoubtedly anti-Marxist and the very openness of the WEA could make it susceptible to the pressure of moderate and moderating ideological tendencies.

A product of, and contributor to, the industrial and political unrest of Red Clydeside, the drive to build independent working-class education gathered pace throughout 1917–18. Socialist Labour Party activists in the Glasgow Plebs League joined forces with the Scottish Labour College elements 'to secure a chain of marxist classes in Glasgow and the West of Scotland'.[13] This was achieved in winter 1917–18, when a hectic combined effort resulted in nearly 40 classes (and many other workshop and community-based informal study circles) in Marxist economics and class-struggle history, delivered to an estimated total of 2,500 worker students in Glasgow and Clydeside.[14]

In the light of this remarkable spread of independent working-class education, the emerging Glasgow WEA branch somewhat pales into insignificance. Teachers and their trade union, the Educational Institute of Scotland (EIS), continued to form the nucleus of the WEA branch formed in wartime Glasgow. William Boyd served as an early branch vice-president, and John Highton, a career civil servant, embarking on a major role in the Scottish WEA, was president. Under their leadership, in 1916–17 classes in economics and Scottish history and literature were negotiated with a receptive school board.[15]

However, the Glasgow record was overshadowed by the more extensive success of branches in Aberdeen and Edinburgh. This was due partly to the formation, in both centres, of three-way joint committees (WEA, school board/local authority, and the university) to facilitate the class programmes recruited by WEA effort, while Glasgow University was conspicuously not formally involved. Between 1914 and 1918, the WEA branch programme in Edinburgh, located at the university, comprised 15 introductory classes and a

2-year tutorial class, while Aberdeen organised around 10 classes, including 2 advanced tutorial classes. This formal, fee-paying, educational programme was manifestly in the WEA subjects reckoned to enhance insight into the complexities of modern society – economics, history and philosophy – with natural history (including evolution) and the world of literature also featuring.[16] Short courses on the politics of citizenship were also held under branch auspices in Aberdeen, Edinburgh and Dundee, forming part of the campaigning public platform aimed at influencing the shape of the expected post-war legislative programmes of political, social and educational reform.

In July 1916, with J. M. Mactavish, general secretary of the WEA, in attendance, a provisional WEA Scottish council was formed at an Edinburgh conference. It pledged to promote the movement throughout Scotland, to put its case before the statutory authorities, win active support from the broad labour and trade union movement at local and national levels and develop a campaigning role for educational advance. Definite signs of a concerted campaign profile emerged during 1917–18, as the five branches and affiliates organised large meetings on national educational reform and post-war recon-struction in the lead-up to the Education (Scotland) Act of 1918.[17] Prominent WEA members in Scotland lobbied and gave evidence to the adult education committee of the Ministry of Reconstruction, which finally reported in 1919. The committee, with majority rep-resentation from the university sector and the WEA, included Robert Climie, then treasurer of the Scottish Trade Union Congress, a veteran trade unionist and ILP socialist from Kilmarnock, who was also a founding member of the Ayrshire WEA branch.[18]

The 1919 Report produced no immediate results in Scotland. However, in one important respect, the WEA had made a start in what was to become a long-haul commitment over the years. Acting with its allies in the EIS, other progressive educationalists, the Scottish Trades Union Congress (STUC), labour politicians and the movement generally, the WEA was concerned not only to secure recognition for continuing adult and workers' education. It also sought to exert political pressure on government for a free, properly resourced state education system from nursery provision through to secondary schooling, and promoted the raising of the statutory leaving age from 14 to 16 years.[19]

At the close of the 1918–19 session, the recently-constituted WEA Scottish Council consisted of five branches with around 500 individual members and 71 affiliated organisations, the great bulk coming from the trade union and labour movement, but also including three local education authorities. This accumulated support included considerable new gains, but the WEA presence on the ground within Scotland was still poorly and unevenly distributed. Its course programme for the year had also been small, totalling only six sessional classes of which five were based in Edinburgh. In order to rise to the challenge of developing a significant and large, popular, working-class base and an educational programme to match, hard decisions had to be faced.[20]

For instance, without compromising its lofty idealism, the WEA had to tackle the issue of the university-level class as its principal curricular offer. Unfortunately, the composition of the student body in the crop of wartime WEA university classes is not known. However, in so far as worker students were among its beneficiaries, and as long as the two- or three-year tutorial course remained the primary 'glittering prize', protracted academic study at university standard was bound to appeal only to a tiny elite of workers who already had the necessary combination of confidence, intellectual ability, time, energy and discipline to cope successfully with the rigours of systematic study at this daunting level. As the EIS journal, complimenting the 'trail blazing' done by the WEA, remarked in September 1918, its classes had been well attended but, so far, had attracted and recruited only among the 'aristocrats of labour'.[21] To move decisively beyond the university precincts into the community and workplace, offering less demanding courses, posed significant challenges. Only thus could the prospect of liberal adult education be opened up to a wider constituency of workers who lived nowhere near one of the four universities, and who either did not aspire to, or were not otherwise equipped for, this level of learning engagement.

TAKING SIDES: POST-WAR DEVELOPMENTS

In the immediate post-war years, the national body of the WEA took concerted action to forge permanent educational links with the organised labour movement and to target its large and growing membership. In Scotland, it committed resources to this effort. In March 1919, it appointed Herbert Highton (brother of John Highton) as full-time organising secretary, his salary being guaranteed by the national office until such time as the Scottish operation became financially independent. Also, following ratification of the Workers'

Education Trade Union Committee (WETUC) scheme in October 1919 between the WEA and the recently amalgamated Iron and Steel Trades Confederation (ISTC), W. H. Marwick was appointed full-time tutor-organiser for course provision for trade union affiliates.[22]

Both these appointments were to prove valuable to the WEA, but the choice of Highton was particularly shrewd politically. John Maclean attacked Highton's appointment in the left-wing press, referring scathingly to the intrigues of the 'wire-pulling' pro-WEA ILP 'gang' in Glasgow, and condemned Highton's role as part of the alleged counter-attack on the growing influence of the Scottish Labour College movement.[23] A Glasgow-based Englishman and skilled engineer who had worked at the giant munitions factory of Weir at Cathcart, Highton had been a trade union activist and branch secretary in the Amalgamated Society of Engineers (ASE) in wartime. Not directly involved with the militant rank-and-file Clyde Workers Committee movement, Highton was a Methodist lay preacher, a Christian Socialist and a staunch member of the Independent Labour Party. By March 1919, he was secretary of the Govanhill branch of the ILP and delegate to the powerful, reconstituted Glasgow Trades and Labour Council. Elected to its parliamentary committee in 1920 and 1921, he helped prepare the historic landslide Labour victory in Glasgow in the 1922 General Election. During 1922–4 he was in an even more influential political position. As president of Glasgow Trades and Labour Council he was, in effect, chairman of the Glasgow Labour Party.[24] In Highton the WEA had enlisted an able, energetic organiser with impeccable mainstream labour movement credentials, and a missionary zeal for the tasks in hand, including a combative defence of the open WEA approach and of high-quality educational work. Moreover, into the early 1920s he was ideally placed to cultivate a network of contacts and secure a solid base of financial and political support for the WEA within the official leadership of the organised labour movement, especially in Glasgow and the west of Scotland.

During Highton's period as organising secretary, 1919–26, over 100 organisational affiliations were secured and maintained annually, some directly to the Scottish council, but mostly to branches at local level. This was attributable to his own driving energy, the untold commitment of branch activists and voluntary members, evidence of growing support from labour movement organisations and developing responses from university partnerships and several local authorities. At the peak of 16 branches, 10 were outside the west of

Scotland. From session 1921–2 until 1925–6, over 2,000 individual members were registered annually although, ominously, over 1,000 belonged to the Edinburgh branch which was soon to secede.[25]

However, a major positive development was the transformation in relationships between the WEA and Glasgow University. Here, a driving force was A. D. Lindsay, a renowned figure in the WEA, adult education, and the university sector in England. Earlier, at Oxford, he had pioneered the joint committee model of liberal adult education tutorial classes with the WEA. On his return to Glasgow in 1922 for two short years as professor of moral philosophy he persuaded the university to form a joint committee on the Oxford model, with attendant funding (initially £500 per year) to provide educational programmes stimulated by WEA demand. This direct financial contribution immediately doubled the size of the WEA core programme in Glasgow and the west of Scotland and, from 1924 until the 1960s, the Glasgow University extra-mural committee became a fixture of the higher education–WEA partnership.[26]

While this initiative can be regarded as a slightly belated and modified outcome of the 1919 Report, the receptive WEA–Labour milieu in Glasgow and the generally progressive left-of-centre outlook of leading academics there had much to do with its early success. The ever-vigilant critics from the Labour College left questioned what they saw as another attempt to boost an ideological alternative to their own efforts.[27] Even so, in political terms Lindsay's Christian Socialist zeal and ILP affiliation, his commitment to extending the role of the university to serve the wider community, and his belief in the value of education for social purpose and democratic citizenship, were ideals which found current and wide recognition, especially in this part of Scotland and, to an important extent, within the WEA fraternity.

Within a short time, key figures in the Labour establishment identified with the WEA, and some became leading members of its principal governing bodies. The most prominent example is Joseph Duncan, whom Highton recruited to the WEA in 1919. Duncan was founder and organising secretary of the Scottish Farm Servants Union and an ardent advocate of adult education. A Labour moderate, a member of the general council of the STUC during the 1920s and its president in 1926, he was also perhaps the ablest trade union leader of his generation. Elected chairperson of the Scottish council of the WEA in 1920, Duncan served it knowledgeably until 1935. Bella Jobson, a full-time official of the Scottish Farm Servants Union, and an influential member of the STUC general council was, throughout the 1920s and 1930s, a mainstay of the Stirling WEA branch and Scottish council treasurer. J. M. Biggar, a prominent Glasgow councillor with a strong Co-op and ILP background, served the WEA at all levels throughout the inter-war period and beyond. C. N. Gallie, of the Railway Clerks Association, was a stalwart advocate of workers' education on the WEA Scottish executive and in the STUC; and James Walker, Scottish organiser for the ISTC and right-wing Labourite, was important as a spokesman for WETUC and for the WEA at STUC level. William Graham, formerly wartime tutor of the WEA Edinburgh economics class, Labour MP for West Edinburgh (1918–31) and a Cabinet minister in the 1929 government, was a parliamentary champion of public funding and wider recognition for the WEA in Scotland. Also of national significance was the early recruitment of John Muir, who in 1916 had been convicted of alleged political sedition as a leading member of the Clyde Workers Committee. Muir had since joined the ILP and moderated his socialist stance prior to election as treasurer of the Scottish council of the WEA in 1920–1. Elected as Labour MP for Glasgow Maryhill in 1922, Muir served in the minority Labour Government of 1924 as parliamentary secretary to the Ministry of Pensions. After losing his seat as MP, he became organising secretary of the national body of the WEA, specialising in education for trade unionists under the WETUC scheme.[28]

During the 1920s, Marwick's resourceful fieldwork for WETUC enabled the WEA to establish a presence in important industrial communities across central Scotland, but particularly in north Lanarkshire. An Edinburgh history graduate, Quaker, and ILP socialist who had been imprisoned as a wartime conscientious objector, Marwick concentrated on organising and lecturing in the Lanarkshire steel towns. In close co-operation with ISTC members, other trade unionists, and Labour party activists, industrial branches were formed in Motherwell and Coatbridge, and student groups in nearby industrial communities. As other trade unions joined the scheme, a WETUC class was often the nucleus of a new WEA branch in areas of Scotland which would not otherwise have been penetrated by the WEA: as in the case of Inverness, for example.

In Scotland, the core subjects in WETUC classes were applied social sciences – economics, economic and labour history, politics and citizenship, issues of industrial democracy, the social psychology of industrial relations, and problems of trade unionism. Public speaking was also a popular offer, building confidence and articulate expression on platforms and in meetings. Sessional and short courses alike were pitched at an appropriate level. Marwick undertook the bulk of the teaching programme, assisted by carefully selected university colleagues and sometimes by guest speakers from the labour and trade union scene. As in the WEA university level classes, written work was encouraged, though rarely submitted. Course timetabling often accommodated shift patterns for iron and steel workers, railway clerks and postal workers, but evening and weekend schools were the norm. Some courses were tailored for a trade union group or sector and, equally, a number of WETUC students every year fed into, and took advantage of, other WEA course programmes.[29]

However, the WETUC strand of work was the first and worst to suffer as a result of the mass unemployment and frequent industrial stoppages of the inter-war period. The correspondent from the west of Scotland commented ruefully in *The Highway*, as early as 1922:

> The continuous unemployment, especially in the iron and steel trades, makes our work among the workers very difficult. Semi-starvation does not tend to an enthusiasm for education in the adult any more than in the juvenile.[30]

In such circumstances, a WETUC class in the industrial town of Coatbridge, on the history of literature, enrolling only two ISTC members, was sustained by an influx of women teachers recruited through the EIS. In 1931, the drastic decline in union membership and dues led the ISTC to withdraw its crucial financial contribution to WETUC, including half of Marwick's salary, and his post was terminated, leaving the WEA in Scotland without a single full-time field-worker or tutor. WETUC classes continued but, after the early 1920s, this strand of provision never formed more than a tiny proportion of the overall WEA programme in Scotland.

In the post-war era, as the WEA in Scotland sought to make a greater impact on the labour movement, it came under sustained attack from the ever rising profile of the Scottish Labour College movement. From 1918–19 the provision of independent working-class education continued to develop apace. In that session, 20 classes were organised in Glasgow alone, where fresh inroads were made into ILP branches. An unspecified number of classes and study circles were organised in other locations in the west, and among militant mining communities in Lanarkshire, the Lothians and Fife. In the 1920s the rival movements achieved a parallel growth in both organisational affiliation and scale of educational programmes, and often competed fiercely for affiliations and allegiance. In 1919–20, while the WEA mustered a creditable total of 21 classes, the Labour College movement again proved that it was not confined to the Glasgow–Clydeside belt. Here, 30 single-term classes ran, and over 50 elsewhere, boosted by successful area conferences from Aberdeen to Edinburgh in the final push to raise the necessary funding for a residential Labour College. The Scottish Labour College ran as a residential centre for one year before closing in 1921. By then, many former members of the British Socialist Party and Socialist Labour Party who had been closely identified with the Labour College movement were preoccupied with building the new Communist Party. Their hostility to John Maclean, who opposed the formation of the Communist Party, also affected their attitude towards the Labour College movement. Therefore, the continuing existence of 'independent working-class education', until then a fluent, often informal, Marxist-oriented political education movement within a wider struggle for socialism, was in danger of becoming a hostage to fortune unless forces on the left were prepared to fight for it politically. It was also under pressure from the revolutionary left in the Communist Party who, by 1922, were about to appropriate the theory and practice of Marxism, transforming it – and political education – into rigid instruments of party building.[31]

Yet, in strategically vital central Scotland at least, reformist labour socialism was in the political ascendant by 1921–2 and, as already suggested, its moderating influences were being exerted within the policies and leading personnel of the growing WEA and in the still flourishing, left-oriented, but essentially non-revolutionary Labour College movement. The Scottish Labour College and associated Plebs League branches were absorbed into the newly-created National Council of Labour Colleges (NCLC) at the end of 1921, with the Edinburgh-based J. P. M. Millar as its first and only general secretary. The formation of the NCLC and its turn to formal relationships with individual trade unions, the TUC and STUC were largely dictated by the rival existence of the WETUC scheme and the continuing challenge of the allegedly pro-capitalist WEA.[32]

Millar was the archetypal champion of non-communist, independent, working-class education, and in his almost obsessive attempts publicly to expose the WEA as a reactionary body, he followed in John Maclean's footsteps as the principal *bête noir* of the WEA in Scotland. He pursued a relentless polemical war against the WEA and its university partners, directing a particular spotlight on the Edinburgh branch. For example, in one episode, he ordered a covert investigation into the political allegiances of all Edinburgh University staff who taught on the large branch programme. The revelation that only one was a known Labour supporter, and the others were avowedly or reputedly anti-socialist, was deemed sufficient proof to indict the WEA for collusion with the corrupt bourgeois influences of the university.[33]

From 1920 the biggest area of expansion for the Scottish Labour College movement was in Edinburgh and the Lothians. Here it presented a serious rival to Edinburgh WEA branch activity which, until 1926, represented the largest WEA programme in Scotland. From a slow start, the Edinburgh and District Committee of the SLC, led by the redoubtable Millar and by Jock Miller, had within a year organised 21 classes with 700 students and had gained 36 organisational affiliations, including the principal trade unions and ILP branches. The Edinburgh Trades and Labour Council had supported the WEA effort from the beginning, but successful political challenges from the left from 1922 resulted in a longstanding adherence to the NCLC. While the Edinburgh WEA branch ceased to exist between 1926 and 1944, the Edinburgh and Lothian district of the NCLC maintained its profile and scale of programme.[34]

In the contest with the WEA, Millar's suspicions about the Edinburgh branch and the university's motives were not unfounded, as there is startling evidence of ideological pressure – in the guise of quality academic teaching – being exerted on worker students, precisely at the high point of post-war militancy and political expectation. George Davie cites the remarkable case of Norman Kemp Smith, modernist professor of philosophy at Edinburgh University who, from 1919, using robust face-to-face argument with workers in WEA classes and in workplace meetings, ostensibly set out to break the influence of Labour College agitators and thereby halt the contagious spread eastwards of Red Clydeside Marxism.

Kemp Smith willingly took the lead in the WEA branch, continuing as elected chairman through the 1920s. As convenor of its advisory committee, acting with the local authority partner, he also directed the large course programme and allocated the academic staff. Rising to over 30 sessional classes by 1926, the branch offered a significant segment of social science courses but, increasingly, a general and specialised arts programme (including harmony, music appreciation, and biblical studies), reflecting more the university's own curriculum and the preferences of a fee-paying Edinburgh middle-class public than a distinctive WEA social purpose. However, it was as lecturer in the large WEA philosophy class and in the branch discussion club that he sought to dissuade students from the doctrines of Marxism, warning against acceptance of an over-optimistic view of human nature and the prospects for a socialist society. Such behaviour could be interpreted in support of the contention that the WEA was being used as an instrument to confront the alleged menace of Marxist influences among workers. In any case, Kemp Smith was a keen advocate of education for citizenship which he encouraged in the WEA programme, and his discernible political agenda by the mid-1920s included a commanding role for the university in its links with the WEA and moderate elements in the Labour establishment.[35]

The sensational secession of the Edinburgh branch in January 1926 commands particular interest. The ostensible reason for the split was rejection of the proposal for a unifying scheme of trade union education – incorporating WETUC, the NCLC, Central Labour College and Ruskin College – under the umbrella of the TUC. The heady rhetoric of the manifesto agreed by the WEA to promote this scheme – 'for the work of securing social and industrial emancipation' – was deemed a threat to the independence of the WEA and a departure from its declared non-party-political principles. Despite clarification and reassurances from Joseph Duncan and Herbert Highton at the dramatic meeting of 8 January, 54 votes to 10 were cast for secession, it being 'obvious from the beginning that the minds of the majority present were decisively made up before the meeting began'.[36] This position was sustained even after the proposed trade union education scheme was aborted in mid-1926.

Although this secession was unique, the split proved damaging in several respects. A highly publicised and politicised episode, it created a furore in the national press, although it also presented opportunities for the WEA to reaffirm its principles publicly. Highton's statement for the Scottish council asserted the independence and respectability of the WEA as an educational organisation: its classes were open to all students, its teaching was non-partisan and non-sectarian in approach; and its tutors and syllabus were accountable to the respective public authorities.[37] Nevertheless, the loss of the Edinburgh branch – with 1,000 members, 2,000 students and large programme – was a huge blow to the credibility, profile and already vulnerable financial position of the WEA in Scotland. Although the principal trade union affiliates had voted against the branch split, they failed to create the nucleus of a revived branch and, instead, after 1928 it was a weakened, isolated WETUC presence which survived for several years in the capital city.[38] Equally galling to the WEA, the breakaway organisation, entitled 'The Edinburgh Workers' Educational Association', continued to exist with a thriving general adult education programme. It did so, albeit in a willing but dependent partnership with the university and local educational authority, and remained unreconciled to the former parent body until 1944.[39]

CONSOLIDATION AND CONTINUING CONTROVERSY IN THE 1930s

Despite the fallout from the Edinburgh experience, by the end of the 1920s the WEA in Scotland had managed not only to stage a recovery as a viable voluntary movement, but also to expand its geographical profile and programmes. In size of programme, the WEA in Scotland peaked in 1938–9 at 200 single-term and full sessional classes, with over 7,000 student enrolments. Into the 1930s short-term grants from the Carnegie and Cassel charitable trusts helped the WEA and Edinburgh university extra-mural committee to pioneer adult education programmes in rural areas of central and southern Scotland. However, the hub of WEA control passed decisively to Glasgow and the West of Scotland, where most of the large local authorities came round to supporting the WEA effort.[40]

Nevertheless, WEA consolidation was accomplished in conditions which somewhat compromised and diluted its distinctive character as a pioneering body and continued to expose the ambiguities in its declared mission. From 1928, within the Glasgow and West of Scotland Joint Committee on Adult Education (Aberdeen and St. Andrews Universities followed suit in their catchment areas) the WEA entered into a more formalised, but increasingly unequal relationship with its higher education and local authority partners.[41] These tripartite bodies undertook co-ordination and supervision of all the adult education effort in their areas of regional responsibility. While the specific role of John MacLeod, the WEA organising secretary based in Glasgow, and that of the voluntary activists, was still to generate educational demand and bring it to the attention and approval of their funding partners – primarily the local educational authorities – those very bodies were becoming more involved in providing and organising non-vocational adult education classes on their own account. In one important sense, they began to do so as a direct result of persistent lobbying carried out by the WEA over the years, and therefore credit for that outcome must accrue to the pioneering body. However, the overwhelming bulk and character of educational programmes emerging from deliberations with local authority partners appears to reflect the priorities of those bodies for a diffuse and wide-ranging provision for the general public: short and sessional classes for personal culture, leisure and recreational pursuits, rather than courses representing a distinctive WEA social purpose.

Moreover, in the 1930s, within the overall programme approved by the joint Glasgow university extra-mural committee, the WEA's social purpose was relegated to a marginal position. The social science subjects – reckoned most essential for providing a vital guide to informed political and community action and as a liberating force for working-class agency – were greatly outnumbered by arts subjects such as English and foreign languages, and by elementary science subjects. Admittedly, it was a result of funding difficulties rather than policy default and lack of demand, that no more than a handful of advanced tutorial classes ever materialised, the norm being one-year and sessional classes. However, on the whole, the curricular imbalance again suggests that the radical cutting edge of WEA social purpose was being blunted by the increasing promotion of other subject areas in both short and advanced courses delivered at the university and in community premises throughout the city and suburbs. [42]

It would appear that both the leading figures in the WEA and the rapidly expanding, 500-strong, individual-member Glasgow WEA branch were keen to recruit for and participate in a diffuse programme to satisfy their own preferences, while maintaining an interest in advocating a more general spread of adult education opportunities *per se*. Certainly, the WEA in Scotland maintained its campaigning role for comprehensive educational advance during the 1930s – raising issues in well-attended and well-publicised annual conferences – but there is an inescapable impression that the predominantly Glasgow-based leadership of the Scottish council and executive displayed a conformist and moderate image in their politics, in their perspectives on workers' and adult education and in their behaviour in committee with university partners.

Ernest Greenhill, senior Glasgow city Labour councillor, past chairman of the Glasgow WEA branch and, from 1936, chairman of the WEA Scottish council, epitomised this stance. For example, always fearful that any part of the WEA programme could be construed as straying into political propaganda, he and John Highton (who was also mindful of his position as a high-ranking civil servant), as WEA representatives on the extra-mural education committee in 1931 agreed to censor a Glasgow branch proposal to show new Soviet films, and to seek the prior approval of the committee on any such further occasions.[43]

To cite this example is not to deny the prevalence of spirited and controversial political discussion in WEA classes in Glasgow or in branch programmes elsewhere. The abiding issue was how to pursue and use the benefits of knowledge, as in the instructive words of the longstanding mission statement of the Glasgow branch:

> to enable every adult in the country to think out clearly and for himself the problems of the day. The wise use of the vote, of membership of political party or trade union, and a dozen other duties, depends on honest, clear, personal thinking. We must not leave ourselves in the power of the agitator or orator of any party.[44]

The multi-faceted Glasgow WEA branch – which in the 1930s and beyond was the 'jewel in the crown' of WEA voluntaryism – exhibited this responsible approach in its eclectic programme. A hive of voluntary activity, it spawned a large number of formal committees, sub-committees and informal clubs based on subject interest groups. For instance, there were active committees for finance, programme, membership and class visits, social events, publicity, literature and libraries, women (for outreach to groups such as Co-operative women's guilds), trade union representatives, and unemployment. Notably, women were prominent as leading members in most committees and clubs, also serving as class secretaries in an extensive programme.[45]

Again, when confronting the issue of educational provision for unemployed workers in the depressed 1930s, the WEA in Scotland sought to steer within safe political channels by adopting and implementing the official and state-sponsored community service approach. John Highton was a founder and executive chairperson of the Scottish Council For Community Service During Unemployment, and the Glasgow WEA branch, in particular, was directly involved, through its unemployment committee, in facilitating unemployed worker access to its general programme and to separate daytime provision. Take-up of liberal studies classes was minimal compared with popular classes held in conjunction with the Glasgow Council For Community Service During Unemployment. Here, recreational, leisure, crafts and allotment gardening programmes characteristically held sway.[46]

This WEA collusion in provision of political palliatives for unemployed workers alienated many trade unionists, and provided one of two grounds for STUC disaffiliation from WEA Scotland in 1936. However, the main issue of debate concerned the continuing feud over ownership and provision of workers' education. Despite forceful interventions by longstanding WEA champions Bella Jobson and C. N. Gallie, conference voted narrowly (75 to 70) for a motion to adopt the NCLC as the only educational organisation worthy of financial support. This decision was not overturned until the 1944 STUC conference, when the enhanced, wartime WEA contribution to trade union and citizenship education was recognised.[47]

Despite such set-piece battles at conference level, during the 1930s there was, in reality, some convergence between the WEA and NCLC in Scotland, at least in the respective education programmes offered to their students. An overview of the type of courses delivered within the Scottish Division (No. 10) of the NCLC reveals a still significant proportion of economics and other social science titles taught, as usual, 'from a working class point of view'. However, this ideologically charged element is greatly outnumbered by practical courses in enabling, organisational skills training such as public speaking, written communication and journalism, and the mechanics of electioneering. It is clear that, while the NCLC in Scotland retained its class war rhetoric, it was essentially no longer a consistently left-wing organisation. It is certainly the case that the Scottish Labour College movement – unlike the WEA – had from the start gained the allegiance of the more militant sections of workers, particularly the miners; but in the climate of defeat, demoralisation and accommodation during the 1930s, the NCLC was in danger of becoming a respectable organisation like its WEA rival. Indeed, scarcely a gadfly on the left, it had transformed itself into a large education and training service agency for the trade unions, the Co-operative movement and the Labour Party.[48]

The NCLC emphasised the need for ownership within the labour movement, and conducted itself with a strident propagandist pitch. The WEA prided itself on objective critical enquiry and on its various partnerships; but despite ideological differences, without the remarkable effort of both as open colleges for workers' and popular education, the political and cultural life of inter-war Scotland would have been immeasurably poorer.

POSTSCRIPT

The WEA in Scotland split into three districts in 1947, aiming to expand its influence throughout the country. However, it did so without ever being granted Responsible Body status by the Scottish Education Department. Consequently, for decades, chronically underfunded and understaffed, the Scottish body remained a poor relation. Moreover, in common with the WEA in England in the post-war era, its identity and mission were still ambiguous.[49] In practice, it served more as a general adult education body than one devoted to promotion of workers' education as such. Its voluntary base also declined. The Glasgow branch dwindled and died by the early 1970s, leaving only a few small branches elsewhere.

Renewal of social purpose, characterised by targeting provision among the large constituency of disadvantaged adults and workers, dates from the middle 1970s. Major commitments, assisted by increased funding and staffing, have included social priority education for community development in deprived areas; the successful pioneering of women's education; creative writing and people's history workshops and publications; and expanded educational opportunities for low-paid and poorly qualified trade union members.[50] Significantly, since the WEA in Scotland was reconstituted as a single entity in 1993, it is this final strand which has risen to prominence within its overall programme and profile. For this writer, it is particularly gratifying that the growing WEA–UNISON Learning At Work programme, concentrated in the public sector, and pursuing a liberal education approach, has become the largest ever undertaking at the end of the first hundred years of the WEA in Scotland. In that primary respect, the WEA can be seen to be fulfilling its historic mission.

NOTES

*Place of publication London unless otherwise stated.*

1.   In this growing historiography, see especially B. Simon (ed.), *The Search for Enlightenment: The Working Class and Adult Education in the Twentieth*

*Century* (Leicester 1990); Fieldhouse and Associates, *History*; R. Lewis, *Leaders and Teachers: Adult Education and the Challenge of Labour in South Wales 1906–1940* (Cardiff, 1993), and R. Duncan, 'Independent Working Class Education and the Formation of the Labour College Movement in Glasgow and the West of Scotland 1915–1922', in R. Duncan and A. McIvor (eds), *Militant Workers: Labour and Class Conflict on the Clyde 1900–1950* (Edinburgh, 1992), 106–28.

2.  R. Duncan, 'A Critical History of the Workers' Educational Association in Scotland 1905–1993', in J. Crowther, I. Martin, M. Shaw (eds), *Popular Education and Social Movements in Scotland Today* (Leicester, 1999), 106–20.

3.  E.g. see William Boyd's comments on this problem in *The Scottish Educational Journal*, 13 Sept. 1918, 282.

4.  For essential background, R. D. Anderson, *Education and Opportunity in Victorian Scotland: Schools and Universities* (Edinburgh, 1983); R. D. Anderson, *Education and the Scottish People* (Oxford, 1995); Ministry of Reconstruction, *Final Report of the Adult Education Committee*, Cmnd 321, HMSO, 1919 for information on Scotland; for useful contextual comment, see also A. Cooke, 'Scotland and the 1919 Report', in A. Cooke and A. McSween (eds), *The Rise and Fall of Adult Education Institutions and Social Movements: Proceedings of the Seventh Annual Conference on the History of Adult Education* (Frankfurt am Main, 2000), 267–77.

5.  Anderson, *Education and Opportunity*; Anderson, *Education and the Scottish People*.

6.  On Boyd and Darroch, see R. H. Bell, 'The Education Departments in the Scottish Universities', in W. H. Humes and H. Paterson (eds), *Scottish Culture and Scottish Education 1800–1980* (Edinburgh, 1983); W. H. Marwick, 'Workers' Education in Early Twentieth Century Scotland', in *Scottish Labour History Journal* 8, 1975, 34–8.

7.  WEA *Annual Reports*, London, 1905–9.

8.  *Glasgow Herald*, 18 Oct. 1909; also in J. B. Barclay, *When Work Is Done* (Edinburgh, 1971), 4.

9.  Duncan, 'Independent Working Class Education'.

10. *Commission of Enquiry into Industrial Unrest: Division No. 7 (Wales)* and *Division No. 8 (Scotland)* (Cmnd. 8668 and 8669).

11. *The Worker*, 3 Nov. 1917.

12. As, for example, R. Fieldhouse, 'The 1908 Report: Antidote to Class Struggle?', in S. Harrop. (ed.), *Oxford and Working Class Education*, new edn (Nottingham, 1987), 30–47: also the essay on the WEA by R. Fieldhouse in Fieldhouse and Associates, *History*; see Jonathan Rose, 'The Whole Contention Concerning the Workers' Educational Association', in his *The Intellectual History of the British Working Classes* (New Haven, 2001), for the most recent contribution to this whole debate.

13. *Plebs Magazine*, Sept. 1917.

14. Duncan, 'Independent Working Class Education'.

15. *The Highway*, June 1917.

16. 1919 Report, 289–91; and relevant pages of *WEA Education Year Book* 1918.

17. *Educational News*, July 1916; *The Highway* for reports throughout 1917–early 1918.

18. Cooke and McSween, *Rise and Fall*, 2000.
19. WEA Scottish Council, *How To Get The Best Out Of The Education Act for Scotland* (Glasgow, 1919).
20. H. Highton's extended report and retrospect on the WEA in Scotland, in *The Highway*, Jan. 1921.
21. *Scottish Educational Journal*, 13 Sept. 1918.
22. WEA Scottish Council, *Third Annual Report*, 1920–1.
23. *The Worker*, 9 Aug., 11 and 25 Oct., 1 Nov. 1919; also Maclean in *Vanguard*, July 1920.
24. Betty Nash, 'A Daughter of the WEA', in *WEA Reportback*, vol. 2, no. 15, Spring 1998, 26–7, on her father Herbert Highton; and my letter of tribute in following issue; Glasgow Trades and Labour Council, *Annual Reports*, 1913–27; Glasgow University Archives, H. E. R. Highton Collection, UGD 102.
25. WEA Scottish Council, *Annual Reports*, 1920–1–1926–7.
26. Glasgow University Archives, SEN1/1/28–29: Glasgow University, Minutes of Senate, 1923–4; D. Scott, *A. D. Lindsay: A Biography* (Oxford, 1971); see also R. Turner, 'Idealists and Liberal Adult Education in the West of Scotland', forthcoming, in *Proceedings of the 8th International Conference on the History of Adult Education*, for a useful discussion of Lindsay and other Hegelian academics at Glasgow; WEA Scottish Council, *Annual Report*, 1924–5; *The Highway*, Summer 1924.
27. See National Library of Scotland, Accession 5120, National Council of Labour Colleges MSS, Box 21(file 8).
28. See entries for Duncan, Graham, Muir, and Walker in W. Knox (ed.), *Scottish Labour Leaders 1918–1939* (Edinburgh, 1984); also for the above, Gallie and Jobson, see Angela Tuckett, *The Scottish Trades Union Congress: The First 80 Years 1897–1977* (Edinburgh, 1986); WEA Scottish Council, *Annual Reports* for 1920s and 1930s.
29. Marwick, 'Workers' Education'; Mitchell Library, Glasgow, Glasgow City Archives, file TD 1163: WETUC Minutes, Scottish District, 1920–36; WETUC Annual Reports, London 1920 and later; *The Highway* also carried regular reports of WETUC activity in Scotland in the early 1920s; see also A. J. Corfield, *Epoch in Workers' Education* (1969), for a history of WETUC, including coverage of Scotland.
30. *The Highway*, Nov. 1922.
31. Duncan, 'Independent Working Class Education', for an account of the Scottish Labour College and sources consulted; see also the discussion of Red Clydeside historiography by T. Brotherstone in the same volume.
32. J. P. M. Millar, *The Labour College Movement* (1980).
33. National Library of Scotland, Acc. 5120, NCLC MSS, Box 21, file 1.
34. Acc. 5120, NCLC MSS, Boxes 77,78,79, NCLC Edinburgh and District Committee minutes, 1919–40; Box 75, Scottish Labour College National Committee minutes, 1923–40.
35. G. Davie, *The Crisis of the Democratic Intellect* (Edinburgh, 1986), 50–3; NCLC MSS, Box 21, files 1 and 2, containing various NCLC–WEA correspondence between 1921 and 1925, including details of Edinburgh WEA branch officers and syllabus.

36. Glasgow City Archives, TD 1163, WEA Scottish Council, minutes of Executive Committee, 16 Jan. 1926.
37. NCLC MSS, Box 21, file 8 and Box 23 contain press cuttings on the branch split.
38. WETUC minutes, Scottish District, 11 Feb. 1928.
39. Barclay, *When Work is Done*.
40. WEA Scottish Council, *Annual Reports*, 1928–9 and following.
41. Glasgow University Archives, ACE 5/5/2/1, West of Scotland Joint Committee on Adult Education, *Annual Reports*, 1928–39; and WEA Scottish Council *Annual Reports*.
42. WEA Scottish Council, *Annual Reports*, 1930s.
43. Glasgow University Archives, ACE 1/1, Glasgow University Extra-Mural Education Committee, minutes, agendas, and papers,1927–35; Minutes of 7 Dec. 1931 for Soviet films decision.
44. WEA Glasgow Branch, *Jubilee Pamphlet 1916–1966* (Glasgow, 1966).
45. WEA Glasgow Branch, *Annual Reports*; *The Adult Student*, no. 1, Dec. 1931, vol. 2, no. 3, 1938 (nine issues), Glasgow.
46. Scottish Council For Community Service During Unemployment, *Annual Reports*, 1933–40; *The Adult Student* vol. 2, no. 1, 1935; WEA Scottish Council, Annual Reports; WEA Glasgow Branch, Annual Reports.
47. Scottish Trades Union Congress, *Annual Reports*, 1936–44; for disaffiliation issue, 1936 Report, 170–2.
48. NCLC MSS, Box 79.
49. Fieldhouse, in Fieldhouse and Associates, *History*; B. Jennings, *Knowledge is Power: A Short History of the WEA 1903–1978* (Hull, 1979).
50. For recent debates, see Duncan, 'A Critical History'.

# 11 The WEA and Workers' Education in Early Twentieth-century Wales

*Richard Lewis*

While no comparative studies exist to confirm or confound the contention, it is a belief widely held that nowhere in Britain did the Workers' Educational Association make more of an impact on social and political life in the twentieth century than in Wales. Certainly by the end of the fourth decade of the century there was some statistical evidence to support the idea that, per head of the population, far more people participated in the classes of the WEA in Wales than in any other part of the United Kingdom.[1] The WEA in Wales evolved in the context of a traditional democratic culture that revered learning and literacy, founded in large measure on a predominant tradition of non-conformist, chapel-based religious observance where attendance at mid-week Bible classes was almost as important as strict observance of Sunday as 'the Lord's day'. It fostered and reinforced the growth of largely untutored book learning. In the mining valley towns and villages especially, the self-taught, well-read working man constituted a small, often significant minority.[2] However, it would be wrong to assume that the Association's success in embedding itself within this culture of text-based Christianity and proletarian erudition was easy or inevitable. Albert Mansbridge had great hopes that his organisation would find support in Edwardian Wales with its increasingly politically active working-class movements and proudly democratic educational traditions that contrasted so markedly with the class-bound structures of England. Yet Mansbridge's optimism was ill-founded; the early history of the WEA in Wales was far from one of easy acceptance and steady growth. The reality was reflected in the comments of the first full-time tutor-organiser of the association in Wales in 1912; when writing of the task in Wales he wrote that 'In all aspects of WEA work *"Nil Desperandum"* is a good motto.'[3]

Edwardian Wales may have been the proud inheritor of a tradition of popular culture, but it is difficult to see any link between that part

of the Welsh experience of the early twentieth century and the establishment of the WEA in Wales. Outside the Welsh-speaking rural
hinterland, Wales was, by and large, an expanding urban and
industrial society where most people spoke and thought in the
English language. Many were English, Scottish or Irish in-migrants
to Wales drawn by the labour demands of the coal industry of the
south Wales valleys, or the mostly coal-related commercial
enterprises of the coastal ports. The little coteries of socially conscious
academics and professionals who allied with trade union enthusiasts
for workers' education to found the WEA in Wales were initially
drawn overwhelmingly from those who came into Wales. Also, the
early WEA found its first footholds in south-east Wales in the most
urbanised, anglicised and cosmopolitan parts of the country. The
organising committee that graced the stage of the Cory Hall in Cardiff
in October 1906 at the founding conference of what became the
WEA in Wales drew very few of its members from the bardic circles,
Welsh literary societies or *eisteddfodau*. Instead, it was led and driven
by men such as P. Wilson Raffan, the Scottish owner of the *South
Wales Gazette*, a weekly paper circulating the western valleys of
Monmouthshire. He used his position to develop a political career as
a radical Liberal, eventually entering the House of Commons as MP
for Leigh in Lancashire in 1910. In 1907 as the first chairman of the
WEA in Wales Raffan stated in terms both stark and unambiguous
what his perception of the purpose of the new organisation was:

> The WEA also realizes that the democracy of this country will, in
> the near future, be called upon to play an important part in the
> affairs of the Empire; hence it is of the highest importance that
> those upon whom the greatest responsibility devolves have such
> knowledge as is necessary, to use the powers wisely and discharge
> their duties in a manner as will bring the greatest good.[4]

It was to be a theme repeated by his successor as chairman, the
philosopher Professor J. S. Mackenzie, a fellow Scot, who declared
his vision of the WEA as creating an educated democracy in Britain
which would be 'under the guidance of the wise subject to the control
and criticism of all'.[5] The ambition was therefore related to a national
political culture that thought in United Kingdom, even imperial,
terms; the Welsh dimension was largely absent from the preoccupations of those behind the development of the WEA in Edwardian
Wales. Rather, it was driven by two related concerns: the growing

belief that the condition of the mass of the people, the manual working class, was increasingly central to political debate; and that the rising political aspirations of the organised working class had to be given some kind of intellectual steer. If the Welsh national question was conspicuous by its absence from the stated concerns of those planning to establish the WEA in Wales in the first decade of the twentieth century, so also was any engagement with the political agenda of radical nonconformity. Almost a century later, it is often difficult to comprehend the extent to which the political landscape of Wales was shaped by the demands of militant religious dissent. Disestablishment of the Anglican state church had been a prime aim of politically active chapel congregations in Wales since the 1880s, and the Liberal landslide of 1906, which left not one Conservative representing a Welsh parliamentary seat, made this an issue that could be translated into legislative action. Temperance, or the limitation or even prohibition of the production and sale of alcoholic drink, was another issue that found active support among the influential ministers and their flocks in both rural and urban Wales. These issues that no longer register at all as factors in electoral life in Wales today, let alone in the rest of the United Kingdom, reflected views of the world that were not easily won over to the concerns that drove those seeking to develop the WEA. Many attempts were made to help the churches and chapels of Wales shift their energies to new agendas, those related to social improvement and economic justice. Such initiatives were by and large unsuccessful; workers' education in Wales developed despite and not because of the power of the chapels.[6]

If the dominant religious affiliation of the Welsh people was less conducive to the development of workers' education than had been hoped by some of its earliest advocates, so was the Welsh language. As has already been stated, it was not in the Welsh-speaking parts of the country that the WEA initially established itself, but in the pre-dominantly English-speaking coastal ports and eastern parts of the south Wales coalfield. The first WEA branch in Wales was founded in 1907 in the coal-exporting port of Barry, a town with a cosmopolitan population and only a small number of Welsh-speaking inhabitants. Even in the north, where Welsh-speaking popular culture was far less threatened by the processes of urbanisation and Anglicisation, the WEA found its first footholds not through the *eisteddfodau*, the Bible classes or the literary circles but through the emphatically English (or even Scottish) university tutorial class movement. More focused and purposeful than the existing range of university extension lectures and short courses already available, the first full university tutorial class in Wales was offered in Wrexham, under the tuition of R. H. Tawney. His Wrexham class has been portrayed as the point at which the WEA was embraced by the existing Welsh culture of enthusiasm for popular education.[7] As a recently published study has shown, this version of events is difficult to sustain. Supported by Oxford University and seen as something of a diversion from the main thrust of their work in Lancashire by both Mansbridge and Tawney, the Wrexham class never really formed the basis of the long-term development of the Association in north Wales after its closure in 1911. Mansbridge did find a way of securing a vague WEA presence in north Wales prior to the outbreak of the First World War, but this was through the tutorial classes organised by the University College of North Wales in Bangor in alliance with the local slate quarrymen's union. This was a genuinely local initiative, based on a partnership between the university college and a key local trade union, in line with WEA thinking but with no organisational link to the venture. Mansbridge's contacts were purely personal and related to his friendship with the principal of Bangor, Sir Harry Reichel, who had developed his enthusiasm for this activity while at Balliol College, Oxford, the intellectual and organisational home of the tutorial class movement.[8] Although from 1910 the WEA claimed to have a district committee which covered the whole of Wales, it was not until the 1920s that the WEA established a significant organisational presence in the north, and then it was based on a very close working relationship with the University College's extra-mural department, a lasting characteristic of the Association in north Wales.

In south Wales there were even greater challenges confronting the WEA before 1914. Despite many efforts by supporters on its staff, the University College of South Wales and Monmouthshire in Cardiff proved to be indifferent to the new Association, preoccupied as it was by its ambitions to build up its physical presence in the town. Sometimes the WEA faced open hostility from some local education authorities that saw it as a rival for scarce public financial support for adult education. The WEA in south Wales was able to pursue a range of strategies that allowed it to create a presence based on local classes and contacts with working-class organisations such as the working-men's clubs affiliated to the south Wales branch of the Club and Institute Union. By the end of 1914 there were 16 local working-men's clubs in south Wales affiliated to the WEA where classes and lectures were organised.[9] However, the real challenge was to secure the support of organised labour in what had by the late Edwardian era already become one the industrial relations storm-centres of Britain. In this regard the key agency was the South Wales Miners' Federation (SWMF), its districts, lodges and officials. With a membership of over 150,000 it had a pervasive influence on the coalfield communities that transcended its role as a trade union. It provided a new communal leadership through its agents and officials that translated into political representation as the union became the basis upon which the early Labour Party displaced, slowly at first, popular liberalism and the chapel-based social and political leadership of late-nineteenth-century industrial south Wales. Despite the efforts of its supporters in Wales, Welsh organised labour proved unenthusiastic about workers' education in general and the WEA in particular. Isolated examples of support cannot hide the fact that prior to the outbreak of the war the Association in Wales made virtually no headway in securing the support of the great coalmining workforce. It was a time of growing conflict between capital and labour, and this may have diverted active trade unionists from long-term commitments to self- and collective educational improvements. However, another factor also came into play, especially in relation to the SWMF: the emergence of an alternative vision of the nature and purpose of workers' education that evolved in the early years of the WEA's existence. The movement for independent working-class education (IWCE) associated with the Labour College movement, with its rejection of support from agencies of the capitalist state, and its commitment to a Marxist-orientated diet of anti-capitalist education based on a 'materialist conception of history', found in many of the young activists of the SWMF some of its staunchest and most effective advocates. A key element of IWCE rhetoric was an abiding hostility to the WEA and its close links to the universities which was to last until well into the 1940s.[10]

The ability of the supporters of IWCE to spread their perception of what workers' education should be was given greater impetus by the fact that in the late Edwardian era, especially in the south Wales coalfield, there was a rising tide of anti-capitalist sentiment amongst the industrial working classes. Battles between capital and labour had a new edge to them that meant that the language of class conflict resonated with young workers. Class-conscious rhetoric and its message that the workers had to secure their own salvation now threw into relief anything which smacked of class collaboration. The WEA's association with middle-class professionals, academics and the universities was viewed with suspicion. They were seen as 'handmaidens of capitalism', spreading pro-capitalist and anti-working-class propaganda. The state was viewed as an agency of class oppression and its funds tainted as a consequence.

While the anti-WEA opinions of the IWCE movement in south Wales caricatured and distorted the intentions of the leading lights of the Association, there was sufficient substance in the critique to make it effective propaganda. By the late Edwardian era and into the war years, the WEA in Wales became a vehicle for a loose coterie of social radicals, academics, civil servants and other professionals living mainly in the Cardiff and Barry areas. Sharing many concerns regarding the social consequences of modern capitalism, they viewed rising class conflict as a threat, not as a means of securing progress and improvement for the mass of the population. In no way unsympathetic to the political aspirations of organised labour, they sought to give it direction. Some of the leading figures of this group were members of the Independent Labour Party (ILP), and were as vociferous in their denunciation of unbridled employer power as any Labour College tutor. However, also prominent were men such as Daniel Lleufer Thomas, the stipendiary magistrate for Rhondda, who had sent many rioting strikers to prison following the major industrial disputes of 1910. Although an advocate of strong but disciplined trade unionism, a staunch supporter of the Co-operative movement and the founder of the Welsh School of Social Science, as chairman of the WEA in Wales he was, inevitably, an easy target for the Labour College activists in the coalfield. Nor was the position of the Association made an easier in this period by the fact that, having failed to attract any significant financial support from local trade unions, it was only kept afloat by virtue of substantial donations from very wealthy individuals, some with strong coal-owning connections.[11]

The early war years were no easier for the WEA in Wales. Matters were made worse by the fact that the Association was deeply split over the war itself. The tutor-organiser John Thomas, an ILP member and devotee of Keir Hardie, opposed the war, as did Hardie himself, on moral and religious grounds. Those who strongly supported the war effort dominated the WEA district committee and matters came to a head with the introduction of conscription; Thomas became a conscientious objector. Thomas was, in effect, forced out of his job.[12] The episode offered yet further evidence for the critics of the WEA that it was in essence an agency of establishment orthodoxy. The late war period offered different challenges. The relative industrial peace of the early war years broke down after 1916, and the south Wales coalfield once again became the centre of national attention as a focus of worker/employer conflict. Appeals to patriotism made less impact when rising house rents and food prices, combined with blatant profiteering, made the anti-capitalist message more credible than ever among key sections of the urban working class. Although there is no evidence that the Welsh working classes turned against the war effort as such, their willingness to take industrial action in pursuit of wage demands, and more alarmingly for the government, the spread of revolutionary socialist ideas amongst the activist elements, prompted a search for solutions in which the role of workers' education took on new relevance and urgency that it had hitherto not possessed. Key players in this process were drawn from the social radical clique that dominated the WEA in Wales. Thomas Jones, the former treasurer of the Welsh District, taken by Lloyd George into the Cabinet Office when he became prime minister, used his contacts and influence to ensure that the WEA had a voice in the debate over responses to the new challenges. The chairman of the Industrial Unrest Commission for Wales, which investigated the causes and possible solutions to the crisis, was none other than Lleufer Thomas. Another member of the social radical clique and sometime WEA tutor, Edgar Chappell, acted as secretary. Lleufer Thomas used the evidence of the rapid expansion of Labour College classes in south Wales to emphasise the need for WEA and university tutorial class provision in the region.[13]

By the end of the war WEA classes were catering for less than a quarter of the number of students attending Labour College classes in the region.[14] The language of class conflict displaced the biblical vocabulary of earlier years among active trade unionists and labour politicians. The Russian revolution and the rise of communism polarised opinion, and the common ground between capital and labour on which the leadership of the WEA in Wales had hoped to construct a sense of civil and social responsibility in the new democratic order had disappeared. In this atmosphere the WEA in Wales struggled to find a new formula that would attract the working-class activist, and wean him or her away from Labour College classes.

This was to be no easy task. In January 1920, *Welsh Outlook*, a journal that was usually very sympathetic to its aims, stated that in its twelve years of existence, the WEA in Wales had made virtually no impact at all. By 1922 the WEA in Wales was perilously close to financial collapse, and the district secretary's salary was reported to be six months in arrears. Once again the Welsh District was kept in existence by heavy subventions from wealthy sympathisers, giving yet more ammunition to its rivals.[15]

That the WEA in Wales survived the immediate post-war years and the beginning of the period of chronic structural unemployment that dogged industrial Wales through most of the inter-war years was due in no small measure to the extraordinary methods and personality of the man appointed as its district secretary in 1919: John Davies. Until his untimely death in 1937, Davies was to keep the Association in existence despite too often 'seeing more pay days than pay packets'.[16] A great networker and fixer, a man of undoubted charm, his unconventional methods – he conducted most WEA business in a popular Cardiff café rather than in his office – many found too eccentric for their taste. Nonetheless, he was a priceless asset to the WEA in Wales, for despite his ability to mix with the wealthy and secure their financial support for the Association, none could doubt his absolute commitment to the organised labour movement. A lifelong member of the ILP, Davies made his name among local trade unionists before 1914 as a journalist on the Welsh labour newspaper, *Llais Llafur*, and as secretary of the Swansea Trades and Labour Council. After war service he worked as the west Wales organiser of the Agricultural Labourers' Union before taking up his post with the Welsh WEA. When struggling to secure and expand trade union support for the WEA, John Davies could speak from experience and with authority about the challenges that faced the working class and the way that adult education could help their struggles. However, just as important to the Association as Davies's links to organised labour was his Welshness. A Welsh speaker, and regular chapel attender, he was committed to developing the Welsh cultural under-pinnings of the labour movement. This meant that with John Davies the WEA in Wales started to insinuate itself into the wider educational and cultural life of Wales, whereas before it had been utterly peripheral. An indefatigable organiser, Davies travelled the length and breadth of Wales promoting the WEA and the cause of workers' education. As was recognised by many in the large number of tributes penned after his death, nobody was more in touch with every facet of Welsh life in the 1920s and 1930s than John Davies.

In 1925 the WEA in Wales was split into two districts: one for the south where Davies remained district secretary, and one for the north. There, a former close associate of the social radicals who dominated the Welsh WEA in the late Edwardian era and war years, the socialist nonconformist minister the Rev. R. Silyn Roberts, became district secretary. The WEA in north Wales still requires its historian, and it is not possible here to do justice to the developments in north Wales or to the key roles of Silyn Roberts and his wife Mary in carving out a special place for the Association in the region. Silyn Roberts was probably as well connected in Welsh educational and cultural life as John Davies, and it is somewhat ironic that with the splitting of the Welsh District in 1925 the Association increasingly became seen as an integral part of Welsh educational and cultural life. By the 1920s the WEA was portrayed as the natural and inevitable successor of earlier Welsh traditions of adult learning, linked to bardic circles and the circulating schools of the eighteenth-century Welsh pioneer in popular education, Griffith Jones. As one early sceptic of this interpretation put it:

In short Griffith Jones, Llanddowror, has been canonised and enshrined as the patron saint of the Adult Education movement in Wales. This historical fiction may gratify the urge to discover reputable national antecedents of the work, or it may serve as an appropriate background to classes in rural areas, but it would tax the powers of our historians to trace the exact sequence between these essentially Welsh institutions and the modern Tutorial Class in industrialised south Wales.[17]

The inter-war years saw the WEA expand its provision and its influence throughout the principality. This expansion was related to developments in its work with the extra-mural departments of the University of Wales's constituent colleges, growing state financial support for adult classes, alliances with trade unions in Wales that were not won over to IWCE and, in the later inter-war years, access to state and voluntary resources devoted to the social-service response to chronic structural unemployment. Yet, the extent to which the WEA was woven into the fabric of Welsh life in the third and fourth decades of the twentieth century was down to the style and personalities of John Davies and R. Silyn Roberts cannot be overstated.

With the benefit of hindsight it is possible to argue that the changing context within Wales allowed the WEA to embed itself, and become, in terms of its impact on the lives of the people it aimed to serve, the most successful area of the UK for the Association. This would be to underestimate the severe challenges that still faced the WEA in Wales. The struggle with the Labour College movement, although it never dominated the work or the thoughts of John Davies and his successors, nonetheless complicated attempts to secure the support of key trade unions in Wales such as the National Union of Railwaymen and – most importantly of all – the south Wales miners. The conflict took on an institutional quality with the creation in 1919 of the Workers' Educational Trade Union Committee (WETUC). It soon became the organisational basis in the districts for the provision of WEA-type classes for members of affiliated unions. Two important and rapidly expanding general unions, the transport workers (TGWU) and the municipal workers (NUGMW) joined the founding steel workers' union (ISTC) in the scheme. John Davies's impeccable trade union credentials, combined with his personal devotion to the labour movement, meant that WETUC in south Wales secured a firm foothold for the WEA in Welsh trade union education.[18]

The IWCE movement responded by the creation in 1921 of the National Council of Labour Colleges, which until its demise in the early 1960s promoted its class-conscious alternative to the WEA. Specifically rejecting state financial support, and regarding the universities as agencies of capitalist propaganda, in the immediate post-war years and in the early 1920s when revolutionary rhetoric dominated debate within the labour movement, the IWCE version of workers' education made some headway amongst many young activists, especially in the south Wales coalfield. Although organisa-tionally separate from the NCLC, the residential Central Labour College (CLC) in London, financially underpinned by the SWMF and its districts, became in the 1920s a finishing school for a whole generation of Welsh miners' leaders and later Labour politicians, including future Cabinet ministers. Two of the latter, Aneurin Bevan and James Griffiths, supervised the creation of the post-Second World War welfare state. Yet it was a flawed institution racked by a whole series of financial scandals and gross organisational incompetence. In these circumstances, and in the straitened times of the late 1920s, the south Wales miners found they could no longer justify the resources devoted to the CLC, which closed in 1929.[19]

The ICWE relied upon the trade union movement to fund classes just as organised labour was to go through one of its most difficult periods in twentieth-century Britain. This dependency was to act as a severe constraint on the growth and impact of IWCE, but it also made the task of the WEA in building up the work of WETUC in Wales very difficult. John Davies was always conscious that the propaganda of the NCLC meant that the commitment of the WEA to the aspirations of the labour movement was under constant scrutiny. The crunch came with the General Strike and great coal lockout of 1926. As a matter of deliberate policy the WEA had decided that all its districts should be seen to be 'taking sides' with the TUC over the dispute. In south Wales John Davies took particular pride in the way that the WEA office and its facilities were put at the disposal of the local strike committee in Cardiff. The collapse of the General Strike and the slow and painful crushing of the miners and their union had a profound effect on John Davies; he was depressed by the consequences for the labour movement, but also for the fate of the workers' education movement, especially in Wales.[20] From its earliest years in Wales the WEA had always been suspect with certain elements of the political right. In the fevered atmosphere of the 1920s, accusations about the left-wing bias of WEA classes and tutors found support, most notably in the *Western Mail*, by this time the main national newspaper in Wales. Accusations that the WEA classes, and even the university tutorial classes, were 'nurseries of bolshevism' surfaced from time to time in its pages.[21] These allegations were strongly refuted by WEA supporters, especially amongst the Board of Education inspectorate for Wales. While the wilder claims were without foundation, there was some substance in the assertion that there was a strong pro-labour and anti-capitalist tone to WEA education, and that its tutors, and especially the young tutors, were not immune to the temper of the times amongst their predominantly working-class students. This was especially because the curriculum was overwhelmingly related to political economy and industrial history. Although in theory the WEA and the NCLC were at daggers drawn, there were many tutors in industrial south Wales who were happy to give lectures and classes for either organisation. The only difference, as one veteran tutor recalled many years later, was that with the WEA 'you were paid'.[22] The suspicion voiced occasionally by some HMIs that one set of tutorial notes might be used when they visited a class and another less politically neutral set when they were absent is borne out by the oral testimony of several former tutors and students.[23] However, with the defeat of the miners, and the chronic problems that afflicted the Welsh economy in the 1920s, the need to maintain state funding for the work of the WEA became more important as trade union funding became more unreliable. Even the WETUC dispensed with the services of its full-time district organiser as industrial south Wales felt the full force of the great slump of the early 1930s. Thus, the WEA became increasingly sensitive to any accusations of partisan political bias that could jeopardise such support.

The alliance with sympathetic trade unions and their leaders remained a key feature of the strategy pursued by the WEA in Wales, but links with the university extra-mural departments and the development of their own, state-funded short courses were ultimately more important. This was so especially after 1924 when the WEA was recognised as a 'responsible body' for the purposes of delivering Board of Education-funded adult education courses. The vital importance of this money is illustrated by the fact that the state grants received by the South Wales District in 1924 was £128, whereas by 1930 it was £970.[24] Of course, the dependence on state funds raised a number of issues with regard to the nature of the WEA version of workers' education, as their Labour College critics were only too keen to point out. From its inception, Mansbridge and other pioneers of the WEA had stressed how it was mainly concerned with raising the educational aspirations of the workers in general and not in raising individuals out of the working class; it did not see itself as an agency of social mobility. In reality, the provision of any form of adult education opened up opportunities to break out of the mine or steel mill. This was just as true of Labour College as it was of WEA classes. IWCE supporters insisted that their form of workers' education trained more effective advocates for organised labour, but the lifestyles of full-time union officials or MPs tended to take them away from that of their members and constituents whether they had acquired their representational skills in NCLC or WETUC groups. The inter-war years saw more and more opportunities for adult education students to gain access to full-time study. From the early 1920s funds made available by charitable bodies such as the Cassel Trust and the Miners' Welfare Fund allowed adult education students to go on to university. At that time, perhaps in part through concern about the way that it might be portrayed to the trade union movement by its critics, the WEA sought to control the trend by trying to tie the grants to a commitment on the part of the students to return to serve their communities after completion of their studies. Increasingly such requirements were seen as unfair and were soon dropped, and by the late 1920s the WEA publicity in Wales would boast openly about the success of working-class students in securing scholarships and university places. By the late 1930s, while still paying lip service to the Mansbridgean ideal of raising the mass not the individual, D. E. Evans, a WEA official in south Wales, gleefully told a meeting of Cardiff businessmen of a former local steelworker and WEA student whom Evans had once visited at his home to find him simultaneously nursing his infant son and translating Virgil from Latin into Esperanto, both of which languages the steelworker had taught himself. This student went on to higher education and subsequently became a university lecturer.[25] It was a story that reflected an emphatic attitudinal shift for the WEA. The strong collectivist tone of WEA publicity in Wales in the Edwardian period, wartime years and early 1920s did not disappear, but the emphasis had shifted to opening up the mainstream of higher educational provision to the talented worker. What the worker subsequently did with such opportunities was not the immediate concern of the WEA.

The most tangible evidence of this shift was the creation of Coleg Harlech, a residential working-men's college established in a millionaire's former residence on the coastal edge of Snowdonia.[26] Aimed unambiguously at the most able working-class students from the WEA and university tutorial classes in Wales, its founder was Thomas Jones. Jones still thought in terms of the worker students being taken away from the economic pressures of their lives for a period of sustained study but then returning to their communities to provide 'wise' leadership to their communities. However, the first warden of the college, and one of Wales's most distinguished adult educationalists, Ben Bowen Thomas, reflected the new perception very clearly:

Ultimately the duty of the adult educationalist lies neither with the industrial worker group nor towards his locality but to the man himself.[27]

This significant shift of emphasis regarding the nature and purpose of workers' education was also reflected in the appointment of John Davies's successor as south Wales district secretary, D.T. Guy. A former coalminer, Dai Guy attended WEA classes from where he gained a scholarship to Coleg Harlech; from there he went to university in Aberystwyth where he read for a degree in Economics.[28]

Perhaps of equal significance is the fact that between leaving Aberystwyth and becoming district secretary, Guy had worked at the Merthyr educational settlement. The educational settlement movement, which was an integral part of the voluntary but often state-supported social service response to the chronic unemployment of the 1930s, created new opportunities for the WEA. Often driven by a strong sense of religious conviction, and established in some of the hotbeds of IWCE activity such as the Rhondda, the settlements were soon making an impact. Similar institutions were established in other parts of the coalfield such as Merthyr Tydfil, Brynmawr and Pontypool. Beyond the settlements there soon grew up innumerable unemployed clubs and related schemes, some run by the Religious Society of Friends, most with some adult educational content. While the IWCE activist disparaged or opposed the activities of 'the Quakers', John Davies, not without some qualms about the long-term consequences, saw opportunities for the WEA to establish itself in the coalfield in a way that it had failed to do when the Labour College movement was at its most influential. By 1934 there were over 93 such schemes operating across industrial south Wales.[29] A Joint Committee for the Promotion of Educational Facilities in the South Wales and Monmouthshire Coalfields distributed grants made available by such bodies as the Carnegie Trust and the Pilgrim Fund. The secretary of the joint committee was the ubiquitous and indefatigable John Davies. Sitting at the centre of this network and working closely with the very influential Thomas Jones, a great enthusiast for the educational settlement and unemployed club movement, John Davies helped to weave the WEA into the very fabric of life in industrial south Wales, just as Silyn Roberts had achieved a similar status for the Association in the predominantly rural north of the country. The result was that in the economically afflicted valleys of the south Wales coalfield, as the shadow of war began to loom in the late 1930s, hundreds of employed and unemployed miners attended the classes and lectures of the WEA, helping to shape perceptions of their world and reinforce a belief in political solutions to the problems that blighted their lives. In fact by 1940 there were very few towns and villages in Wales where there was not some form of WEA activity.

Through adapting to change, John Davies and Silyn Roberts had given the WEA a relevance to the shifting social and economic agendas that confronted adult education in the 1920s and 1930s. Yet, however pivotal these men were, the WEA in Wales succeeded above all because it engaged the enthusiasm and the commitment of dozens of tutors and class secretaries, and, most important of all, thousands of students who found in its classes and tutorial groups unique opportunities to develop intellectually. Because of the peculiar circumstances that obtained in Wales in the years just before the Second World War, the WEA gained a distinctly Welsh identity that had been so conspicuously absent before 1914. The war and the post-war years saw the end of chronic structural unemployment and with them went the unemployed clubs and the charitable schemes. New initiatives, such as the attempt to rebuild on a new basis the alliance with organised labour associated with the trade union pilot schemes of the 1950s, occupied the energies of the Association in very different economic circumstances from those of the inter-war years. Full employment and a huge expansion of further and higher education in the 1960s and 1970s confronted the WEA in Wales and eroded its role as an opportunity agency. However, the changing nature of work, and especially the growth of female employment and the wider equal opportunities debate provided the Association with new challenges. The economic recessions of the 1980s and early 1990s to some extent revived the role of the WEA as a provider of adult educational support to the districts in Wales blighted by long-term joblessness. Despite these shifting agendas and priorities, and through various debates about its role and relevance, the WEA in Wales has retained its distinct identity and its engagement with Welsh educational, cultural and political life. Perhaps nowhere is the extent to which the WEA in Wales is still woven into the fabric of Welsh public life more visible than in the way that so many of its former employees from the 1970s have become prominent local, national and even international politicians. Although always remaining rigorously non-partisan, the WEA has been an important vehicle for those who wished to follow the political public-service pathway. This has mainly benefited the Labour Party in Wales but, as one recent study has shown, the WEA legacy has also aided the Welsh nationalist strand of political activity.[30] If in the early years of the twentieth century the WEA in Wales failed to acquire a role and identity, the work of its pioneers ensured that that by the last decades of that century no social or political history of Wales could be complete without reference to the work and contribution of the Workers' Educational Association.

NOTES

*Place of publication London unless otherwise stated.*

1. Harold Marks, ' Some WEA Statistics: How Efficient are the Districts', *The Highway*, xxxii (Mar. 1940). In the 1937–8 session the South Wales District had the highest proportion of manual workers attending its classes of any district in the UK: *31st Annual Report of the South Wales District of the WEA.*
2. For a recent study of the Welsh autodidact tradition and its relationship to miners' institutes and libraries see Jonathan Rose, *The Intellectual Life of the British Working Classes* (New Haven, 2001), 237–54.
3. *Fifth Annual Report of the Workers' Educational Association for Wales* (1911–12).
4. *South Wales Daily News*, 1 Dec. 1907.
5. *Glamorgan Gazette*, 1 Nov. 1911.
6. See for example Christopher Turner, 'Conflicts of Faith? Religion and Labour in Wales, 1890–1914' in D. R. Hopkin and G. S. Kealey (eds), *Class, Community and the Labour Movement: Wales and Canada, 1850–1930* (Cardiff, 1989), 67–86 and R. Pope, *Building Jerusalem, Nonconformity, Labour and the Social Question, 1906–1939* (Cardiff, 1998), 31–70.
7. Ron Brooks, ' Rochdale, Wrexham and the University Tutorial Class Movement in North-west Wales, 1907–1914', *The Welsh History Review*, xx, no. 1, June 2000, 62–88.
8. Brooks, 'Rochdale, Wrexham and the University Tutorial Class Movement'.
9. *WEA for Wales, Eighth Annual Report, 1914–15.*
10. A detailed account of the struggle between the WEA and the Labour College movement in south Wales can be found in Richard Lewis, *Leaders and Teachers, Adult Education and the Challenge of Labour in South Wales, 1906–1940* (Cardiff, 1993).
11. Lewis, *Leaders and Teachers*, 39. For the wider influence of the Cardiff/Barry coterie see Richard Lewis 'The Welsh Radical Tradition and the Ideal of a Democratic Popular Culture' in E. Biagini (ed.), *Citizenship and Community: Liberals, Radicals and Collective Identities in the British Isles, 1865–1931* (Cambridge, 1996).
12. Lewis, *Leaders and Teachers*, 105.
13. Lewis, *Leaders and Teachers*, 134–5.
14. Lewis, *Leaders and Teachers*, 134–5.
15. Lewis, *Leaders and Teachers*, 144.
16. The distinguished Welsh historian, John Davies, has recently produced a very insightful study of the life and work for the WEA of his uncle, after whom he was named. It can be found in 'John Davies and the Workers' Educational Association in South Wales', *Llafur, Journal of Welsh Labour History*, viii, no. 1 (2000), 45–68. Many of the references to the work of John Davies in this chapter are taken from this article and from Lewis, *Leaders and Teachers*.
17. P. S. Thomas, 'Adult Education in Swansea', *Cambria*, Spring 1931.
18. Lewis, *Leaders and Teachers*, 152–90; Davies, 'John Davies', 48.
19. R. Lewis, 'The Central Labour College: Its Decline and Fall, 1919–1929', *Welsh History Review*, xii, no. 2 (1984).

20. Lewis, *Leaders and Teachers*, 172.
21. See P. Stead, *Coleg Harlech: The First Fifty Years* (Cardiff, 1977), 31.
22. Interview with A. J. Lush, transcript held at the South Wales Miners' Library, University College, Swansea.
23. Lewis, *Leaders and Teachers*, 184.
24. *23ʳᵈ Annual Report of the South Wales District of the WEA, 1929–30*.
25. *Western Mail*, 18 Mar. 1938.
26. The best and most accessible account about the origins and early development of Coleg Harlech can be found in Stead, *Coleg Harlech*. For the remarkable life and times of Thomas Jones see E. L. Ellis, *T. J.: A Life of Dr Thomas Jones, CH* (Cardiff, 1992).
27. B. B. Thomas, 'Adult Education and the Industrial Worker' (substance of an address to the World Conference on Adult Education, Cambridge, August 1929), reprinted in *Welsh Outlook*, Oct. 1929.
28. Lewis, *Leaders and Teachers*, 206.
29. J. Davies, 'Time to Spare' in *Wales and the New Leisure* (Llandysul, 1935), 7.
30. The list includes Neil Kinnock, Rhodri Morgan, Ron Davies, Wayne David, Allan Rogers and Llewellyn Smith. For the influence of the WEA on Plaid Cymru see Davies, 'John Davies', 61.

# 12 Women's Involvement in the WEA and Women's Education

*Zoë Munby*

The WEA was founded in 1903 as An Association to Promote the Higher Education of Working Men. Two years later it was renamed the Workers' Educational Association, in part in recognition of the legitimate claims of working women to higher education. From the earliest days the WEA championed the rights of working-class men *and* women to study:

> A report like this must fail to give any impression of the steady pursuit of knowledge under incredible difficulties which is carried on patiently by women who have been at work in dressmakers' rooms or in mills through long days.[1]

The new organisation willingly provided a platform and organisational base for women in the labour and suffrage movements to campaign for women's educational rights. Yet today the WEA shows few signs of these early feminist influences. This chapter explores the extent to which women's involvement, interests and priorities have shaped the organisation as it reaches one hundred years.

The picture we hold of women's involvement in the WEA will vary widely. If we are familiar with the organisation, it is likely that our understanding will be very specific to a time and place – the WEA is a federation and within that federation local voluntarism has carved out local cultures. In the past decade the organisation has been refashioned as a single body, but locally programmes and patterns of voluntary activity remain diverse. It is also possible that we have a common sense of how the organisation conducted itself in its earliest years; it is likely that we believe women not to have been important. However, it is possible to offer fragmentary evidence which reveals how unexpected and innovative women's involvement could be.

Some of the earliest classes organised by the WEA were for women only and these examples begin to suggest ways in which women have contributed to the organisation and how important the WEA was in women's lives. In 1910 in Reading 70 women crammed into a new women-only class organised by the WEA; the class, unusually for the WEA, was embroidery. In the same year, in Newcastle upon Tyne, a women's class, 'Pioneer Women of the Nineteenth Century', was being organised. By 1911 women in Chorley were studying 'The Psychology of the Child Mind' and WEA women's study circles extended across London. In 1912 women in Battersea attended a women-only class, 'Nineteenth Century Novelists', and had organised a concert to raise funds for a children's Christmas party. These examples suggest that there is a rich body of evidence of women's involvement in the WEA that needs sifting and analysing.

We know surprisingly little about the numbers of women who attended WEA classes. The collection of student statistics by the organisation reflected the demands of the funding it attracted. In the early days the WEA's only consistent source of grant aid was for students studying the three-year tutorial classes, so tutorial students were recorded from the beginning. However, the educational programme on offer from the WEA was far wider, as the examples above illustrate, and the statistics from these non-grant-earning classes were not consistently recorded.[2] In national annual reports student numbers for tutorial classes are reported from the earliest days; occupational data for those classes is added from 1919–20, and reporting from then on extends to encompass those shorter courses that were progressively able to earn grants for the Association. The WEA published student numbers for *all* provision, and separated out men and women only for a brief period from 1954–5 to 1965–6.[3]

In addition to the financial imperative, an important influence on what was recorded, and on what was reported, was the value attached to the tutorial classes. These were seen as *the* academic rationale for the organisation's existence until well after the 1939–45 war. The tutorial class, demanding a commitment to weekly classes with regular essay writing, over a three-year period, was a major commitment for anyone. It was a significant difficulty for working people, difficult for women who had any domestic responsibilities and almost impossible for a married woman with children. Women tutorial students were mainly young, or single, and in most cases in jobs such as teaching and clerical work. Despite the great obstacles, there were women-only tutorial classes organised as an element in the women's work of the organisation. Women students, as a percentage of tutorial students, increased from 9 per cent in 1910–11 to 32 per cent in 1919–20, then levelled out. For many in the WEA the main goal of the tutorial system remained the education of male manual workers and these figures were greeted with faint embarrassment.[4] What is probably more significant is that women did *not* break through to become a majority of tutorial students.

For the relatively small numbers of women tutorial students the impact of this model of education was extraordinary: here is Maude Royden, an Oxford tutorial class lecturer, describing her Oldham women's class, studying Shakespeare, in 1908–9.

> They not only stayed the course but, at the close of each class, accompanied me down the street to the railway station still arguing and discussing, stood on the platform while I, my head out of the carriage window, continued the class, and made their last contributions to the discussion in shouts above the roar of the train as it pulled out of the station. Can you beat it?[5]

Despite the impact of exceptional teachers such as Maude Royden, the significance of the tutorial system was that it demanded something that many women could not give and so the great surge in women's take-up of educational opportunities within the WEA had least impact on the tutorial classes. The tutorial class, along with trade union education, the other 'flagship' WEA provision, were the only two categories of class in which women did not overtake men. In this way women's engagement in the WEA remained relatively invisible.

A search for statistical evidence of women's involvement in the WEA exposes the extent to which the official value afforded to the tutorial classes overshadows other WEA work, a remarkable tradition of what was known as 'pioneer' work and which would today be known as 'outreach' and 'informal community education'. These lecture programmes, study circles, single talks and social groups were part of the tradition from the earliest years, but this work was only recorded in detail sporadically. Much of the hard statistical evidence of work with women is lost, or was never recorded. Were it possible to calculate the numbers of women involved in the pioneer work of the WEA, a reading of annual reports suggests that women were the majority of WEA students from some time in the 1920s.

Pronouncements on the scale, and significance, of women's involvement in the WEA have been made at regular intervals over the past 100 years, but the basis of these pronouncements was the statistics that *were* published. These were occupational, collected from tutorial classes until the 1940s, when for a short period they were recorded for all WEA provision. The category 'housewives, domestics' from 1919–20, altered to ' home duties and nursing' in 1937–8, was used to pass as a measure of women's involvement. This category, in its own right, is problematic, blurring as it does unpaid home labour and paid domestic work. The debate tended to ignore, at the same time, other occupational categories likely to incorporate women.

There are further problems with the conclusions drawn from these statistics. The WEA's founding objective was the opening-up of opportunities for working-class men – and then people – to university-level education. The tutorial classes were important as a measure of the *standard* of study; there was also a need to measure the organisation's ability to attract working-class students. This did involve some debate, from the earliest days, as to what could be considered working class, but the safe definition was always the manual worker. 'Housewife' was used, on more than one occasion, as an unproblematic category, implicitly representing a middle-class leisured existence, to contrast with the working-class manual worker. Of course, this was wrong on several counts: as already discussed, the whole category as constructed by the WEA included women involved in paid work, who, by any standards, would be identified as working class. For those women who were housewives, no attempt was made to categorise them by their own employment prior to marriage, or by the employment status of their husbands. We can describe the WEA housewife at different periods; here are examples, offered not as evidence of class, but to illustrate the problem.

Mary Toomer of Lincoln branch in the period 1911 to the 1930s was a housewife. Her husband was a Co-op grocer. Apart from her domestic duties she managed to fit in activism in the suffrage movement, in the Women's Co-operative Guild, as a founder member of the WEA branch, political demonstrations, work with unemployed people and membership of Lincoln Education Committee. She was much more the working-class labour movement activist that the WEA aspired to educate than the title 'housewife' indicates. She is not untypical.

Dorothy Tams attended WEA classes in the 1930s as a housewife. She married relatively late, having been a stalwart of the tutorial classes in North Staffordshire and a member of the District committee in her twenties, when she was single. She was the daughter of a pottery worker, a widower. Dorothy made her way to high school and teacher training college. She married a railwayman, Eric Tams, who she had met through the WEA: *he* made the journey from the railways, to Ruskin College, to an organising job with the WEA and back to Staffordshire as the district secretary. In the 1930s he was a railway worker and she was a housewife. Was this a working-class housewife or a middle-class housewife?

There was, however, no consistent WEA position on women and class. Alongside fears that 'the housewife' would divert the organisation from its true path, there is evidence of a real sense of understanding of the constraints on women's lives and a desire to develop a realistic educational offer that met women's needs. From 1911 afternoon classes specifically for women not in paid work become a standard, if not extensive, element in the WEA repertoire. The initiative comes from the women's committee and women's officer, but the logic appears to have been accepted fairly widely.

No day or time is really suitable to a married woman of the working class; one has to get the least unsuitable time, and that is sometimes in the afternoon and sometimes in the evening.[6]

Afternoon classes for women and particularly for women's organisations such as the Women's Co-operative Guild, were a feature of the WEA programme in many Districts from this first decade, almost without a break up to the present day.

The category of 'housewife', *is* more prominent in post-1945 WEA literature. This reflects the relative affluence of this period, the ideological pressures on women in that period to fashion a job of home-making and the actual increase in the number of women, from all classes, staying at home. Post-war propaganda emphasised the 'proper' role of wives and mothers as homemakers, rather than wage earners. It is also true that a number, possibly a large number, of these housewives *were* middle class. *The Highway* published its first 'As a housewife' article from a student in 1947 and they appeared consistently from that period until the 1970s.

Having got the last of my children safely settled at school all day I felt free to try to do something outside the usual routine of household chores.[7]

The tone of these contributions does suggest subtle differences in education and expectations. The debate which these changes generated in the 1950s polarised between positions defending the historical mission of the WEA and those who argued that the organisation should reposition itself as a generalist provider of liberal education, in a soon-to-be-classless society. Yet women discovered the WEA in part because, irrespective of class, they experienced the 'double burden' of domestic and paid work. Women remained, and arguably still remain, disadvantaged educationally, even when they were relatively comfortable in material terms. Expectations and aspirations could be low.

> I made up my mind to go; I didn't tell my husband where I was going when I asked him to baby-sit, in case he laughed at my 'going back to school', I told him a half truth – that I was going out to see a friend whom I had in fact persuaded to go along with me for support.[8]

It could be argued that the WEA was achieving its mission to address educational disadvantage by providing education for women, in this period, as in earlier ones, yet this was not the way the organisation saw the shift in the composition of the student group. For the WEA, then and even now, disadvantage is centrally identified with class, and working-class students are engaged in manual labour.[9] Housewives and women were welcomed into the WEA, given a platform in the publications of the organisation, whilst WEA policy debates failed to explore, let alone incorporate, an understanding of women's position.

The support offered to women has been both groundbreaking and non-existent. The story of childcare in the WEA reflects all these contradictions. In 1916 a class in Birkenhead offered a crèche alongside a women's study circle. Margaret McMillan, nursery pioneer, socialist and children's rights activist was a vocal member of the WEA in the early years and wrote about her attempts to establish a WEA women's branch alongside her world-famous Deptford nursery, so that mothers could study while their children attended the nursery. These two early examples appear to owe more to partnerships, in the case of Birkenhead, with the settlement movement, than a WEA belief in the need to support mothers. The real developments in childcare occurred alongside the influx of post-war housewives. In 1948 a daytime psychology class established its own crèche in London; there was a crèche from 1952 in Hampshire; from 1960 in Glasgow; from 1966 in Lincoln; 1969 in Hertfordshire and Darlington and so on. The early childcare emerged as a demand from existing classes of women and was organised and staffed voluntarily. Toys and rudimentary resources were donated. Gradually there is evidence as the 1960s progressed of poorly paid staff, in some instances; where this occurred, the costs were borne by the mothers.

The distinctive change in the 1970s was the appearance of crèches organised by WEA staff, where courses were being run as project-funded District programmes. This decade saw a revival of work targeting particularly deprived working-class communities and a growing sense that substantial student support was needed to attract groups of students who did not fit earlier WEA patterns of recruitment. The work developed in pockets of innovation. Meanwhile, WEA branch programmes were only very sporadically offering crèches and were still reliant on volunteer organisation, although there is evidence of partnerships developing sometimes – with the Women's Royal Voluntary Service and the Pre-school Playgroups Association (PPA), now the Pre-school Learning Alliance. One extraordinary initiative that appears to have emerged and been lost was West Lancashire and Cheshire District's attempt to revive the summer school tradition in 1976 and 1977, with Pontins Leisure Fiesta Week, incorporating full day-care for several hundred children.

In the early 1980s childcare as a feature of the WEA's educational offer moved up the agenda. There was the first crèche at a national event, the first national meeting concerned with the implications of offering childcare, several research projects and at least two publications and the first crèche at a biennial conference. Although childcare has become a feature of much District-led community education within the WEA in the last two decades, the provision of crèches for branch classes has become less common. It could be argued that this reflects the ageing membership of WEA branches, and the extent to which branches are less likely to be concerned with recruiting new, younger students. Patterns of women's employment have shifted to shorter periods at home with children but this statistic disguises the gap between women whose earning capacity is sufficient to make paying for childcare a viable option and those for whom this is not possible. Women at the bottom of the skills/earning ladder are still unlikely to return to work until their children are in full-time education, or beyond. These women use crèches when they are available. There are external pressures which have influenced the slow-down in the development of childcare support for women in WEA classes – the 1989 Children Act and the 2001 move to OFSTED registration have progressively tightened the law surrounding childcare. Yet this has occurred at a period in time when adult education funding has begun to incorporate childcare costs. The WEA did not record complete student numbers for its first 50 years (and thereby leaves us unable to map women's involvement accurately), nor has it systematically recorded childcare provision or numbers of children registered. Impressionistically, childcare is an established but localised feature of District provision, now at the end of the WEA's first century and a relatively rare feature of branch provision. Rather than celebrating the achievement of the diverse community childcare that the WEA achieves, however unevenly, the invisibility of childcare in the organisation implies the lack of importance attached to it.

The picture that emerges of women's involvement in the WEA is one of contradictions: innovative, early, voluntarily-run crèche provision and a lack of action when state funding opens up the possibility of secure childcare as a feature of adult education. The WEA – setting out its stall for state funding 100 years ago on a platform of addressing disadvantage – does not develop strategies to use these funds. The WEA has sponsored radical provision that matched women's needs at many periods in its history; yet the argument for supporting women students with childcare alongside courses is no more an automatic entitlement now than it was in 1903.

Despite these shifting patterns in support for women with children and women in the home, women have always been WEA students and in the majority from well before the organisation officially recognised that this was the case. In exploring how important the WEA was to women, an important factor will be the women who worked and volunteered for the WEA. These included women committed to developing women's work and women's education, as well as the many important and influential women who worked across the organisation as a whole.

The WEA National Women's Advisory Committee (WAC) was established in 1907 at the invitation of the WEA national executive. Its members brought the credibility of the organisations they represented into the WEA, as well as a sense of what working women needed or wanted by way of education. Some of the original figureheads disappeared over time; some were local representatives whose significance it has not been possible to establish. Mrs Tawney and Gertrude Toynbee were included because of their relationship to important men in the movement, yet they remained involved and supportive. Miss Zimmern, sister to the tutorial lecturer A. E.

Zimmern, may have been introduced to the WEA via a family connection, but she chaired the women's advisory committee, was active in fundraising for women's education, and was on the committee as a representative of the Women's Industrial Council. Marion Phillips, of the Women's Labour League, took a serious interest. The two figures from the wider world of women's politics who were most publicly identified with building WEA women's education were Muriel Madams, of the Co-operative movement, and Margaret McMillan. McMillan had by 1907 something of a cult following for her groundbreaking work in nursery care and education.

Another significant group was the small number of women who worked for the universities as extension lecturers and staff tutors for the tutorial classes. Maude Royden was the first woman to work as an Oxford extension lecturer and became a committed teacher of women's tutorial classes for the WEA. She combined the work with suffrage activism, and her commitment to women's education was clearly and directly linked to her belief that women needed to organise separately to achieve equal rights with men. She wrote extensively on women's education in *The Highway*, particularly with a concern for women's access to higher education. Helen Stock was another significant tutorial lecturer for the Oxford Delegacy who taught women-only classes; her involvement with the Kettering Co-operative factory class probably influenced the career of Sophie Green, who was to become a WEA organiser. Other women such as Helen Wodehouse and Alice Cameron, in the Midlands and Yorkshire, Edith Morley in Reading and Mabel Atkinson in London, while carving out careers at a time when women academics were few and far between, taught some women-only classes. Slightly later there was an influential group of young women, recent university graduates, for whom the 1939–45 war created opportunities. Employed by the universities as in the case of Bridget Sutton and Gladys Malbon in North Staffordshire, or as WEA staff tutors and tutor-organisers in the case of Dorothy Martin in Northern District, Janet Walters in Eastern District, Phyllis Angrove in Cornwall and Elizabeth Monkhouse (see plate 8) in Eastern District and Scotland. Although much of their work was initially concerned with 'war work', which included classes in women's hostels, these tutors did not approach the work with a prior interest in working with women and do not appear to have had a specifically feminist agenda. They were also isolated within an organisation that saw them as substitutes in wartime conditions. They were influential as role models and as the first substantial group of women employed by the WEA, other than in a clerical capacity.

Women as teachers and organisers also championed the wave of women's education beginning in the 1970s: by this period they were more likely to be employed directly by the WEA and were explicitly operating within a feminist agenda. In Scotland, Jean McCrindle, from 1960 to 1963 in Glasgow, broke new ground with women's classes and crèches at a period which was otherwise a low point in women's work; from the 1970s Jean Barr in the West of Scotland, and Chris Aldred and Margaret Marshall in the North of Scotland, developed programmes of women's work. There were significant groups of women employees in Northern and North-western Districts, developing new work with working-class women. London District had appointed Lucie Manheim to work with women's groups in 1970 and a programme of *Women's Studies* classes developed. Alongside these teaching and organising initiatives were women developing feminist theory, within the context of an emerging women's education curriculum. The women's branches were the third influence in this process, and voluntary activity was closely intertwined with the business of organising and teaching. Sue Crane, recruited via Portsmouth's 'Mainly for Women' class as a single mother with a young child, worked her way through the WEA's branch voluntary structures and on to the Women's Education Advisory Committee (WEAC). Alongside this voluntary involvement, she began teaching for the WEA and returned to study for a degree. Even more than in earlier periods, the distinctions between taught and teacher, paid organiser and voluntary activist, broke down in the context of WEA women's education which developed as an intervention within the work of a wider movement.

Separate women's education championed by university lecturers, teachers and paid WEA organisers can be seen as the work of middle-class women with a feminist agenda to raise the consciousness of working-class women. In many senses it was just this. But this is not the whole story. A significant number of women from working-class backgrounds used the WEA as a route for educational advancement and took that achievement back into the organisation as teachers. Fragmentary evidence suggests that the first wave of WEA 'pioneer' classes was frequently the work of women. In North Staffordshire the pioneer work from 1911 was at the suggestion of a woman in a tutorial class. It would appear that this period of voluntary work involved both middle- and working-class women. The record of women's education in the WEA is fragile, much of it disappearing with the minutes of sections and branches, and the names of the women who organised and taught the great wave of voluntary women's education from 1910 to 1930 are lost.

An exception to this is the case of Sophie Green, an employee of the Kettering Co-op clothing factory, a tutorial student who was appointed as tutor-organiser in Kettering in 1919. It is unclear how the radical decision to appoint a working-class woman with no formal educational qualifications was taken. The post was one of three that were created to develop the pioneer work of the Association, and her appointment was seen as a strategy to build the approaches developed in the voluntary movement. She organised and taught an enormous programme for 20 years, prioritising work with women, although her record is not exclusively in this area. Her programme is exceptional both for the range of the curriculum she promoted, from strong tutorial classes and courses lasting one term, to outreach work in single lectures and work with young people. She built the movement locally: by supporting women tutorial students with individual coaching, by the development of social initiatives. She continued her own education over the years, winning a scholarship to the women's summer class at Bryn Mawr College, USA. The reports of her work illustrate the wider value that all records of adult education struggle to convey. More than numbers and class titles, anecdotes such as this speak of value added to people's lives.

> throughout the past winter Miss Green has run a Social on alternate Saturday evenings, to which the young people have come ... (it) has done a good deal for young women working in Kettering but living away from home, who have been brought in touch with a new group of people. Though it may be difficult to express it on paper, there is considerable evidence that Miss Green is a source of power and strength in and around Kettering.[10]

A further way in which working-class women influenced and contributed to the WEA was via their involvement with the Co-operative movement. The Women's Co-operative Guild as a partner in WEA women's education is a crucial component in the work of the WEA. For many working women there was a triangle of commitment: to the Guild, to the WEA and to the suffrage movement. Harriet Cory in Reading, Mary Toomer in Lincoln, and Ada Sutcliffe in

Huddersfield shared a commitment that linked the education of women via the WEA to wider social change for working people in general and women in particular. The organisation of the Guilds, linked to the local store and the highly valued membership of the Co-op that carried with it the 'divi', was a ready means of reaching women, and it was overwhelmingly a working-class organisation. The format of the weekly Guild meetings was a business session followed by education. The Guild nationally provided model educational programmes and speakers' notes for local women giving talks. There was an expectation of regular opportunities for practical sessions (an icing demonstration from the Co-op baker), an explanation of Co-op trading principles and some exploration of wider social issues. The WEA contributed both single lectures and courses for Guilds on a scale that was significant and long term.

The WEA/Co-operative Guild partnership offered working-class women a means of influencing adult education; this was also one manifestation of those WEA classes organised for women *only*. Work with the Guilds begins in 1912 and for many years their classes were radical in subject and focused on women's rights and women's position. The work continued in Midlands and Northern Districts until the early 1980s. Over the years the Guildswomen and their courses became less radical, but their course requests still focused on women's concerns. As mass education of working-class women in the twentieth century the WEA/Guild partnership must stand as a significant achievement. To the extent that it offered a space for exploration of women's lives and place in society, it can also be understood as the only real example of large-scale working-class women's education ever attempted.

What has emerged in the WEA from these and many other kinds of women's classes, from 1910 until the present day, is a women's education curriculum. The significant feature of the work is how consistent the programme has been throughout almost 100 years. Women's involvement in adult education has been about redressing inequalities experienced from school years, about trying to break through into higher education or achieve occupational advancement, as well as collective experience and mutual support. It has also been about a desire for personal development and satisfactions which men rarely express. In mainstream and mixed adult education classes this emotional engagement can easily become directed at the tutor, an impressive figure who brings a new world of culture and knowledge. Women students have long been victims of the male tutor who offers emancipatory ideas within a formal framework that allows of no transformative experience.

> ENDOCRINE: The miserable worm! The rank coward! He preaches freedom to us, emancipation, throw off your chains! Find your true selves! And he himself is *afraid*! He wouldn't *dare*, to try and *practise* what he preaches! (*Her voice rises.*) He tells us to find our soul-mates, and then he runs away from me and hides behind his wife's petticoats! (*She glares in front of her.*) ... I tell you this. You will never find your freedom; the WEA will never find its soul; until all tutors in every district are annihilated!
> *Death of a Tutor, A Drama of WEA Life!* (1932)[11]

WEA women's education is an attempt to find that freedom and that soul.

However, an element in the women's education curriculum has been practical 'women's subjects', subjects informed by traditional female roles – hygiene, home nursing and embroidery in the early years metamorphosing into food hygiene certificates, First Aid, and crafts today. The persistence of these subjects has from the earliest years generated a debate. Are they appropriate subjects for the WEA? Is this all we want for women by way of education? Margaret McMillan used the pages of the WEA publication *The Highway* to support women's education that was not narrowly tied to 'mothercraft'. Her 1909 contribution to the debate is a powerful call to action:

> The working class girl is not a distinct species. It is not in her nature, and its general law of development, that she differs from those so-called upper-class girls, but only in her prospects and circumstances. But surely the most important thing she has to do is to *alter* these, and how can she alter them if she *accepts* them?[12]

The reason for the persistence of these courses relates to reaching women who may not have decided that a wider educational adventure is for them. They have been and continue to be used as a means of building classes of working-class women and responding to the educational priorities that they identify. The distinctive feature of WEA women's education is that these courses are usually seen as the beginning of a journey.

By the autumn (1910) a sort of Gallup Poll (with signatures) on 'What subjects do you wish to study' was taken through all the women's organisations of the town. Rather to our dismay, embroidery and cooking topped the list – and these were not 'WEA subjects'. ... the class of 70 went merrily on for several sessions. Stitchery provides great opportunities for talk and discussion and so it was that this class became the starting point for other new ventures.[13]

Health classes are another core element in the women's education curriculum. In 1911 Littleborough branch organised a programme of lectures on women's health and was thrown into disarray when 500 women turned up. The numbers did not decline as the series continued. Children's and women's health as a major concern reflects the burden of health care falling on women in a pre-National Health Service society and subsequently, after 1948, the continuing dissatisfactions with the service to women and a medicalised understanding of health. An innovative programme of women's health discussion groups developed in North-western District in the 1980s, informed by feminist consciousness-raising groups and campaigns, becoming a national project. Women's health remains an important curriculum area, but two developments sprang from this in the 1980s that have been the focus of recent debate around women's education: assertiveness training and counselling. The WEA women's health agenda follows contemporary trends and preoccupations: today exercise, diet and aromatherapy feature.

Literature – books and reading – is one of the most important curriculum areas for the WEA as a whole and has been *the* most important for women. Within women's education literature, and women's writing in particular, have been important from the earliest years. The emphasis for women has been on the opportunity for an imaginative understanding of their situation and an escape from the limitations of their daily lives. Most of the early women's tutorial classes were Literature classes:

The women are asking for Shakespeare and poetry – because it is so near to life – and because it is so far away.[14]

The new development within this curriculum area in the 1970s was women's creative writing groups, and publication, linked to the concern of the women's movement with exploring and analysing women's experience. In recent years work with immigrant and refugee women has continued and developed this tradition.

As literature offered working women a means of imaginative engagement with their lives, so history opened up a world where possibilities for a more significant place in the world, and pride in women's achievements, could emerge. Sophie Green wittily offered two courses for women in Rothwell in 1925–6: 'Pioneers of the Women's Movement' (successful) and 'Great Men of the Nineteenth Century' (less successful). There were large numbers of women's history courses from 1910 to the 1930s which tended to focus on reclaiming and celebrating achievements – 'Famous Women', 'Historical Position of Women' and some social history such as 'History of the Home'. The WEA in the 1970s was one of the testing grounds for the developing women's history, with women like Sheila Rowbotham and Sally Alexander working with their classes to present research and explore women's lives which had been 'hidden from history'. The histories from both periods invited the student to re-examine how we have arrived at where we are today, to encourage a critical understanding of the world.

Social sciences and current affairs have been another major element in the curriculum, and again, from a perspective of women's lives: 'Women in Local Government', 'Modern Day Problems', 'Citizenship and Home Problems', 'Economic Position of Women', taking any contemporary issue and examining it from a woman's perspective. The scope of this curriculum area was not exclusively focused on women's immediate concerns: in 1914–15 a London girls' club ran a WEA 'newspaper' class. In 1931–2, 90 London women trade unionists attended a WEA Saturday school on 'Industrial Conditions in India'[15] and in the inter-war years numerous Women's Co-operative Guild classes explored 'World Problems'. Social sciences were particularly in demand in the Women's Co-operative Guild and re-emerged with dramatic effect in 1970s women's studies.

In the mid 1970s, a group of women in the Labour Party, myself included, wanted to organise ourselves as women to discuss 'women's issues'. ... So, it was suggested that we start a WEA class ... We decided to meet fortnightly and invite speakers in a variety of subjects concerning women's oppression. The topics we covered were, for example: Women and Health, Women and Trade Unions, Images of Women, the Equal Pay and Sex Discrimination Acts and the Politics of Housework.[16]

Social science subjects in more recent years are more likely to appear as a component in women's education within a framework of 'Return to Learn'-type education. For example, in the 1980s the national WEA/UNISON educational partnership gave rise to the programme 'Women, Work and Society'.

The examples above illustrate Margaret McMillan's rallying call to 'alter, not accept' women's prospects and circumstances, yet her understanding of 'circumstances' was wide – she was concerned that working-class women's lives were without beauty and pleasure – she believed that the flowers in her nursery were as significant as the food.

The last element in the WEA women's education curriculum is the engagement in the pleasure of music, dance and drama. Morris dancing and folk dancing flourished in the inter-war years; drama and elocution were increasingly popular in the same period, in branch programmes as much as in women's education. Perhaps allied to the pleasures of drama, the use of role-play in student-centred teaching techniques has become a standard tool in women's education; but it is music and singing that have been the significant feature of 'creative' women's education. In 1913 the Dudley women chain makers, fresh from a successful strike, requested a singing class. A year earlier the WEA in Birmingham had a prizewinning 'working girls' choir'[17] as part of their thriving music section. Wensleydale and District branch, possibly nervous of the probity of having too much fun, tried some innovative mixed curriculum classes in 1914–15 with 'Modern Europe and Singing', and 'French and Singing'. Singing groups and classes were a particular feature of work with London girls' clubs in the inter-war years, and were popular with women war workers during the Second World War. In the 1980s and 1990s women's choirs and singing classes appeared in several Districts, from the Dearne Valley women's choir in Yorkshire South, the Choir for Women Who Think They Can't Sing in Staffordshire and the Bristol women's choir.

The outline of a WEA women's education curriculum offered above is intentionally loose. It is intended to draw out the common features of education offered to women-only groups, within the WEA, over a long period in time, rather than to argue for a definition of women's education. Outside this framework are the Return to Learn and New Opportunities for Women (NOW)-type courses for women who are returning to study after a break, which usually involve written work and usually accreditation. Emerging in the 1970s and increasingly significant in the early twenty-first century, the students on these programmes are mainly, or entirely, women, whether or not the course has been advertised as women-only. Apart from the NOW programmes few courses start from a perspective of addressing women's needs. They owe more to the tutorial tradition than they do to women's education. It has been suggested that, just as the counselling trend has led women towards individual solutions, so Second Chance education can lead women to individual advancement, rather than a concern for collective change. The same, if slightly nuanced, criticism could be levelled at the growth in the past five years or so in 'family education' within the WEA (see plate 10). The debate around women's education that has emerged within and beyond the WEA centres on what women's education is, and whether it has been diluted or diverted from the 1980s onwards. The extent to which these trends do exist reflects a series of changes in women's lives in the 1980s and beyond: increased pressures to earn and survive in a society which has dramatically reduced social care, a growth in inequality and the loss of many traditional community organisations and frameworks.

The contribution of the WEA to establishing a women's education curriculum is nevertheless significant, however weakened that strand of education is within the Association today. This work has emerged in an organisation where there were more women than men students and where there were some facilities for their particular support needs, yet it can be argued that the culture of the organisation does not reflect this tradition. What impact have women had on the management of the WEA? From the early days the WEA did see women as an important constituent of working-class education; the national committee invited a group of influential women to form a women's advisory committee in 1907. The work of this committee was initially 'to discuss the education of working women with a view to making recommendations to the executive'. It continued to advise, expanded by considerable numbers of other women, from 1907 to 1915. It ran an annual 'round table conference', concerned with the higher education of working women, and the routes offered to this within a dramatically expanding WEA women's education.

Alice Wall was appointed as 'special organiser' for women in 1910 – a significant appointment given that initially the organisation nationally could only boast of employing a general secretary, an assistant secretary and Alice Wall, with the support of three clerical workers. The WAC also moved strategically in 1911 to establish a place for women in the democratic structure of the organisation, steering a motion through the executive that encouraged WEA branches to include women in their committees as representatives of women's organisations, and to promote the formation of women's committees and sections.[18]

In this second objective they were spectacularly successful. Women's committees and sections had been formed in 1910 in South London, Reading and Birmingham; five more appeared in 1911 and by 1914–15 there were 34 branches which had either women's committees or secretaries, out of a total of 179 branches. Alice Wall resigned from her post in 1912 (on marriage) and was replaced by Ida Hony, who continued energetically to promote the development of women's sections and committees, and the classes, lectures and study circles which they organised. During 1911 there were 18 such classes and lectures reported in *The Highway* and by 1914–15 76 women's classes, numerous study circles and lectures – there were 50 women's lecture programmes in London alone, consisting of 130 individual lectures. It was pointed out that these figures only represent the activity reported to Ida Hony and that the actual scale of women's work was larger.[19]

The strategic role of the WAC was lost in 1915, when the executive reported a decision to review the function of this committee, in the light of the growth of local organising for women. Some functions of the WAC were passed to the large and influential London women's committee, which had many members in common. From 1915, with no paid women's officer, the recording of the work suffered and it is unclear to what extent this reflected a real decline. It seems probable that the retrenchment that the whole organisation experienced during the war years had an impact on women's education. There is a resurgence in women's education and local committees and sections from 1925 until the early 1930s. By the mid-1930s separate WEA women's structures appear to have withered away, except in London District where a women's committee survived until the outbreak of the Second World War.

It was almost 40 years before separate organisational frameworks for women's education resurfaced within the WEA. In the second wave of women's education in the early 1970s the classes appear first, then local structures and finally, in 1979, a national Women's Education Group, which changed its name almost immediately to the Women's Education Advisory Committee (WEAC). Women's education was welcomed back into the national structures of the WEA with considerably more caution on this second occasion. The original group consisted of three women and four men, supported by a male national officer until the appointment of Eileen Aird as a national officer in 1984, who then acquired responsibility for women's education, amongst other work. When Aird left in 1989, national responsibility for women's education was not prioritised, her post was not replaced and WEAC disappeared from the scene. At this point in time the national focus for women's work might again have been lost, except for the initiative of two women working at national office – Halina Hassett, who had been Aird's assistant, and Kate Fisher, a research officer on a temporary contract. They organised a national women's education weekend in spring 1991, and used this event to alert women in the WEA nationally to the situation. From that meeting an informal Women's Education Advisory Group (WEAG) was formed, which in turn lobbied for the reinstatement of the Women's Education Committee (WEC) which was achieved in 1993. Women's branches declined in numbers during the 1990s; a sampling of District reports suggests that women's education also declined, although the pattern is uneven as in some Districts, such as Northern Ireland, there was a great expansion of women's work.[20] Whilst WEC developed as a national organising focus for women's education it was relatively unsupported. A one-day-a-week post to support the committee from 1993 was increased to a half-time post in 1995, and in 2001 a full-time national post for women's education was established.

If, in 2002, one year away from our centenary, we have re-established a national full-time post for women's education it has arguably still a fragile relationship to the structures of power. The WAC of 1910 had two representatives sitting on the national executive, respected within the organisation as the voice of working women. Ninety years on, women's education is represented within management structures via a single representative on the national executive and on the national education committee, supported by one of the national co-ordinators.

WEA 'founding fathers' Tawney, Mansbridge, Temple and others saw knowledge and education as the path to citizenship and equality of opportunity. Some women, in both periods of intensive feminist intervention in the WEA, were questioning whether the ways in which the movement offered education would 'work' for most women and attempted to forge a different model of women's education. However superficially impressive the account of women's education in the WEA may appear, work with women and women's roles remains marginalised within the organisation. The power of the first women's education committee was significant, yet it was brushed aside in wartime with apparent ease. The re-establishment, since the 1970s, of a women's committee and national worker has occurred within a larger and more complex organisation and WEC, the voice for women within the management structure, is much smaller given the scale of the organisation as a whole. In its centenary year the WEA will have an all-male team at the national office – a male general secretary, deputy, education, finance and European officers. District secretary posts have, since the 1990s, increasingly gone to women, but women district secretaries stay in post for relatively short periods of time, whereas most men remain until retirement, and therefore carry the power of established positions. Male candidates dispropor-tionately take senior management posts. None of this should surprise, as it reflects the inequalities that permeate society. It seems almost churlish to make this point, in an organisation that has been at the forefront of so much women's work, but it can still be argued that there has been a relative failure of women's education in the WEA, and a lack of support for women in education.

Structural inequalities in a long-established voluntary organisation are unsurprising but it helps our understanding of the Association today to ask how this manifests itself. Funding is central to the inequality of women's education within the WEA and tangible evidence of the failure of the organisation as a whole to take women's concerns into its mainstream. A thread of separate funding runs throughout this story. The first national women's worker post was created in 1910, supported by WAC fundraising, on the understand-ing that the Association's main funds bore none of the cost.[21]

All women's pioneer work outside tutorial classes was taught by volunteer women tutors. Sophie Green's post was paid for from a special grant from the Cassel Trust. The Co-operative movement paid for work with the Guildswomen. In the 1960s and 1970s women paid for crèches themselves and worked in them as volunteers. The first request for a national women's education post in 1979 was delayed as the NEC sent the WEAC on a fruitless search for external funding; once established, the post rapidly fell victim to central cuts. Sue Crane argued in 1986 that the organisation was getting women's education 'on the cheap':

Part-time tutors, unpaid for outreach and development, in reality then subsidise this work themselves; voluntary members often do the same. ... Part-time tutors have been known to use their income to subsidise their voluntary work with the branch, others have used their fees to pay crèche workers where such an arrangement has not been available through a branch or district.[22]

The Margaret James Fund, established by a private bequest in the 1940s to support women WEA students who were going to university, was used from 1992 to fund women's education. This was a successful strategy to achieve mainstream funding for women's education, although it is debatable how much impact this has in the scale of the total budget of the organisation. Project funding fuelled the growth of second-wave women's education. The WEA clearly has a need to generate short-term and project funding, but it is significant when a whole area of work relies almost exclusively on such funding. Even within the sprawling culture of the last 30 years where government, European and charitable project funding have made a major impact on the organisation, priorities within the WEA's national bidding regimes have not successfully addressed women's concerns.

It is clear that the waves of separate women's education that the WEA has experienced have their origin outside the organisation and that the urgency and significance of the work is driven by more than educational priorities. The 1909–15 period and 1970s to mid-1980s exactly mirror the high tide of suffrage organisation and the rebirth of feminist organising. The women who joined the WEA and within its structures worked for women's education in both periods often came from a traditional WEA recruiting ground of socialist, radical Christian and local political activism. At these two periods great numbers of those women were increasingly dissatisfied with the obstacles experienced in making that political vision significant for women, and specifically for working-class women. The WEA was a vehicle whereby women could be offered a means to explore social oppressions, the significance of the dominant culture, their own lives. Over the years the WEA was effectively the educational provider for a great number of women's organisations – in adult schools, girls' clubs, townswomen's guilds, the Young Women's Christian Association, the Girls' Friendly Society and the Women's Institute. These organisations originated in broadly similar concerns for women's spiritual, social, educational or political isolation. The WEA played the same role in labour movement women's organisations such as women's sections in the Labour Party and trade unions and in the Women's Co-operative Guild.

Many women within the WEA would not share the concern expressed here at the marginal position of women's education, or protest at the lack of support for childcare – a benign paternalism can be preferable to harsher alternatives. Women's contribution to the WEA, as volunteers and paid workers, has been significant and at points in time, inspirational. The energies of women voluntary members are the force that still drives much of the organisation. Within the WEA's essentially liberal governance, the power of senior staff and senior voluntary members rested and rests with men. However important individual women's contributions have been, without positive discrimination, changes in processes, structures and attitudes, women will not breach that power. The radical challenge of women's education, and its critique of male power, have no place in the WEA. The significance of women's work within the WEA lies outside the Association, in the contribution it has made to women's organisations and the wider world of women's education. There is, though, an opportunity, after one hundred years, to acknowledge the difficulties we inherit with the power of the voice of the founding fathers. Whilst recognising that the vision which Mansbridge, Tawney and others had of an organisation which brought university-level education to the male manual worker was important in its time, we should be able now to accept that this was never achieved on anything other than an individual level. If the WEA can turn away from the historical edifice it has constructed – and defended – over the years, it may be able to learn more from the real WEA achievements of work with women and women's education.

## NOTES

*Place of publication London unless otherwise stated.*

1. *WEA Annual Report,* 1909–10, 13.
2. Data in reports varies from district to district, and thus national reports had to assemble what common statistical records were possible. Fragmentary evidence in the form of registers and class reports exist in some district archives, but the only source nationally for student numbers are the national annual reports. This commentary on national student numbers has had to reflect what was published, rather than what statistics were collected, although in some local cases this information is far richer.
3. *WEA Annual Reports,* 1903–83.
4. R. H. Coates, 'A Tutor's Memories', *The Highway,* Mar. 1939, supplement, iii.

5. Women's Library, Maude Royden MSS, quoted in Lawrence Goldman, *Dons and Workers. Oxford and Adult Education Since 1850* (Oxford, 1995).
6. Alice Wall, 'Women in the WEA', *The Highway*, Sept. 1912, 186.
7. Edwina Page, 'The First Plunge in a Tutorial Class', *The Highway*, Feb. 1949, 95.
8. Judith Jones, 'The WEA – A Best Buy?', *WEA News*, 1965, 15–16.
9. J. R. Williams, 'How Do We Stand With the Workers?', *The Highway*, Jan. 1934, 18–19, and numerous other contributions.
10. *WEA Eastern District Annual Report,* 1928–9, 8–9.
11. Written by John Mack, staff tutor, and performed at the Oxford summer school in 1932. All parts were based on real protagonists in the WEA in north Staffordshire.
12. Margaret McMillan, 'The Claims of the Practical in Education', *The Highway*, Nov. 1909, 58.
13. Thames and Solent District WEA archive, Reading Branch file, Ruth Hinder, correspondence.
14. Maude Royden, 'Classes for Women', *The Highway*, Feb.1909, 78.
15. *London WEA Bulletin,* 1921–32, 3.
16. 'Battling on Every Front but One', article by a participant in a Yorkshire group in *WEA Women's Studies Newsletter*, May 1984, new series, 1.
17. Birmingham Central Library, Social Studies Dept., Birmingham WEA Branch minutes, 1911–12.
18. National Archive, WEA CENTRAL 1/2/1/2, general minute book, 1903–8, executive committee, Jan. 1911.
19. *WEA Annual Report,* 1914–15.
20. This assessment is supported by an article 'Women's Education in the WEA: Building on Our Past, Working for the Future' by 'Amen Sister', in *WEA Reportback*, Autumn 1994. It is revealing that the article is anonymous.
21. National Archive, WEA CENTRAL 1/2/1/2, general minute book, 1903–8, executive committee, July 1910.
22. Sue Crane, 'Women and the Voluntary Movement: Learning to Win', *Breaking Our Silence* (WEA pamphlet, 1986).

# 13 Literature, Cultural Studies and the WEA

*Derek Tatton*

Literature has been a fairly consistently popular subject in adult education for more than 150 years – roughly, an average of 10 per cent of all programmes over the whole period. With specific reference to WEA provision, the following summary illustrates the broad pattern:

> *Literature:*12 per cent of all courses in 1910; 8 per cent in the 1920s, 20 per cent in 1930; then, with some small fluctuations, an average of 10 per cent through each decade until the present.
>
> Compare this with dramatic fluctuations in popularity with other subjects within the WEA curriculum:
>
> *Social Studies*: 50 per cent early years; to 68 per cent in 1944; to less than 5 per cent in the 1990s.
>
> *International Affairs*: 22 per cent in the 1940s to less than 2 per cent from the 1970s.
>
> *History*: 5 to 12 per cent for decades; then 25 per cent after the Second World War. Subsequently, with local history and archaeology – prominent as a very popular subject cluster with at least 15 per cent.
>
> *Economics*: 18 per cent in the 1930s; 5 per cent in the 1950s; 2 per cent in the 1970s. Not listed (because so few courses) from the 1990s.
>
> *Art (Appreciation):* low down for most decades of the twentieth century.
>
> *Art (practical – painting, etc.)* often frowned on, not encouraged and even banned from WEA/responsible body classes until the 1970s (because regarded as LEA territory).[1]
>
> In the year 2000, *Arts and Crafts* constituted the most popular subject band of all WEA classifications: 19 per cent of total student hours. History, including local history and archaeology: 16 per cent; ICT (which had not, of course, featured in the WEA curriculum for the first 90 years or so): 10 per cent; Literature, with communications, media and creative writing: 9 per cent; social science: 1 per cent.[2]

## WHY HAS LITERATURE SO CONSISTENTLY HELD ITS PLACE IN THE CURRICULUM?

Literature in early adult education and throughout the WEA's first century has always embraced a broader definition than 'imaginative writing of high quality' – it has covered an extraordinary range of classes, courses, themes, often inter-disciplinary, and not easily conforming to formal 'academic' definitions or boundaries. So, classes in *language* and literature, essays, biography, letters, journals, diaries, creative *writing*, aspects of history (classic 'Histories', 'The Bible as Literature'), film, TV (drama, sit-coms, 'soaps', docu-drama) lyrics, the study of advertising, cultural studies – all have been included, or have claim to be included, within the WEA Literature curriculum.

Raymond Williams and Terry Eagleton have theorised about definitions of 'Literature' and its development within the academy. Williams, helped by his own 15 years' experience as an adult education tutor, argued for a complete continuum of language, literature and communications across orthodox subject boundaries.[3] Eagleton, in his seminal *Literary Theory – An Introduction* (1983) asks 'What is Literature?'[4] His answer illustrates how English Literature for many years, through the nineteenth century and well into the twentieth, had to struggle to escape the charge that, in contrast with the Classics, 'English' was a non-subject. Meanwhile, as both Williams and Eagleton acknowledge, Literature was recognised and valued within adult education and the WEA before it was accepted as a subject, on a par with 'the Classics', in universities and schools – moreover, this is not the only example where adult education has been in advance of the academy.

## TRADITION AND INNOVATIONS

Looking back over two centuries of adult education and the various kinds of Literature courses, one might be tempted to agree with the cynic's comment on theories of education: 'Stay where you are, keep doing what you're doing – you'll end up being an innovator.' It's not that simple, of course – there have been changes, developments and there may even have been progress and a raising of standards.

Nevertheless, it is important to see that some issues keep returning: the Victorian mechanics' institutes are especially interesting in relation to issues of student control, the influence of social class attitudes and ideological pressures on curricular development. The issues raised in them on priorities in subject choice and promotion were open and explicit from the earliest years. The mechanics' institutes, as George Birkbeck's biographer says, came 'under the control of the moneyed classes and became props of orthodoxy and respectability instead of independent working class organisations'.[5] There were objections to political and religious discussions in the mechanics' institutes – some Literature was kept out for this reason. A curriculum devoted primarily to the natural sciences had already by the 1840s embraced an increasingly popular programme of Literature courses with the now predominantly middle-class students. The pattern became clear – decline in Sciences accompanied an increase in Literature and Fine Arts.

The London Working Men's College experience was rather different. Here there was a deliberate attempt to break from some of the restrictions of the mechanics' institutes, particularly the ban on politics and controversy. The college started with political science at the forefront but History and Literature became more popular, with the college then trying to get back to politics through massaging the curriculum: 'Political Themes Illustrated by English Literature' (but only eight students enrolled for this).[6] As historians of the college found, students were 'interested in problems in the first instance, not subjects narrowly defined'.[7] This was especially the case with self-educated adults like many of the radicals in the Chartist movement. In the Chartist Halls at Manchester, Oldham, Leeds, Birmingham and other cities and towns, educational activities were to the fore and men like Thomas Cooper would give lectures and lead discussions not just on political and social issues but also on science, literature, the fine arts, morals and theology. *The Northern Star* devoted almost an entire broadsheet page to 'Literature'.

Within the university extension classes, issues of class, gender and curriculum became significant. Middle-class women experienced 'democratic readings' from the Romantic poets but as Sheila Rowbotham has pointed out: 'It was not a simple question of left and right, for they chose their heroes and mentors from both camps higgledy-piggledy – King Alfred and Oliver Cromwell, John Wesley or William Morris, Ruskin, Dante, Carlyle ... Hardy, Dickens.'[8] And, as another recent book describes this formation:

> they attracted lower-middle-class women, especially school teachers and those involved in welfare work. They formed the biggest single group in university extension ... and many were pioneers in the

women's suffrage movement. This group was the most persistent in demands for courses in English and History, as against science or economics or other more overtly political subjects.[9]

At the start of the twentieth century during the formative years of socialism and the WEA, therefore, the ideological revolt was moral, ethical, and aesthetic as much as it was economic and political. However, this was immediately problematic because in the early decades the controversies around Ruskin College, the Plebs League, the Labour Colleges and the WEA involved a shared dominant assumption about values in relation to the hierarchy of issues/subjects: economics, politics and social studies were top priority, as study and debate in these spheres would directly aid the emancipation of the working class. An example of how this scale of values operated ideologically is offered at the height of the Ruskin College conflict in 1909. Principal Dennis Hird was encouraged to stop teaching Sociology and Evolution and to move to teaching 'less controversial subjects such as Literature and Temperance'.[10] This prejudice against Literature was active in the movement for decades. In 1925, a contributor to *Plebs* complained about the 'dangerous tendency' whereby the journal was giving space to poetry and Literature: 'in the old days (*Plebs*) confined itself to things that mattered.'[11] Some in the WEA took a similar view. George Thompson, district secretary in Yorkshire in the 1920s, 'wanted sanction refused for non-serious subjects such as Literature and Music'.[12] These were popular with women, and that was a key part of the problem, linked also to the spiritual/materialist dichotomy which Thompson summarised in this way:

A distinct word of warning to those who are having so much to say about spiritual values in adult education. The Metaphysical Interpretation of Adult Education may be a song that echoes sweetly in the cloister but it will sound very different in the steel mills, down the pit, in the factories and on the docks.[13]

CONTENT AND PEDAGOGY

There have been several detailed analyses of Literature courses in the WEA and these help inform and qualify generalisations made about the significance of the subject over the first century of the Association. A study was made of all extant syllabuses of Literature classes promoted by the Oxford tutorial classes committee since 1909 and a report on this survey was written for *Rewley House Papers* in 1960.[14] The survey was divided into three sections: popularity, subject-matter, and method. On the popularity of Literature, the report stated that the subject had always been fairly important in adult education 'though the Tutorial Class Movement did not take kindly to it at first' and Oxford's first Literature class did not begin until 1917, in Stoke-on-Trent.

Under the heading of 'subject matter' it was reported that Victorian Literature was one of the most popular subjects in the early years, when the most popular contemporary authors were Wells, Bennett, Shaw and Galsworthy. Forster, Lawrence, Eliot and Joyce 'were ignored until the 1930s, and James and Hopkins did not appear on syllabuses until the very late 1930s. ... With foreign authors a more enlightened picture emerges largely because of the continuous popularity of the drama ... Dostoevsky was introduced as early (*sic*) as 1925, along with Ibsen.' The influence of Empson, Leavis, Murray and Richards can be seen by the later 1930s when their books appear on book lists and 'after a modest time-lag of about 5 years, this critical ferment begins to have an influence in adult education.' 'Public Expression' had been taught at summer school back in 1920, and a 'Culture and Environment' emphasis is noted after the 1939–45 war. Classes on 'The Cinema' were run from 1950.

On the 'Method of Teaching Literature', the report says that, in the early years, the 'lecture technique of teaching was predominant, and in these courses the approach was formal and academic'. A tendency to crowd syllabuses was noted. The 'second Literature class at Kettering in 1918 proceeded by single lectures, from the roots of our Literature, through Middle English and the drama to the pre-raphaelites in 24 weeks'. A course ran through the session 1937–8 on 'The Place of Poetry' from Chaucer to the twentieth century. But there was a 'shift gradually to less formal discussions of the writer's quality and ability', and 'strikingly apparent in recent years is the great reduction in texts listed ... to be studied ... Practical criticism has triumphed', concluded the report.

Another survey of Literature classes provided by the WEA was carried out at about the same time by a working party which presented a substantial report to the 1960 WEA national conference.[15] *Aspects of Adult Education* reported that three subjects had been chosen 'for detailed analysis': economics, science and literature. The working party was concerned to note that economics had declined sharply in WEA programmes, but they wondered whether it could be argued that shifts in 'consumer preference' must be accepted ... and the 'movement must adapt itself'. It was difficult to draw a line between education for 'social purpose' and education for 'personal enrichment', Literature being seen as a subject which stood on the boundary. But the authors were a little wary of it, lest it was 'taught in such a way that it becomes an avenue of escape'. The working party had read and considered 160 syllabuses from the 1958–9 session, roughly one-quarter of the total of WEA Literature classes that year. They divided the courses into groups according to approach to the subject: general (20 courses); specific period (41); specific form (17); specific point of view (25); drama (44); other (13).

In observations on these syllabuses they had noted, with admiration, a 'pioneer tutorial on foreign literature' where one year was to be spent on French, one year on American and the final year on Russian writing. However, they were scornful of a class called 'How to enjoy reading' which attempted to study 20 novels, 18 poets, 8 plays and 'for good measure', 5 biographies. 'Specific period' courses are often 'as much history (of a kind) as Literature'. 'Specific form' courses were almost equally divided between the novel and poetry, with two or three on biography. 'Specific point of view' covered a wide range of titles like' Morality, Love and Religion', or 'Literary Landscapes'. A quarter of the 'drama' courses were on Shakespeare; a few were on Greek drama but modern drama was the most popular.

LITERATURE COURSES IN THE EASTERN DISTRICT 1950–78

Using guidelines from the above two reports, I reviewed Literature courses in the Eastern District for selected years between 1950 and 1976, two from each decade, using broadly the same categories as the working party. I then conducted a more detailed analysis of 300 Literature syllabuses taught in the Eastern District from 1968 to 1978.[16]

In the year 1951–2 there was a total of 38 Literature courses, divided as follows:

- 10 general;
- 10 specific period;
- 14 specific form;
- 4 specific point of view;
- 0 others.

In the year 1961–2: 56 courses, divided as follows:

- 8 general;
- 8 specific period;
- 31 specific form;
- 0 specific point of view;
- 9 others.

In the year 1975–6: 72 courses divided as:

- 13 general;
- 11 specific period;
- 30 specific form;
- 18 others.

I also listed those dealing with exclusively twentieth-century Literature – between a third and a half of all courses each year.

Other courses included 'Mass Media' (five of these in 1960–1); English Language (only two over the whole period of nearly three decades); creative writing, and children's Literature (a big increase in the 1970s, with eleven courses in 1975–6: 15 per cent of total). Courses on specific points of view included 'Town and Country in Poetry and Fiction'; 'The Family in Twentieth Century Literature'; 'Feminism in Literature'.

Within 'specific form', drama was most popular (an average of eight per year), followed by the novel (six per year), poetry (three per year); TV drama from the early 1970s (three per year); biography (two per year) and film (two per year).

Only 57 syllabuses in the 1968–78 sample dealt with works before the nineteenth century; 85 with the nineteenth century; 33 across a wide time-span; 125 with the twentieth century.

Adult education students have always shown a strong interest in modern Literature. This is surprising given that the tutors themselves rarely studied this literature when they were at college and university. Also, the closely related subject of modern/contemporary history is often less popular than, say, archaeology. It seems then that Richard Hoggart was right and that many adult students have felt that Literature – especially modern Literature – will 'speak to their condition'. The Oxford Extra-mural Delegacy Report in 1958 stated that: 'this intense interest in contemporary literature undoubtedly contains an important element of concern for society.'

My own review of the range and orientation of the 300 syllabuses corroborates this:

- a syllabus on the post-war novel states 'that it offers a representation of what is happening in society';
- a class in Wisbech on modern American writing was told that students will be exercising a dual discipline – reading Literature and looking critically at American society through the imaginations of its writers;
- a syllabus on 'Literature since the War' states that 'the individual at odds with society is the theme running through all the works selected'.

As we have seen, in the 1920s and 1930s, the 'Shawlsworthy' syllabus was a particular favourite. By the 1960s Shaw, Wells and Galsworthy had all but disappeared. The most frequently mentioned writer on the 300 syllabuses examined was D. H. Lawrence, with Hardy not far behind. The period spanned by these writers was the one which tutors and students favoured first. Shakespeare and Dickens held a steady place, of course, but women novelists, especially George Eliot, the Brontës and Virginia Woolf were mentioned more frequently than Henry James or Conrad. E. M. Forster and James Joyce were there but Orwell was on more syllabuses. Although contemporary writers were widely discussed, the preference was for works which have been around for 10 or 15 years. It was rare for a class to study works newly published or performed in the last year or two. Thus, in the 1970s works from the late 1950s and the 1960s by Pinter, Osborne, Amis, Murdoch, Drabble, Golding, Sillitoe and so on predominated in the contemporary Literature syllabuses.

There was some attempt to appeal to local loyalties: 'East Anglian Men of Letters' and 'Essex books and people', but local Literature does not have the same appeal as local history. Sometimes there was a remarkable lack of interest in local writers – John Bunyan was not considered in Bedford or Bedfordshire during the whole twelve years surveyed, despite there being a relatively high number of Literature courses in that county. Some of the well-known names from Irish, Welsh and Scottish writing appeared quite regularly. Drama was the most international of forms with Brecht, Ibsen, Pirandello, Chekhov, Sartre, Beckett and Arthur Miller appearing as frequently as any English playwright apart from Shakespeare. Very little poetry in translation was studied over the decade reviewed and it was a small group of foreign novelists, mainly from France and Russia, that appeared with any frequency. Solzhenitsyn was widely studied between 1971 and 1976. Goethe, Dante, Homer and Horace were mentioned rarely, if at all.

The crowded syllabus, noted critically in the earlier reports, featured here too. A class on biography was burdened with 23 texts recommended for set reading in a 12-week course. Another course of the same length on the Victorian novel focused on 13 novels recommended for reading and discussion. If a syllabus is attempting to cover vast territory, taking as read a wide range of books, then we can assume that the tutor necessarily becomes lecturer, or at least that the sessions become very tutor-centred. In cases like this it seemed that tutors were simply reproducing in method and approach, if not in content, what they experienced in lectures at university and college. The result was likely to be a course dominated by the tutor and those students already 'well-read', strengthening the tendency for these courses to become middle class in membership and orientation.

## LITERATURE AND CULTURAL STUDIES IN THE WEA

It is clear then that the WEA has often reflected, through its curriculum, negative and positive features in society generally. Literature titles and approaches have been influenced by ideology and fashion: 'Shakespeare, the Patriotic Writer' during the 1914–18 war, through (allegedly) 'Lenin and the Lakeland Poets' in the 1920s to 'Booker Prize Winners' in the 1990s. At its best, this freedom and flexibility has enabled WEA students and tutors to make a significant contribution to the emergence and quality of British cultural studies. This is a core theme of Tom Steele's book, *The Emergence of Cultural Studies 1945–1965* which is sub-titled *Cultural Politics, Adult Education and the English Question*. The book offers a richly documented and subtle examination of the prehistory of cultural studies tracing its roots in the work especially of W. E. Williams, Richard Hoggart, E. P. Thompson and Raymond Williams, through the WEA. The first Williams is less well known, but merits the recognition accorded here for his editorship of the WEA journal *The Highway* during the 1930s and 1940s when it was a 'model of radical cultural exchange and featured many of the major writers on culture of the period'.[17] The son of a Welsh carpenter, he became secretary to the British Institute of Adult Education 1934–40, director of the Army Bureau of Current

Affairs (ABCA), which he founded, 1941–5, director-general of the Arts Council 1951–62. He 'crowned all these achievements by his collaboration with Allen Lane in creating the vast Penguin and Pelican library of popular editions' – his obituary in *The Times* said he was 'one of the greatest and most effective mass educators of his time' (April 1977).[18] W. E. Williams and George Thompson, the Yorkshire district secretary, were two iconic figures in the 1930s and their conflicting views on the question of 'culture' reflected the main dilemma confronting the WEA. It was undoubtedly the key debate within the adult education movement – Tom Steele characterises this debate in the pages of *The Highway* (1939) as:

> A symbolic engagement between W. E. Williams, as signalling the modernising metropolitan element wanting to popularise the WEA's provision to a wider social public and Thompson as a provincial Yorkshire traditionalist atavistically bent on class warfare.[19]

In the post-war period and especially from the 1950s it is clear that the WEA's provision did extend to a wider social public and this was the period when pioneering 'Cultural Studies' – now an industry – began in WEA classes.

It is interesting to note that Edward Thompson in the 1950s argued that 'we now have, even among sections of our working class movement, the values of private lives growing up – the private fears and neuroses, the self interest and timid individualism fostered by pulp magazines and Hollywood films.'[20] Richard Hoggart too, but from a different political perspective, was concerned about the impact of mass culture and especially its newest and most powerful element, TV, on the sturdy independence of the working class:

> Most mass entertainments are in the end what D. H. Lawrence described as 'Anti-life'. They are full of corrupt brightness, of improper appeals and moral evasions. To recall instances; they tend towards a view of the world in which progress is conceived as a seeking of material possessions, equality as moral levelling, and freedom as the ground for endless irresponsible pleasure.[21]

As we have seen, many courses in the WEA were engaging with these broad issues over this whole period and earlier with a wide range of tutors. Raymond Williams knew this from the inside and shortly before he died, realising that the history of 'cultural studies' was being distorted he made sure he put the record straight:

> when I moved into internal university teaching and at about the same time Richard Hoggart did the same, we started teaching in ways that had been absolutely familiar in Extra-mural and WEA classes, relating history to art and literature, including contemporary culture, and suddenly so strange was this to Universities they said 'My God, here is a new subject called Cultural Studies'. But we are beginning I am afraid, to see encyclopaedia articles dating the birth of Cultural Studies from this or that book in the late 1950s. Don't believe a word of it. That shift of perspective about the teaching of arts and literature and their relation to history and to contemporary society began in Adult Education, it didn't happen anywhere else.[22]

## GENDER

Bernard Jennings, WEA President 1981–91, wrote in 1978: 'The traditional work acquired a slightly musty odour. It became identified with courses in literature and music for middle class, middle-aged ladies.'[23] Where did the odour come from? It's hard to escape the view that Literature contributed. Complex issues of class and gender are operative here. In the early decades men predominated in Literature courses as elsewhere, but in every single year since 1924 there have been more women than men in WEA Literature classes. This obviously had an impact on what was taught and how it was taught (with more women tutors involved than with most other subjects). Bernard Jennings made his observations in the context of comment on WEA developments since the 1950s. He was expressing the widely held view, based on the shift in the Association's student membership and course provision: a decline in the proportion of working-class students (mostly male) which accompanied in a fairly neatly patterned way the increases in the percentage of 'liberal arts' students in the classes. When these courses were offered as a 'consumer choice' in a growing adult education 'market' they had a ready appeal to the already 'educated' – mainly middle-class women.

There remained a deep and lasting suspicion that the 'avenue of escape' can too easily be taken in Literature, arts and music classes which could also be fashionable for those who wished to be 'cultured persons', as Hoggart recognised. But quite different kinds of motivation were always active. This is an account given by a member of a Literature class I taught in Luton in the 1970s, quoted in Rose's *Intellectual Life*:

> On one occasion when dad and I, together with other workers who had been compelled to leave school early, were attending a WEA class, we discussed what books would be interesting and easy to read and be especially suitable for those who had not read a book since leaving school and I was then introduced to a work by Thomas Hardy. ... This was the first serious novel I had read up to this time in which the heroine had not been of 'gentle birth' and wealthy, and the labouring classes as brainless morons. This book made me feel human and even when my employers talked at me as though I wasn't there, I felt I could take it; I knew that I could be a person in my own right.[24]

'Struggling to be a person in my own right' is how many younger women described their commitment in the 1970s, to the women's movement.

Many Literature classes contributed to, or were affected by, women's studies in the 1970s: a development which had claim to be 'the first radical issue for many years to come out of the voluntary movement of the WEA'.[25] *The Women's Studies Newsletter* was launched in 1977 and within two years the newsletter and Women's Studies classes had become a major force in WEA affairs with women's education issues provoking some of the most intense and thoroughly argued debates at the 1979 and 1981 WEA national conferences.

## WRITING, PERFORMANCE AND COMMUNITY ARTS

*The 1919 Report* emphasised the importance of creative writing from within the movement – this was making, could make, a distinctive contribution to working-class culture, the report argued.

> The (adult) class should be the starting point for activity, individual and collective, on the part of the students. In some classes ... it is the practice for the students to give dramatic performances as a conclusion to the session's work, and such experiments should become a regular feature of classes in literature. Attention should be given to the possibilities of dialect literature

... Students should be encouraged to write, and to write in their local language and with the material offered by the scenes and life which are familiar to them.[26]

A fair amount of writing, of all kinds, was done over the years, (though never as much as the *1919 Report*'s authors had advocated). The best advice to tutors continued to carry this message and valuable work came out of WEA classes. Fred Kitchen's *Brother to the Ox* (1939) is the classic example of what could emerge.[27] This autobiography published in 1939 is an exceptionally impressive record of country and urban work written from experience by a man who had been farm labourer, miner, coke worker and navvy. Fred Kitchen was encouraged to write the book in a WEA class. Raymond Williams, in noting that this book is 'one of the very few direct and unmediated accounts of a rural labourer's life' devotes as much space to Fred Kitchen in his seminal work *The Country and the City*, as he does to major known writers.[28] A. J. J. Ratcliff in his book *The Adult Class* (1938) wrote about a Literature class which ran in the early 1930s 'in a certain mining area' in which written work was completed in abundance. The best work came from a man in his seventies who wrote his first play, which was successfully acted. His novel, a leisurely regional and industrial one, was published afterwards, week by week, in the local newspaper.[29] Few published books came out of WEA classes, but with *Brother to the Ox* we may include Samuel McKechnie's novel *Prisoners of Circumstance*, James Whittaker's autobiographical work and the most well known, *Love on the Dole* by Walter Greenwood.

In the 1970s a new emphasis on writing came from different directions: the Adult Literacy campaign; Ruskin College *History Workshops* and important linked developments in oral history; community publishing projects, and the establishment of bookshops specialising in radical or 'alternative' publications. There was a fresh, organised attempt to get working-class people to write and publish their work. University and WEA adult education was influenced and involved. For example, the Scotland Road Writers' Workshop in Liverpool from 1973 was formative, and other similar workshops followed in Liverpool and elsewhere. In Hackney, the growth of *Centerprise* publications from the early 1970s was extraordinarily creative, leading to similar initiatives in Bristol, Birmingham and the North East. Representatives from nine of these groups met in 1976 to form the Federation of Worker Writers and Publishers.

The early *Centerprise* work was done in partnership with the Hackney WEA Branch:

> In using the WEA people have been responding to, and putting new life into, its traditions of self-organisation, local democracy and student control of the planning of courses.[30]

There were some battles, however, between the WEA Branch and the London District over the relative merits of academic qualifications and of local knowledge and informally acquired skills for the tutor of a class.

The early Federation challenged what it saw as orthodox and restricting definitions of 'Literature' itself and collided with the Arts Council Literature panel over a grant application for funding a worker for the Federation:

> no recommendation for grant-aid from the Literature budget can be forthcoming. The members were of one voice in judging the examples of literature submitted: they considered the whole corpus of little, if any, solid literary merit.[31]

This view was contested, of course, and the conflict at this juncture involved widely different judgements about 'community arts' in particular. Greg Wilkinson of the *Commonword Workshop*, stating the Federation's case to Sir Roy Shaw, at the Arts Council, was rather dismissive of 'Community Arts': 'As for the Worker Writers' movement, this is not some therapeutic sideline to be nodded off to Community Arts ... a sort of ... bargain basement ... where everything is possible as long as it's cheap.'[32]

From an adult education point of view, Writers' Workshops and Community Arts developments had this in common: during the 1970s they helped to break the rigidities between the *practical* on the one side and the *academic* and the *appreciatory* on the other. This didn't occur without conflict and deep tensions being worked through, and the WEA (and its Literature tutors in particular) were in the thick of these.

Before taking his position as secretary-general at the Arts Council, Roy Shaw had been WEA Literature tutor and director of the extra-mural department at Keele University. At Keele he had provoked considerable controversy when he attacked the WEA in print as a 'rather ineffective organisation, particularly for working class adult education',[33] and he launched the Keele University Community Education Programme, independent of the WEA, concentrating work within the mining village of Silverdale. The programme ran for ten years through the 1970s with Bill Parkinson (formerly lecturer in Literature at Bristol University and a WEA tutor) appointed organising tutor for the project from 1972. There were not just tensions between university and WEA but inside the project itself, with sackings and disillusionment causing bitterness. Bill Parkinson characterised the department's ideological method of extending culture and the arts: 'It was like carrying a B52 air-strike on the village: load the aircraft with cultural goodies and drop them on the village. They never questioned the kind of things they were dropping.'[34] Ten years later a community play, *Go See Fanny Deakin*, written by Joyce Holliday and organised through the WEA, had striking success in Silverdale and established WEA networks in the village which have survived through to 2002.[35] The contrast between university and WEA approaches to the village of Silverdale in this little drama is salutary.

## THE WEA GOLDEN AGE – BACK TO THE FUTURE?

Many people now look back to a WEA 'golden age'; so many, including authoritative historians of adult education, that there must be an engagement with the likelihood that Literature and Cultural Studies formed part of this phenomenon. For example, Jonathan Rose summarises at the end of his book: 'The withering away of the autodidact tradition is a great loss.'[36] His preface has prepared the reader for this decline and fall:

> Thereafter (from 1945) the working class movement for self-education swiftly declined, for a number of converging reasons. This then, is a success story with a downbeat ending.[37]

Lawrence Goldman concludes his history of Oxford University adult education: 'that sense of mission, that very reverence for education in the labour movement, has declined in recent decades.'[38] Tom Steele also looks back to the period of the 1960s as being the age of innovation for cultural studies in extra-mural/WEA adult education.[39]

Each is right, of course, in terms of the argument about fundamental change in the British labour movement and this having a decisive impact on the WEA. However, we should be wary about generalisations and value-judgements which imply that the WEA's radical mission has ended. At least, we need a nuanced appraisal of specific changes and their implications for current and future WEA developments. Robert Lochrie, general secretary of the WEA, reviewing Rose's book in the WEA's current in-house journal, *Learning for Life* (2001), gives it the highest praise but expresses two reservations that are pertinent. Rose constantly uses the term 'autodidact', which can be derogatory, whereas many of those quoted in his book experienced rich informal and formal education, in adult education courses, for example. More crucial to our argument here, Lochrie emphasises that Rose contributes to the view (expressed by other reviewers) that 'this kind of intellectual life belongs to some past golden age', and Lochrie makes the point that expansion of opportunities in formal education has not necessarily led to enrichment of adult individual lives.[40] It may be the case too that contemporary culture and collective social life are weaker, despite material improvements and greater early-age formal education.

Over the past 20 years the WEA has engaged in some exciting new work focused on working-class communities, targeting the disadvantaged. Branches and volunteers were not able to do this effectively and this work has almost exclusively been led by professional field staff, tutors and organisers. This work has included some innovative developments in writing: 'Roots' courses, for example, where students with minimal schooling and no formal qualifications have been encouraged to write about their experiences as children and adults. They have also been prompted to read other people's accounts, including short stories and novels. At the same time within the WEA developments in workplace learning, community learning, improved training and pedagogy, new evaluation procedures, and a focus on educational progression have all been positive developments. The Association has also continued the 'Cultural Studies' work (for example, honouring Raymond Williams through the annual residential weekends on themes from his writings, since 1988, at the Wedgwood Memorial College in Barlaston); organising courses leading to special lectures and publications of significance – for example, the annual Robert Tressell Memorial Lectures, arising from local Hastings branch courses, published as a book in 1988.[41] In all these ways, arguably the WEA recently has been engaged in work just as relevant, focused and important as in earlier decades, in the last century.

254 A Ministry of Enthusiasm

However, concurrently, there has been a decline in the number of branches during the 1990s (continuing the decline from the peak of 1,000 branches in the 1960s and 1970s). There has also been a reduction in the range and number of courses run by many urban branches. This has had an impact on Literature/Cultural Studies in the WEA in the obvious sense that WEA branches in some towns and villages are simply not there now to organise these courses, and they have not been replaced by anything else in formal adult education, as there has also been a reduction in LEA classes in this sphere. Filling this vacuum, perhaps, we have the growth of the University of the Third Age (U3A), informal reading/book groups and the Federation of Worker Writers and Publishers (now funded by the Arts Council) with a membership of 65 independently-organised writers' workshops. Hence, we have a relative decline in the significance of the WEA in literary and cultural spheres.

The important arguments about political and cultural trends since the 1980s also have a resonance in the WEA which, as we have seen, has always been sensitive to general trends in culture and society. The collapse of communism and the triumph of market-driven economies has led, inexorably, to a relocation of adult education within a market framework. Thus, in Lawrence Goldman's *Dons and Workers* a key concluding argument develops from Goldman's review of the University of Wisconsin adult education idea: to expand individual adult access to university resources. In other words, this Wisconsin model represents a more individualist, market-led model of adult education than the British tradition, and Goldman concludes:

> For a (British) society belatedly beginning to embrace and understand the meaning of mass higher education, the American model is proving to be a better guide to fulfilling new functions and meeting new demands than the old adult tradition.[42]

Yes, there can be gains from a consumer-led, individual access model: it has been good to get rid of some rigidities and dogmas in the old British adult education tradition so that, for instance, art/painting classes and WEA language courses now flourish. However, this brings with it the open market for bridge, flower-arranging, and 'leisure courses' generally, which are problematic when they begin to dominate, as they can, in a lowest-common-denominator environment.

This is where we engage with a very contemporary and contentious argument about crude market forces leading to a 'dumbing down' in media and cultural affairs. Dennis Potter famously called his cancer 'Rupert', because of the damage he believed a Murdoch-driven media empire can do to the body politic. Since Potter's death it is arguable that media moguls like Murdoch and Burlusconi (with the concomitant ethos of money-power, ratings, competitiveness) exert an influence more powerful and more extensive than ever.

Ken Loach, whose views on this are similar to Potter's, expressed the view, in 2001, that TV drama in Britain could not now present the kind of 'Wednesday Play' which enabled *Cathy Come Home* and many other radical dramas to be seen by large audiences. In receiving an award from Melvyn Bragg he, polemically, referred to the time (11.30 pm) when the excellent *South Bank Show* was being broadcast. His point was that serious and intelligent programmes struggle to get through in a ratings-dominated culture. These are not just 'old Left' voices from the past. The reaction to the chairman of the BBC's speech to the Westminster Media Forum in March 2002 revealed an extremely broad swathe of opinion (broadcasters, writers, politicians) showing concern for BBC standards which Gavin Davies had sought to defend by stating that those who complain about 'dumbing down' are 'white middle-class southerners'. The *Guardian* led a two-page feature on this issue (14 March 2002) by highlighting Richard Hoggart, 'cultural critic', and his contribution, in which he wrote: 'It is highly unfashionable today to use any language of judgment.' Hoggart makes his judgement very clear: too many TV programmes 'encourage a mindless, cruel competitiveness and a disguised ... contempt in the makers for those at whom they are directed ... They aim ... chiefly at the lowest common denominator in taste wherever it is to be found.' Martin Kettle (son of Arnold Kettle, first Open University professor of Literature) wrote on the same issue, opposing Gavin Davies: 'We live in measuring times ... Nothing escapes the modern measurers.'

It is a measure of how the WEA has lost cultural clout and significance when one considers that The Pilkington Report (1962) on broadcasting welcomed and considered detailed representations from the WEA on the future of broadcasting. Hoggart was a member of the Pilkington Committee and his WEA perspective then was a major influence (as Raymond Williams was later to emphasise) on the Report. By contrast, the WEA's influence on media policy or even

educational issues generally from the 1980s has been so marginal as
to be non-existent.

In celebrating the centenary of the Association it may be
appropriate to avoid bland self-congratulation by revisiting some of
the 'unfashionable' older WEA arguments which, as Hoggart
demonstrates, remain current. William Temple, archbishop of
Canterbury and WEA president said six decades ago: 'Business is
concerned with people as they are; Education is concerned with
people as they may become.' An extra-mural director (another
Literature tutor) retiring in the early 1990s said in his valedictory
speech: 'We should measure that which is valuable but not just value
that which is measurable.' Teasing out and debating the implications
of these thoughts would present a challenge to the post-modern
illusions which are corroding WEA culture and so much more.

At the beginning of the twenty-first century we have all the
problems of famine, poverty, war, terrorism, massive and increasing
inequality, globalisation, environmental crises and so on – yet the
WEA in 2002 is running fewer courses on these major topics as a
proportion of its provision than ever before; meanwhile, courses on
bridge, Christmas flower-arranging and cake decoration flourish in
some branch programmes, as a glance through District Annual
Reports in the 2000s reveal. George Thompson and the others were
too dogmatic when warning about 'escapism' through Literature or
whatever, but their social and political vision provoked debate which
gave focus to the WEA's work, including Literature and Cultural
Studies. The challenge for the WEA now is to reconnect all the good,
positive, targeted work and the new broader curriculum with that
earlier vision, through a revived social and political education-for-
citizenship movement for the twenty-first century. No small task!

## NOTES

*Place of publication London unless otherwise stated.*

1. These percentages are taken from the subject analyses provided by the
   National Office of the WEA (National Archive).
2. Percentages based on the student hours summary provided with the WEA
   membership folder, 2002.
3. R. Williams, *Politics and Letters* (1979), 325.
4. T. Eagleton, *Literary Theory – An Introduction* (Oxford, 1983), ch. 1.
5. T. Kelly, *George Birkbeck* (Liverpool, 1957), 58.
6. J. F. C. Harrison, *A History of the Working Men's College* (1954), 61.

7. Harrison, *Working Men's College*, 26–7.
8. S. Rowbotham, 'Travellers in a Strange Country: Responses of Working Class Students to the University Extension Movement 1873–1910', *History Workshop Journal* (Autumn 1981), 72.
9. T. Steele, *The Emergence of Cultural Studies, 1945–1965* (1997), 36.
10. P. Yorke, *Ruskin College 1899–1909* (Oxford, 1972), 32.
11. *Plebs*, May 1925, 209.
12. Margaret Cole, *The Life of G. D. H. Cole* (1971), 108, note 1. This was Thompson's view of Literature in the 1920s, according to Margaret Cole. He later modified this view somewhat.
13. G. H. Thompson, 'Progress and Aims in Adult Education', *Tutors' Bulletin*, April 1945, 9. Quoted in Steele, *Emergence of Cultural Studies*, 12.
14. D. Butts, 'The Development of Literature Teaching in Oxford Tutorial Classes', *Rewley House Papers* III no. 7 (Oxford, 1958–9),13–19.
15. 'Aspects of Adult Education: A Report' (1960), 39–41.
16. D. Tatton, 'The Tension between Political Commitment and Academic Neutrality in the WEA' (PhD, Open University, 1987).
17. Steele, *Emergence of Cultural Studies*, 72.
18. Steele, *Emergence of Cultural Studies*, 73.
19. Steele, *Emergence of Cultural Studies*, 72–8.
20. Quoted by Steele, *Emergence of Cultural Studies*, 164, from E. P. Thompson, 'William Morris and the Moral Issues of Today' in *The American Threat to British Culture* (1951), 29.
21. Steele, *Emergence of Cultural Studies*, 164, from R. Hoggart, *The Uses of Literacy* (1957), 340.
22. R. Williams, 'The Future of Cultural Studies' in *The Politics of Modernism* (1989), 162.
23. Bernard Jennings's address to the National Council Meeting of the WEA, 17 June 1978: 'A Policy for the Association's Future' – printed in *WEA News*, Autumn 1978, 6–7.
24. J. Rose, *The Intellectual Life of the British Working Classes* (New Haven, 2001), 275, quoting from Edith Hall, *Canary Girls and Stockpots* (Luton WEA Branch, 1977), 39–40.
25. Report on WEA National Meeting on Women's Education, London 8 Dec. 1979, *Women's Studies Newsletter* no. 12, Winter 1980, 15.
26. *The Ministry of Reconstruction Adult Education Committee, Final Report – 1919*, 89–90.
27. F. Kitchen, *Brother to the Ox* (1940).
28. R. Williams, *The Country and the City* (1975 ed.), 314–15.
29. A. J. J. Ratcliff, *The Adult Class* (1938), 75–6.
30. D. Morley and K. Worpole (eds), *The Republic of Letters – Working Class Writing and Local Publishing* (1987), 124.
31. Charles Osborne, Literary Director, Arts Council of Great Britain, quoted in Morley and Worpole (eds), *Republic of Letters*, vi.
32. Morley and Worpole (eds), *Republic of Letters*, 135.
33. R. Shaw, 'Why Keele is appointing a Field Officer for Working Class Education', a five-page 'note' for University of Keele, Department of Adult Education, dated May, 1971. para. 7. See the public expression of

this view in his article, 'Universities and the WEA: Myths and Reality', *Adult Education*, May 1971.
34. Taped interview with Bill Parkinson, University of Keele, Nov. 1982.
35. Joyce Holliday had established a reputation for plays (adaptations of Arnold Bennett novels and documentary dramas) written for the New Victoria Theatre, Stoke-on-Trent. Fanny Deakin was a well-known North Staffordshire communist and this community play, involving scores of local residents, chronicled her life.
36. Rose, *Intellectual Life*, 464.
37. Rose, *Intellectual Life*, 11.
38. L. Goldman, *Dons and Workers. Oxford and Adult Education since 1850* (Oxford, 1995), 326.
39. Steele, *Emergence of Cultural Studies*, chs. 1 and 9.
40. WEA, *Learning for Life* vol. 1, no. 3 (Autumn, 2001), 30.
41. D. Alfred (ed.), *The Robert Tressell Lectures, 1981–1988* (WEA South Eastern District, 1988).
42. Goldman, *Dons and Workers*, 316.

# 14    From Day Release to Lifelong Learning: Workplace Education and the WEA after 1964

*Peter Caldwell and Stephen K. Roberts*

Despite the creation and achievements of WETUC from 1919, developments in workplace learning in the WEA were slow. As John Holford has shown in this volume, an important reason for this was unease within the movement over the price the WEA would pay for extending its reach to those whose interest in education was defined not by a devotion to learning for its own sake, but by their need for training to become more effective trade unionists. 'Liberal adult education', the WEA's watchword, had meant during the heyday of WETUC the delivery of programmes to trade unionists of humanities and social science content of comparable shape, texture and quality to those enjoyed in WEA branches. With Tawney still making speeches after 1945 that extolled the need to prevent trade union students and others from falling away from the standards set by the earliest WEA students in their personal 'sacrifices of time and energy', and the national leadership uneasy about being drawn into providing 'training' for 'functionaries', the 1953 working party report marked a willingness in some quarters to abandon long-held assumptions. Even so, adherence to the 'gold standard' of the tutorial class was engrained in the WEA, and continued to dominate the thinking of officers and voluntary members long after the statistics of declining enrolments should have set off alarm bells and new ways of thinking.

In 1954, three pilot schemes, in Cleveland, Port Talbot and on Tyneside, provided material for a report by Hugh Clegg and Rex Adams to the 1959 WEA national conference. Their argument was that there was no contradiction between 'education' and 'training', and that the two could be reconciled through a notion of 'industrial studies' that built from the student's workplace experience to the wider social, economic and political context. The WEA helped to pioneer day release courses for trade unionists during the 1950s and 1960s, and thus ushered in a format for course delivery that was to thrive for many decades. Organisationally, though, it was an initiative by the TUC, rather than the WEA, which determined the future pattern of educational activity for trade unionists.

Trade unions had changed enormously since the founding of the WEA. Amalgamations before and after the 1939–45 war had left them leaner and fitter, and had seen them through the worst of the inter-war slump and depression. They played a full part in the war effort, being brought into partnership with government on an industry-by-industry basis. Far from drawing the unions' teeth, however, the Joint Production Committees of World War II enhanced trade unionists' political awareness and in some cases, their militancy.[1] After the war, unions became integrated into the fabric of national public life as never before, because of the victory of the Labour Party at the 1945 general election; a development which was not arrested when that government was voted out of office in 1951. Consensus on the need to work with unions, a powerful force in the country, was spread across governments of the 1950s, 1960s and 1970s of whatever political hue, and was shared by Winston Churchill, hardly a natural labour movement ally.[2] Against this background, unions had more of a stake than ever before in wishing to develop the quality of those who held lay office at local level. For them and for the TUC, therefore, hand-wringing arguments about the primacy of what was becoming to be described as the 'Great Tradition' of liberal adult education carried less weight than strategies for ensuring that union representatives performed their tasks willingly and effectively. From 1947 the TUC began providing training programmes of its own, and encouraged member unions to take union education seriously. From this period can be dated the first appointments of full-time union education officers.[3]

As union expectations of adult education rose, and as their involvement in it on their own account expanded, it became increasingly clear that the WETUC fare of a general WEA curriculum microwaved for trade unionists could not continue. The TUC with WEA agreement wound up WETUC in 1964, and replaced that relationship with a new one, in which the balance of power reflected the changed worlds of trade unionism and adult education. A TUC education committee now supervised its provision of all courses, and scrutinised each syllabus. Regional education officers liaised with WEA district secretaries and tutor-organisers to provide day-release courses in a formula by which the TUC-approved curriculum was delivered by WEA tutors in the districts, which were reimbursed the teaching costs under the longstanding 'Responsible Body' arrangements with the Ministry of Education and its successor, the Department of Education and Science. A by-product of these 1964 changes was the killing-off of the WEA's arch-rival, the NCLC. In the post-war climate, the rhetoric of enmity between the two bodies appeared more tired than ever, as the NCLC depended in its latter days entirely on the TUC for survival, in a way that the WEA never did. Begun in a period when the arguments had some vitality and meaning, the WEA–NCLC conflict had deteriorated into an arcane ritual war dance among a minority of the *cognoscenti* of adult education. Justifiably, it has been concluded that 'the formal takeover by the TUC in 1964 represented the extinction of an exhausted vein of socialist pedagogy'.[4]

In 1968, the TUC published *Training Shop Stewards*, followed by further policy statements in 1973 and 1975. Enshrined in these statements was the TUC view that the training of representatives should focus primarily on their role in 'furthering the aims and policies of the union', that its methods and purposes should be determined by unions, not other bodies, and that training should take place in an educational environment, free from constraints by employers or managers.[5] These were pronouncements that left the WEA with little to do in the fields of educational policy-making and administration, but gave tutor-organisers and tutors enough scope for local pedagogic innovation to make the work more than simply the delivery of prescribed content. After all, the aims of these courses, classically organised into day-release programmes of ten days, one day a week, included confidence-building and enhancing motivation among the students.

The growth of this type of provision was given a great boost in the 1970s during the years of the Labour governments. The notion of a 'social contract' between the government and the unions was a dominant public policy idea. Government would look after unions' interests in return for self-imposed restraint, in which public-sector unions would not pursue inflationary pay increases. A spin-off from this union–government relationship was specific grant support from the DES for trade union studies courses. Furthermore, when the report of Sir Lionel Russell on the future of adult education was published in 1973, it allocated to the WEA four special categories of work in which it had claimed expertise in its evidence to the committee. They were education for those in urban areas, socially and culturally deprived; work in an industrial context, mainly trade union studies; 'developing greater social and political awareness', and 'liberal and academic study below the level of university work'. Much thought was devoted by the WEA over the following decade and more into working out precisely what might be meant by the second two categories. Social and political education as a subject area had long been languishing in the WEA and elsewhere, and the general programme was difficult to disentangle or distinguish from university provision in extra-mural departments, where there was in any case an issue (though often unaddressed) about what 'university standard' meant. Despite these ambiguities, the WEA rose to the challenge laid down by Russell. Thirteen new tutor-organisers were appointed between 1974 and 1976 to work in the 'priority areas' the report had identified, and the WEA was especially successful in social education, providing programmes for a wide range of socially disadvantaged groups, including working-class women, those with learning difficulties, single parents and prison inmates.

The Russell report obviously gave the green light to trade union studies, and a great increase was noticeable in the scale of provision, stimulated naturally enough by the provision of direct government funding for trade union courses, which reached £1,000,000 in 1978–9. In 1974–5, 5,022 class meetings were held in trade union and industrial studies, the vast bulk being organised with the TUC. By 1976–7 this had risen to 6,955 meetings, a 38 per cent increase. In the latter year, the class meetings in this area of WEA work accounted for 21 per cent of the total WEA provision. The TUC itself attributed the increase to the introduction of health and safety courses following the explosion of interest in the topic culminating in the Health and Safety at Work Act of 1978 and the introduction of statutory safety representatives. Before 1975 virtually non-existent, these courses were taken by over 27,000 safety representatives in 1978–9 alone. The basic units of delivery through the 1970s and 1980s were separate Stage One ten-day courses for general representatives and for health and safety representatives, followed up by offerings at Stage Two, with options for further study in particular topics. Between 1975 and 1984, some 114,803 students completed the Stage One general course.[6] This was the great success story of trade union education in which the WEA shared. Attempts at more ambitious programmes in which the WEA was a partner, such as a Social Science Research Council project of 1975–8 involving special

BBC television programmes, study books, postal courses and face-to-face tuition (a mini-Open University approach) were less successful.[7]

In 1975 the TUC called on the DES to regard union education as a high priority, and in 1978, the WEA national planning committee reported the TUC's expectation that there would be a 'year-on-year increase of 30 per cent in its class provision'.[8] Nonetheless, this whole area of work continued to depend upon a prevailing set of assumptions between government and unions about mutual political co-operation, from which the WEA was a beneficiary. After a wave of localised and well-publicised public sector strikes in the winter of 1978–9 – the so-called 'winter of discontent' – the writing was on the wall for the union–government relationship, epitomised in popular comment as 'beer and sandwiches at Number Ten', a perceived cosy symbiosis between the Wilson–Callaghan Labour governments and the big players in the TUC. In fact, the government perception that trade unions could be helpful extended back to 1945 and indeed to the war years, and had been shared by Conservative administrations, so when a frontal attack on these notions was launched by the Thatcher government elected in 1979, it was more than just a rejection of policies of the mid-1970s. Spectacular confrontations took place between the government and the unions, most notably with the miners in 1984–5, and extensive legislation was passed to curb union activities.

No sooner had the new Conservative government taken office than the TUC education department had to report a sharp decrease in the number of enrolments on its courses, and this was the pattern established for the decade. Although there was some recovery by the late 1980s, the public climate, poisoned by a hostile mass media, had swung against trade unionism. From 1980–81, TUC meetings up and down the country reported that 'employers had become more obstructive in granting paid release; were challenging course syllabuses on grounds of relevance; and, were taking a very narrow view of what constituted industrial relations issues'.[9] Unsurprisingly, fewer union members volunteered as lay officers, and there was a reluctance by many to stick their heads above the parapet of defence against Thatcherism. A survey of shop stewards in the mid-1980s found that larger firms were more likely to take a relaxed view of granting paid release than small companies, public-sector organisations and shops.[10] Yet, it was remarkable that there were still new volunteers coming forward to fill what are often in their nature thankless tasks. There was actually a sea change in the type of people becoming representatives. In the perception of the TUC, it was being found that

> today's union workplace representative was likely to be younger ... and less open to influence from the traditional pattern of high-density union organisation in the private sector. Many representatives considered their main problems to be in generating commitment to, and interest in trade union activities and issues at workplace level, and the greater demands today for communicating more effectively with members.[11]

In other words the new representatives of the late 1980s were not likely to be familiar with the culture, mechanisms and processes of the union movement of its Butskellite heyday, and would have particular need for an educational offering in which communication skills and confidence-building were prime ingredients. In this change lay the basis of new approaches in workplace learning.

Trends in trade union education had not in any case always worked to the benefit of the WEA, even in days of plenty. When WETUC was wound up, the WEA lost its control over curriculum content, and was left to try to relate its voluntary ideals, classically enshrined in the branch structure, to its new role as provider of day-release courses. Another loss was the long WETUC tradition of weekend schools, which disappeared when it was recognised that these once-popular and effective meetings now catered only for a small minority. The increased funding of the 1970s and the expansion of the curriculum to include health and safety did not see a flow of money into the bank account of the Association. The local authority technical colleges (from the late 1970s more usually called 'further education colleges') by 1977–8 were providing nearly 80 per cent of the TUC courses, cutting down the WEA's share from 50 per cent in the period 1964–76 to a mere 20 per cent. The TUC naturally talked more to its largest providing sector than to its (by now) minority shareholder, and regional TUC education officers, empowered by direct DES funding, enjoyed greater local powers of choice over competing providers. An effect was of course to develop the local networking and horsetrading skills of WEA staff, not so much of district secretaries as of the specially-appointed trade union studies tutor-organisers.[12] Moreover, positively, much was done in local WEA delivery to encourage informal and participative approaches to learning that lay firmly within the WEA tradition. In addition, the WEA was able to provide a locus for fostering wider interest in trade unionism, in places where 'industrial branches' or 'trade union studies branches' (the terms seem to have been used interchangeably) were founded. By the later 1970s these included Oxford, Bristol, Telford, Coventry, Liverpool, London, Manchester and Leeds. Some branches successfully brought together the new audience of trade unionists, increasingly younger, white-collar activists including many women, with the WEA tradition of interest in labour history and international studies, as well as promoting interest in trade union topics of a more specific, technical kind.

Workplace learning had become heavily dependent on government policy, and the 1980s inevitably saw a great shake-up in the pattern of provision. An index of decline was that in 1980 it was estimated that the WEA could account for a maximum of only 9 per cent of industrial tutors in the United Kingdom.[13] The effects of the decline in TUC day release courses were uneven in the WEA. All districts cut their day release provision between 1979 and 1987, some drastically and with indecent haste, as in the cases of the then Bucks., Berks. and Oxon. District, the Eastern, North Staffs., South-western and Western Districts. At least it could be said that the WEA's overall share of TUC provision stayed roughly the same, but this was an optimistic gloss on a serious retreat. A 1989 report concluded that 'it has become evident that the WEA can no longer claim to be a national provider of trade union education', a shocking admission given the tradition of WETUC and the golden days of only a decade earlier.[14] The report called for a recovery and a consolidation of existing work, noting in passing that the regions of the country where WEA trade union tutors, both full- and part-time were most plentiful, were the English midlands, south-east and north-west England. It was, however, able to report a number of WEA local initiatives that offered possibilities of a way forward. A WEA tutor-organiser in the West Midlands District was in 1983 seconded to the TUC to establish union courses for Asian workers, building on an existing inner-city programme. In 1987 the London District worked with Brent NALGO women's group to provide courses for women trade unionists in Brent, and the South-eastern District worked with the print union, the National Graphical Association, to develop courses in the many small firms typical of that industry. An important theme in these experiments was 'lateral thinking' in which the shared needs of trade union students and other WEA student groups were emphasised. During the early 1980s in particular, the skills of trade union tutors were deployed in programmes designed to address the social dislocation of unemployment. Unwaged people and part-time workers were the target groups for WEA courses in TUC centres for the unemployed, courses on credit unions and for tenants' groups were aimed at community activists, and a broad span of those not in full-time employment were recruited to Second Chance to Learn courses, which the WEA introduced successfully in the West Midlands and the Thames Valley. Though the model of Second Chance was drawn from provision on Merseyside that had grown out of community development initiatives in the 1970s, the pattern of one whole day a week for a course lasting at least ten and in some cases up to 30 weeks obviously owed much to trade union education precedents, and to the WEA informal and student-centred traditions of learning. In the West Midlands model of Second Chance, and doubtless elsewhere, a benefit for the WEA itself was the collaboration between trade union studies tutors and some of those whose efforts had been mainly deployed in the general academic programme, thus helping to combat a pattern of demarcation of professional activity that had begun to appear in WEA Districts since the rise of the TUC scheme and the demise of WETUC.

The government's negative attitudes towards manufacturing industry in general and to labour-intensive, heavy industry in particular did nothing to help trade union education, and the TUC was frozen out of policy-making. The WEA's contribution in this field and in all fields was also affected by innovations in education policy. The Responsible Body system of direct funding for adult education to the WEA, university extra-mural departments and local education authorities which had been in place for most of the WEA's existence was scrapped in 1989. The universities had become disenchanted with the restrictions as they saw them of the special funding arrangement, probably because they foresaw that as higher education expanded, the concept of 'extra-mural' as opposed to continuing education would be fatally undermined as more and more adult learners entered the higher education mainstream. (The perspective from within extra-mural departments themselves was naturally very different.) No serious resistance to reform came therefore from the university sector. At the same time as the writing appeared on the wall for the RBs, the Education Act of 1988 shook up the whole educational system, and had massive implications for adult learning, in the WEA as elsewhere. One analyst concluded that adult learners and the educational offering put before them were affected by at least 80 per cent of the 238 sections of the 1988 Act.[15]

The WEA as it stood in the 1980s had more to lose than either of the other categories of Responsible Body, and in 1989 a serious threat to its continued existence was thrown up when it was proposed by the DES that the Association should receive future funding through the LEAs. This was at best to disregard the 'great tradition' of liberal adult education, as most LEAs had no deep-rooted interest in WEA-style academic studies, but on the other hand the 1988 Act was by no means a death knell for continuing education as such. Local authorities, like the WEA itself and the university departments, had in fact been initiating schemes of work with adult learners that included access and second chance education and provision for disadvantaged groups. Many local authority initiatives of this kind stemmed not from departments of education but from economic development units, unemployment units and a range of socio-economic agencies which had not existed among metropolitan and shire authorities before 1979. An optimistic reading of the 1988 Act therefore stressed its potential for mainstreaming adult education, which would be admittedly at the expense of the now threadbare 'great tradition'.[16] The LEAs were being given a brokering and co-ordinating role under the 1988 Act that in fact they were ill-equipped to perform, and undermining any optimistic view of the government's intentions was its avowed disenchantment with local authorities in general, and with county councils in particular.

By the late 1980s, the union movement had been restructured, as a response to massive changes in the nature of the British workforce. A new unionism had emerged which was marked by a shift away from the collectivist traditions and willingness to exert industrial muscle in bargaining situations which paradoxically had flourished under accommodating Labour governments. Trade unions in the 1990s were more likely to see themselves as serving the needs and aspirations of members in a broader context than the narrowly industrial. With the decline of funding for trade union studies and of the Responsible Body arrangements, the WEA needed a new formula for workplace learning as much as did the unions. The first schemes of Return to Learn, a partnership between the public-sector National Union of Public Employees (NUPE) and the West Mercia District of the WEA in 1989 offered a model for a way forward. The important elements of confidence-building and personal development which had underlain the whole tradition of British workplace learning under WETUC and the TUC day-release scheme were now brought forward to hold centre stage in the rationale of the new courses. In the day-release programme, the conveying of information was a primary aim of tutors and a main expectation of students. By contrast, the new courses put an emphasis on the building up of study skills from scratch, using as primary materials students' own personal experiences and moving outwards and forwards from there. Course books were organised under the headings 'Writing', 'Investigating your Community', 'The Media', 'Fact and Opinion', 'Observing a Meeting', 'Statistics and Figures' and 'Writing a Short Story'. Much of this would have struck a chord with any survivors of the WEA in its earliest days, though it differed considerably from the general WEA programme of its own time, influenced as it was by post-1945 extra-mural department assumptions and practices. A difference between this model and the TUC–WEA partnership was that the curriculum was developed by WEA tutor-organisers and tutors, not handed down by the union.

From the beginnings in the west midlands, NUPE Return to Learn was extended under the auspices of the union to north-west England, Scotland, Yorkshire and Humberside.[17] An important ingredient in the courses was accreditation. This was and is the system by which students can gain educational 'credits' for their learning achievements. The system was validated and moderated by Open Access Federations, regionally organised consortia of higher and further education providers in a framework that had national validity but was free of formal examinations that would have deterred all but a few of the students who took up the courses. A national credit framework was developing at the time, which gave these credits transfer value for those proceeding to other kinds of courses. There was initially some resistance to the notion of credit among sections of the WEA voluntary movement, on the grounds that the WEA was proclaimed itself to be committed to a non-examination educational framework. This response was ironic in the light of the pre-1960s WEA's preoccupation with the 'gold standard' of the tutorial class, but was often the product of misunderstanding as to what 'credit' was.

NUPE Return to Learn proved a highly successful and adaptable formula. By 1996 the programme had expanded to be available in all of the regions covered by the new 'super-union' UNISON, formed from a merger of three public sector unions including NUPE.[18] By 1998 6,000 students had completed it.[19] Its flexibility and adaptability were inherent, and were suited to the new 'post-Fordist' climate of the world of paid employment. Programmes could be tailored to the needs of specific groups of union members; forms of open learning could be developed to take account of learners' needs; the curriculum could be developed and reviewed by students and tutors working co-operatively, and the courses could lead to a variety of outcomes according to individual students' needs. There is substantial evidence that students were not those typical of trade union studies of the 1970s and 1980s. A study of 1995 found that 80 per cent were women, 42 per cent were employed part time, 76 per cent earned less than £11,500 p.a. and 91 per cent left school at 16 or earlier.[20] Significantly, this model of trade union education succeeded in attracting thousands of ordinary members who held no position or office in the union. While some trade union educators argued that this diverted resources from training core activists, there was evidence to suggest that it helped to encourage new types of activism and active membership amongst previously under-represented groups.

The co-operative principles of learning in Second Chance courses and UNISON Return to Learn led naturally to the Voluntary Educational Advisor (VEA) scheme, by which former students advised intending new students and new learners while on their courses. VEAs could themselves earn credits for their learning, thus continuing their own educational progression. Just as the early WEA envisaged learning as a highway not as the conventional ladder, so these WEA students were challenging the orthodox distinctions between education and training, studying and volunteering, learning for personally-defined goals and for employment progression.

The planned routeing of government funding to the WEA via local educational authorities never bedded down. The creation instead in 1992 of the Further Education Funding Council for England worked with the grain of developments in workplace learning and in other community education and social education projects of the WEA. It was only the branch traditional academic programme that was left again looking isolated by these developments, especially so since its natural local allies, the university departments of adult or extra-mural education, came under the ministrations of a different funding council. Much of the WEA's work that had been codified in the Russell priority groups was now incorporated in a schedule of the Act which listed vocational courses, courses preparing students for public examinations, access to higher education courses, courses in what used to be called Adult Basic Education (ABE) and courses leading to independent living and improved communication skills for those with special learning difficulties.[21] This work inevitably came to be called 'Schedule 2 work'. Many of the new Open College Network-approved new programmes in second chance and workplace learning fell into the Access category, and thus attracted FEFC funding on a favourable tariff, since the basic mechanism of state funding for adult education was to be payment by results. Units of funding were clocked up on the basis of successful student throughput.

If this regime had been imposed on the WEA in 1980 it could well have quickly killed off the Association, but a decade and more of living in the funding wilderness had put sections of the WEA, particularly its field staff, on their mettle and able to respond quickly to the new challenges. By another irony of history, the WEA's academic programme, the direct descendant on most people's reckoning of the tutorial classes, was corralled into the 'Non-schedule 2' area, a catch-all description of learning programmes without measurable outcomes and therefore not deemed worthy of FEFC support, or at least not at premium rates. To try to prove that there could be measurable learning outcomes on branch and other general programmes, the WEA commissioned a Nottingham University continuing education specialist to develop a scheme for assessing outcomes in uncertificated, liberal academic, adult education. It was certainly not what WEA students wanted, but in some cases it facilitated some thoughtful reflections on what the purposes of these courses really were.

While for most WEA observers it seemed that nothing but ill was coming from government policies towards the funding of adult education, there has been a trend at work since 1980 that has not yet at the time of writing (July 2002) been reversed or significantly mutated. It is thus becoming the equivalent of the Responsible Body arrangements in durability and orthodoxy. It is the principle that adult basic education and access provision, and programmes designed to produce measurable outputs and student progression, are more worthy of public funding than leisure-based courses or courses of open-ended academic study for its own sake. The effect is to discourage total academic flexibility and the notion that students can take a subject wherever their inclinations take them: the essence of much of the WEA tradition. On the other hand, however, coupled with the transformation of British universities from elite to mass higher education institutions, the new regimes have sent more working-class 'mature' students to higher education than at any time in British history. Under the New Labour governments from 1997, trade unions have not been ushered back into Number Ten for either beer and sandwiches or their New Labour equivalent. Nevertheless, the new government has granted unions a role, has commended schemes such as UNISON Return to Learn, and has broadened the policy-making community with a stake in workplace learning.

The last five years of New Labour to 2002 have seen significant developments in the capacity of trade unions to stimulate and facilitate the growth of workplace learning and the WEA, especially through its partnership with UNISON, has played an important role in this. There has been a recognition that in a rapidly changing labour market, with an emphasis on adaptability and transferable skills, there is an important role for a more liberal strand of education in the workplace. UNISON Return to Learn, which was developed as a scheme for union members to study in their own time, has increasingly provided the centrepiece of learning partnerships with employers. These partnerships benefited several thousand low-paid employees and included the key ingredient of paid release from work, helping to address the problem of shortage of time that is often a major obstacle to participation in adult learning. These learning partnerships linked in with union strategies to open up career paths and greater training opportunities for their members, thus widening the bargaining agenda and underlining the relevance of unionism to the modern employee.

The WEA is particularly proud of its contribution to the National Health Service Individual Learning Account scheme. This is a national partnership between the NHS, UNISON and the WEA with its origins in the NHS Plan's commitment to improve educational and training opportunities for non-professional staff. The partner organisations have been working successfully since early 2001 to provide serious and well-resourced training (some of it tailor-made by UNISON and the WEA) for the thousands of front-line NHS staff such as health care assistants and catering and domestic staff, who have traditionally missed out on training opportunities.

The potential contribution that trade unions can make to address adult basic skills needs has been widely acknowledged. Networks of union representatives and workplace officers have daily contact with millions of workers and have often built up a relationship of trust that is essential in drawing employees into learning. Many of the successful projects sponsored by the Union Learning Fund have been designed to develop relevant and accessible approaches to workplace basic skills. Central to this strategy has been the establishment of a layer of union representatives, Learning Reps or Learning Advisers, who specialise in encouraging interest in learning, providing information and encouragement to potential learners and pushing the employer to provide suitable facilities. The WEA has been in the forefront of these developments. It has demonstrated in particular the value of adult education approaches such as labour-intensive outreach and promotional activities, that help to lay the groundwork for successful provision. One dimension of this work has been the use of electronic learning, and the WEA was closely involved in establishing *CareConnect*, UNISON's Learn Direct hub that is pioneering ways to harness the flexibility and appeal of information technology to the building of workplace learning.

More generally, the report of Helena Kennedy QC into widening participation in further education provided a basis on which to build an agenda for access, and the appointment of a minister for lifelong learning was a token of serious intent in the whole subject of unlocking the potentialities of the adult population in the interests of the economy and society. The Union Learning Fund will encourage innovation in trade union education, and is thus a valuable innovation, even if it is not a restoration of direct funding. Positive comments about unions flowed from the National Advisory Group on Continuing Education and Lifelong Learning (NAGCELL) Report, *The Learning Age*, and the report by Klaus Moser, *A Fresh Start*. The WEA brings to these developments a century of experience of its own. The issue is not merely that of ensuring the best take-up of existing provision. The adult education tradition, of which the WEA has been an important part, has been based on curriculum development and innovation, building programmes for students' needs and promoting the idea that education should be available for everyone.[22]

## NOTES

*Place of publication London unless otherwise stated.*

1. R. Croucher, *Engineers at War 1939–1945* (1982); K. Laybourn, *British Trade Unionism c.1770–1990* (Stroud, 1991), 163–80.
2. R. Jenkins, *Churchill* (2001), 853.
3. R. Fieldhouse, 'The Workers' Educational Association' in Fieldhouse and Associates, *History*, 183.
4. J. McIlroy, 'Independent Working Class Education', in Fieldhouse and Associates, *History*, 269.

5.  TUC, *Review of the TUC's Education Service: General Council Report* (1987), 3.
6.  *The Industrial Tutor*, iv, no. 3 (1986), 55.
7.  'The WEA and the Trade Union Studies Project' (unpublished WEA report, n.d. circa 1978).
8.  TUC General Council Report, 'Review of Trade Union Education Services', 1975; WEA unpublished paper, 'The Allocation of Resources to WEA Trade Union and Industrial Studies Provision', planning committee, 5 Jan. 1978.
9.  TUC, *Review of the TUC's Education Service: General Council Report* (1987), 8.
10. *The Industrial Tutor*, iv, no. 3 (1986), 54.
11. *Review of the TUC's Education Service* (1987), 9.
12. P. Caldwell, 'The WEA's Work in Trade Union Studies', *The Industrial Tutor* (Sept. 1979), 4–5; C. Baker and P. Caldwell, 'The Future of the WEA's Trade Union Studies Work', *WEA Trade Union and Industrial Studies Newsletter*, Jan. 1978.
13. A. Nash, 'British and American Labor Educators: A Comparative Analysis', *Labor Studies Journal*, iv pt. 3 (1980), 248.
14. WEA, *Trade Union Education and the Future of the WEA* (1989), 5.
15. UDACE (Unit for the Development of Adult Continuing Education), *Adults and the Act, The Education Reform Act 1988 and Adult Learners* (Leicester, 1988), 373.
16. P. Caldwell, 'Reforming Adult Continuing Education', *Education Policy*, v no. 4 (1990), 373–80.
17. NUPE Education, 'R2L, Return to Learn' (1992).
18. P. Caldwell, 'UNISON Return to Learn: A Flexible Model for Lifelong Education?', unpublished paper for 4th International Conference on Learning and Research in Working Life, Steyr, Austria, July 1996.
19. A. Munro and H. Rainbird, 'The New Unionism and the New Bargaining Agenda: UNISON-Employer Partnerships on Workplace Learning in Britain', *British Journal of Industrial Relations*, xxxviii no. 2 (2000), 231.
20. H. Kennedy, *Return to Learn: UNISON's Fresh Approach to Trade Union Education* (1995).
21. Listed in Fieldhouse and Associates, *History*, 104.
22. P. Caldwell, 'Adult Learning and the Workplace' in H. Rainbird (ed.), *Training in the Workplace* (Basingstoke, 2000), 244–63.

# 15 WEA Values in the Twenty-first Century

*Julia Jones*

At the plenary session of the Workers' Educational Association National Conference at Manchester in 2001, the general secretary was asked about the marketing of the organisation. His reply was that marketing the WEA was peculiarly difficult because there is no single statement that can be made about it that is true of every part. 'Except', he added hastily, 'that it is a Good Thing'.[1]

In an age that is anxious about image presentation, branding, and market niche, this inability to express the WEA's *raison d'être* in a single sound bite could be considered a fatal weakness. The GPO at the beginning of the twenty-first century is no longer a General Post Office so renames itself *Consignia* for the global market (and back again to *Royal Mail*); the AEEW joins with MSF to become *Amicus*; National Power conceals past disappointments as *Innogy*; and Andersen Consulting re-brands as *Accenture* to put 'a greater accent on the future'.[2] We, in the Workers' Educational Association, comprise more workless than working people; it's more fashionable to provide learning opportunities than education and the nature of our formal association has changed fundamentally in recent years. Should we be commissioning an expensive consultancy firm to re-brand us as something high-sounding and fatuous, *Studiá*, perhaps, with a re-design of our re-designed logo and corporate colour schemes with endorsement from a focus group? Possibly not ...

What has intrigued me as a relative newcomer to the WEA and working in a county, Essex, that has frequently found itself at odds with both District and national policy, is how tangible a dynamic the Association does still possess. Despite its muzzy strapline and anxious all-things-to-all-people promotional literature, on the ground the WEA retains an ability to be proactive in a variety of contexts and to reinvent itself whilst remaining loyal to its central tenets. The purpose of this chapter is to explore some possible reasons for this. It is based on less than a decade's experience of the WEA; firstly as a sessional tutor employed to teach literature on the WEA general programme in Essex from 1993, then as an outreach[3] development worker looking at the learning needs of 'vulnerable' parents, finally as a member of the Eastern District field staff managing the WEA community programme in Essex until the time of writing in 2002.

If the general secretary of the WEA finds it hard to make universally applicable statements about what it is exactly that it does these days, anyone looking at the activities of the organisation in this single county of Essex will feel some sympathy with him. On the one hand Essex has more individual branches than any other English county – more than some entire Districts. There may be a choice of three or four general programme classes a week in the larger towns, two courses a year in the villages. Branch members are typically past retirement age, broadly middle class and cleave to the liberal studies curriculum. The Essex Federation has retained its joint university courses longer than any other county in the Eastern District. The Essex community (outreach) programme on the other hand offers personal development, ICT, skills for parents and volunteers and is currently the only location in the country where the WEA works directly in a prison. The majority of its students are aged 25–35 and exist within the means-tested benefit system, usually on income support. This means that many of them are from that statistically camouflaged sector of society which doesn't even feature on the unemployment register.

At first glance the only common denominator between these two WEA programme groups might be that they are comprised of the work-less – the retired magistrate on the one hand – the lifer on the other. What has happened to the WEA's USP (Unique Selling Point), its promotion of higher education for Working People?[4] It's a question that's been troubling the organisation since before its first half century. In his fiftieth anniversary address in 1953 R. H. Tawney insisted that the function of the Association must remain inseparable from its title – though he was careful to qualify its first word.

> We interpret the word 'workers' in no narrow sense; but our primary mission, proclaimed from hundreds of platforms and in scores of pamphlets, is to the educationally underprivileged majority.[5]

Forty years earlier, in 1914, his explanation had sounded less embattled. The WEA, he had argued is not limited by articles of association to one specific purpose. Its aim is to articulate the educational aspirations of Labour, to represent them to the proper authorities, to stimulate into activity, when it exists, the organisation through which they can be satisfied, to create it when it does not.[6]

The shift in tone from the facilitator to the missionary may betray anxiety:

movements, like individuals, should beware when all men speak well of them ... when a cause has achieved a modest measure of success, its adherents should redouble their vigilance to ensure that it is not merely floating with the current but inspired by specific and distinctive aims ... and judges its activities by the degree to which they promote the attainment of them.[7]

Nevertheless, after 1953 Tawney's single-issue organisation was quietly rejected and what has been termed 'the drift to universal provision' continued.[8] When, in 1966, the WEA constitution was again revised, more than 60 years of commitment 'to Promote the Higher Education of Working People' was watered down 'to stimulate and to satisfy the demand of adults, in particular members of workers' movements, for education'.

Currently (2002) the charitable purpose of the Association 'is to promote adult education based on democratic principles in its organisation and practice, through the participation of its voluntary members'. The certainty, the charisma, in the language of the early days has vanished. Explicit recognition of workers in the headline statement has been taken out and the recognition of the role of the WEA's voluntary members sounds as if it has been tacked on. Whatever would Tawney say?

There is more at stake here than slapping a preservation order on a quaint old moniker. The W-word matters. The development of modern adult education from the mid-nineteenth century has been intimately connected with changes in the organisation of work – particularly with the phenomenon of industrialisation.[9] Industrialisation impacted profoundly on political and social institutions and, intimately, on families and on the gender expectations of men and women. Education was seen, variously, as a means of gaining new skills, improving individual quality of life and enabling collective action. 'The twentieth century', writes

Fieldhouse, 'inherited a strong tradition of socially purposive adult education'.[10] The WEA was a beneficiary of this – the tradition of voluntary self-help, of education to enhance the quality of life and the expectation that education could and should contribute to political and social action. As Tawney rather beautifully described it: 'Like all working class movements the Workers' Educational Association moves in a path worn smooth by the vanguard of the anonymous.'[11]

The big structural changes made by the mid-twentieth century – universal suffrage, the entitlement to free secondary education, a welfare state posited on the nuclear family and 40 years of male bread-winning – might seem to freeze-frame the gains made during the first 50 years of the WEA's existence. Yet, relationships between patterns of work, social and domestic structures and expectations of education have not remained static. Towards the end of the twentieth century it became fashionable to add the prefix *post-* to most accepted social descriptors – post-modern, post-industrial, post-Fordist, post-Enlightenment – and to assent to claims that we were experiencing a new industrial revolution.

> Historians looking back at the closing decades of the twentieth century may well identify our own times as the crucial period of a new industrial revolution. Certainly they will identify some profound changes in the nature of work ... already we can see that there are pervasive effects on economic organisation and living standards, on family and household structure, and on community and social cohesion.[12]

This extract comes from a post-graduate course reader produced for the Open University. If the WEA has not lost touch with the resonance of its own name it may once again have a special role to play in ensuring that education (or 'lifelong learning') does more than offer people sticking plaster solutions to the new range of problems and injustices emanating from the changing world of work. 'One of the motivating factors that has affected the involvement of working class communities in education has been the desire to understand and promote social and collective responses to the needs and challenges of their lives.'[13]

This does not mean that all its students and voluntary members must be workers. Very often it has been worklessness, whether it be for the retired, the unemployed or those who have never entered the job market that has focused attention on what work means to people.

It is more than the provision of livelihood – though none of us must ever forget how much that matters:

> Employment ... provides a time structure for the day, the week and the year, enforces regular activity, establishes structured social networks outside the family, links the individual to goals and purposes that transcend his/her own and is the basis of personal identity and status.[14]

Much the same, on a smaller scale, could be said of education, which may be one reason why, as traditional social networks are perceived to fragment under the urge to 'lead one's own life',[15] our government promotes versions of the 'Lifelong Learning' agenda as a form of social control. Perhaps the late 1990s fad-phrase 'social *inclusion*' sounds more benign than social *control* but the sceptical will draw their own conclusions from the official lists of those workless people at whom Lifelong Learning initiatives should be aimed. They do not usually include the retired or the independently supported spouses of Middle England. Groups to be targeted are the 'disadvantaged' (who cost the state money) or the 'disaffected' (who might destabilise it). Is there a covert establishment hope that education might replace religion as the opiate of the masses? The expectation of the WEA pioneers was that, if education enabled people to extend their understanding of the world, it might also contribute to their changing of it.

The WEA relationship with the world of employment has always been indirect and its role in the 'partnership of labour and learning' complex. At its foundation it concerned itself with those aspects of people's human development, their social, cultural, intellectual aspirations for which no educational provision was made by the state – because such provision was not directly required for the working class to function at work. One hundred years later it is having to redress the balance to deal with those aspects of people's human development for which work is necessary – and for which no provision is made now that un- and under-employment are a structural feature of British society. Learning however is no adequate substitute for labour any more than labour without learning was sufficient to kindle 'the real glow of life'.[16]

Over the course of a century, however, the WEA has moved from being 'a working-class body in the sense that it is an educational expression of the working-class movement'[17] to being complimented thus:

> The WEA has helped to equip the more vulnerable in English society to make their voice heard and has provided one of the most effective platforms for the caring, articulate middle-classes.[18]

There is an acceptance, in the second statement, of the social separation between 'the more vulnerable' who are to be helped and 'the caring, articulate middle-classes' up there on the platform which is disquieting. The fragmentation of the industrial working class has left many of its members vulnerable. 'Your own life, your own failure', as Beck puts it.[19] Feelings of isolation and low self-esteem are endemic amongst people living in the most difficult circumstances. The WEA, of all organisations, needs to retain 'the idea of social solidarity which is the contribution of the working classes to the social conscience of our age'.[20] This is both an educational and an ethical issue dependent on understandings of democracy.

One apparently paradoxical aspect of the WEA's relationship with the world of work is its reliance on voluntary effort – work for which no one is paid. Just as attitudes to and expectations of paid work have changed over the past century so have attitudes to and expectations of the non-paid. But this has not, to my knowledge, received the same degree of theoretical or sociological study. In a period that is busily seeking Third Ways, the vol'n'com (voluntary and community) sector, in which the WEA is currently located, receives plaudits, access to the funding market but little real power. This is partly because the sector is not well understood and partly, I suspect, because status at the beginning of the twenty-first century is far more firmly linked to salary level than it was at the outset of the twentieth. Volunteer is assumed simply to mean amateur, rather than having-different-expertise. Throughout the English education system (I apologise for my parochialism) there are willing non-paid workers, but their status and function within their several organisations are frequently anomalous – even when they comprise the governing body. There is a huge range of issues, assumptions and expectations to be unpicked around educational volunteering – many of them historical and others connected with social class. For the WEA this is of central importance and needs research even more urgently than co-ordination or management.[21] A model that essentially derives still from the original, inspired partnership of nineteenth-century educational philanthropy with early twentieth-century labour movement activism deserves some radical reconsideration with a century on the clock.

As education has grown globally into a major source of employment as well as increasing its role as a prerequisite for employment, there has frequently been unease and even disagreement within the WEA around its allocations of responsibility to its paid and unpaid labourers. At the time of writing, the Association is looking with more urgency into the ways in which the commitment and effort of its voluntary members can be extended from its traditional home in the branch organisation to permeate the workplace and community programme. That in itself will make little difference if issues of power are not openly – and reflectively – debated.

The WEA today – together with educational institutions in every sector – is ever more inescapably shaped by the 'new managerialism',[22] – and volunteers are notoriously hard to manage. Within my own county the voluntary members of the Essex Federation gained a degree of notoriety for approaching their role with an Awkward Squad's seriousness and were roundly ticked off for it in the Eastern District's 75th year commemorative history.

> Despite its justifiable pride in its voluntary and democratic principles the WEA cannot simply allow its members to act however they like. The WEA has obligations which at all costs it must strive to fulfil. Some of these relate to its heritage – its traditional concern for rigorous academic study of socially-relevant subjects and its traditional mission to the educationally under-privileged. Others related to its receipt of government and local authority funds.[23]

It's not only that relationships can be difficult between voluntary members who have a governing role and paid professionals who must manage (that's an English constitutional fact of life); the situation in the WEA has historically been complicated by the decentralised relationship between the national executive and the districts.

It has also been complicated by disagreement about the degree of closeness that it is proper for a voluntary organisation to have with the government. Resolution of this becomes more acute as yet more public services are re-privatised. Increasingly politicians of both parties are tempted to use the 'not-for-profit' sector to take the edge off this extension of the market principle and to implement manifesto idealism cost-effectively (i.e. cheaply) at 'the grass-roots'. Combined, however, with a bidding culture and stringent data-collection and audit requirements this forces the vol-orgs to adopt ever more comprehensive management systems very similar to the statutory providers. Where the implementation of such systems is not well handled, this can give rise to feelings of anger and alienation in voluntary members – and indeed tutors and students as well.

This is not new for the WEA. Since its receipt of the first tranche of Board of Education funding (from 1907) it has been externally accountable and subject to inspection. Its managers are thus open to accusations of government toadyism from outsiders and their own members and often encounter fierce resistance to what may be intrin-sically worthwhile initiatives. 'At the heart of public sector managerialism is the claim that the objectives of social and educational services can be promoted more efficiently and to a higher standard if the appropriate management techniques are deployed.'[24]

In the 1970s, for instance, the WEA had mapped out for itself – at a national level – areas of work which the Russell Committee (1973) recognised as being 'a logical development of the Association's traditional concern for the underprivileged' and suitable for government funding. Delivery, however, proved difficult – as the then WEA assistant secretary explained:

> The 'democratic rights of the voluntary movement' were rediscovered, refurbished and re-introduced against the centralised imposition of three of the four Russell categories – (a) 'education for the socially and culturally deprived', (b) educational work in an industrial context', and (c) 'political and social education'. The fourth category – 'liberal and academic study' – the bedrock of most branch provision, tended to become increasingly detached from the other three categories in ensuing internal and external discussions.[25]

The 'very nature of the WEA' at that period – a voluntary self-governing movement with a federalist constitutional structure, authority residing in the Districts and determination of the programme firmly in the hands of class members – brought it close to being unmanageable. Members' democratic rights in the red corner vs. accountability to national democracy (taxpayers' money) in the blue. Those who were left un-provided were the workers and the weakest – those who should have been at the heart of the Association but who had dropped unnoticed from its governance as their industrial and class base had fragmented.

By the mid-1990s, when I became involved with the WEA, all sectors of education had undergone more than a decade of Thatcherism. Centralisation, strong management and accountability were in the ascendant. In some areas, notably schools, this had been coupled with a constitutional boost for the largest group of volunteers in the country – school governors. For the WEA, however, survival choices had culminated in the decision to incorporate all the English Districts into a single Association with effect from April 1993. They – and the Scottish Association (but not the Welsh and Northern Irish Districts) – became subject 'at all times ... to the ordinance of the National Executive Committee'.[26] As the District management began the implementation of new procedures, the Essex Federation discussed secession.

Roger Fieldhouse describes the WEA as suffering an 'identity crisis' at this period and locates this around the central issue of the engagement of the voluntary member, quoting from the fifteenth Albert Mansbridge Memorial lecture:

> Its core activities are by and for its members, but the discourse of 'provision' and the funding conditions mean that more and more of its work is done for others who are not members and whom existing members do not see as sharers in the inherited WEA project. It will not be long before an open decision will have to be made: will it continue to organise learning activities mainly for members and assume that all learners in all its classes are seriously offered the choice of becoming members? Or will it transform itself openly into an association of members contributing subscriptions to help others gain access to learning?[27]

If alternatives for the WEA were as unappealing as these – become a self-perpetuating clique or pay out philanthropically – one might feel that there's a lot to be said for avoiding 'open' decisions! The constitutional position of members was changed in 2001 with a reversion to the pre-1966 opting-in system. At the time of writing it is too early to assess what effect this change may have on voluntary activism. All that can usefully be memoed is that an activist is not necessarily a democrat and that compliance with external forms of democracy does not automatically ensure social justice and equality of opportunity for all.

Fieldhouse differentiates almost in passing between 'the idea of democracy as government by an active membership' and the Association's ' "ethos of democracy" in the class where the direction of learning is determined by the students'. In fact, this distinction is crucial as it focuses attention on the processes of class organisation and the styles of teaching and learning within the group. It is these I believe that provide the clue to the true nature of 'the inherited WEA project'. With gratitude to Paulo Freire I would like to describe this legacy as the WEA's pedagogy – a pedagogy that, at its best, is based on mutual respect; that involves each student as the prime volunteer, valuing their individual experiences as an adult and their potential as a contributor to society. As the introduction to the most recent edition of *Pedagogy of the Oppressed* has it:

> There is no such thing as a neutral educational process. Education either functions as an instrument that is used to facilitate the integration of the young into the present system and bring about conformity to it, or it becomes 'the practice of freedom' the means by which men and women deal critically and creatively with reality and discover how to participate in the transformation of their world.[28]

For all the upheaval around centralisation through the 1990s and again with the advent of the Learning and Skills Council, the WEA has retained a set of guidelines for action that are close to those established in 1903. Today these key statements are described as *aims*:[29]

- Stimulating and responding to the demand of adults for liberal education, through the direct provision of courses and other activities;
- Providing in particular for the needs of working class adults and of those who are socially, economically or educationally disadvantaged;
- Providing educational programmes for appropriate organisations concerned with the collective needs of adults in the community and in the workplace;
- Generally furthering the advancement of education to the end that all children, adolescents and adults may have full access

to the education needed for their complete individual and
social development.

In the first, and later, drafts of the constitution these guidelines were
termed *objects*, viz: to promote the higher education of working men
primarily by the extension of university teaching, also (a) by the
assistance of working-class efforts of a specifically educational
character and (b) by the development of an efficient school
continuation system.[30] In 1906 the movement reduced its offer to
'assistance' in the development of an efficient school continuation
system but committed itself additionally to (c) the co-ordination of
popular educational effort.

With some re-wordings these statements have remained consistent
through a century of constitutional tinkerings. Their authors at least
seem clear that the 'inherited WEA project' is to propagandise for
education – education that is intended to foster the worker's
individual personal development as well as social and cultural understanding. Syntactically, however, these public commitments are
neither *aims* nor *objects* – both of which might, theoretically, be
attainable in time. They are *strategies*, ways of working, therefore not
time-bound. As a contribution to explaining how it is that the WEA
retains its potential to motivate people to change their lives on the
ground, while occasionally appearing almost stymied by self-doubt
at the centre, this may be more important than it seems.

There is a WEA way of doing things across its different programmes
which is motivating and identifiably consistent – even if the things
that WEA agents (paid workers, voluntary members, funding partners)
see as needing to be done may vary according to time, place and
individual circumstance. In a fragmented, self-doubting, post-
industrial age, this is a significant attribute. Another striking feature
of these commitments is their variousness. I would argue that the
inherited WEA project has always been pluralistic – opportunistic even
(in the cause of promoting education) – and that it is in fact fortunate
that its internal diversity has tended to preclude the adoption of 'single
issue' approaches, whether they proceed from a lecturer's calls for
clarity, the advocates of specific curricula or the writers of prescriptive
national courses. When the WEA becomes mono-cultural – in an
educational sense – its days may then be numbered.

Looking at the current four ways of working it's obvious that, while
no one programme can hope to undertake them all, they provide a
useful check-list. This may be particularly helpful to the tutor-

organiser – a.k.a field staff member, programme manager or whatever title is in vogue for that constitutionally powerless, but quintessentially WEA, employee. Samuel Johnson defined a lexicographer (himself) as 'a harmless drudge'. This may have been how the role of the tutor-organiser was conceived, but (declaring a current interest in this as a field staff member) I personally warmed to a recent description of tutor-organisers as social and educational 'entrepreneurs'[31] and would think of Mansbridge himself as an entrepreneur, an opportunist, an inspired, ethical fixer. The tutor-organisers I have met engage variously with district management, voluntary members, partners, students and representatives of the other educational institutions on their patch. Moreover, as the WEA has been pulled in more firmly to address national educational priorities (and accept yet more national funding) the tutor-organiser is increasingly likely to find her-/himself in conference with providers from the statutory sector on whatever is the burning learning issue of the day.

In the 'Kennedy' era,[32] when I was first appointed, the keynote issue was Widening Participation. Working closely with LEA and FE colleagues in Essex it became obvious that there was a WEA *modus operandi*, unwritten, as far as I knew, but dinned into me with varying degrees of emphasis by both the district secretary and by the Essex Federation chairman.[33] This was to involve partnership working at all levels and vesting ultimate control of the learning process in the students. I was to ensure that teaching and learning methods were participatory and that students' life experiences were valued. The crucial qualities were to be consultation and respect.

These WEA approaches related crucially to process rather than product and helped reassure me that, although the students I was meeting on our emergent community programme were generally younger, poorer and living in more extreme circumstances than the branch members with whom I had previously worked, we were identifiably functioning as part of the same organisation. The facts that their motivation for learning was driven as much by personal need as by expectations of social pleasure and that the liberal studies curriculum offer left them cold, were ultimately of secondary importance.

'Outreach' programme students' rejection of the liberal studies curriculum (literature, history, philosophy, music – all that I instinctively thought of as 'culture') in favour of assertiveness, ICT and parenting skills – was hard to accept. Although the WEA curriculum in Essex may be unusually strongly polarised, I believe that others will understand my distress. The Association's first publicly funded, inspected, and praised educational product was the tutorial class, with its associated liberal studies curriculum and radically participative teaching and learning methods. It was indeed something to be proud of and has for many years helped shape the WEA's view of its own identity.

In his compassionate and compelling book on the *Intellectual Life of the British Working Classes* Jonathan Rose has investigated the dreams, struggles, triumphs and frustrations of the aspirant working-class scholars who sought this way out of spiritually claustrophobic everyday lives. He recognises that one attraction, other than intrinsic satisfactions, offered by study of 'the best that has been thought and written'[34] was access to the culture of the class where power lay. But in designer culture, Cool Britannia, that is no longer an option. 'The old classics-orientated autodidacts have disappeared, along with the factories who employed them.'[35]

Actually there are many who are still alive and well and enjoying their continuing education on the WEA general programme. That is to be celebrated. However, what Rose is saying ties in with the sociologists' explanation that, as employment patterns have changed in this post-industrial age of structural under-employment (known as 'flexibilised working'), so class identities have been weakened and their accompanying cultural understandings fragmented into lifestyle choices.[36] This is where it seems to matter that the WEA retain its special understanding of the link between working patterns and (compensatory) educational need. This must include understanding of the educational needs of the workless. In his chapter on 'the destandardisation of labour' Ulrich Beck describes how 'wage labour and an occupation have become the axis of living in the industrial age. Together with the family this axis forms the bi-polar co-ordinate in which life in this epoch is situated.'[37]

If, in the twenty-first century this is no longer the case, alternative reactions are possible. One, in Beck's phrase is to 'privatise the risks' – blame the non-employed[38] for their own situation and suggest that all education need do is offer them the chance to 'up-skill' and all will again be well. Such is the strength of this political message – promulgated by governments in one New Deal initiative after another – that it is widely believed and by the victims themselves. The WEA, as part of adult education, would be in breach of its humane obligations if it did not offer such upskilling opportunities where they are missing; and if that is what class members request –

that is what the WEA provides. ICT has decisively outstripped history as the Association's most-studied subject.

The motivation of these students is not entirely different from those early WEA recruits who, as Rose has shown, did use access to liberal culture as a class stepping stone as well as a method of widening horizons and enriching the intellectual content of their everyday lives. (I'm sure Tawney's students would have demanded access to the Internet!) T. W. Price, a student of the first tutorial class and later a district secretary, stated matter-of-factly, 'Working class students never seek to get knowledge for its own sake and this is quite healthy.'[39]

However, if today's truth is that there will never, in the global economy, be a return to full, standardised employment with its distinctive accompanying patterns of family, class and culture, what can the WEA do, as it once did, to promote holistic educational responses to a collective situation?

This is where the concept of a WEA pedagogy may help. The Association is right to remember its early tutorial classes with pride, because what was special about them was the curricular process – the variety of teaching and learning approaches, the emphasis on active participation, the social bonds formed and the mutual respect between tutor and students in the labour/learning partnership.[40] This is replicable whatever the subject content and, in a microcosmic way can enable every student to be part of an 'ethos of democracy'.

'Adult education', wrote Mansbridge, 'is concerned with every legitimate activity and expression of man'. He foresaw that a partnership of Labour and Learning would inspire a demand for education 'which would not be confined purely to intellectual subjects because only a small proportion of normal men and women are by nature students'.[41] There were far more WEA students than ever made it to the tutorial classes[42] and the pioneers of the WEA were pragmatic in their acceptance that content and teaching styles should be appropriate to students' interests and learning preferences if education were to be accessible to all.

'Two main ideas have always dominated the policy of the Association', wrote T. W. Price.

The first of these is that the highest educational facilities in the land should be accessible to any person who desires them and has the capacity to profit by them ... and the second great principle underlying the WEA programme is that the education supplied should be of the character desired by working class students.[43]

At the time of writing we have not, as a nation – despite compulsory secondary education to 16, despite the expansion of the further and higher education sectors, despite a decade's overt espousal of 'widening participation' and the current trumpeting of support for 'lifelong learning' and 'inclusivity' – yet achieved that first great goal of educational accessibility. There is no space here to do more than refer the reader to Veronica McGivney's canonical surveys of the individual and institutional reasons for this and reiterate, if this is necessary, her insight that 'another way in which exclusion is perpetuated is through the curriculum.'[44]

Price saw that access to university-type education – as in the tutorial classes – was not appropriate for all:

Beyond those thousands (of potential scholars) are the millions whose educational demands are of a more elementary kind: whose needs are for the knowledge of essential facts, and the development of powers of judgement and a mental alertness that will make them proof against cant and shibboleths – the satisfaction of this demand too is part of the claim made by the WEA on behalf for the working classes of this country.[45]

The education described here is concerned both with functionality (the 'essential facts') and empowerment ('proof against cant'). The language of 'claim' and 'demand' is the language of social justice and it is needed as much today as in the early years of the twentieth century. However, Price writes confidently from within 'the working class movement', whereas such assumptions of class-collective interests are no longer possible today. The process of individualisation[46] has eroded working-class identity from within far more fundamentally than the politicians of the 1980s and 1990s have attacked organised labour from without.[47]

Yet inequality remains and once again deepens. 'At the level of people, the system isn't working', said the president of the World Bank of the global economy in 1999.[48] This is both between and within nation states, the internal record of the United Kingdom in recent years being particularly poor. So on whose behalf does the WEA now speak? How can we help the general secretary?

The WEA speaks, propagandises even, as it has always done, for Education. Education 'in particular' for the disadvantaged, the disaffected, the vulnerable, the impoverished, the excluded – all those who are living , in any sense, on the wrong side of the tracks. We could follow Freire and call them The Oppressed. They are up against the system just as much as Yesterday's Heroes were – those 14-year-old elementary school leavers working the 54-hour weeks for pitiful pay and poor conditions.[49]

Whilse recognising that globalisation has exported much blatant workplace oppression, we know that our national system still bears heavily on many of us and we in turn oppress one another. We also know that, with the traditional supports of family, neighbourhood, faith, and class frequently fragmented, there are new understandings to be reached about the internalisation of oppression, its domestication and privatisation. This may seem a discomforting terminology. The facts are not easy to live with either. The WEA currently works nationally in partnership with Women's Aid. One of the most depressing details I have noticed is a sign in a local refuge reminding women that, as they knew what it is like to be hit, they should know not to hit their own children.

Facts and language that challenge our expectations may also make us think – and that's what the WEA believes that education's for. Otherwise, why not simply leave the weakened and unhappy to the care of health and social services?

The twentieth century has been termed the 'Century of the Self'.[50] It is a period that has seen ever more sophisticated (and materialist) understandings of the human psyche being used in conjunction with the revolutions in mass communication to manipulate people's emotions for the benefit of the powerful. Consumerism, advanced marketing techniques and financial deregulation have been the engines of spectacular capitalist growth across the globe. 'Indeed, for the first time in history, the whole planet is either capitalist or highly dependent on capitalist economic processes.'[51] It is not surprising that workers' education and education for empowerment (in Freire's terminology, for 'liberation') still matter – just as they did in the days of T. W. Price. The workers of Price's day have retired, or lost their jobs, or never found them. The WEA project is pluralistic and fragmented as is the society it serves. Yet, the Association retains a unity that is based on an inherited pedagogy and its continuing propagandist belief in the value of education. 'Not until equality of educational opportunity has been won in its entirety and not until the supreme importance of education as a social force is so universally recognised that there is no longer need to stimulate educational enthusiasm will the WEA admit that its work is done.'[52]

## NOTES

*Place of publication London unless otherwise stated.*

1. Robert Lochrie, WEA biennial conference, Manchester, 12 May 2001.
2. Oliver Burkeman, 'If the name fits ...', *Guardian* 8 Jan. 2001.
3. For a useful definition of outreach see V. McGivney, in *Learning for Life*, Spring 2001, 21. In the later 1990s it became usual to refer to such targeted work as the 'community programme' whilst the branch courses were referred to as the 'general programme'.
4. There is also a small workplace programme in Essex, two or three courses a year during this period. I use the word 'work' in this chapter as paid 'on the books' employment as opposed to home responsibilities, volunteering, or part-time, undeclared, cash jobs in the 'informal' sector.
5. 'The WEA and Adult Education' (1953) in R. H. Tawney, *The Radical Tradition* (1964).
6. 'An Experiment in Democratic Education' (1914) reprinted in *The Radical Tradition*, 75.
7. 'Experiment in Democratic Education', 83.
8. Fieldhouse and Associates, *History*, 184.
9. Fieldhouse and Associates, *History*, 1–4.
10. Fieldhouse and Associates, *History*, 45.
11. 'Experiment in Democratic Education', 75.
12. Council of Churches of Britain and Ireland, 'The Changing Nature of Work' (1997) in J. Ahier and G. Esland (eds), *Education, Training and the Future of Work* (1999), 14.
13. G. Coyne, 'Towards a Programme for Adult and Community Learning', *Learning for Life*, Spring 2002, 10.
14. Faith Robertson Elliot, 'Economic Restructuring and Unemployment' (1996) in Ahier and Esland (eds), *Education, Training*, 201.
15. U. Beck, 'Living Your Own Life in a Runaway World: Individualisation, Globalisation and Politics' in A. Giddens and W. Hutton (eds), *On the Edge. Living with Global Capitalism* (2000), 164–74.
16. *Trodden Road*, 69.
17. WEA 1939 policy statement.
18. M. D. Stephens, *Adult Education*, 104.
19. Beck, 'Living Your Own Life', 167.
20. Tawney, 'Experiment in Democratic Education', 74.
21. Currently (2002) there is a newly appointed co-ordinator for Voluntary Education Advisers (VEAs), and the National Executive Committee has discussed a paper by Marion Young (2001) entitled 'Preparing for the Future'.
22. Geoff Esland *et al.*, 'Managerialising Organisational Culture' in Ahier and Esland (eds), *Education, Training*, 160.

23. V. Williams and G. J. White, *Adult Education and Social Purpose* (Cambridge, 1988), 158.
24. Esland *et al.*, 'Managerialising', 67.
25. M. Doyle, 'Reform and Reaction: The WEA Post-Russell' in Jane Thompson (ed.), *Adult Education for a Change* (1980),130.
26. Fieldhouse and Associates, *History*, 167.
27. Fieldhouse and Associates, *History*, 167.
28. Richard Shaull, introduction to P. Freire, *Pedagogy of the Oppressed* (20th anniversary edn Harmondsworth, 1996).
29. 'One of Us', WEA membership pack, 2001.
30. Articles of constitution drafted at provisional executive committee meeting 14 July 1903.
31. Cliff Allum in an appreciation of Richard Copley, *Learning for Life*, Spring 2002, 14.
32. Helena Kennedy's Widening Participation Committee was set up in 1994 and reported in 1997: H. Kennedy, *Learning Works: Widening Participation in Further Education* (Coventry, 1997).
33. Respectively, Carolyn Daines and Arthur Brown.
34. Ex-chief inspector of schools, Chris Woodhead, in an exposition of extreme curricular positions on *Start the Week* , BBC Radio 4, 11 Mar. 2002.
35. J. Rose, *The Intellectual Life of the British Working Classes* (New Haven, 2001), 463.
36. Ulrich Beck, *Risk Society (*1992) esp. part 2, 'The Individualisation of Social Inequality', 87ff.
37. Beck, *Risk Society*, 139.
38. I use this term to include impoverished people such as those on Income Support, who are not counted in unemployment figures. Note 4 includes the definition of 'work' that I am using.
39. Price, 81.
40. See Tawney, 'Experiment in Democratic Education', 77 for a description.
41. *Trodden Road*, 55.
42. I was particularly interested to learn of a WEA initiative with the unemployed at the Hollesley Bay Labour Colony in 1909.
43. Price, 81; compare also Tawney, 'Experiment in Democratic Education', 76.
44. V. McGivney, *Fixing or Changing the Pattern?* (Leicester, 2001), 65.
45. Price, 80.
46. Beck, *Risk Society*, 87.
47. W. Hutton, *The State We're In* (1995), 28–9.
48. Jeff Faux and Larry Mishel, 'Inequality and the Global Economy' in Giddens and Hutton (eds), *On the Edge*, 93.
49. June Jones and Julia Thorogood, *Yesterday's Heroes* (Ingatestone, 1986), 101 (one of a series of four volumes of reminiscences produced for Age Concern Essex. Original material in Essex Record Office).
50. Adam Curtis, four-part BBC TV series, Apr. 2002.
51. Manuel Castells, 'Information Technology & Global Capitalism' in Gidden and Hutton (eds), *On the Edge*, 52.
52. Price, 92.

# 16   WEA Voices

The writer of this article entered the office of the Workers' Educational Association in January 1909. The Association then had two rooms in a rather shabby office building in Buckingham Street, a turning off the Strand. The rooms were small and the ceilings low and the staff consisted of Mansbridge and, if I remember rightly, two typists, but there were occasional voluntary helpers to be found in the office.

Mansbridge was then 33 years old and at the height of his powers, tall, good-looking, full of vitality. The West Country burr in his voice ... was undoubtedly an asset. His personality was remarkable, it seemed to fill the office and his entry was like a battery being re-charged. The effect he had on people was indeed striking; I have seen visitors leave his room with heads up, eyes shining, stepping as if they were walking on air, absolutely exalted. I am sorry if this sounds like a rhetorical exaggeration, but 'exalted' really is the word; it was a phenomenon that had to be seen to be believed. His energy was amazing; he was constantly dashing about the country, starting new centres, converting the doubters, inspiring the faithful, stimulating the beginning-to-get-tireds into fresh activities. Mrs Mansbridge always kept his bag packed with duplicate night things, shaving kit and the like, so he had only to grab his case and rush off, knowing that everything needed would be there. All this expenditure of energy seemed to spring from an inner compulsion that would not let him rest. One might sometimes wonder if all these journeys were really necessary, but Mansbridge relied to a great extent on his personality to achieve his results, and where personal contacts were possible he was nearly always successful. He was a very good speaker – considerable natural eloquence charged with passionate and obvious sincerity. Other qualities that impressed me were his kindliness, his cheerfulness and self-confidence. There must have been many times when the financial position of the Association gave rise to considerable anxiety, but his worries were never noticeable to the ordinary members of the staff, and I have never known anyone who had fewer hesitations or doubts about matters of policy – his policy was the right one, and it was achieving results ...

On 10 June 1914, Mansbridge was suddenly stricken down by a mysterious illness that was eventually diagnosed as cerebro-spinal meningitis. That he recovered at all is remarkable, but progress was very slow. Towards the end of 1915, when the Association had virtually been without a general secretary for more than a year, it was clear that it was not likely that he would, within a reasonable time, be able to resume the responsibilities of the office, and he therefore resigned ...

The new people wished the Association to be regarded as the 'educational wing of the labour movement' and the question at issue was whether this aim was compatible with the original declared policy of the WEA, 'non-political' or, indeed, with their own amended version, 'non-party political'. Mansbridge had been at pains to emphasise, in every possible way, the impartial nature of the Association. He sought to secure the support and participation of people of as many types and shades of opinion as possible – almost like a collector seeking to complete a set. The early tutors included not only distinguished socialists ... but also such orthodox economists as Henry Clay (afterwards Sir Henry Clay) – and at least one Conservative. From another point of view they ranged from J. G. Newlove (Union of Post Office Workers and Ruskin College) to that gentle aristocrat, the Hon. Gerard Collier (see plate 6). The famous 'Westminster Lectures' given by J. H. B. Masterman in the Houses of Parliament had an average attendance of a thousand or more, a large proportion being trade unionists. There was a different chairman each week and these included A. J. Balfour and Sir William Anson (Conservatives), J. Ramsay Macdonald and G. N. Barnes (Labour) and R. B. Haldane and L. V. Harcourt (Liberal). I well remember Will Crooks moving a vote of thanks with a most amusing speech. For several years in pre-1914 days the national treasurer was T. Edmund Harvey, a leading Quaker, ex-warden of Toynbee Hall and a Liberal MP. Under the new regime a Liberal MP as treasurer of the Association was as unthinkable as a Liberal MP as treasurer of a constituency Labour Party ... I remember Mactavish trying to close the only staff party held in my time at the central office with the singing of 'The Red Flag'. I remember that on the occasion of a com-memorative number of *The Highway* (probably the WEA's silver jubilee) it was pointed out to the then editor, Mrs Wootton ([later] the life-peeress, Lady Wootton) that she had invited messages from a variety of people but not from a Conservative, and her answer, 'Oh, I just could not bring myself to ask for greetings from a Tory' ...

W. H. Hosford, 'The Triumph and Tragedy of Albert Mansbridge', unpublished paper.

\* \* \*

I was introduced and chatted to [Albert Mansbridge] himself for whom I had an admiration amounting almost to hero worship. This was for me a truly memorable experience. Since most of the students attending my first WEA class were like myself engineering craftsmen working long hours on munitions work during world war one we held our meetings on Sunday afternoons. That we should choose to desecrate the Sabbath in this way so annoyed the chairman of the [Bath] education committee, Alderman S. W. Bush, a strict Sabbatarian that even if he was president of the branch he threatened to withhold the grant which the LEA then paid to the WEA and still continues to pay down to the present day ... Much to our relief however the alderman relented after listening to a deputation of branch representatives.

Ted Ashman, in M. Turner, *A History of the Workers' Educational Association, Bath Branch 1912–87* (Bath, 1987)

\* \* \*

The purpose I thought adult education might fulfil for me was to fit me to undertake more important and more congenial work in the Working Class Movement. My first contact with the WEA came at the very crescendo of my enthusiasm for the Trade Union and Labour Movement—and I was not satisfied with the job of giving out bills at a meeting. I was ambitious in that I wanted to make a bigger contribution, and I had enough common sense to realise that the only possibility of my being able to make that contribution was by training myself for the job. The motive which impelled me to the adult educational movement was as much egoistic as altruistic, but not more so.

*Learn and Live* (1933)

\* \* \*

I started at the Morrison Busty, one of the new collieries within a few miles of where I lived, in 1929, and renewed my acquaintance with the pit. At the same time, I took up WEA class studies on Economics and also (as this wouldn't provide me with the possibility of a job) evening classes in English, shorthand and accounts, studies which I felt would probably enable me to get a clerical job of some kind. By that time, I was almost 19 years of age and beginning to have a different attitude to many things. I became involved in the union lodge ... [Later, in the 1930s] it was all part of my left-wing education. The WEA ran its classes, the NCLC ran its classes, the Left Book Club was publishing books about economics, politics, economic and social history, drama and so forth.

Maurice Ridley, in *But the World Goes on the Same* (1979)

\*   \*   \*

My main reason, of course, was that after my baby was born, if he was to be put to bed, etc. at a proper hour, all our evening occupations away from home had to be curtailed. Living in a village with no library or other public facilities the winter nights in consequence were apt to become monotonous, and since my husband was very engrossed in his wireless and did not object to staying in and listening to the child, and as I felt I was getting dull and 'ruttish' and wanted to get out of the ordinary run of things, I decided to give the WEA a trial.

*Learn and Live* (1933)

\*   \*   \*

As a shift worker, from my joining Tutorial Classes right up to the present I have obviously made more sacrifice than I care to remember, but it was well worth it. I remember attending a Tutorial Class held in the University, wearing clogs, and washing when I arrived there. It was extremely difficult to keep awake during some lectures. I sometimes closed my eyes, this was when we were working long days, but I heard it all. I got up at 3.30 a.m., finished at 2 p.m., hurried home to wash and change and get some dinner, back to the station, use three trains to my destination, arrive back home at 10.30 p.m., write out my daily report, wash, etc., to bed and up again at 3.30. I did this for twenty-four weeks and was never late at either work or class.

*Learn and Live* (1933)

*   *   *

I hadn't a clue what the WEA was, but it was somewhere to go. Maybe there would be some eligible males going too. I was thirty-seven, the years were clocking up on me. I had my horoscope cast, everything was right except I would have two marriages, but would have difficulties in both and I would do better with an older partner. What a laugh, here I was an old maid not even a spec of a male around, however as I am supposed to be optimistic, who knows.

The teacher arrived at the class wearing a vivid green coat, orange coloured hair and a face that looked as though the trams had criss-crossed utterly out of control. Before the session had finished I was hooked. To hell with fellows, this was interesting.

We started with D H Lawrence. His first book, *The White Peacock*, was one of the books given to me by my friend who went to Brazil. I had read it, but I couldn't get home fast enough to read it again.

We were studying James Joyce, to my delight there were passages in the book that were familiar to me and not the others, due to the mixture of Irish Catholics and Protestants who lived round us in our home town. I chuckled at the character called Pissy Burke, it reminded me of a friend of Dad's called Shitta Malcolm.

Nancy Dobrin, *Happiness: A Twinge of Conscience is a Glimpse of God* (1980)

*   *   *

I stayed away from the Guild to please him—which it did not. I stayed away from the Women's Section of the Labour Party. I did not give up the WEA. If I had, he would not have been any more pleased. I did do what I could to make him feel differently – but it was no use.

*Learn and Live* (1933)

*   *   *

I remember – during an acute phase of loneliness... – attending for the first time a WEA class. About fifty young people – most of them in their early twenties – were present, and most of them seemed to know each other. In all probability they had attended similar classes. The subject was a fashionable one – psychology. For nearly an hour the lecturer spoke. He spoke briskly and competently but not, I thought (my work and reading and experience of life had given me some knowledge of psychology) not very intelligently or originally. When he had finished he said, 'Shall we all join in general discussion', and sat down. Immediately – just as though someone had pressed a switch – those boys and girls turned their chairs towards each other and began talking away about psychology. Just like automatons. It was almost frightening ... After some time I left abruptly for the nearest pub, where harsh things were being said about Aston Villa.

Ah well, I thought, and had another go – a drama class this time ... The lecturer droned, and he droned, and he droned. ... But at last – after about an hour – the lecturer reached his climax. He had to – the dear little chap was almost out on his feet. He threw away the beard he might have been mumbling into, and said impressively: 'Urhh!' He frowned at one of the women – who came-to with a start – and said severely, 'J B Priestley!' I nearly giggled, and the lecturer said 'J B Priestley. Urh – novelist. Urh – dramatist. Urh – essayist'. And after a pause, almost awesomely: 'Man urh man – m-a-n of GEE-nius!' And with that I got up. And I went out. And in the same pub they were arguing furiously about the Wolves.

John Petty, *Five Fags a Day* (1956)

*   *   *

At Toynbee Hall [WEA class] I had the good fortune to have C. E. M. Joad as my tutor in philosophy and English literature, and spent five years under him with the greatest benefit to myself. In those days he was quite a young man and never dreamt of the fame he was to achieve on the 'Brains Trust' on the BBC in later life. My brother, who also went to Toynbee Hall when I did, took a dislike to Joad from the start, saying that he suspected he was a bit of a *poseur*; but I at first was greatly impressed with him because of his obvious brilliant intellectual gifts. However, after a few months I began to see that my brother's view was correct, because it was becoming clearer and clearer that it was a sort of philosophical game that Joad was playing with us in our class, and that he, as an individual, had no really deep and vital beliefs to express or defend at all.

Harry Benjamin, *Adventure in Living* (1950)

*   *   *

Despite my upbringing in what we used to call 'the Labour Movement', I had never even heard of the Workers' Educational Association when, at the end of my first year in the University of Hull, the vice-chancellor – Principal Nicholson as he was called – made desultory conversation at a lunch he gave for the executive of the students' union. He asked me if I was going to work during the vacation and I replied, with some embarrassment, that I had signed up for six weeks paid canvassing with the Labour Party. Why, he asked, should I be reluctant to talk about my political inclinations? To reinforce his reassurance, he described his own record. It included a deep involvement with the WEA.

In fact Nicholson was one of the great men of the Association's early years and therefore should have not suggested that the WEA had political connections. But the idea of educating the toiling masses stuck in my mind. When I graduated and became a 'management trainee' in the steel industry, I visited the offices of the South Yorkshire District and offered my services. I appeared on the following year's programme as tutor for a course in twentieth-century history – the notion of contemporary history had not been invented. By the third lecture there were still only five 'students' on the register. In consequence the class was cancelled.

I did not enjoy being a putative captain of industry. And I wanted to be a candidate in the City Council elections. So, when I saw an advertisement for WEA Sheffield organiser I applied for the job. The district secretary, Raymond Rochelle, told me that it was not really a suitable post for a graduate and that in a couple of years a vacancy for tutor-organiser might arise in one of the outlying regions of his empire. But I could not wait. The regional committee – much to the annoyance of the local branch – agreed that I could augment my wages (and improve my status) by taking courses both of the WEA and the Sheffield extra-mural department. I had visions of encouraging heroic workers to ever-improving levels of scholarship.

In some parts of the region, my romantic illusion was very near to reality. The extra-mural department had a special relationship with the Derbyshire miners. One tutor wrote the union's official history. All of them took classes which combined genuine education with political commitment. But not me. I addressed groups of bored middle class ladies. One 'student' walked out of a class because when I quoted Lytton Strachey he was (at least by implication) critical of

Queen Victoria. It was the heyday of Kingsley Amis and I lived in constant expectation of one of the middle class ladies trying to seduce me. None of them ever did – even tried, I mean.

I worked for the WEA for two years, then I went off into more regular employment with the National Health Service – leaving behind fewer classes in Sheffield than when I began. I had enjoyed the job. But I always felt in casual employment. In those days I needed the discipline of nine to five and a daily routine. Thank heavens the House of Commons changed all that.

Roy Hattersley

*   *   *

I got let in for a course of 8 lectures to the WEA at Port Talbot, some way from here. Did I tell you how I got let in for these? Thought a professorial olive-branch was a pistol to the old head? And the titles? The first, any road, is the world of Ernest Hemingway. Fuck that. Took me all day yesterday to prepare. Would gladly pay £50 (=2 × my honorarium from the course) not to do it. After a too-quick shave, bolting poached egg on haddock, I staggered down the road, bleeding and belching, insisted on a large whisky, got to the huge bus-area, couldn't find the recommended bus ('Oh no, there's no number 4 now', 'Oh no, you want the 42, that's your bus'), was taken over half South Wales, asked for the grammar school as directed, 'which one? the county or the secondary?', said it was one by a bus-stop, was put down at one not by a bus-stop, remonstrated, was told I must want the one by the bus-stop, two stops back, walked through freezing horrible Port Talbot, pissed in gents, failed to shake cock enough and drenched left leg, arrived 40 minutes late, class *still there*. Lecture tolerable, though old man talked much of Izaak Walton, back in time for double whisky and pint of bitter, met Swansea's most horrible man in bus up to Uplands.

Kingsley Amis to Philip Larkin, 19 Feb. 1957, from *The Letters of Kingsley Amis* ed. Zachary Leader (London 2001)

*   *   *

Like thousands of trade unionists across central Scotland, I owe a lot to the WEA. My involvement with them came after the partnership was agreed between them and the National Council of Labour Colleges (NCLC). As a result of that deal both organisations were joint sponsors of day courses and weekend conferences to train union activists in negotiating skills and to equip them with a wider perspective on equal rights and health and safety. These classes also provided a relaxed environment in which I could meet activists from outside my own plant or union and therefore were instrumental in helping me build up my political perspective.

The main formative figure at these classes was Tom Sweeny who was the full-time Scottish representative of NCLC. Tom never quite forgave the WEA for intruding on his empire, but applied himself with total commitment to training two generations of shop stewards. Curiously, his other great passion was ballroom dancing. At the end of a class he would unwind by reminiscing about his achievements on the dance-floor with the same enthusiasm that he had talked about at the negotiating table.

Michael Martin MP, Speaker of the House of Commons

*   *   *

From August 1966 until May 1970 I was tutor-organiser in industrial studies for the South Wales District of the Workers' Educational Association. The work was demanding, the hours were long. There could be disappointments when an under-subscribed course had to close or when a class failed to magnetise enough students to even start.

But no pressure or frustration was ever great enough to outweigh the main experience of being part of the WEA – unalloyed delight, spiced with inspiration ...

The South Wales district secretary at the time, and long before it, was David Thomas (D. T.) Guy. D. T., a former industrial worker, adult student, university graduate by his early 30s, acquaintance of Mansbridge, friend of Tawney, was a cultured, thoroughly Welsh, benign giant of a man. He led his district committee, students, tutors and organisers by appearing not to insist on anything whilst at the same time making it mildly but absolutely clear that he expected – and tolerated – nothing but the best. The reason for that was strong and simple: to him the purpose of the WEA was to conduct an unstinting mission of enlightenment. Of course, he never articulated his purpose in such a grandiose way – but the result of his mixture of zeal and benevolence, passion and kindness was compelling. It meant that everyone on D. T.'s staff would do anything to avoid letting him down. No management was ever less theoretical or didactic. No management ever provided a sharper spur to effort.

Naturally, the students also had much the same effect on me. People who have done a day's work and can show insatiable curiosity, can consume everything on a reading list, can sustain their attention for a two-hour lecture and discussion session are testing students. When they approach a class series on 'The economics behind today's news' with piercing questions about the welfare of the yen or the shortcomings of incomes policy, they are impressive. But they become terrifying to the tutor when they can listen to thirty minutes on 'Mao, the Cultural Revolution and the Contradictions of Communism' – and then demonstrate that visits to China as merchant seamen, or to Hong Kong as soldiers, or a life long interest in the People's Republic have given them encyclopaedic knowledge. Imagine being a twenty five year old, damp-behind-the-ears tutor turning up at the Aberdare Trades and Labour Council to speak on 'The rise of fascism' and being confronted by a class of 27 people, 8 of whom had been International Brigaders in the Spanish civil war ... Such experiences were very character forming.

Bill Gregory, a seaman before the First World War, a soldier, a 1920s insurrectionary, a Depression barber, an Oxford graduate, Second World War intelligence agent and post-war extra-mural and WEA tutor was one of the finest teachers that any adult could hope for. Brilliantly laconic, funny, an instructor-by-aphorism, he was my role model. I was starting in adult education as he was in semi-retirement in his early 70s so I naturally asked him for professional tips. 'Oh, I don't give advice. It's much better for you to find your own way', he said. But, pressed insistently, he eventually said reluctantly 'Well, I suppose there is one little bit of guidance I can give: in adult education – and in politics too if you are the right kind of stuff – always aim a little bit above their heads. If you do that, people will reach up. But if you aim at their bellies, like some do, then they'll think with their balls'. It wasn't elegant, I suppose. But to me, it was the innermost secret of the trade. So I tried, without Bill's charisma arsenal, to follow his guidance.

Kindness, tolerance, the willingness of experienced students to teach fresh faced tutors made survival possible. That, in turn, strengthened performance – particularly in the (then) novel shop stewards' day release courses. As the South Wales WEA broke new trails at Fords, Hoover, ICI, and other large and small employers in the late 1960s, I learned very quickly that the key to successful and fulfilling workers' education was the development of students' self confidence. Classfuls of assertive, capable shop floor representatives had only negative memories of their last encounters with education and training in school or National Service. For much of the time they'd been taunted by teachers and instructors with what they *didn't* know and what they *couldn't* do. So, despite being tigers across a negotiating table, they naturally began the courses with inhibitions and self doubt. The WEA classes, where encouragement was a teaching method, where emphasis on what students *did* know was essential, and where hectoring or humiliating teaching techniques were absent disorientated some at first. But as familiarity and security grew, self-assurance quickly flourished, and the classes became places of vitality and enjoyment. Many of the men and women who came to our courses blossomed manifestly. Most stayed in their jobs but, among the ones that didn't, several went on to become full-time union officials and 18 men and 1 woman who came to the classes run by my fellow WEA tutors and me between 1966 and 1970 were university graduates by the mid 1970s. There really cannot be much that is more fulfilling for any teacher than to see students taking the risks – and making the sacrifices – involved in changing the whole course of their lives through using the opportunities of adult education provided by the WEA.

The innovative industrial classes were quickly and easily established in some places, and several companies gradually extended such day release courses on industrial relations, labour economics, communications, organisational and representation skills from union representatives to middle management. Other encounters were not as easy. A departmental boss in a south Wales steel works expressed his disgust at the provision of worker's education in company time by complaining 'You are just going to turn these bastards into bright bastards'. I couldn't help responding with 'Well we'll take care not to waste time on a hopeless case like you then'. It wasn't diplomatic or well advised – and it could have been disastrous. But fortunately the managing director thought it was very funny and the course got under way.

As word of the industrial day release classes got around, demand increased. By the autumn of 1968 it was obvious that our limited resources for daytime teaching were very stretched. In the belief that it would ease the pressure from the firms asking to set up courses I therefore encouraged my colleagues to make a market response: we increased the charges from an absurd shilling per lecture – maximum

5 shillings a day – to £5 a day. It didn't work. The inverse demand phenomenon set in as companies equated higher fees with higher quality. Applications for our services increased. It helped District financing but it also meant an extra heavy work programme. Happily, after 1970, extra training officers were recruited and supply moved towards demand.

Evening and day classes were followed by Saturday Schools and weekend courses, mainly for the TUC. Those events presented a logistical challenge for any tutor with a love of sport, and the most important documents at our District course planning meetings were rugby, soccer and cricket fixture lists. It wasn't just my obligations to the local cricket club that made it a necessity – any Workers' Educational Association that fixed a Saturday School which clashed with a Rugby International would deserve no mercy.

On the one occasion that a Saturday School at the Bluebell Inn, Caerphilly did collide with our International – Wales v. Ireland in 1969 – we conceded to culture and watched the game on TV. The title of that particular class was then extended from 'Why Enoch Powell is wrong' to 'Why Enoch Powell is completely wrong' and held six weeks later so that the lecture didn't go to waste ...

My enjoyment didn't just come from being a tutor. Organising others for classes had its appealing results too. Jeff Cocks, later principal of Pontypridd College, used to pack Rhondda classes with his spellbinding twentieth century history courses – mainly because, he said, 'I did ten minutes of ignition and then the students blazed away about their own ideas and experiences for two hours. I learned a lot more than I taught'. Gareth Griffiths, later of the University of Western Australia and brilliant author of *The Empire Writes Back* did a weekend school in Caerleon College on Joseph Conrad and the students from other courses on 'The Common Market' and 'The economics of holidays' deserted their classes to learn what *Heart of Darkness* was *really* about. Glenys, my wife, taught a Co-operative Women's Guild evening class in the Rhymney Valley for three pre-pregnancy years. It was a sort of educational love-in as far as I could see – and it had pedagogic benefits too. Glenys would start to speak when the big hot water urn at the back of the class was switched on and she would end exactly 18 minutes later when the gushing steam signified that brew-up time had come. The result was the nicest file of less-than-20 minute-lectures on 'Development depends on Women', 'The Pankhursts', 'Equal Pay for Equal Work' and many similar consciousness raisers that anyone could wish for.

Although, over a gap of 30-odd years, there's always a danger that 'distance lends enchantment to the view' I must say that the memories of my time with the WEA are marvellous and all my mind pictures are sunlit. Or nearly all ...

I began my job with the WEA on 22 August 1966 and one of the first courses that I managed to arrange was a weekly series of Thursday night current affairs classes in the Social Democratic Club in a Merthyr valley village whose name was then, even in the rest of South Wales, almost unknown. With the enthusiastic support of two local councillors, Dai Tudor and Maldwyn Brace, the class quickly took root. The sessions were lively and argumentative – and they usually extended to closing time. By 20 October there were over 50 students on the roll. I was proud, exhilarated, eager. This was what I *really* wanted to do.

On the morning of Friday 21 October 1966, the gigantic Pant Glas tip towering above the primary school in that village slid down in a massive avalanche of slurry. A total of 116 children and 28 adults were killed. The name of Aberfan instantly became known across the world as a definition of preventable tragedy.

I heard the news on the car radio. With Glenys – on half term holiday from a school in the next county – I was in Aberfan within half an hour. We had formed no real idea of the appalling scale of the disaster. I even took a shovel to help with the digging. One look told us how puny that hope was. We left the village to make way for the miners with their equipment. No-one knew then that even their skills would not be enough.

Two weeks later, I started the Thursday evening class again – not with any serious educational purpose, but because going into the village as someone who was not an insider but not quite an outsider just seemed the right thing to do. Amazingly, the class re-formed, although – naturally – with smaller numbers. Gradually, as the months passed, it moved from being an opportunity for conversation to divert minds to becoming a mixture of current affairs discussion and rehearsal of arguments to put to the Official Public Inquiry. When I went to the village years later, former class members said to me that it was useful. In the words of one 'It helped us to *organise* our anger'.

The Aberfan class continued until my time with the WEA ended when the 1970 General Election campaign began. The people who came to the Thursday night sessions, like their families and neighbours in the village, dealt with misery in superhuman ways. Their grief was indelible. But so was their spirit. Like countless others that I met only because I worked for the WEA, those people gave me much more than I could have ever given them. My gratitude has never faded.

Neil Kinnock

\*   \*   \*

I worked for the WEA as the tutor-organiser for Edinburgh and SE Scotland from the 1970 General Election (when I was defeated) until the first General Election of 1974 when I was elected.

I took over the job from the late Ian Jordan, whose commitment to dissent and passion for teaching came in equal proportions. Two decades later a journalist asked me who had been the greatest political influence on my thinking. I imagine he expected me to come up with a well-known Labour figure such as Bevan or a theorist such as Tawney, and looked startled and perplexed when I gave him the unknown name of 'Ian Jordan, a former WEA tutor-organiser'. But it was true. Ian and my contacts through the WEA taught me more about the reality of injustice and the case for social rights than I would ever have got out of books.

The money-spinner which was the backbone of our then work programme was a series of about one hundred evening courses which attracted around 2,000 adults per year. Organising lectures for such a large programme was demanding. Making sure the lecturers lasted the length of the course was sometimes more challenging than retaining the students. I have never forgotten the conversation when I rang up the wife of a lecturer to enquire why he had missed his class the night before to receive, after a pause, the response 'You mean he wasn't at the evening class last night?'

The evening class programme provided a paradox which might have been a parable of our times. Despite our best efforts to attract the real workers, the evening classes were aggressively colonised by the middle classes. With the naivety of youth I thought a class in metal sculpture might bridge the gulf and harness engineering skills for the purposes of a liberal education. The course was enthusiastically taken up by an all-graduate entry from the Edinburgh bourgeoisie. Real metal workers do not find an evening with yet another oxyacetylene torch a great way to spend their leisure hours.

But bless them, all those keen middle-class adults provided a solid financial foundation on which we could run courses on trade union rights and social realism. The trade union weekends were much the most congenial part of the job. By 1 am on Saturday night we'd almost convinced ourselves that the revolution was really coming. Well, if not the revolution, at least the certain defeat of the Heath Conservative Government.

And that did come. I launched my last evening class on the day Heath called the election that ended in his exile. There was a three-day week and a general blackout because of the last successful miners' strike. I was sent to a small town just south of Edinburgh to register a class at the local secondary school. I had no idea where it was and it was impossible in the blackout to see a single sign. Fortunately I saw two 14-year-old girls and deduced that they were bound to know the whereabouts of the local secondary school. I drew up beside them but before I could ask where I could find the school they both screamed 'Help, help' and vanished into the darkness. I have often wondered whether my political career would have ended there and then if I had not found the secondary school before they found a policeman.

Robin Cook MP

*   *   *

On a personal basis, my only contact with the trade union movement was being a member of the NUJ for about a year when I worked with the *Glasgow Herald* newspaper and then spending about four years negotiating with the trade unions when I was on the staff of the Clyde Shipbuilders Association.

Coming from a quiet middle-class background I was brought up in an environment where there was grave suspicion of trade unions as organisers of revolutions with no respect for the worthwhile traditions of our community. However in negotiations with trade union officials and personal contact with the unions I changed my sentiments entirely and I never came across a single official who broke his word or ignored signed agreements. I also found them to be persons of character and high standards.

During my employment with the shipyards and in the press the WEA came to my notice and when I became an MP in Glasgow I had even greater contact. It became clear that the WEA was a worthwhile and non-bureaucratic organisation which was designed basically to ensure that unused educational talents of so many people engaged in rather unexciting and boring jobs could be utilised and developed and the most significant part of the work was that its aim was purely educational with no secret agenda. I suppose that another thing that attracted me to the WEA was that it never sought to emphasise itself as a world-shaking organisation but always simply got on with the job and did it very well. On looking back on my many years in public life I think there are few organisations in respect of which my feelings are so positive – it did a great job and did it well and never sought any medals for the work it did.

Sir Teddy Taylor MP

\*    \*    \*

It seems to me that the WEA does not address the needs of the really poor. It appeals to the upwardly-mobile middle classes who are already educated. Moreover, the organisation doesn't seem able to attract young people. It seems to me a grouping of middle-aged and retired people.

I feel the WEA syllabus is at fault here. There should be more on offer than the usual 'handicrafts and hobbies' courses. There should also be basic 'survival' courses like cooking on a budget. The WEA does not offer education as I understand it. To me education should help people cope with and make sense of the world they live in.

One example that comes to mind here was a WEA funded residential weekend school, organised by its TUBE [Trade Union and Basic Education, Manchester-based] project, on Working with the Black Communities. The title of the event – 'Tools for Taking Control' – appealed to me because, as a black woman, I have very little control over my life. Therefore, I had high expectations of the course and really thought I'd be given all the answers to all the questions I ever wished to ask!

This, of course, did not happen, but it was a delight to talk with other black people, both Afro-Caribbean, and like myself, Asian, and exchange experiences in a supportive way. We learnt to draw an individual and group profile of where we were in our lives and what resources we possessed to make decisions and choose options. We also role-played various skills, such as presenting a clear argument, chairing a meeting and so on. We also looked at the strategies needed to make our needs known to those bodies who have the power to meet them, such as local government, educational institutions, etc. ... We saw how education empowers people and how we seemed to have missed out on this education.

We could not, of course, cover everything properly in one weekend and I was still left with many questions. Nevertheless, I found it a valuable experience and a step in the right direction.

Shamsa Butt, North-western District, 1989

\*    \*    \*

I first became interested in Tai Chi in the 1980s when visiting China and watching people in the parks. It was later, after illness and retirement that I joined classes initiated by the WEA. At that time the slow sustained movements appealed to me and did not seem too difficult! I hoped Tai Chi would help alleviate the various aches and pains I was suffering and help me to relax.

Initially I found the movements extremely difficult. My body and brain didn't seem to connect and I experienced considerable frustration. I observed others in the group and several were experiencing similar difficulties. Tai Chi is certainly more complex than it had first appeared. Our tutor was extremely helpful and understanding. When I began to relax and look outside myself I recognised his professionalism and skills. He is very aware of individual needs and provides appropriate and balanced sessions. He works with the group, pairs and individuals, and leads through example by demonstration ...

Hy Murdock, WEA class, Leicester 2001

\*    \*    \*

I work in an elderly persons' home and resource centre in Handsworth Wood, and am employed by Birmingham Social Services. Whilst in my position as shop steward I received a pamphlet informing me of WEA/NUPE's Return to Learn course. I decided after twenty years away from study this was a challenge I could not refuse. When I first saw the workbook I was impressed by the structure and especially the easy-to-follow instructions. There was a choice of topics that interested me including creative writing and note taking. I overcame my fear of maths by learning to do percentages for the first time. The interview assignment also taught me how to ask questions objectively. At the present time I am continuing with my work with the elderly, but Return to Learn has given me the confidence to take on the added responsibility to become a senior shop steward and to apply for training such as trade union studies and a computer course.

I am also contemplating possible full-time further education in subjects such as trade unionism, politics or social history. I found the course enjoyable, not too difficult but time consuming and also I needed self-discipline and self-motivation. The weekend schools were a great experience with everyone 'in the same boat'. I became aware that learning can be fun.

John Ward, Birmingham WEA/NUPE Return to Learn, 1992

\* \* \*

I had previously attended a course at Willowbrook School that had helped my daughters learning and I had enjoyed this. A friend and I saw some information about the Helping in Schools course which was being run at a neighbouring school. We inquired as to whether it could be run at Willowbrook. It was over twenty-five years since I had been to school. I felt I was too old to start learning again. Would I be able to take anything in? If I could, would I be able to remember anything? Despite these feelings I was also excited. As the weeks went by I was fully committed and I was gradually beginning to realise that I wasn't stupid or thick. It was hard work and very involved. Two lessons each week and two hours per week working in a classroom environment with children and homework.

As the end of the course loomed I felt a little flat; I did not want it to finish. It was hard for me to understand my own feelings. I felt my confidence and self-esteem had had a real boost. I was starting to believe in myself. I was finally doing something for me. I went to see Mr Osborn the head teacher at Willowbrook School to see if we could carry on using the classroom and if more courses could be arranged. He started off by dashing my hopes and saying that the room that we had been using was being turned into the new nursery block. Then my hopes started to rise: we could use the mobile that the nursery were at present using once they had moved. We could have a classroom and a crèche. The whole place needed re-decorating. That would cost money: how could we manage that?

Fortunately there was an article in the local paper saying that the Prince's Trust were looking for projects to undertake. After assessing what needed doing they agreed to take it on. They came armed with brushes and paint, bricks and mortar and set about the mammoth task of transforming the mobile. We then set about gathering toys together for the creche, desk and chairs for the classroom and anything else that we could get our hands on that might possibly be useful.

I had achieved what at one time I would have thought impossible. I had completed a folder of work that included a project, something I had never done before. I had pushed, and achieved a centre for other people to be encouraged to take up some sort of learning and was able to say 'Look I have done it, and if I can you can.' I look at the centre and feel very proud I was partly responsible for that and feel it would not have been possible if I wasn't given the chance through the Helping in Schools course to realise I had got potential.

Sue Armstrong – Helping in Schools course, East Midlands, 2001

\*   \*   \*

For me the WEA has been a way of life since the 1940s. So much more than a network of classes, the WEA is the source of some of my deepest friendships. The voices of countless tutors and fellow-students made some sense out of the confused babble of ideas that was all I carried away from a wartime education.

In a small town in West Dorset, with no aspiration higher than a secretarial course at the 'Tech' I stumbled upon the WEA. I forget how. Here Miss Clifford – no first names then – communicated her burning enthusiasm for the Origins of the Novel between bites upon her evening sandwich. A vivid eccentric, she paced the cracked boards of a side room in the Friends' Meeting House in a pair of crumpled black suede boots and gave ... ? nothing short of inspiration.

What stood out for me, raw from the closeted academy where I had persistently 'failed', was the equality, the belief that everybody had an opinion worth hearing. Miss Clifford addressed me as though I had something to give to individuals in that group who were old enough to be my grandparents – as they also spoke to each other, and to me! In time I learned, dry-mouthed, to share my thoughts with them. It had begun: empowerment through the WEA, a crucial part of my life for five decades – still giving me a Voice in the twenty-first century.

Don't imagine the relationship has been continuous – or dewy-eyed. I have been critical, served on committees, on the London District council even, and grumbled – particularly at what I perceived as red tape. There have been gaps of five years, eight years, more. I've attended courses in many different geographical areas. How to return for instance, after years of isolation in 'the sticks' in the 1950s?

– period of immersion in children and chores ... Suddenly we moved to Guildford, and somebody stuffed a WEA leaflet through the door! Dry-mouthed once more, and blushing like a teenager, I took a three-year Psychology course with Dr. Alexander from Goa. I had hardly heard of Goa or Psychology. The first time I opened my mouth I feared the earth might open, but. ...

The 1960s was a wonderful time to be involved. By then I was a branch secretary, and things were changing. The traditional pattern of evening classes was extending and widening – under protest from traditionalists at first. Morning and afternoon classes, classes with a creche on site – then, wildly innovative, today, taken for granted. For the first time too we got out of the schoolroom – pond-dipping, exploring country churches. There was even a series of farm walks. On the social side, because the WEA gives 'so much more', there were theatre trips – not to mention whole weeks away at summer school. We met students from the trade unions, from similar organisations in other parts of Europe – another source of lasting friendship ...

Since I came to Yorkshire the WEA has again given me a Voice – literally, as performance poet, in response to the encouragement of a Creative Writing class. And the relationship with the WEA is going strong – is it a love affair, a marriage, or just a beautiful friendship? I'll settle for friendship. Thank you.

Sheila Naish, Yorkshire North District, 2002

# Notes on Contributors

.

**John Atkins** is WEA Brussels officer and a former tutor-organiser in the WEA North-western District. He is the author of *Neither Crumbs Nor Condescension: The Central Labour College 1909–1915* (Aberdeen, 1981).

**Peter Caldwell** is district secretary, WEA West Mercia District, and has written extensively on workplace learning.

**Sean Creighton** is secretary of Labour Heritage and works as policy officer for the British Association of Settlements and Social Action centres. His historical interests include the labour movement and UK Black and Asian history.

**Rob Duncan** has been a WEA tutor-organiser in Scotland since 1980. A specialist in labour and community history, he is the author of several books and articles and serves as chair of the Scottish Labour History Society and edits its journal.

**John Field** is deputy principal of the University of Stirling, and was professor of lifelong learning at Warwick University. Among his many publications are *Lifelong Learning and the New Educational Order* (Stoke-on-Trent, 2000).

**Lawrence Goldman** is fellow and tutor at St. Peter's College, Oxford and author of *Dons and Workers. Oxford and Adult Education Since 1850* (Oxford, 1995). He is president of the WEA Thames and Solent District.

**John Holford** is professor in the Department of Educational Studies, University of Surrey and is director of postgraduate programmes in the department. He is a former WEA tutor-organiser, and is the author of *Union Education in Britain* (Nottingham, 1994).

**Bernard Jennings** is professor emeritus of adult education at the University of Hull and a former WEA president. Among his recent publications is *The WEA in Australia. The Pioneering Years* (Sydney, 1998).

**Julia Jones** formerly managed the WEA community programme in Essex. Her previous publications include *Margery Allingham: A Biography* (1991), and she is currently studying for a doctorate.

**Richard Lewis** is deputy director of the School of Arts and Media at the University of Teesside, and author of *Leaders and Teachers: Adult Education and the Challenge of Labour in South Wales, 1900–1940* (Cardiff, 1993).

**Zoë Munby** has been WEA tutor-organiser in Stoke-on-Trent and Staffordshire since 1987. In recent years she has supported and developed student autobiographical writing and publication and radical local history programmes.

**Stephen K. Roberts** is editor of the 1640–60 section of the History of Parliament, and was a tutor-organiser in the WEA West Mercia District. He has written a number of books and articles on the period of the English revolution.

**Meredith Kwartin Rusoff** is an independent scholar living and working outside New York City. She received her Ph.D. from Northwestern University, Evanston, Illinois, and is revising her dissertation, 'They Hoped for Yesterday: British Social Criticism in the Early Twentieth Century', for publication.

**Derek Tatton** is principal of Wedgwood Memorial College, Barlaston, Staffordshire, and a former WEA tutor-organiser.

# Index

Districts *continued*
  South Wales, xi, xiii, 206, 300–5
  South Western, x, xii, 134, 265
  Southern, xiii, 140
  Welsh, 205
  West Mercia, 94, 267
  West Lancashire and Cheshire,
    221
  West Midlands, xii, 86, 89, 93,
    265
  Western, xi, 265
  Yorkshire, xi, 114, 136
    South, 132, 135, 136, 298
      branches, 136
      statistics, 136
Dover Wilson, John, 43
Duncan, Joseph, WEA activist, 184,
  189

Eagle, E. C., historian, 4
Eagleton, Terry, academic, 239
Edinburgh Trades and Labour
  Council, 188
Edinburgh, University of, 188
Edinburgh Workers' Educational
  Association, 190
Education Act, 1944, xiii, 71, 145
Education Act, 1988, 266–7
Education (Scotland) Act, 1918, 181
Educational Institute of Scotland
  (EIS), 180, 186
Educational Settlements Association
  and movement, 88, 145, 211,
  220
Elsdon, K. T., historian, 143, 145
Emery, Albert, student, 52, 53, 56
Essex Federation, 275
Evans, Brendan, historian, 145
Evans, D. E., WEA officer, 210

Federation of Worker Writers and
  Publishers, 250–1, 254
Fieldhouse, R., historian, 3, 58, 108,
  131, 139, 140, 142, 179, 195,
  277, 282, 283
Fircroft Residential College,
  Birmingham, 49, 82
First World War, 204
Fisher, H. A. L., 71

Fisher, Kate, adult educator, 233
forces, armed
  adult education in, 135
Foreign Office, 136
Freire, Paulo, 283
Furniss, Henry Sanderson, 101–4,
  107
Further and Higher Education Act,
  1992, 269
Further Education Funding Council
  (FEFC), xiv, 269–70
  Schedule 2, xiv, 270
Fustian Society, 13

Gallie, C. N., WEA activist, 185,
  193
'Geddes cuts', xii
General Strike and miners' lock-out,
  1926, 208
George, Reuben, WEA activist, 7
Gill, L. V., WEA activist, 44, 45–6,
  61
Girls' Friendly Society, 235
Glasgow Council for Community
  Service During
  Unemployment, 193
Glasgow, University of, 184
Goldman, L., historian, 3, 252, 254
Goldstein, Joseph, author, 169
Gore, Charles, 6, 7, 13, 14, 35, 64,
  97
Graham, William, advocate of
  WEA, 185
Green, Ernest, district secretary,
  124, 132, 134, 135, 137, 142–3,
  144, 145, 146, 147, 148, 157,
  169
Green, Sophie, tutor-organiser, xii,
  223, 225, 229, 234
Green, T. H., 14, 64, 98, 106
Greenhill, Ernest, WEA activist, 192
Greenwood, Arthur, 114–15
Greenwood, Walter, 250
Gregory, Bill, tutor, 301
Griffiths, Gareth, tutor, 303
Griffiths, James, 207
Griffiths, Maud, student, 52, 53
Guy, D. T., district secretary,
  210–11, 300–1